LIBERTY'S DAUGHTERS

BOOKS BY MARY BETH NORTON

The British-Americans
Women of America (edited with Carol Berkin)
Liberty's Daughters

LIBERTY'S DAUGHTERS

*The Revolutionary Experience of
American Women, 1750–1800*

MARY BETH NORTON

LITTLE, BROWN AND COMPANY   BOSTON–TORONTO

FIRST EDITION

LIBRARY OF CONGRESS CATALOGING IN PUBLICATION DATA

Norton, Mary Beth.
  Liberty's daughters.

  Bibliography: p.
  Includes index.
  1. Women—United States—History—Colonial period,
ca. 1600-1775—Sources 2. Women—United States—
History—Revolution—1775-1783—Sources. 3. Women—
United States—History—1783-1815—Sources.
4. Women in politics—United States—History—
Sources. I. Title
HQ1418.N67   301.41'2'0973   79-25245
ISBN 0-316-61251-0

VB

Designed by Janis Capone

*Published simultaneously in Canada
by Little, Brown & Company (Canada) Limited*

PRINTED IN THE UNITED STATES OF AMERICA

For
Judith Long Laws, Carol Berkin, Linda Waugh,
Lydia Bronte, Pauline Maier, and Calista Sullivan:
Friends and Colleagues

CONTENTS

ILLUSTRATIONS

ACKNOWLEDGMENTS

Many persons and institutions contributed to the writing of this book. The Meigs Fund of Cornell University assisted in the payment of general expenses throughout my research. An N.E.H. Younger Humanists Fellowship in 1974–1975 supported me at the Charles Warren Center, Harvard University, where I completed the bulk of the New England research and worked out the broad outlines of the project. Stimulating conversations with other Warren Center fellows that year, especially Robert V. Wells, helped me to shape my topic more precisely than had been possible previously. In 1977–1978 I was privileged to hold a fellowship at the Shelby Cullom Davis Center, Princeton University, where I wrote the first draft and participated regularly in the Davis Center seminar on the history of the family, led by Lawrence Stone. An early version of the first chapter was presented to the seminar in November 1977, and I learned much from the vigorous criticism offered on that occasion.

All researchers recognize that their work would be far more difficult without the advice and assistance of archivists. Because almost all current manuscript indexes and catalogs inadequately describe women's papers, I am even more indebted than usual to the knowledgeable staffs of the many libraries I visited. My sincere thanks go to them all, for without their help this book would have been impossible to write. I am also grateful to the staff of the Catalog of American Portraits at the National Portrait Gallery, and to the Hirschl and Adler Galleries, New York (especially Ms. Susan Menconi), for their assistance in locating and obtaining illustrations.

I have been aided by a number of Cornell students, whose work is cited in footnotes when appropriate. In particular, I would like to thank Norman Bloch, Sabrina Toma, Margaret Kassner, Suzette Witschi, and especially Mark Cunha, for their invaluable assistance. Roberta Ludgate's typing skills made the preparation of the final manuscript exceedingly easy, and Leslie Y. Arnold's deft editorial hand removed numerous redundancies and superfluous statements.

Invitations to present papers at a number of universities and professional meetings during this Bicentennial era gave me the opportunity to try out many of the ideas that have been incorporated into the book. I have also profited from the comments of friends and colleagues who read all or part of the manuscript. My special thanks go to Carol Berkin and Michael Kammen, who both read the entire second draft; to Mary Maples Dunn and Nancy Falik Cott, who offered key suggestions; and to Louise Tilly and Peter Wood, whose special perspectives provided me with cogent and useful criticisms, although both will think I ignored too much of their advice.

Finally, I wish to thank the women to whom this book is dedicated, for their warm friendship and unstinting support have sustained me for more than a decade.

PREFACE

In eighteenth-century America, women's lives centered upon their homes and families. Thus this book, too, necessarily concentrates upon the familial realm. Its guiding assumption is that colonial women's attitudes toward themselves, their families, and the world around them were shaped by a combination of their own daily experiences and society's expectations of them. Accordingly, it carefully delineates the range of female roles, emphasizing the troika that defined the life of the mature woman — wife, mother, and household mistress — but paying attention as well to a female's earlier experience as daughter and her later one as widow.

When I began to research this topic in 1972, I wanted to address a series of questions never previously asked by scholars of early American history, and to include both blacks and whites in my study.[1] In particular, I hoped to examine eighteenth-century women's self-perceptions, the influence of their sexual identity on all phases of their lives, and, perhaps most importantly, the impact of the American Revolution upon them. At the outset I was not at all certain that my goal could be reached, for the sources were reputedly sparse, unrevealing, even (it was said) nonexistent. Yet such pessimism proved completely unwarranted. My research into the published and unpublished papers of approximately 450 eighteenth-century families, coupled with the study of government records housed on both sides of the Atlantic, has uncovered a wealth of material and has led me to question historians' common assumptions about the lives of colonial women.

Perhaps the most central of these — one that has been largely accepted until very recent years — is the notion that the preindustrial American woman's essential economic contribution to the household gave her a social status higher than that of both her European contemporaries and her nineteenth-century descendants. (Of course, such an observation applies only to whites, although authors have not explicitly made a racial distinction.) It has long been contended that white female colonists were relatively equal partners within the home, that they often engaged in business activities outside the household, that gender roles were not sharply defined, and that women consequently developed high self-esteem.[2]

The conclusions reached in the pages that follow challenge that construct on every point. Eighteenth-century Americans proved to have very clear ideas of which tasks were properly "feminine" and which were not; of what behavior was appropriate for females, especially white females; and of what functions "the sex" was expected to perform. Moreover, both men and women continually indicated in subtle ways that they believed women to be inferior to men. Far from having a high status and an excellent opinion of themselves and their abilities, most of the white women who lived in pre-revolutionary America turned out to display low self-esteem, to have very limited conceptions of themselves and their roles, and to habitually denigrate their sex in general.

These findings therefore call into question the generally accepted chronology of women's history, which — to put it too simplistically — argues that following a "golden age" of equality (which for some authors encompasses only the seventeenth century but for most includes much of the eighteenth) white women "lost status," declining into the presumed helplessness of rigidly defined sexual spheres that culminated in the Victorian era. Some scholars of the nineteenth century have begun to challenge the latter part of this formulation by emphasizing the potential for the development of "domestic feminism"; when their conclusions are viewed in conjunction with mine, it appears that the older theory should now be abandoned.[3]

One of the hallmarks of the traditional approach to the history of early American women has been a failure to discuss the American Revolution in any detail. In the standard chronology, the chief villain causing woman's "decline and fall" was industrialization, and so the previous centuries were seen as a halcyonic, premodern whole, leaving no conceptual space for a consideration of the Revolution. Those scholars who have examined women's lives in the revolutionary era have confined themselves to an anecdotal treatment of women's contributions to the war effort and have neglected to inquire into the long-term impact of the conflict on female Americans. Recently, Joan Hoff Wilson explicitly investigated that crucial subject, but she concluded that the Revolution had little effect upon women, except perhaps a negative one.[4]

Yet evidence from other times and places suggests that wars in general, and revolutions in particular, can have a major impact upon women's lives. Anne Firor Scott's analysis of the Civil War and William Chafe's of the Second World War show how those conflicts significantly affected American women. Recent works on the French Revolution and the English Civil War conclude that those internal upheavals altered women's experiences in measurable ways. Moreover, an anthropologist's cross-cultural study of female status indicates that one of the chief factors influencing women's roles is the presence or absence of men. In times of war, she argues, the balance of work roles and, indeed, of the exercise of some types of power, necessarily shifts from male to female because of men's prolonged absence from the home.[5]

My study of the American Revolution is more in accord with these discussions of other societies and chronological periods than with the conventional literature of American women's history. In my opinion, the Revolution had an indelible effect upon American women, but its consequences cannot for the most part be discovered in the public world of law and politics, where they have previously been sought. The postrevolutionary years brought no widespread reform of legal codes, no universal enfranchisement of women, no public feminist movement. Instead, the 1780s and 1790s witnessed changes in women's private lives — in familial organization, personal aspirations, self-assessments. In short, the Revolution's impact is more accurately revealed in an analysis of women's private writings than in an examination of formal actions implemented by men.

But there is a potentially serious drawback to a concentration on women's writings as the primary source of evidence, for only about half the white American female population in the eighteenth century may have been sufficiently literate to sign a name to a will.[6] Moreover, that minimal level of competence by no means implied the ability to write an occasional letter, much less to correspond regularly with friends or relatives or to keep a diary. As a result, despite the large number (368) of unpublished collections of family papers that I consulted, my findings cannot be said to be based upon a representative cross section of the American female populace.

Nevertheless, I would argue that this book accurately depicts many aspects of the lives of all eighteenth-century American women, not just those from the middling and upper ranks of society. The regional coverage is broad, from the St. Lawrence River in the north to St. Augustine in the south to Kentucky, Ohio, and Louisiana in the west. Further, the opinions and actions of poor, illiterate white and black women were often noted by travelers and other observers, by their masters and mistresses, or by government officials. Such indirect sources must be used with care, but they can provide information about women who did not leave written records of their own. In addition, much of the book is concerned with the universals of female lives — courtship, marriage, pregnancy and childbirth, child rearing, and household work — and in spite of obvious variations arising from race, wealth, or place of residence, these common experiences of femininity made women in many ways more alike than different. Accordingly, for the purposes of this book, it seems possible to allow the literate portion of the female population to speak for their illiterate counterparts.

The book is divided into two sections. The first, composed of five chapters, traces the constant patterns of women's lives, those aspects of their existence that remained basically the same during the last half of the eighteenth century, both before and after the Revolution. The second, with four chapters, examines some new trends that first appeared in the revolutionary and postrevolutionary years. This rather complex organization results from the fact that the material did not fit a neat chronological framework. Indeed, as will become evident in the later chapters, the picture was further complicated by the appearance of varying patterns within the postwar trends. Some of the new ways quickly supplanted the old, but in other instances new styles developed alongside old ones, paralleling but not completely replacing them by 1800.

The last chapter and the conclusion indicate the ways in which I think these late eighteenth-century trends were related to nineteenth-century developments. On the other end of the chronological scale, though, I mean to imply no specific interpretation of women's experiences prior to 1750, and especially not before 1700. The lives of colonial women in the seventeenth century might have been similar to or different from those I describe in the mid-eighteenth century; I do not know which, nor do I intend to speculate about a subject on which there is at present such inadequate information.[7] I would simply observe in passing that, if I have learned anything from my research, it is that most of the widely held assumptions about the lives of colonial women cannot withstand careful scrutiny.

Part One

THE CONSTANT PATTERNS
OF WOMEN'S LIVES

Chapter One

જી

THE SMALL CIRCLE OF
DOMESTIC CONCERNS

THE HOUSEHOLD, THE BASIC UNIT OF EIGHTEENTH-CENTURY AMER-
ican society, had a universally understood hierarchical structure. At
the top was the man, the lord of the fireside; next came the mistress,
his wife and helpmate; following her, the children, who were expected
to assist the parent of their own sex; and finally, any servants or
slaves, with the former taking precedence over the latter. Each family
was represented in the outside world by its male head, who cast its
single vote in elections and fulfilled its obligations to the community
through service in the militia or public office. Within the home, the
man controlled the finances, oversaw the upbringing of the children,
and exercised a nominal supervision over household affairs. Married
men understandably referred to all their dependents collectively as
"my family," thereby expressing the proprietary attitude they so
obviously felt.[1]

The mistress of the household, as befitted her inferior position,
consistently employed the less proprietary phrase "our family." Yet
she, and not her husband, directed the household's day-to-day activities. Her role was domestic and private, in contrast to his public,
supervisory functions. As the Marylander Samuel Purviance told his
teenaged daughter Betsy in 1787, "the great Province of a Woman"
was "Economy and Frugality in the management of [a] Family."
Even if the household were wealthy, he stressed, "the meanest Af-

3

fairs, are all and ought to be Objects of a womans cares." Purviance and his contemporaries would have concurred with the position taken in an article in Caleb Bingham's *The American Preceptor,* a textbook widely used in the early republic: "[N]eedle work, the care of domestic affairs, and a serious and retired life, is the proper function of women, and for this they were designed by Providence."[2]

Of course, such statements applied only to whites, for no eighteenth-century white American would have contended that enslaved black women should work solely at domestic tasks. But the labor of female slaves too was affected by their sexual identity, for they were often assigned jobs that differed from those of male slaves, even though such tasks were not exclusively domestic. Appropriately, then, an analysis of black and white women's experiences in eighteenth-century America must begin with an examination of their household responsibilities.

I

"I have a great and longing desire to be very notable," wrote a Virginia bride in 1801, declaring her allegiance to the ideal of early American white womanhood. In this context, the adjective "notable" connoted a woman's ability to manage her household affairs skillfully and smoothly. Thus the prominent clergyman Ezra Stiles asked that his daughter be educated in such a way as to "lay a founda[tion] of a notable Woman," and a Rhode Islander wrote of a young relative that she "Sets out to be a Notable house Wife." When the Virginian Fanny Tucker Coalter exuberantly told her husband, John, "I'm the picture of bustling notability," he could have had no doubt about her meaning.[3]

The characteristics of the notable wife were best described by Governor William Livingston of New Jersey in his essay entitled "Our Grand-Mothers," which was printed posthumously in two American magazines in the early 1790s. Decrying his female contemporaries' apparent abandonment of traditional values, Livingston presented a romanticized picture of the colonial women of the past. Such wives "placed their renown" in promoting the welfare of their families, Livingston asserted. "They were strangers to dissipation; . . . their own habitation was their delight." They not only practiced economy, thereby saving their husbands' earnings, but they also "augmented their treasure, by their industry." Most important, "they maintained good order and harmony in their empire" and "enjoyed happiness in their chimney corners," passing on these same qualities to the daughters they carefully raised to be like themselves. Their homes, in short, were "the source of their pleasure; and the foundation of their glory."[4]

Although other accounts of the attributes of notable housewives were couched in less sentimental form, their message was the same. Ministers preaching funeral sermons for women often took as their text Proverbs 31, with its description of the virtuous woman who "looketh well to the Ways of her Household and eateth not the Bread of Idleness." So too drafters of obituaries and memorial statements emphasized the sterling housewifely talents of the women they eulogized. Such a model of female perfection did not allow a woman an independent existence: ideally, she would maintain no identity separate from that of her male-defined family and her household responsibilities. A man like James Kent, the distinguished New York lawyer, could smugly describe himself as "the independent . . . *Lord of my own fireside*," while women, as William Livingston had declared, were expected to tend the hearth and find "happiness in their chimney corners."[5]

These contrasting images of autonomy and subordination were translated into reality in mid-eighteenth-century American household organization. Although the mistress directed the daily life of the household, her position within the home was secondary to that of her husband. She was expected to follow his orders, and he assumed control over the family finances. In 1750, the anonymous author of *Reflections on Courtship and Marriage*, a pamphlet long erroneously attributed to Benjamin Franklin, told men that it "would be but just and prudent to inform and consult a wife" before making "very important" decisions about monetary matters, but evidence drawn from a variety of sources indicates that few colonial husbands followed this advice. Instead, they appear to have kept the reins of financial management firmly in their own hands, rarely if ever informing their wives about even the basic details of monetary transactions.[6]

The most comprehensive evidence of this phenomenon comes from an analysis of the claims for lost property submitted by 468 white loyalist refugee women after the Revolution. The claims procedure as established by Parliament and carried out by a commission appointed for the purpose required that American loyalists prepare detailed written statements of their losses of property and testify orally about those statements. Because each claimant wanted to receive the maximum possible return on her claim, there was no reason for her to withhold any information from the commission or to feign ignorance of a particular item of property that had belonged to her family. As a result, claims prepared by female refugees, the vast majority of them widows of loyalist men, accurately depict the dimensions of the world in which they had lived prior to the war. If they had participated in economic decision making, the claims documents would demonstrate that fact by revealing their knowledge of their families' financial status. But instead the claims uniformly disclose loyalist women's insulation from the external affairs of the household and their confinement to a wholly domestic realm.

The evidence of women's ignorance of financial affairs takes a variety of forms in the claims records. Rural wives often were unable to place a precise value on tools, lands, or harvested grain, even if they knew a farm's total acreage or the size of the harvest. Urban women frequently did not know their husbands' exact income or the cost of the houses in which they lived. The typical wealthy female was not aware of her husband's net worth because she did not know the amount of his outstanding debts or what was owed to him, and poor women occasionally failed to list any value at all for their meager possessions. Women of all descriptions, moreover, shared an ignorance of legal language and an unfamiliarity with the details of transactions concerning property with which they were not personally acquainted. The sole exceptions to this rule were a few widows who had already served several years as executrices of the family estates; some wives of innkeepers, grocers, or other shopkeepers who had assisted their husbands in business; and a small number of single women who had supported themselves through their own efforts.

Loyalist husbands, then, did not normally discuss economic decisions with their wives. The women lacked exactly that information which their husbands alone could have supplied, for they were able to describe only those parts of the property with which they came into regular contact. That the practice in these loyalist homes was not atypical is shown when one looks at patriot families as well.

American wives and widows alike repeatedly noted their lack of information about their husbands' business dealings. "I don't know anything of his affairs," a Virginian resident in London wrote in 1757; "whether his income will admit of our living in the manner we do, I am a stranger to." Elizabeth Sandwith Drinker, a Philadelphia Quaker, commented years later, "I am not acquainted with the extent of my husband's great variety of engagements," quoting an apposite poem that began, "I stay much at home, and my business I mind." [7] To such married women, their spouses' financial affairs were not of immediate import. But widows, by contrast, had to cope with the consequences of their ignorance. On his deathbed, a New England cleric surprised his wife with the news that she would have "many debts to pay that [she] knew nothing about," and her subsequent experience was replicated many times over — by the Marylander whose husband left no records to guide her administration of his estate, by the Virginian who had to tell her husband's employer that he had evidently neglected to maintain proper rent rolls, by the New Yorker who admitted to her son-in-law that she had known "very little" of her spouse's affairs before his death. [8]

It might seem extraordinary that colonial men failed to recognize the potential benefits — to their children and their estates, if not to themselves — of keeping their wives informed about family finances. Yet the responsibility was not theirs alone. Married women rarely appear to have sought economic information from their husbands, whether in anticipation of eventual widowhood or simply out of a desire to understand the family's financial circumstances. [9] On the contrary, women's statements reveal a complete acceptance of the division of their world into two separate, sexually defined spheres.

"Nature & Custom seems to have destined us for the more endearing & private & the Man for the more active & busy Walks of Life," remarked Elizabeth Willing Powel, a leader of Philadelphia society, in 1784. A similar sense of the character of the difference between male and female realms shone through the 1768 observation of a fellow Philadelphian of Mrs. Powel, the teenager Peggy Emlen, who described the men she saw hurrying about the city streets: they "all seem people of a great deal of business and importance, as for me I am not much of either." Men shared this same notion of the dichotomy between male public activity and female private passivity. In 1745, an essayist warned women that they were best "confined within the narrow Limits of Domestick Offices," for "when they stray beyond them, they move excentrically, and consequently without grace." A New Englander twelve years later worried that women might want "to obtain the other's Sphere of Action, & become Men," but he reassured himself that "they will again return to the wonted Paths of true Politeness, & shine most in the proper Sphere of domestick Life." [10]

If women were accordingly out of place in the world beyond the household, so men were not entirely at home in the female realm of domestic affairs. The family property may have been "his" in wives' terminology, but at the same time the household furnishings were "hers" in the minds of their spouses. Wartime letters from American husbands confirm the separation of male and female spheres, more because of what they do not contain than as a result of what they do. When couples were separated by the Revolutionary War, men for the most part neglected to instruct their wives about the ordinary details of domestic life. Since they initially sent explicit directions about financial affairs, their failure to concern themselves with household management would seem to indicate that they had been accustomed to leave that realm entirely to their wives. Only if they had not previously issued orders on domestic subjects would they have failed to include such directives in their correspondence. [11]

The evidence, then, suggests that female whites shared a universal domestic experience that differentiated their world from that of men. Their lives were to a large extent defined by their familial responsibilities, but the precise character of those obligations varied according to the nature of the household in which they resided. Although demographic historians have concentrated upon determining the size of colonial households, from the standpoint of an American woman, size — within a normal range — mattered less than composition. It meant a great deal to a housewife whether she had daughters who could assist her, whether her household contained a helpful servant or a demanding elderly relative, or whether she had to contend with a resident mother-in-law for control of her own domestic affairs. [12]

But ultimately of greater significance were differences in the wealth and location of colonial households. The chief factors that defined a white woman's domestic role arose from the family's economic status, which determined whether there would be servants or slaves, and from the household's location in a rural or urban setting. With a similarity of household roles as a basis, one can divide eighteenth-century women into four groups: poor and middling white farm women, north and south; white urban women of all social ranks; wealthy southerners who lived on plantations; and the female blacks held in bondage by those same wealthy southerners.

II

A majority of white women in eighteenth-century America resided in poor or middling farm households, and so it is reasonable to begin a discussion of female domestic work patterns with an assessment of their experience. Their heavy responsibilities are revealed most vividly in accounts left by two city families who moved to rural areas, for farm women were so accustomed to their burdensome obligations that they rarely remarked upon them.

Christopher Marshall and his wife abandoned Philadelphia when the British occupied the city in the fall of 1777, shifting their large family to Lancaster, Pennsylvania. There Marshall marveled at his wife's accomplishments, at how "from early in the morning till late at night, she is constantly employed in the affairs of the family." She not only did the cooking, baking, washing, and ironing, all of which had been handled by servants in their Philadelphia home, but she also milked cows, made cider and cheese, and dried apples. The members of the Palmer family of Germantown, Massachusetts, had a comparable experience when they moved in 1790 to Framingham, about twenty miles west of Boston. Mary Palmer, who was then fifteen and the oldest daughter in the home, later recalled that her father had had difficulty in adjusting to the change in his womenfolk's roles. "It took years to wean him from the idea that we must be ladies," she wrote, "although he knew that we must give up all such pretensions." Mary herself thrived in the new environment. "Kind

9

Residence of David Twining, 1787, by Edward Hicks. Courtesy of Abby Aldrich Rockefeller Folk Art Center, Williamsburg, Virginia. In the mid-1840s, Hicks painted from memory this scene of the farm on which he was raised, showing the multitude of activities in which the members of the family were involved. In the foreground, his foster mother teaches him to read.

neighbors" taught her mother how to make butter and cheese, and the girls "assisted in the laborious part, keeping churn, pans, cheese-hoops and strainers nice and sweet." After she married Royall Tyler and set up housekeeping in Brattleboro, Vermont, Mary continued to practice the skills of rural housewifery she had gained as a teenager. Between managing her dairy in the summer and supervising spinning and weaving in the winter, not to mention raising five children, she observed, "I never realized what it was to have time hang heavy." [13]

Mary Palmer's recollections disclose the seasonal nature of much of farm women's labor. Such annual rhythms and the underlying, invariable weekly routine are revealed in the work records kept by farm wives like Sarah Snell Bryant, of Cummington, Massachusetts, and Mary Cooper, of Oyster Bay, Long Island. Each week Mrs. Bryant devoted one day to washing, another to ironing, and a third at least partly to baking. On the other days she sewed, spun, and wove. In the spring she planted her garden; in the early summer she hived her bees; in the fall she made cider and dried apples; and in mid-December came hog-killing time. Mary Cooper recorded the same seasonal round of work, adding to it spring housecleaning, a midsummer cherry harvest, and a long stretch of soapmaking, boiling "souse," rendering fat, and making candles that followed the hog butchering in December. In late 1769, after two weeks of such work, she described herself as "full of freting discontent dirty and miserabel both yesterday and today." [14]

Unlike the laconic Mrs. Bryant, who simply noted the work she had completed each day, Mrs. Cooper frequently commented on the fatiguing nature of her life. "It has been a tiresome day it is now Bed time and I have not had won minutts rest," she wrote in November 1768. One Sunday some months later she remarked, "I hoped for some rest but I am forst to get dinner and slave hard all day long." On those rare occasions when everyone else in the household was away, Mary Cooper understandably breathed a sigh of relief. "I have the Blessing to be quite alone without any Body greate or Small," she noted in late October 1768, and five years later another such day brought thanks for "some quiate moments which I have not had in weeks." [15]

Perhaps one of the reasons why Mrs. Cooper seemed so overworked was her obsession with cleanliness. Since travelers in rural America commented frequently upon the dirt they encountered in farmhouses and isolated taverns, it seems clear either that cleanliness was not highly valued or that farm wives, fully occupied with other tasks, simply had no time to worry about sweeping floors, airing bedding, or putting things away. Mary Cooper's experience suggests that the latter explanation was more likely. Often describing herself as "dirty and distrest," she faithfully recorded her constant battle against filth. "We are cleaning the house and I am tired almost to death," she wrote in December 1768; the following spring, after seven straight days of cleaning, she complained, "O it has been a week of greate toile and no Comfort or piece to Body or mind." Another time she noted with satisfaction, "I have got some clean cloths on thro mercy some little done to clean the house," and again, "Up very late But I have got my Cloths Ironed."[16] Obviously, if a farm woman was not willing to invest almost superhuman effort in the enterprise, keeping her household clean was an impossible task.

Mary Cooper's diary is unique in that it conveys explicitly what is only implicit in other farm wives' journals: a sense of drudgery and boredom. Sarah Snell Bryant would record that she had engaged in the same tasks for days on end, but she never noted her reaction to the repetition. This sameness was the quality that differentiated farm women's work from that performed by their husbands. No less physically demanding or difficult, men's tasks varied considerably from day to day and month to month. At most — during planting or harvest time, for example — men would spend two or three weeks at one job. But then they would move on to another. For a farmer, in other words, the basic cycle was yearly; for his wife, it was daily and weekly, with additional obligations superimposed seasonally. Moreover, men were able to break their work routine by making frequent trips to town or the local mill on business, or by going hunting or fishing, whereas their wives, especially if they had small children, were tied to the home.[17]

Rural youngsters of both sexes were expected to assist their parents. "Their children are all brought up in industry, and have their time fully employed in performing the necessary duties of the house and farm," remarked a foreign visitor to a western Pennsylvania homestead in 1796. His inclusion of both sons and daughters was entirely accurate, for although historians have tended to emphasize the value of boys' labor to their fathers, extensive evidence suggests that girls were just as important as aides to their mothers. The fifteen-year-old Elizabeth Fuller, of Princeton, Massachusetts, for example, recorded occasionally baking pies, making candles, scouring floors, mincing meat for sausages, making cheese, and doing laundry, in addition to her primary assignments, spinning and weaving. Nabby and Betsy Foote, sisters who lived in Colchester, Connecticut, likewise noted helping their mother with housework, again in conjunction with their major chores of sewing, spinning, and weaving. When the parents of Ruth Henshaw, of Leicester, Massachusetts, called her home in mid-July 1789 after she had been visiting a relative for four days, saying, she recounted, that they "could not Subsist with out me any longer," they were only expressing what is evident in all these diaries: the labor of daughters, like that of wives, was crucial to the success of a farm household.[18]

Brissot de Warville, an astute foreign traveler, recognized both the value of women's work and the clearly defined gender role distinctions visible in rural life in his observations upon a fellow Frenchman's Pennsylvania farm in 1788. It is a "great disadvantage," Brissot remarked, that "he does not have any poultry or pigeons and makes no cheese; nor does he have any spinning done or collect goose feathers." The reason: he was a bachelor, and "these domestic farm industries . . . can be carried on well only by women."[19] Brissot's friend had two women indentured servants, so he did not lack female labor as such; what was missing was a wife or daughters to supervise the servants. Significantly, neither he nor Brissot seems to have considered the possibility that he could himself keep poultry or learn enough about cheesemaking to direct the servants. That was clearly "woman's work," and if there was no woman present, such work was not done, no matter how pressing the need or how great the resulting loss of potential income.

Yet in some frontier areas the gender role divisions so apparent in more settled regions did blur, although they did not break down entirely. Farmers' wives and daughters occasionally worked in the fields, especially at harvest time. Travelers from the East were unaccustomed to the sight of white female fieldworkers and wrote about it at length. In 1778, for example, a doctor from Dorchester, Massachusetts, told his wife in some amazement that he had seen Pennsylvania German women "at work abroad on the Farm mowing, Hoeing, Loading Dung into a Cart." A New Hampshire farmer, by contrast, matter-of-factly recorded in his diary his use of female relatives and neighbors for field work. In that same colony in the early 1760s the pendulum swung the other way, and men helped with women's work. In the winters, recalled one woman many years later, "the boys did as much Knitting as the Girls, and the men and boys also did the milking to spare the women."[20]

Backcountry women had to cope with a far more rough-and-ready existence than did their counterparts to the east and south. The log cabins in which many of them lived were crudely built and largely open to the elements. Even the few amenities that brightened the lives of their poor contemporaries in areas of denser settlement were denied them; the Reverend Charles Woodmason, an Anglican missionary in western South Carolina, commented in 1768 that "in many Places they have nought but a Gourd to drink out off Not a Plate Knive or Spoon, a Glass, Cup, or any thing — It is well if they can get some Body Linen, and some have not even that." Later in the century, one woman on the Ohio frontier, lacking a churn, was reduced to making butter by stirring cream with her hand in an ordinary pail. Under such circumstances, simple subsistence would require most of a woman's energies.[21]

How, then, did frontier women react to these primitive conditions? At least one group of pioneer men termed their wives "the greatest of Heroines," suggesting that they bore such hardships without complaint, but other evidence indicates that some women, especially those raised in genteel households, did not adapt readily to their new lives. Many, like a Pennsylvanian, must have vetoed their husbands' plans to move west because of an unwillingness to exchange a civilized life for a residence in "what she deems a Wilderness." Others must have resembled the Shenandoah Valley woman, a mother of eight, who descended into invalidism shortly after her husband moved her and their children to what their son described as a "valuable Farm but with a small indifferent house . . . & almost intirely in woods."[22] Perhaps, like a female traveler in the west, the Virginian "felt oppress'd with so much wood towering above . . . in every direction and such a continuance of it." This was not a unique reaction: a Scottish immigrant, faced with his wife's similar response to the first sight of their new home, comforted her by promising, "[W]e would get all these trees cut down . . . [so] that we would see from house to house."[23]

At least in this case the husband knew of his wife's discontent and reacted to it. In other instances, the lack of communication between spouses resulting from their divergent roles appears to have been heightened on the frontier, as wives deliberately concealed their unhappiness from their husbands, revealing their true feelings only to female relatives. Mary Hooper Spence, who described herself as having been beset by "misfortunes" ever since the day of her marriage, lived with her husband on the "dreary & cold" island of St. Johns (now Prince Edward Island) in the 1770s. In letters to her mother in

Boston she repeatedly told of her loneliness and depression, of how she found a primitive, isolated existence "hard to bear." By contrast, her husband characterized their life as "happy" and reported to a relative that they were "comfortably" settled. Likewise, Mrs. Joseph Gilman, said by her husband to be pleased with living in the new settlement of Marietta, Ohio, in 1789, later recounted that on many occasions while milking their cows she would think of her New England home, "sob and cry as loud as a child, and then wipe her tears and appear before her husband as cheerful as if she had nothing to give her pain."[24]

To point out the apparent dissatisfaction of many frontier women with their lives in the wilderness is not to say that they and others did not cope successfully with the trials they encountered. To cite just one example: Mrs. Hutchens, a Mississippi woman whose husband was kidnapped and whose slaves were stolen, pulled her family together in the face of adversity almost by sheer force of will alone. Her son subsequently recalled that she had told her children they could survive if they were willing to work. Accordingly, she and her three sons cultivated the fields while her daughters did the housework, spun cotton, and wove the fabric for their clothing. By the time her husband returned seven years later, she had prospered sufficiently to be able to replace all the slaves taken by the robbers.[25]

The fact that Mrs. Hutchens put her daughters to work spinning and weaving is significant, for no household task was more time-consuming or more symbolic of the female role than spinning. It was, furthermore, a task quintessentially performed by young, single women; hence, the use of the word "spinster" to mean an unmarried female and the phrase "the distaff side" to refer to women in general. Farm wives, and especially their daughters, spent a large proportion of their time, particularly in the winter months, bending over a flax wheel or loom, or walking beside a great wheel, spinning wool. No examination of the domestic sphere can be complete without detailed attention to this aspect of household work.

Before 1765 and the subsequent rise in home manufacturing caused by colonial boycotts of British goods, spinning and weaving as ordinary chores were largely confined to rural areas of the northern and middle colonies and the backcountry South. Planters and even middling farmers who lived along the southeastern coast and city residents

At the Loom, by an unknown artist, c. 1795. Courtesy of Archives of American Art, Smithsonian Institution, Roll ND/47, American Folk Art Gallery, Downtown Gallery Papers. The subject of this naive painting, one of the earliest depictions of an American woman at work, appears to be embroidering an elaborate coverlet.

throughout America could usually purchase English cloth more cheaply than they could manufacture it at home, and so they bought fabric rather than asking their wives, daughters, or female slaves to spend the requisite amount of time to produce it. But rural women outside the plantation South spent much of their lives spinning. They began as girls, helping their mothers; they continued after their marriages, until their own daughters were old enough to remove most of the burden from their shoulders; and they often returned to it in old age or widowhood, as a means of supporting themselves or making use of their time. Not all farm women learned weaving, a skill open to men as well, but spinning was a nearly universal occupation among them.[26]

Rural girls understood at an early age that spinning was "a very proper accomplishment for a farmers daughter," as the New Jersey Quaker Susanna Dillwyn put it in 1790. Susanna's niece Hannah Cox began trying to spin on an "old wheel which was in the house" when she was only seven, so her mother bought her a little new wheel, upon which Hannah soon learned to spin "very prettily." Similarly, the tutor on Robert Carter's Virginia plantation observed that his small pupils would tie "a String to a Chair & then run buzzing back to imitate the Girls spinning." Such playful fascination with the process of cloth production later turned for many girls into monotonous daily labor at wheels or looms during the months between December and May. The normal output of an experienced spinner who carded the wool herself was four skeins a day, or six if an assistant carded for her. Teenaged girls like Elizabeth Fuller, who were less practiced than their mothers, produced on the average two or three skeins a day. After a long stint of spinning tow (short coarse linen fibers) in January and February 1792, Elizabeth exploded in her diary, "I should think I might have spun up all the Swingling Tow in America by this time." Later that same year, she switched to weaving, at last completing her annual allotment on June 1. In three months she had woven 176 yards of cloth, she recorded, happily inscribing in her journal, "Welcome sweet Liberty, once more to me. How have I longed to meet again with thee." [27]

But clothwork, which could be a lonely and confining occupation, as Elizabeth Fuller learned, could also be an occasion for socializing. Rural girls sometimes attended "spinning frolics" or quilting bees, many of which lasted for several days and ended with dancing. [28] Even more frequently farm women "changed work," trading skills with others experienced in different tasks. Mary Palmer recalled that after her family moved to Framingham her mother would change work with other women in the area, "knitting and sewing for them while they would weave cotton and flax into cloth" for her, since as a city dweller she had never learned that skill. In a similar way Ruth Henshaw and her mother repaid Lydia Hawkins, who warped their loom for them, by helping her quilt or making her a pair of stays. Ruth regularly exchanged chores with girls of her own age as well; in December 1789, for example, she noted, "Sally here Spining Changeing works with Me," while ten days later she was at Sally's house, carding for her.[29]

From such trading of labor farm women could easily move on to work for pay. By 1775 Betsy and Nabby Foote had taken that step. Nabby, like Lydia Hawkins of Leicester, specialized in warping webs and making loom harnesses; her sister Betsy worked in all phases of cloth production, carding wool, hatcheling flax, and spinning, as well as doing sewing and mending for neighbors. In the rural North and South alike white women spun, wove, and sold butter, cheese, and soap to their neighbors, participating on a small scale in the market economy long before the establishment of textile factories in New England and the consequent introduction of widespread wage labor for young northern women.[30]

Given the significance of spinning in women's lives, it is not surprising that American men and women made that occupation the major symbol of femininity. William Livingston had declared that "country girls . . . ought to be at their spinning-wheels," and when Benjamin Franklin sought a wedding present for his sister Jane, he decided on a spinning wheel instead of a tea table, concluding that "the character of a good housewife was far preferable to that of being only a pretty gentlewoman."[31]

Compelling evidence of the link between spinning and the female role in the eighteenth-century American mind comes from the observations of two visitors to Indian villages. Confronted by societies in which women did not spin but instead cultivated crops while their husbands hunted and fished, both the whites perceived Indian sex roles as improper and sought to correct them by introducing the feminine task of spinning. Benjamin Hawkins, United States agent for the Creek tribe, admired the industrious Creek women and encouraged them to learn to spin and weave. This step, he believed, would lead to a realignment of sex roles along proper lines, because the women would be freed from dependence upon their hunter husbands for clothing, and they would also no longer have time to work on the crops. The men in turn would therefore be "obliged to handle the ax & the plough, and assist the women in the laborious task of the fields." A similar scheme was promoted by the Quaker woman Anne Emlen Mifflin, who traveled in the Seneca country as a missionary in 1803. Men should work in agriculture, she told her Indian

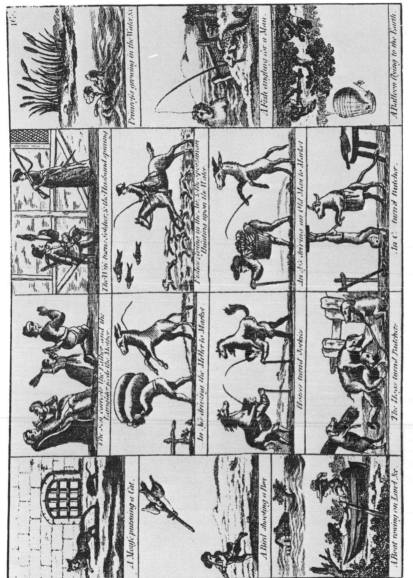

English Role Reversal Prints. From Catchpenny Prints: 163 Popular Engravings from the Eighteenth Century *(Dover Publications, New York, 1970). The fact that the creator of this series of role reversals chose to show a man spinning demonstrates that occupation's symbolic character. Note, too, the panel illustrating the reversal of parental and children's roles.*

audience, so that women would be able to learn spinning and dairy management, which were "branches suited to our sex," as opposed to "drudging alone in the labors of the field."[32]

As Mifflin's comment shows, women, too, found spinning a necessary component of femininity, a fact best illustrated by reference to Elizabeth Graeme Fergusson's poem "The Contemplative Spinner." In 1792, Mrs. Fergusson, one of the leaders of intellectual life in republican Philadelphia, composed a poem in which she compared her spinning wheel to a wheel of fortune, leading her to a series of observations on life, death, and religion. But the wheel did more: it also reminded her of other women, linking her inextricably to "a train of Female Hands / Chearful uniting in Industrious Bands." And so, she wrote:

> *In such Reflections I oft passed the Night,*
> *When by my Papas solitary Light*
> *My Wheel I turnd, and thought how others toild*
> *To earn a morsel for a famishd Child.*[33]

To Elizabeth Graeme Fergusson, spinning symbolized her tie to the female sisterhood, just as to Benjamin Hawkins and other eighteenth-century men that occupation above all somehow appertained to femininity. It is consequently ironic that the one factor that differentiated the lives of urban women most sharply from those of their rural counterparts was the fact that they did not have to engage in cloth production. Women who had access to stores saw no point in spending hour after tedious hour at the wheel or loom. Not, at least, until doing so came to have political significance in the late 1760s, as Americans increasingly tried to end their dependence on British manufactured goods.

III

Although urban women did not have to spin and weave, the absence of that time-consuming occupation did not turn their lives into leisured ones. Too often historians have been misled by the lack of lengthy work entries in urban women's diaries, concluding therefrom that city "ladies" contributed little or nothing to the family welfare. Admittedly, white urban women of even moderate means worked shorter hours and at less physically demanding tasks than did their rural counterparts, but this did not mean that their households ran themselves. Women still had the responsibility for food preparation, which often included cultivating a garden and raising poultry. The wives of artisans and shopkeepers also occasionally assisted their husbands in business. Furthermore, their homes were held to higher standards of cleanliness — by themselves and by their female friends — than were the homes of farm women like Mary Cooper. Even if they could afford to hire servants, they frequently complained that supervising their assistants took almost as much time and effort as doing the work themselves.

Middling and well-to-do urban women who described their daily routines in letters or diaries disclosed a uniform pattern of mornings devoted to household work, a late dinner at about two o'clock, and an afternoon of visiting friends, riding, or perhaps reading quietly at home. Although some women arose as late as eight o'clock (which one female Bostonian termed "a lazy hour"), others, including Abigail Adams, recorded that they habitually rose at five. A Pennsylvanian summed up the common practice in a poem:

> *Like a notable house wife* I rise with the sun
> *Then bustle about till the business is done,*
> *Consult with the Cook, and* attend to the spiting [*sic*]
> *Then quietly seat myself down to my* kniting —
> *Should a neighbour step in we* talk of the weather
> *Retail all the* news *and the* scandle *together,* . . .
> *The* tea things removed *our party disperses,*
> *And of course puts an end to my* very fine verses.[34]

The chores that city women performed in the mornings resembled those of farm wives. Their diaries noted hours devoted to washing and ironing, cooking and baking, sewing and knitting. Like that of their rural counterparts, their labor was affected by the seasons, although less consistently so: in the autumn they preserved fruit and stored vegetables, and early in the winter they salted beef and pork and made sausage. Yet there were differences. Most notably, urban dwellers made daily trips to large markets, where they bought most of their meat, vegetables, cheese, and butter. Rebecca Stoddert, a Marylander who had moved to Philadelphia, marveled that her neighbors quickly killed chickens they had purchased without "think[ing] of fatting them up," a practice she deplored as wasteful and shortsighted.[35]

Although urban women were not burdened with the major stock-tending and clothmaking chores that devolved upon farm wives, some of the time thus saved was devoted to cleaning their homes. Many of the travelers in rural areas most horrified by dirty farmhouses and taverns were themselves urban women, who had adopted standards of cleanliness for their homes, clothes, and beds that were utterly alien to farm wives. Certainly no rural woman except Mary Cooper would have written a journal entry resembling that of a Philadelphian in 1781: "As we were whitewashing & cleaning house this day I seemed anxious, I fear over anxious to have every thing clean, & in order." Another Philadelphia resident, the Quaker Sally Logan Fisher, seems to have painted, whitewashed, or wallpapered her house each spring, even though she remarked in April 1785 that it was "troubelsome work indeed, the pleasure afterwards of being nice, hardly pays for the trouble." Other wives in smaller towns similarly recorded their commitment to keeping their homes neat and clean.[36]

Cleaning, though, was perhaps the only occupation at which city dwellers of moderate means expended more energy than women living in agricultural regions. One of the benefits of residing in a city or a good-sized town was the availability of a pool of female workers who could be hired at relatively low rates. If a woman decided that she could not afford even a minimal payment, she could take a girl into her home as a sort of apprentice in housewifery, compensating her solely with room, board, and clothes. Independent female wage earners will be discussed in chapter 4, and here attention will focus on servants who actually resided in middling and wealthy households.

The mistresses of such homes felt caught in a dilemma. On the one hand, servants were impertinent, lazy, untrustworthy, careless, and slovenly (to list just a few of their complaints), but on the other hand it was impossible to run a household without some help. The women who offered themselves for hire were usually either single girls or elderly widows; only in rare cases can one identify white females who spent their entire lives as servants.[37] Instead, girls worked as maids, cooks, or laundresses for a few years before marriage, often for a series of employers. From the diaries and letters of mistresses of urban households one gains the impression of a floating population of "young Giddy Headed Girls" who did largely as they pleased, knowing that with the endemic American shortage of labor they could always find another position. Few seem to have stayed in the same household for more than a few months, or a year at most, before moving on to another post. For example, in just the five years from 1794 to 1799, Deborah Norris Logan, Sally Logan Fisher's sister-in-law, employed at least ten different female servants in fairly rapid succession. Among them were two widows, some immigrants from Ireland and Germany, a pair of sisters, and several girls.[38]

Deborah Logan had no daughters to assist her in the home, but even if she had, she, like other urban mothers, would not have expected them to contribute as much work to the household as did their rural counterparts. City daughters from well-to-do homes were the only eighteenth-century American women who can accurately be described as leisured. The causes of their relative lack of employment have already been indicated: first, the work of an urban household was less demanding than that of a farm, so that mothers and perhaps one or two servants could do all that was necessary; and, second, city girls did not have to produce the cloth supply for the family. Accordingly, they could live at a relaxed pace, sleeping late, learning music and dancing, spending hours with male and female friends, and reading the latest novels.[39]

This is not to say, as some historians have argued, that these young women were entirely idle and decorative, for they did extensive amounts of sewing for their families. Girls began to sew at an early age — Hannah, Sally Logan Fisher's daughter, was only eight when she made her first shirt — and they thereafter devoted many hours each day to their needles. Most of their tasks were mundane: mending and altering clothes; making shirts for their fathers and brothers; and stitching apparently innumerable aprons, caps, and shifts for themselves, their mothers, and their aunts. Such "common sewing" won a girl "no great Credit," the New Englander Pamela Dwight Sedgwick admitted in 1789, but at the same time, she pointed out to her daughter, "[I]t will be thought unpardonable negligence . . . not to doe it very nicely." Sometimes girls would work samplers or make lace, but even the wealthiest among them occasionally felt apologetic for spending a considerable amount of their time on decorative stitchery. Betsy DeLancey, a daughter of the prominent New York family, defended such evidently frivolous employment to her sister Anne in 1768 by referring to Proverbs: "I must be industrious and make myself fine with my own Hands, and who can blame me for spending some of my time in that manner when it is part of the virtuous Womans Character in the Bible." [40]

In poor households, daughters' sewing skills could contribute significantly to family income, as may be demonstrated by reference to the Banckers of New York City. Christopher Bancker was an alcoholic, and his wife Polly tried to support the family by working as a seamstress. Yet she alone could not "du the whole," as she wrote in 1791, and so her two oldest daughters, Peggy and Betsy, also sought employment as seamstresses. Even with the girls' help the family experienced severe economic difficulties, yet the combined income of wife and daughters, coupled with charity proffered by reluctant relatives, kept the Banckers out of the poor house. Peggy and Betsy — and, by implication, other urban girls as well — thus proved to be economic assets to their families in a way that sons were not. The best that could be done with the two oldest Bancker boys was to send them out of the household to learn trades, so that they would no longer be a drag on family resources. Not until they had served apprenticeships of several years, with the expenses being borne by relatives, could they make positive contributions to the support of their parents and siblings. But their sisters had been "apprenticed" to their mother, and so they had developed salable skills at an early age. The other side of the coin was the fact that the Bancker boys' advanced training eventually paid off in higher wages, whereas the girls had little hope of ever improving their position, except through a good marriage. [41]

Because sewing was readily portable, and because they lived so close to each other, well-to-do urban girls frequently gathered to work in sizable groups. While one of their number read, usually from a popular novel, the others would pass the afternoon or evening in sewing. Like farm girls, they created an opportunity for socializing out of the necessity for work, but as a result of their proximity they were able to meet more often, more regularly, and in greater numbers. One sewing group called itself the "Progressive Society" and confined its reading to edifying tracts. "Our design is to ameliorate, by every probable method, the morals, opinions, manners and language of each other," one of the members wrote, explaining why they excluded cardplaying, gossip, and men from their meetings.[42]

In addition to sewing, city girls, like their rural counterparts, were taught what one of them termed "the mysteries of housewifery" by conscientious mothers. Sally Logan Fisher began to instruct her daughter Hannah in "Family affairs" when she was just ten, so that she would become "a good Housewife & an active Mistress of a Family." Daughters did some cooking, baking, and cleaning, helped to care for younger siblings, and on occasion took charge of the household. Sometimes they acquired this responsibility only when their mothers became ill, but in other cases adults deliberately adopted it as a training device. Abigail Adams, who believed it "an indispensable requisite, that every American wife, should herself know, how to order, and regulate her family," commented approvingly in 1788 that her son-in-law William Stephens Smith's four sisters were "well educated for wives as well as daughters" because "their Mamma had used them to the care of her Family by Turns. Each take it a week at a Time."[43]

The words chosen by Mrs. Adams and Mrs. Fisher revealed a key difference in the domestic roles of urban and rural girls. Farm daughters learned to perform household tasks because their family's current well-being required their active involvement in daily work, whereas city girls acquired domestic skills primarily so that they could eventually become good wives and mothers. The distinction was crucial. Urban daughters participated sporadically in household tasks as a preparation for their own futures, but farm girls worked regularly at such chores as a direct contribution to their family's immediate welfare.[44] The difference points up the overall contrast between the lives of urban and rural white women. In both city and farm, women made vital contributions to the success and survival of the household, but in rural areas those contributions were both more direct and more time-consuming.

IV

Wealthy southern women were directly responsible for even fewer household tasks than northerners with comparable means. But northerners who moved south soon realized the falsity of an initial impression that "a mrs of a family in Carolina had nothing to doe but be waited on as their was so many negros." Anna Bowen, a young Rhode Island woman who first went to South Carolina to visit a married sister and subsequently married a planter herself, told another sister in 1790 about the problems of running a large household. Required to "think incessantly of a thousand articles of daily supply," she sometimes did not know "which way to turn," Bowen admitted, but, she added confidently, "I shall learn in time."[45]

The daily schedules of mistresses of large plantations resembled those of wealthy urban women in the North, with the exception of the fact that social visits were confined to one or two afternoons a week because of the distance between plantations. The mornings were devoted to household affairs, although white southerners spent their time supervising the work of slaves instead of doing such chores themselves. The day began, sometimes before breakfast, with what one southern man termed "Grand Rounds from the Kitchen to the Larder, then to the Poultry Yard & so on by the Garret & Store Room home to the Parlour." After she had ascertained that the daily tasks were proceeding as planned, the mistress of the household could spend some time reading or playing music before joining her husband for dinner in early to mid-afternoon. Afterward, she would normally turn to needlework until evening, and then again to reading and writing.[46]

The supervision of what were the largest households on the North American continent involved plantation mistresses in varied activities, almost always in the role of director rather than performer. What were small-scale operations on northern farms — running a dairy, raising poultry, tending a garden — were magnified many times on southern plantations, but they remained within the female sphere. Chores that northern women could do in a day, such as laundry, took nearly one week of every two on at least one South Carolina plantation. Food management, easily accomplished in small northern urban families with access to markets, occupied a significant amount of time and required much forethought on large plantations, where each year's harvest had to feed perhaps one hundred or more people for months. White women, it is true, did not usually make the decisions about how many hogs to kill or how many barrels of corn to set aside for food and seed, but they did manage the distribution of food once it had been stored, not to mention the supervision of its initial preservation. Furthermore, they coordinated the manufacture of the slaves' clothing, spending many hours cutting out garments or superintending that work, in addition to making, altering, and mending their families' clothes.[47]

Such women invariably aroused the admiration of observers, who regularly commended their "industry and ingenuity," their "very able and active manner," or their character as "worthy economists" and "good managers."[48] Surviving correspondence indicates that the praise could be completely deserved. A prime example is provided by the Marylander Hannah Buchanan, who in August 1809 returned alone to Woburn plantation while her husband remained in Baltimore on business. She reported to him in anger that the white couple they had left in charge did not have "the smallest idea of the proper economy of a Farm." Among the abuses she discovered were a misassignment of slave women to nonessential tasks, a lack of planning for the slaves' winter clothing, and extremely poor handling of food supplies, including such errors as allowing the slaves to have wheat flour, consuming all the pork, and having no vegetables at all. "This is miserable management," she declared, and set herself to correct the situation. A month later the work on winter clothes was coming along "Wonderfully," and she was filled with ideas on how to prepare and distribute the food more efficiently. Although she expressed a desire to rejoin her husband in the city, she proposed, "[L]et me direct next year and you will spend less believe me and the people will live much better."[49]

Appropriately, then, the primary task of girls from wealthy southern families was to gain expertise in running large estates. Like their northern counterparts, they did some cooking and baking and a fair amount of sewing, but their household roles differed from those of both farm and city girls. Whereas one New England father told his daughter, "[L]earn to work as fast as you can to make Shirts etc & assist your Mother," Thomas Jefferson advised his younger daughter, Maria, who was usually called Polly, that she should know how to "manage the kitchen, the dairy, the garden, and other appendages of the hous[e]hold." Teenaged girls like Eleanor Parke (Nelly) Custis accordingly served as "deputy Housekeeper" to the mistress of the family, who in her case was her grandmother Martha Washington.[50] If this training was successful, parents could look with pleasure upon the accomplishments of such excellent managers as Martha Jefferson Randolph, who assured her father in 1791 that at Monticello under her direction "there is as little wasted as possible," or Harriott Pinckney Horry, whose fond mother, Eliza Lucas Pinckney, had herself managed three South Carolina plantations in the 1740s while she was still a teenager. "I am glad your little wife looks well to the ways of [her] hou[se]," Mrs. Pinckney told her new son-in-law within a month of his marriage, especially remarking upon her daughter's ability to run a "perfectly neat" dairy.[51]

In the end, being a good plantation mistress involved very different skills from those of the usual notable housewife of northern communities. Most importantly, the well-to-do southern white woman had to know how to command and direct the activities of others, often a great many others, not just the one or two servants common to northern households. It was less essential for a wealthy female southerner to know how to accomplish tasks herself than it was for her to know how to order blacks to perform them, and to ensure that her orders were carried out. Thus when the Virginian Elizabeth Foote Washington, who feared that she would not survive until her baby daughter reached maturity, decided to leave her a book of household advice, she devoted most of its pages to hints on the management of slaves. A mistress should behave with "steadiness," she advised; she should show the servants that she would not be "impos'd upon." The most important goal was to maintain "peace & quietness" in the household, and to this end a mistress should be careful not to complain about the slaves to her husband or her friends. Such a practice would make the servants grateful and perhaps encourage their industry, she wrote.[52]

As it happened, both the daughters born to Mrs. Washington died in infancy, and so her detailed delineation of the way to handle house servants was not passed on as she had hoped. But other white southern girls early assumed the habit of command. A telling incident involved Anne, the daughter of James Iredell, the North Carolina attorney and eventual associate justice of the Supreme Court. At the early age of four, she showed how well she had learned her lessons by "strutting about in the yard after Susanna (whom she had ordered to do something) with her work in her hand & an Air of as much importance as if she had been Mistress of the family."[53]

The story of Anne Iredell's behavior inevitably forces one to confront a difficult question: how did Susanna, a mature black woman, react to being ordered about by a white child? Or, to broaden the issue, what sort of lives were led by the black women who, with their husbands and children, constituted the vast majority of the population on southern plantations? Many female slaves resided on small farms and presumably worked in both field and house, but the discussion here will concentrate upon larger plantations, for it was in such households that most black women lived, since the relatively small proportion of white families who possessed slaves tended to own large numbers of them.[54]

Significantly, the size of these plantations allowed the specialization of domestic labor. White northern farm wives had to be, in effect, jills-of-all-trades, whereas planters often assigned slave women more or less permanently to particular tasks. A wide variety of jobs were open to black women, jobs that demanded as much skill as those performed by such male artisans as blacksmiths and carpenters. The slave list prepared by Thomas Middleton for his Goose Creek, South Carolina, plantation in 1784 included a dairymaid, a nurse, two laundresses, two seamstresses, and three general house servants. On other plantations women were also employed as cooks, spinners and weavers (after the mid-1760s), midwives, and tenders of poultry and livestock.[55]

Female blacks frequently worked at the same job for a number of years, but they were not necessarily restricted to it for a lifetime, although practices varied from plantation to plantation. Thomas Jefferson used children of both sexes under ten as infant nurses; from the ages of ten to sixteen he assigned girls to spinning and boys to nailmaking; and then either put them into the fields or had them learn a skilled occupation. Even as adults their jobs might be changed: when Jefferson went to France as ambassador in 1784, his "fine house wench" Dinah, then twenty-three, began to work in the fields, continuing at that assignment at least until 1792. The descriptions of slaves bought or sold on other plantations likewise showed women accustomed to different occupations. Colonel Fitzgerald's Nell, aged thirty-four, was "a stout able field wench & an exceeding good Washer & Ironer"; her daughter Sophy, eighteen, was a "Stout Wench & used to both field & [hou]se Work." [56]

All field work was not the same, of course, and women who labored "in the crop" performed a variety of functions. Evidence of work assignments from both the Jefferson and Washington plantations shows that there were some field jobs reserved for men, most notably cradling wheat and cutting and hauling timber for fences, but that women sometimes built fences. Women plowed, hoed and grubbed the land, spread manure, sowed, harrowed, and at harvest time threshed wheat or husked corn. At Landon Carter's Sabine Hall plantation in Virginia two women, Grace and Maryan, each headed a small gang of female fieldworkers. [57]

On outlying quarters, most women were agricultural laborers, with the occasional exception of a cook or a children's nurse. But female slaves raised at the home plantation could sometimes attain a high level of skill at conventionally "feminine" occupations. White masters and mistresses frequently praised the accomplishments of their cooks, seamstresses, and housekeepers. In a typical passage, Alice DeLancey Izard, a wealthy South Carolinian returning home after a long absence, commended her dairymaid Chloe because she found "the Dairy in excellent order, & plentifully supplied with Milk, & Butter," further observing that Chloe "has made little Chloe very useful in her line." [58]

Mrs. Izard thereby called attention to the transmission of skills among generations of female blacks. Thomas Jefferson's censuses of his plantations demonstrate that women who were house servants tended to have daughters who also worked in the house, and the

An Overseer Doing His Duty. The Papers of Benjamin Henry Latrobe, Maryland His-
torical Society. In 1798, Latrobe sketched these female slaves at work in a recently cleared
field near Fredericksburg, Virginia.

inventory of a Pinckney family plantation in 1812 similarly included
a mother-daughter midwife team. Indeed, midwifery, which was most
likely an occupation passed on from woman to woman rather than
one taught deliberately by a master, was one of the most essential
skills on any plantation. Slave midwives were often called upon to
deliver white children as well as black, and masters recognized the
special demands of their profession. In 1766, the midwife at Landon
Carter's Fork Quarter, who was also the poultry tender, left her post
to deliver a baby, an act resulting in the death of four turkeys. Even
the petulant Carter realized that her midwifery duties came first, and
so he did not punish her.[59]

In this case, a conflict arose between the midwife's divergent duties
within her master's household. More commonly, slave women must
have had to contend with contradictory demands placed upon them
by their plantation tasks and the needs of their own husbands and
children. Only a few aspects of the domestic lives led by black women
within their own families can be traced in the records of white plant-

ers, for masters and mistresses did not, on the whole, concern themselves with the ways in which female slaves organized their homes. Yet occasional comments by slaveowners suggest that black women carefully made the most of what little they had and were even able to exercise some entrepreneurial initiative on occasion. Slave families occasionally maintained their own garden plots and supplemented their meager food and clothing allowances through theft or guile. Further, black women established themselves as the "general Chicken Merchants" in the plantation South. Whites often bought fowls from their female slaves instead of raising chickens themselves, as a means, Thomas Jefferson once explained, of "drawing a line between what is theirs & mine."[60]

That some black women had a very strong sense indeed of what was "theirs" was demonstrated on Nomini Hall plantation in the summer of 1781. Robert Carter had authorized two white overseers to begin making salt, and in order to accomplish that task they commandeered an iron pot from its two female owners. Joan and Patty, the aggrieved slaves, awaited their chance and then removed the pot from the saltworks. After the whites repossessed it, the women dispatched Patty's husband, Jesse, to complain to Carter about the treatment they had received. Carter sided with the women, agreeing that their pot had been taken in an "arbitrary" manner, and he ordered it returned to them.[61]

One could argue that Joan and Patty were emboldened to act as they did because they anticipated that Carter, a well-meaning master who eventually emancipated his slaves, would sympathize with their position. But bondwomen less favorably circumstanced also repeatedly displayed a desire to control as much of their lives as was possible under the conditions of servitude. Robert Carter's relative Landon was quick to anger, impatient with his servants and children. He frequently had recalcitrant slaves whipped, a tactic to which Robert rarely resorted, yet the women at Sabine Hall were no less insubordinate than those at Nomini. If Robert Carter's "Young & Stout" Jenny deliberately had fits "upon her being reprimanded," Landon Carter's Sarah pretended to be pregnant for a full eleven months so that she could avoid work, and Criss sent her children to milk his cows in the middle of the night in retaliation for a whipping. Similarly ingenious was James Mercer's Sall, who in August 1777 convinced her master that she had consumption and persuaded him to send her to the mountain quarter where her parents lived. That summer he ordered that she should be well fed and allowed to ride six or seven miles on horseback each day until she recovered her health, but by the following year, Mercer had concluded she was faking and directed that "she must turn out at all events unless attended with a fever." [62]

The same willful spirit asserted itself when masters and mistresses attempted to move female slaves from their accustomed homes to other locations. A North Carolina woman who was visiting Boston wanted to have her servant Dorinda sent north to join her, but learned from a relative that Dorinda "would by no means go to Boston or, from Cape Fear." Some years later a Pennsylvanian who had sent a slave woman to Cuba to be sold learned that she had managed to convince the white woman accompanying her that she should be returned to her Philadelphia home, because she was "Very Unhappy and always Crying." And "Miss Charlotte," an East Florida black, demonstrated her autonomy by her reaction to a dispute over who owned her. One of the two whites involved reported that she lived with neither of them, but instead "goes about from house to house," saying "now she's a free woman." [63]

Charlotte, Sall, Dorinda, and the others gained at least a little freedom of movement for themselves, but they were still enslaved in the end. All their victories were minor ones, for they could have only limited impact upon the conditions of their bondage. White women were subject to white men, but black women had to subordinate themselves to all whites, men, women, and children alike. The whites demanded always that their needs come first, before those of black women's own families. Female slaves' work lives were thus complicated by conflicting obligations that inflicted burdens upon them far beyond those borne by most whites.

V

White Americans did not expect their slaves to gain satisfaction from their work, for all that masters and mistresses required of their bond servants was proper behavior and a full day's labor. But white women, as already indicated, were supposed to find "happiness in their chimney corners," to return to William Livingston's striking phrase. Men certainly believed that women should enjoy their domestic role. As a Georgian told his married sister in 1796, "I am sure that those cares which duty requires to your husband, and your child — must fill up every moment of time — and leave you nothing but those sensations of pleasure — which invariably flow — from a consciousness of having left no duty unperformed." Women too anticipated happiness from achieving the goal of notable housewifery. "Domestick oeconomy . . . is the female dignity, & praise," declared Abigail Adams's younger sister, Elizabeth Smith, in the late 1760s, and a Virginian observed to a friend nearly forty years later that she had "always been taught, that within the sphere of domestic life, Woman's chief glory & happiness ought to consist."[64]

The expectation, then, was clear: domesticity was not only a white American woman's inevitable destiny, but it was also supposed to be the source of her sense of pride and satisfaction. Regardless of the exact shape of her household role — whether she was a rural or an urban wife, or the mistress of a southern plantation — she should find fulfillment in it, and she should take pleasure in performing the duties required of her as mistress of the home.

Unsurprisingly, women rarely found the ideal as attractive in reality as it was in theory. But the reasons for their dissatisfaction with the restrictions of notable housewifery, which required them to be consistently self-effacing and constantly employed at domestic tasks, are both illuminating and unanticipated.

First, it must be noted that Mary Cooper was alone among her contemporaries in emphasizing the difficult, fatiguing nature of housework as the primary source of her complaints. Only she wrote of "the continnel cross of my famaly," only she filled her diary with accounts of weariness and endless drudgery.[65] Women's unhappiness with their domestic lives, in other words, stemmed not from the fact that the work was tiring and demanding. Their husbands' labor was also difficult, and in eighteenth-century America there were few models of a leisured existence for either men or women to emulate. Rather, women's expressed dissatisfaction with their household role derived from its basic nature, and from the way it contrasted with their husbands' work.

As has been seen, farmers' lives were much more varied than those of their wives, not only because they rarely repeated the same chore day after day in immediate succession, but also because they had more breaks from the laboring routine. The same was true of southern planters and of urban husbands, regardless of their occupation. The diaries of planters, professional men, and artisans alike demonstrate that their weeks were punctuated by travel, their days enlivened not only by visits with friends — which their wives also enjoyed — but also by a variety of business activities that took them on numerous errands. It was an unusual week, for example, when Thomas Hazard, a Rhode Island blacksmith, worked in his shop every day without any sort of respite from his labors, or when Ebenezer Parkman, a New England clergyman, did not call on parishioners, confer with neighbors about politics, or meet with other ministers.[66]

Against the backdrop of their husbands' diverse experiences, the invariable daily and weekly routines of housewifery seemed dull and uninteresting to eighteenth-century women, especially those who lived in urban areas, where the housework was less varied and their spouses' opportunities for socializing simultaneously greater. "The same cares and the same wants are constantly returning in domestic Life to take up my Time and attention," Pamela Dwight Sedgwick told her husband, Theodore, the Massachusetts Federalist, in words that reappeared in other women's assessments of their lives. "A continual sameness reigns throughout the Year," wrote Christian Barnes, the wife of a Marlborough, Massachusetts, merchant, and Mary Orne Tucker, a Haverhill lawyer's wife, noted in her diary that she did not record her domestic tasks in detail because "each succeeding day with very little variety would present a compleat history of the last."[67]

New England city dwellers were not the only women who made such observations about the unchanging character of their experiences. The transplanted Rhode Islander Anna Bowen Mitchell reported from her new South Carolina home in 1793, "[T]he detail of one day . . . would be the detail of the last six months of my life," while hastening to add that her days were not "insipid," but rather filled with "heart-soothing tranquility." A Virginia planter's wife was more blunt about her situation in 1785, describing herself and her friends as "almost in a State of vegitation" because of their necessary attention to the "innumerable wants" of their large households.[68]

She thus touched upon yet another source of housewives' discontent with their lot: the fact that their all-encompassing domestic responsibilities left them little time to themselves. In 1755, a New England woman remarked longingly to a correspondent, "[T]he little scraps of time that can be rescued from Business or Company, are the greatest cordials to my tired Spirits that I meet with." Thirty years later Pamela Sedgwick echoed her sentiments, telling her unmarried friend Betsy Mayhew, "[W]e that have connected ourselves in the famely way, find the small circle of domestic concerns engross almost all our attention." Sally Logan Fisher too commented, "[I] find so much to do in the Family that I have not all the time for retirement and improvement of my own mind in the best things that I wish," revealingly referring to her domestic duties as "these hindering things." Again, such complaints were not confined to northerners. A young Virginia wife observed in 1769 that "Domestick Business . . . even deprives thought of its Native freedom" by restricting the mind "to one particular subject without suffering it to entertain itself with the contemplation of any thing New or improving." A wry female poet made the same point in verse: "Ah yes! 'tis true, upon my Life! / No *Muse* was ever yet a *Wife*," she wrote, explaining that "Muses . . . in *poultry yards* were never seen," nor were they required "from Books and Poetry to Turn / To mark *the Labours of the Churn*." [69]

The point of all these remarks was the same, despite their divergent geographical and chronological origins. White American women recognized not only that their domestic obligations were never-ending, but also that their necessary concentration upon those obligations deprived them of the opportunity to contemplate "any thing New and improving." So Elizabeth Smith Shaw told her oldest sister, Mary Cranch, in 1781, several years after her marriage to the clergyman John Shaw, "[I]f Ideas present themselves to my Mind, it is too much like the good seed sown among Thorns, they are soon erased, & swallowed up by the Cares of the World, the wants, & noise of my Family, & Children." Abigail Adams in particular regretted her beloved younger sister's preoccupation with domestic concerns during her second marriage, to another clergyman, who boarded a number of students. In February 1800 she told Elizabeth (then Mrs. Stephen Peabody) that her "brilliant" talents were "en-

Elizabeth Smith Shaw Peabody, by Gilbert Stuart, 1809. Oliver B. James Collection of American Art, University Art Collections, Arizona State University, Tempe, Arizona.

cumbered" and "obstructed" by her household chores, lamenting "that the fire of imagination should be checked, that the effusions of genious should be stifled, through want of leisure to display them." Abigail's characterization of the impact of domestic responsibilities on her sister's life bore little resemblance to William Livingston's glorification of those same activities: "The mind which is necessarily imprisoned in its own little tenement: and fully occupied by keeping it in repair: has no time to rove abroad for improvement," she observed. "The Book of knowledge is closely clasped against those who must fullfil there [*sic*] daily task of manual labour."[70]

Even with their expressed dissatisfaction at the endless, unchanging nature of housework, one might theorize that late eighteenth-century American women could nevertheless have found their domestic lives meaningful if they and their husbands had highly valued their contributions to the family well-being. But such was not the case. Women revealed their assessments of the importance of their work in the adjectives they used to describe it: "my Narrow sphere," my "humble duties," "my little Domestick affairs."[71]

Always the words belittled their domestic role, thereby indicating its low status in contemporary eyes. Modern historians can accurately point to the essential economic function of women within a colonial household, but the facts evident from hindsight bear little relationship to eighteenth-century subjective attitudes. In spite of the paeans to notable womanhood, the role of the household mistress in the family's welfare was understood only on the most basic level. Such minimal recognition did not translate itself into an awareness that women contributed to the wider society. Instead, just as a woman's activities were supposed to be confined to the domestic sphere, so, too, was any judgment of her importance. Americans realized that a successful household needed a competent mistress, but they failed to endow that mistress with an independent social standing or to grant to her domestic work the value it deserved. Notable housewifery was conceived to be an end in itself, rather than as a means to a greater or more meaningful goal. As such, it was an inadequate prop for feminine self-esteem.

Accordingly, it comes as no surprise to learn that women generally wrote of their household work without joy or satisfaction. They spoke only of "the discharge of the necessary duties of life," of "perform[ing] the duties that are annex'd to my Station." Even the South Carolinian Martha Laurens Ramsay, described by her husband, David, as a model wife, regarded her "self denying duties" as "a part of the curse denounced upon Eve," as a penalty to be endured, instead of as a fulfilling experience. The usage was universal and the message unmistakable: their tasks, with rare exceptions, were "duties," not pleasures. The only Americans who wrote consistently of the joys of housewifery and notable womanhood were men like William Livingston. In contrast, Christian Barnes found the household a prison that offered no intellectual stimulation, describing it as a place where women were "Chain'd down to domestic Dutys" that "Stagnate[d] the Blood and Stupefie[d] the Senses."[72]

Yet still women did not question the overall dimensions of the ideal domestic role. Sometimes, to be sure, they inquired about its details, as when Esther Edwards Burr, Jonathan Edwards's daughter, and her close friend Sarah Prince carried on a learned discussion about the precise meaning of the parts of Proverbs 31 that outlined the virtuous woman's daily routine. But ultimately they saw no alternative to domesticity. Many were simply resigned to the inevitable, for they had few options. Certainly some expressed the philosophy that "the height of happiness is Contentment" with one's lot, that although their life had "no great veriety . . . custom has made it agreable . . . and to desire more would be ungreatfull."[73] More probable, though, is the fact that the household duties women found unsatisfying were intertwined in their own minds with responsibilities from which they gained a great deal of pleasure. Their role as mistress of the household, in the end, constituted but a third of their troika of domestic duties. They were wives and mothers as well as housekeepers, and these components of domesticity gave them the emotional and psychological rewards they did not receive from running their households efficiently.

Chapter Two

꽃

THE IMPORTANT CRISIS
UPON WHICH OUR FATE DEPENDS

MARRIAGE, IT WAS GENERALLY SAID IN EIGHTEENTH-CENTURY AMERica, brought a "Great Change" to a woman. She who had been a "rattlepated, lazy" girl was transformed overnight into a "sedate Matron." Certainly a bride's newly acquired domestic responsibilities altered her life: running a household was quite different from assisting one's mother, wherever a girl had lived prior to her wedding. Yet there was more to the shift in women's circumstances at marriage than simply the assumption of added household obligations. Colonial men and women alike believed with an English author that "marriage draws a broad line of discrimination, separating the female sex into two classes." Although men explicitly described married women as superior to their single counterparts, women did not share that value judgment. Nevertheless, they still divided the members of their sex into two different, equal, and exclusive clubs. Thus an unmarried Pennsylvanian observed to a married relative in 1779: "Cousin Sally is going to quit our Sisterhood, and enter herself into your society." [1]

Behind this apparently exaggerated perception of change lay the solid basis of reality. When a white woman married, she did not move from independence to dependence, for all her life she had been dependent on her parents, especially her father. But there were two key distinctions between her previous dependence and her new status. First, although she had had no opportunity to choose the family into

40

which she was born, she did have some control over the selection of a husband. This was both a benefit, giving her influence upon her own future, and a source of considerable anxiety, since she might make the wrong choice. Second, her marital status was enshrined in law in a way that her single state had not been. As a married woman, a *feme covert*, her dependence was legal as well as actual. In a good marriage, her status under the law would mean little, but in a poor one the consequences could be serious.

A colonial black woman's legal status did not change when she married: she remained a slave. But through marriage she, too, acquired new responsibilities that had to be fulfilled despite her obligations to the larger biracial household of which she was a part. Colonial black women as well as white often had affectionate and long-lasting relationships with their husbands, but to begin an examination of eighteenth-century matrimony with an analysis of happy marriages would not prove very enlightening. Since wives in such unions had little reason to reflect upon their subordinate position, the greatest insight can be gained by looking first at those who had direct experiences with marital discord that forced them to confront the realities of their status.

I

"I often Run over in my mind, the many Disadvantages that Accrues to our Sex from an Alliance with the other," a New York girl remarked to a close friend in 1762, but "the thought of being Do[o]med to live alone I Cant yet Reconcile." Indeed, she added, "the Appellation of old Made . . . I don't belive one of our Sex wou'd voluntarily Bare."[2]

All the evidence from mid-eighteenth-century America demonstrates the accuracy of her observation. A white spinster's lot was unenviable: single women usually resided as perpetual dependents in the homes of relatives, helping out with housework, nursing, and childcare in exchange for room and board. Even when a woman's skills were sufficient to enable her to earn an independent living, her anomalous position in a society in which marriage was almost universal placed her near the bottom of the social scale. The debilitating depression that must have afflicted many spinsters is especially evident in the fragmentary diary of Rebecca Dickinson, a Hatfield, Massachusetts, seamstress. One night in 1787, when she was forty-nine, Dickinson wondered to herself, "how it came about that others and all the world was in Possession of Children and friends and a hous and homes while I was so od[d] as to sit here alone." On another occasion, after drinking tea with her married sister and some friends, she returned to find her dwelling "dark and lonesome." Then, she observed, "[I] walked the rooms and cryed myself Sick."[3]

Given the unattractiveness of such a life, it is hardly surprising that throughout most of the eighteenth century white girls saw no alternative to matrimony. To marry was to take "the dark leep," as Pamela Sedgwick called it, to step from the well-lighted familiar existence of a parental home into a shadowy future governed by a husband one might have misjudged. Yet the options perceived by colonial women encompassed only whom, not whether, to wed. They assumed they would marry, and they recognized the significance of that transition in their lives. Thus Elizabeth Smith Shaw both congratulated and commiserated with her niece Nabby Adams on her wedding to William Stephens Smith in 1786. "The Sensations you experienced upon quitting your Father's Family were such, as I can easily conceive — What I suffered myself upon the like occasion, Time can never efface," Elizabeth recalled. "To bid adieu to our former Habitation, & to give up the kind Gaurdians [sic] of our youth, & place ourselves under quite a new kind of Protection, cannot but strike a reflecting Mind with awe, & the most fearful Apprehensions — as it is *the* important Crisis, upon which our Fate depends."[4]

Although Nabby left no record of suffering "fearful Apprehensions" about marriage, some of her contemporaries did. Just before her wedding to Lund Washington, Elizabeth Foote wrote in her journal, "I hope I have prepared my self for the worst that may happen — that is — if my marriage should prove a unhappy one." Anne Emlen, the pious Quaker who later became a missionary to the Seneca nation, had similar thoughts on the very day of her wedding to Warner Mifflin. In her diary she described the "gloom that has overspread my mind," revealing her fears that her depression presaged "some heavy curses" and "outward trials of rather a sore nature" that would come with matrimony. "May I be able to endure to the end, in the fire & in the furnace," she prayed. Another Pennsylvanian, Anna Rawle, informing her mother, Rebecca Shoemaker, of her engagement to John Clifford, mused seriously, "[I]f I am to be unhappy I console myself with reflecting on the shortness of life, and that at the end of it the enquiry will not be if it was passed pleasantly, but well." [5]

Such statements as these might well seem inexplicable in an era when romantic love had been firmly established as the basis for marriage in both England and America. Surely, one would suppose, white women eagerly looked forward to marrying the men they loved. To a certain extent, they did; but, like a Virginian, they also admitted to "some very serious reflections on the occasion . . . of becoming the wife of the man [one] prefer[s] to all others." These somber thoughts derived from women's remarkable perception of the meaning of marriage: it would determine their "future happiness or misery," it would "Cast the Die" for the remainder of their lives. As Eliza Lucas Pinckney commented succinctly in 1745 shortly after her own wedding, matrimony was "a nice affair for if we happen to judge wrong and are unequally matched there is an end of all human felicity." [6]

In contrast to such intensely personal, deeply felt female concerns about marital decision making, young men exhibited what can only be called a kind of detachment. Their correspondence contained long disquisitions on the nature of matrimony, all of them radically different from women's writings on the subject. Instead of expressing a belief that marriage would determine their fate, young men told each other that matrimony was "a Debt to Society," an "indispensible Duty" that had to be fulfilled unless the greater good would be served by "the Celibacy of some of its Members." Women never said anything comparable to the statement of a Virginian who wrote matter-of-factly in 1779 that "no Man who has helth youth & Vigour on his side can when arrived to the Age of Manhood do without a Woman." [7]

The divergent male and female perceptions of the significance of matrimony in their lives reflected the variations of reality. Marriage did fix white women's fates in a way that it did not affect men's. To be sure, an unhappy marriage could be distressing to both parties, but men's work lives transcended the home, whereas women's did not. Especially if they were city dwellers, men could find sexual outlets beyond marriage by visiting prostitutes, and if their wives were inadequate housekeepers or poor mothers they could hire servants to do the same work. But a woman had no such alternatives. The double standard prevented her from seeking sexual satisfaction with a man other than her husband, and her life was largely defined by her household. Her dependent status made her peculiarly vulnerable to the effects of her spouse's failings.[8]

To understand fully the source of women's apprehensions about marriage, then, one must examine closely the circumstances of wives trapped in unsatisfactory unions. Estimating the extent of marital incompatibility in eighteenth-century America is extremely difficult, but recent research suggests that the rates of discord were probably comparable to those of the present day. Whatever the precise incidence of matrimonial difficulties, anyone reading the private papers of colonial families immediately becomes aware of one crucial fact: all eighteenth-century white women knew of other women who were unhappily married, and so they constantly had before them examples of what their own fate could be. Thus the Philadelphian Elizabeth Graeme chose what might otherwise appear to be a peculiar way of consoling an acquaintance whose young daughter had just died. "Allow your self to think what your Daughter may have missd," she counseled. A married woman's life was "[h]ard and painful even with a kind and tender partner; but if it is our fate to be conected with A Tyrant; it is then a temporary Hell." In exchange for that, the girl had acquired "at least a habitation of rest; if not a mansion of Glory."[9]

Women who were themselves involved in marital trials clearly perceived their dependent status, their lack of options, and the insufficient protection afforded them by the law. The first two themes pervaded the poetry composed by Grace Growden Galloway, the desperately unhappy wife of the Pennsylvania politician and eventual loyalist Joseph Galloway, in the 1750s and 1760s. Years later her daughter Betsy tried to explain the verses to her own children with the comment, "Your Grandfather was a good man, but your G[ran]dmother . . . had great sensibility." The poems themselves present a harsher picture, alternating themes of male deceit and perfidy with descriptions of a "wretched Wife / Whose doom'd with him to spend her Life." In one fragment, a woman reminisces to a friend about the days of their youth: "t'was then / We was foolis[h] & silly enough to belive men." In another the author advises,

> *never get Tyed to a Man*
> *for when once you are yoked*
> *Tis all a Mere Joke*
> *of seeing your freedom again.*

Still other verses express a longing for "the holy Vestals Cot" or lament,

> *. . . I am Dead*
> *Dead to each pleasing thought each Joy of Life*
> *Turn'd to that heavy lifeless lump a wife.*

A number of the poems recount Grace's loneliness and her despair at how Joseph had changed since their courtship, when, she recalled, "Native Eloquence flowed from thy Tongue." Now, she wrote in the spring of 1759, "[I] find Myself Neglected Loathed Dispised." Although it is impossible to know how much Grace herself had contributed to the marital problems, one might speculate on the basis of these poems that the ambitious Joseph had deliberately courted the only daughter of the wealthy doctor Lawrence Growden with an eye more to financial advancement than to affection.[10]

Mary Cooper, that overworked Long Island housewife, did not write poetry, but she echoed Mrs. Galloway's themes in a diary entry written on her wedding anniversary in 1769: "[T]his day Is forty years since I left my fathers house and come here and . . . I think in every respect the state of my affairs is more than forty times worse." She, Mrs. Galloway, and other women like them could not escape from their unhappy marriages, not only because of their financial dependence upon their husbands but also because of their legal status. Referring to precisely that, a New Englander in 1757 excused her failure to write to a male friend with the remark, "[Y]ou know I am a Femme Covert and cannot act for myself."[11]

She meant it as a joke, but there was a bitter truth behind her humor. Under the common law the colonists inherited from England, married women legally became one with their husbands, and so they could not sue or be sued, draft wills, make contracts, or buy and sell property. If they earned wages, the money legally belonged to their husbands; if they owned property prior to marriage, any personal estate went fully into their husbands' hands and any real estate came under their spouses' sole supervision. Furthermore, the children of the marriage fell entirely within the custody of the father.[12]

But the picture was not wholly bleak, for *femes covert* did enjoy some protections under the common law. Most notably, they had a right to dower in their husbands' estates, guaranteeing them a life interest in approximately one-third of the family property at his death. Related to dower right was the common colonial requirement that wives be "separately examined" prior to any sale of real estate, because of the potential impact on their dower. Usually, though, obtaining the wife's consent was a mere formality, and, as Marylynn Salmon has recently shown, at least one colony (Pennsylvania) did not even adopt this common-law protection until the 1770s. But on occasion the requirement could give a woman a genuine weapon to wield against a husband's wasteful ways. Such was the message forcefully conveyed by a Pennsylvania resident who had been unable to prevent her husband from sending the family into bankruptcy, when her Maryland granddaughter was being asked to agree to a property sale. Show "prudence and fortitude," the grandmother advised, and "never give your consent. . . . When you married, the estate was equally yours, and dearly have you earned it. I allow that it seems hard that a wife should deny to pay her husband's debts, but they are not just debts. How many wives are now suffering the utmost misery by complying with the wishes of such a husband!"[13]

Despite the provisions for dower and separate examination, the common law offered married women inadequate legal protection. And so there developed in England and America the parallel system of equity, the guiding principle of which was a devotion to the spirit rather than the letter of the law. Equity permitted the drafting of antenuptial agreements, or marriage settlements, which could preserve for a woman some control over the property she brought to a marriage and in addition allow her to bequeath that property to persons of her own choice. A woman who understood her rights under equity, therefore, could ensure her future financial security before entering into matrimony. Although some historians, notably Mary Ritter Beard, have emphasized the ability of female colonists to negotiate such antenuptial contracts, recent scholarship suggests that few women took advantage of this opportunity, whether because of ignorance, neglect, belief that guarantees were unnecessary, or perhaps inability to persuade their fiancés to agree to the proposal. Accordingly, the unhappily married wife who could rely on equity's protections appears to have been more the exception than the rule.[14]

Provisions of divorce laws in the Anglo-American world are also crucial to an understanding of the position of *femes covert*, for divorces were almost impossible to obtain in the eighteenth century. Marriages, once contracted, were regarded as perpetual, and so divorce *a vinculo*, which allowed the injured party to remarry, was permitted only if some condition predating the union (such as impotence or a prior marriage) rendered the ceremony itself invalid. Divorce *a mensa et thoro*, the more common form, was essentially a legal separation agreement, sometimes combined with an award of support to an innocent wife. Granted for such causes as adultery and abusive conduct, divorce of this sort did not normally allow remarriage.[15]

Because of the difficulties of winning a legal divorce, many colonial couples simply separated by mutual agreement or ended their unions through the desertion of one of the parties. In such cases, women had to bear a special burden, since in the absence of their husbands and without a separation agreement they were unable to conduct business or to earn money that could not later be claimed by their spouses. Such were the problems that beset Rachel Wormley, of Wellfleet, Massachusetts, who believed that her husband, who had deserted her some years earlier, was also a bigamist. "Sir you Cant imagon the unesenes it gives me to sumtimes hear won thing and sumtimes another and not rearly to know how the afear is," she told the lawyer Robert Treat Paine in 1764 as she urged him to assist her. "It is not liveing with out a husband that gives me soo much unesenes," she assured him; "I think my self a thousen times haper than those that are obliged to live with a bad one." Rather, the difficulty was caused by the uncertainty as to her status at law. Was she married or not, was she *feme covert* or *feme sole?* The Massachusetts government finally resolved the question the following year when it accepted the evidence of her husband's bigamy and annulled her marriage.[16]

The same legal dependence that caused trouble for Rachel Wormley after her husband's desertion also helped to dissuade wives from running away or even filing for divorce. Abigail Gardner Drew, a Nantucket resident who compared her situation unfavorably to that of a galley slave, explained her reasoning thus: "I would willingly fly . . . but it is more than I can bear to have the one who occasions my unhappiness to enjoy . . . that property I have endured so many hardships to obtain, and I turned once more in to the wide World bereft of Interest and friends." An identical train of thought must have motivated the Massachusetts women who waited nearly twice as long as men after an offense before petitioning to separate from their spouses. Wives were both more resigned to adverse marital circumstances and less able to find alternatives to matrimony than husbands. So the Virginian Mary Ellis, who found it "humiliating" to be "the *property* . . . of a man" she had "necessarily ceased to love," deserted her husband and children in April 1801, only to return soon thereafter. A year later she once again threatened to leave, seeing "nothing before me but horror, and despair," but she nevertheless appears to have remained at home.[17]

Two well-documented cases of marital separation in eighteenth-century America show the realities of *feme covert* status and the manner in which legal disabilities impinged directly upon women who were enmeshed in unhappy unions. Nancy Shippen, a teenaged Philadelphia belle, in 1781 allowed her father, the socially conscious Dr. William Shippen, to push her into marriage with a wealthy man she did not love. Less than a year later she deserted her husband, Henry Beekman Livingston, returning with her baby to her parents' home. There she lived in a peculiar state of suspension between marriage and spinsterhood, sharing the care of her daughter with her mother-in-law and describing herself as "a wretched slave — doom'd to be the wife of a Tyrant I hate." Every attempt Nancy made to free herself from Henry ended in failure: there was no legal separation in 1785, no divorce in 1789. When her husband that same year threatened to bring suit to obtain formal custody of their daughter, the best legal advice Nancy's uncle Arthur Lee could give her was to talk privately to the wives of the justices of the Pennsylvania Supreme

Court. "It is the cause of humanity," he told his niece, "& in that cause the female voice is irresistible." Lee's confidence that no judge would "decide against humanity & you" obscured the vital fact that Mrs. Livingston had no legal standing to challenge her husband. In the end, Henry decided the matter by seeking (and evidently winning) a divorce in 1791 on the grounds of Nancy's desertion.[18]

The same legal handicaps characterized the very different case of the New Hampshire farm wife Abigail Bailey. After she had been married to her husband, Asa, for twenty-two years, Mrs. Bailey made the horrifying discovery that he had forced one of their daughters into an incestuous relationship. When she finally confronted him with her knowledge, asserting that she intended to stop his "abominable wickedness," Asa told her that she "was under his legal control; and he could overrule all |her| plans as he pleased." Although Abigail was able to throw her husband out of the house by threatening him with their daughter's promise to testify against him, she could not make Asa agree to a property settlement. Repeatedly he returned to the house to play upon her fears that she was incapable of "taking the whole charge of so great a family, and mostly young children, and all of [its] numerous affairs, without head or helper."

After several years, Asa at last consented to a settlement, but he told her they would have to travel into New York to complete the sale of their farm. Mrs. Bailey suspected a trick, but in her desperation she nevertheless agreed to accompany her husband. Once they crossed the state line, Asa announced triumphantly, New York laws "are far more suitable to govern such women as you, than are the laws of New Hampshire," and he abandoned her in the rough frontier town of Unadilla, returning alone to their home in order to settle their affairs. Realizing that if Asa was successful she would lose both her property and her children, Abigail embarked on a solitary journey of 270 miles back to New Hampshire, fortunately arriving in time to have her husband arrested.

Yet even then she had to resort to a ruse in order to regain control of the children, who were in the custody of one of Asa's friends. A sympathetic attorney informed her that "the law had given a man a right to move his children where he should think best," but also pointed out that "no law could prevent [her] attempting to alarm the man." Accordingly, relying on the ignorance of Asa's confederate, she threatened him with arrest unless he surrendered the children to her. Frightened, the man complied, and the imprisoned Asa finally agreed to a property settlement, in exchange for which Abigail dropped the charge of incest, a capital crime in New Hampshire.[19]

Perhaps the most illuminating aspect of this incredible tale is the way in which Abigail Bailey's detestable husband continually referred to her *feme covert* status as he tried to thwart her attempts to win her freedom. He was intensely aware of the power the law gave him over his wife, and he wielded it to the utmost, even to the extent of deliberately luring her into a jurisdiction where his common-law authority was magnified by local statutes. Although she was victorious in the end, her triumph resulted not from the law — with the partial exception of the fact that New Hampshire's incest penalty eventually gave her a powerful club to use against her husband — but rather from her employment of a legally groundless threat. Like Nancy Shippen Livingston, she had to rely not on the letter of the law but on the authorities' willingness to bend and stretch the statutes in order to protect her from the husband whom the law defined solely as her protector.

Mrs. Bailey and Mrs. Livingston obviously represent not the colonial norm but the extreme. Nevertheless, an understanding of their legal dilemma is crucial to a comprehension of the rational judgment that lay behind the fears white women expressed as their wedding days approached. It was not by chance that when Abigail Adams in 1776 urged her husband, John, to "Remember the Ladies" in the nation's "new Code of Laws," she did not ask that women be allowed to vote but rather that husbands' "unlimited power" over their wives be curbed. "Remember all Men would be Tyrants if they could," she reminded him; "why then, not put it out of the power of the vicious and lawless to use us with cruelty and indignity with impunity"?[20]

Abigail Smith Adams thus revealed in forthright fashion her conclusion that the major problem facing women in the revolutionary era was their legal subordination to their husbands. That subordination had little direct impact on her and other happily married wives, but it still hung like a sword of Damocles over the head of every white female American contemplating or experiencing matrimony. The secondary status of wives in the household and in the law may not have deterred women from marrying, but it nevertheless had major consequences for the conduct of courtship and marital relationships in colonial America.

II

The fact that women had no real alternative to an irrevocable marriage led to the development of two protective social mechanisms designed to prevent them from making a mistake in the choice of a husband. The first established strict rules of behavior for girls of marriageable age — rules that women violated only at their peril. The second insisted on parental involvement in marital decision making. Both were intended to guarantee that girls would not marry or surrender their virginity on impulse, for rash acts could, as Eliza Lucas Pinckney had said, bring "an end of all human felicity." Above all, young women had to ensure that they would be able to contract a good marriage, for upon that "crisis" their future hinged.

Knowing that, as one author put it, "contempt and infamy invariably follow the want, and even a suspicion of the want" of virtue, girls assiduously guarded their reputations. In the 1750s, Helena Kortwright, a New Yorker who later described herself as having been a "giddy girle" with a "poor empty head," still "never suffered any [beaux] to approach [her] too nearly, had a very great aversion to familiarity of any sort, kept them always at a proper distance." Half a century later, Eliza Southgate of Maine lengthily described to an inquiring cousin her relationship with an occasional escort after persistent rumors had raised questions about the propriety of her behavior. And in 1787, two sisters even expressed concern lest their brother's withdrawal from a courtship at a late stage would be "the means of retarding other Men from paying their Addresses" to the young woman in question, for "most of them would feel a reluctance at taking one that has been so much a friend of another." [21]

Many genteel young men understood the constraints that governed their female friends' behavior, and they adopted a stilted, formal mode of discourse when they communicated with their loved ones. For example, when "Alexis" proposed to "Zephyra" — courting couples often employed romantic pseudonyms — in 1761, he began, "I am at last resolved to make this the soft Messenger of what my faultering Tongue on every Occasion refuses to utter, & to save your native Modesty the uneasiness of a Blush by the presence of one who perhaps (which Heaven forbid) is disagreeable." Even contemporarics mocked the artificiality of this style, yet there was a reason for it. Girls complained about men whose conversation in mixed company consisted of *"little Cupids* by wholesale, with *Hearts, darts, hopes, fears, heartaches,* & all the etcetera superfluous of the *tender passion."* One said, "[T]he only Beau within my reach is the serene Hugh of Huntingdon, and I am sure he is what the Philosophers have so long been in search of, a perfect Vaccuum." However, the system they satirized was ultimately designed to protect them from excessive intimacy before marriage.[22]

In spite of all the precautions, transgressions were bound to occur, and the genteel young people's descriptions of such incidents in diaries and letters indicate the strength of the social mores they had ignored, if only briefly. "I'm told that Madam *Flora Diner* has taken a miff in consequence of your soliciting her chastity," wrote one young Massachusetts man to another in 1789. "You should always be scrupulously delicate with those females whose virtue is so perfectly established." When he referred to "that soft tender pensive glow of injured innocence" his friend would see on Flora's face upon "fall[ing] in company" with her, he hastened to add that he did not mean "falling down at the same time & in the same place with Miss Flora — God forbid!" A like event clearly occurred during James Iredell's ardent courtship of Hannah Johnston, for one day in the spring of 1773 he offered profuse apologies for having "unintentionally offended" her "noble Delicacy" the night before. He "very justly deserved" her censure, Iredell admitted, assuring her, "I will not disoblige you again in the same manner." Patty Rogers, a Massachusetts diarist in her early twenties, in 1785 recorded a relevant exchange with the acquaintance she called Philamon: "In the course of the evening he took some liberties that would not have been *strictly decent* had they come to light — It gave me *pain* — Surely thought I he must have mistaken my Charecter — Dont you *hate* me said I? I hate you P[att]y no indeed — why — what made you ask that? — Because you treated me Ill ass if you thot me a bad girl." [23]

Patty Rogers's choice of words is revealing. She, presumably like Flora Diner and Hannah Johnston, did not want to be thought a "bad girl," and she regarded Philamon's advances as an indication of his negative evaluation of her moral character. But the onus lay on her. In telling him that he would hate her for allowing such liberties (which included his putting a hand on her breast) instead of accusing him directly of a sexual transgression, she revealed her belief that the duty of restraint was hers rather than his, and that the primary burden of guilt for transcending the bounds of propriety would also be hers. Her perception was correct. The double standard was firmly in force, and women who engaged in premarital sex, or who were merely suspected of having done so, had greatly lessened their chances for a good marriage. Obeying the rules of propriety could not guarantee that a girl would find a worthy husband, but careless behavior on her part would almost certainly lead to an unfavorable result. That was why many genteel young women adhered so carefully to strict standards of behavior.

Even some girls from poorer families resisted pressures placed upon them by suitors far more importunate than genteel young men who understood the rules. Letters received by Sally Pomfret, the daughter of a North Carolina farmer, differ dramatically from those addressed to her well-to-do counterparts. "Let not your chiefest glory be immurd in the nice casket of a Madenhead withhold not what thou shoulest [sic] communicate," implored one of her admirers. A second despaired, "[Y]our Coldness to me I am afrade will Cause me to run Crasey," and a third cried, "[I]f it be a crime in mee to love O Most Adoriable it is your fair self, that hast raised such tumults in my breast, that I never since had my thoughts sease one Minuet of you since I had the Pleasure of your sweet Company." Although Sally's suitors were unrestrained in their language, the contents of their pleas suggest that she had been successful in fending off their advances, thereby protecting her marriageability. That such was not always the case with poor whites, though, is evident in a 1775 letter addressed to Lucy Gaines, the housekeeper on a Virginia plantation. "My deear love and the delite of my life," it began; "[I] very well remembur the great sattisfaction we have had in Each others Company. . . . I can nevor forgit your preshus lips as I have Cist so offten and am very desiours to make them my one." [24]

Lucy Gaines's relationship with another suitor, Anthony Frazer, the plantation's overseer, illustrates what could happen when young women failed to avail themselves of the protections afforded by the social code. John Harrower, the tutor on the plantation, thought Lucy "a tender hearted, agreeable, good girle & one that is strictly virt[u]ous, honest, & modest," and so he watched with concern as she became deeply involved with the footloose, irresponsible Frazer. Harrower's description of the affair was couched in nautical terminology filled with double entendres (as in, "I seed the Anthony Man of War & the Lucy Friggat . . . engaged Yard Arm & Yard Arm" or they were "Moor'd head & stern along side of each other in Blanket Bay"), but his satirical approach did not cover his suspicion that Anthony's intentions were other than honorable. Finally he took a hand in the matter, inquiring directly into Anthony's motives. When he concluded that the overseer did not intend to marry the housekeeper, he urged her to refuse to spend any more nights with him without an explicit promise of marriage. Gaines, though, ignored Harrower's advice, and she eventually left the plantation after Frazer simply abandoned both her and his job without warning in April 1776. [25]

Lucy Gaines's subsequent fate is unknown, but in two other cases it is possible to trace the later lives of women who bore children out of wedlock and who had accordingly violated the moral code more visibly than she. Janette Day, a New Englander, described the emotional impact of the experience when she revealed that after the birth of her daughter, "[I was so] sunk in my own Opinion I had nothing to Support me." She had lost any sense of "Internal Satisfaction" and self-respect. But Day was fortunate enough to be aided by a wealthy Boston widow, Elizabeth Murray Smith, who loaned her sufficient funds to open a small school. "Your very Acts of Benificence seemed to give me a Merit in my own Eyes, and in those of the World," declared the grateful woman, describing herself as having been "Helpless Friendless almost reduced to want" before Mrs. Smith, "the instrument in the Hand of a kind Providence," had come to her assistance. [26]

Janette Day eventually went to Scotland to marry a suitor who was willing to overlook his wife's past indiscretions. A far less satisfactory marriage was the ultimate fate of Rachel, a Virginia girl from a prominent family who bore an illegitimate son to one of the French officers who served at Yorktown. Rachel's friends, who believed her "lost to every thing that is dear to Woman," still sympathized with her plight, while her guardian, an elderly aunt, displayed understandable ambivalence about the child. "Oh her agony was indescribable whenever the sweet unoffending babe was brought into her presence," recorded Rachel's contemporary, Betsy Ambler. "Sometimes with her eyes shut she would kiss him, then send him away, and in a moment order that he might be brought back again." Rachel's disgrace also "soured" her younger sister's temper, for the older girl's behavior had affected her sister's marriageability as well as her own and had also led to family conflicts over inheritance. Reflecting upon the situation, Betsy Ambler concluded that the incident demonstrated how "a departure from Female rectitude . . . involves a family so irremediably." When her son was approximately ten years old, Rachel married "an obscure man in her neighborhood," and she eventually bore two more children.[27]

Although Betsy Ambler's father, who was the executor of Rachel's father's estate, and other family friends tried to persuade the French officer to marry Rachel, he rejected their pleas. In his obstinacy, he was aided by the fact that he was not a member of the Virginia community and did not need to concern himself about the Americans' opinion of him. In the opposite circumstances — that is, when an illegitimate conception resulted from the sexual activity of young people subject to the same social mores — the result could be quite different. Recent research into the premarital pregnancy rate in the late eighteenth century has indicated that in some New England towns as many as one-third of the brides were pregnant at the time of their marriage. This startling statistic has been variously interpreted either as evidence of a mutual youthful search for sexual fulfillment or as proof that men were becoming more adept at exploiting women. But it can also be read as an indication of the social pressures enjoining marriage upon sexually active couples. As has been seen, the clichéd script that threatened pregnant women with abandonment by their lovers had more than a little truth to it. Consequently, marriages that followed conceptions, such as the one Robert Treat Paine contracted in 1770 with his lover, Sally Cobb, show middling and well-to-do American men's respect for the proprieties of conduct. That respect may have been forced, since in Paine's case one can assume that his legal and political career would have suffered had he not legitimized the son born only three months after his wedding.[28] But enforced behavior was no less real or visible than voluntary action, and the result was the same: the woman was safely, if not quite respectably, married.

By no means did all cases of premarital pregnancy in eighteenth-century America represent weddings caused solely by social pressure and contracted against the will of one or both parties. Frequently, mutual consent was involved, as young people simply anticipated their wedding night, allowed the New England custom of bundling (in which a courting couple spent the night in bed together, supposedly fully clothed) to lead to indiscretions, or decided to present their parents with a fait accompli that demanded consent to a marriage that had not gained prior approval. But regardless of the circumstances, families still censured premarital pregnancies. A Virginia woman, for example, refused to visit her seriously ill daughter, who had had a baby seven months after a wedding the family had opposed, despite the fact that the girl "Cald out for her Mammey but as other Times No Mammey Could be found." The mother's heartlessness was condemned by her in-laws, who accused her of "cast[ing] of[f] all Bowels of Compassion" for her daughter, yet she evidently held firm in her refusal to see the young woman.[29]

If children wanted to avert such an impasse with their parents, they had to consult them at a much earlier stage in the process of mate selection. Usually, studies of parental involvement in their children's courtship take a male perspective and stress the potential conflict between boys seeking independence and fathers wishing to impose their will on their sons.[30] But girls, who wanted above all else to avoid making a mistake that might ruin their lives, often deliberately sought the advice of parents and friends as they reached decisions about whom to marry. Far from resenting their elders' interference, they generally welcomed it.

Thus Jemima Condict, a young New Jersey woman who had fallen in love with her first cousin and had been told by friends that "they dont think it is a right thing . . . it is forbid," decided in 1775 to ask for her mother's opinion: "& see if I could be Convinst one way or tother." Jemima's mother was reluctant to interfere, yet after her daughter persisted she admitted that "She had thought a great Deal about It & for her part Could Not see but that It was right & as for its being forbid She did not think there wos such a Place In the Bible." Jemima ended the conversation still wishing, "with all my heart I New the Right way & Could be made To Chuse it," but four years later she married the man in question.[31]

Eighteenth-century parents normally proved less reluctant to comment on their daughters' marital plans than did Mrs. Condict, but the girls paid similar respectful attention to opinions offered more freely. For example, Susan Vergereau, the "Zephyra" whose courtship correspondence was quoted earlier, delayed her wedding to "Alexis" (William Tennent III) for two years, until her parents, who were communicants of the Church of England, had become reconciled to the fact that he was a Presbyterian minister. By the same token, Nabby Adams decided not to marry Royall Tyler, a law student with a reputation for "practicing upon Chesterfields plan," after her father, John, adamantly opposed the match, even though her mother favored it. When Nabby finally chose a husband, she picked her father's secretary, William Stephens Smith, a man he obviously favored. Shortly after the wedding, Abigail Adams expressed the hope that Nabby would "bless the day, that a Sense of duty & fillial affection overpowerd every other consideration." Unfortunately, though, Nabby Adams Smith, like that other dutiful eighteenth-century daughter Nancy Shippen Livingston, found herself married to a man who lacked the very dependability her father had sought for her. Although John tried to put the best face on his daughter's subsequent unhappy experience with an irresponsible spouse whose business failures and frequent, lengthy, and unexplained absences brought her trouble for the rest of her life, Abigail did not allow herself similar illusions. "I make no reflections but in my own Breast," she told her sister Mary in October 1797 while Abigail was visiting her then-deserted daughter. "It is some comfort, to know that she has not been the cause, and that she could not prevent the misfortunes to which she is brought." [32]

Jane Bruce, the daughter of an Orangeburg, South Carolina, store-keeper, was not as willing as Nabby Adams or Susan Vergereau to submit to her parents' wishes, yet even so, their opposition to her marital plans caused her to hesitate for months after her fiancé, the Connecticut-born Samuel Jones, asked her to elope. "If I was sure it would give uneasiness to none but myself I . . . never would disobey him [her father]," she explained to Samuel. And so she wavered indecisively, as one of her friends put it, "between allpowerfull love and filial affection," telling Samuel first that they had to forget each other, next that she would marry him despite her parents' displeasure, then returning to her original position. Finally she requested the opinion of her closest female friends, in effect substituting their judgment for that of her parents. When they approved the match, she at last agreed to elope. After she had become Mrs. Jones, her friends served as her intermediaries as she sought reconciliation with her parents, but it was nearly ten years before her mother, by then widowed, fully accepted the marriage. [33]

Since she did not proceed with the wedding until she had ascertained that her friends favored her action, Jane Bruce's behavior confirmed the observation that the choice of a marital partner for an eighteenth-century American daughter was normally a collective, rather than an individual, decision. Young women like her readily accepted the involvement of others in their selection of spouses. Although they did not always agree with their elders' conclusions, they knew the value of a parental assessment of their suitors. So Matilda Lawrence Schieffelin, a New Yorker who had married a British army officer without her parents' consent, told them that she hoped her younger sister would not follow her "rash example," for even though her marriage was happy she could easily have been "deluded" because she had failed to consult them. "I am anxious lest my Sister should be equally indiscreet," she wrote in 1780, "but hope and entreat she may rely on your care, and marry some person whom you know and approve." [34]

While daughters consequently sought the opinions of their parents when they considered marrying, they and their elders differed significantly in their assessments of the appropriate criteria to use in judging a proposed match. Indeed, even mothers and fathers disagreed with each other on that important matter.

To fathers, and sometimes to young men as well, financial matters were often paramount. This meant both that fathers carefully investigated the financial status of their daughters' suitors and that the fathers of young men did not want their sons to marry girls with no resources. "Gerles without a porsion Stickes long on hand," observed a North Carolina Scot succinctly in 1779, and accounts of marriages thwarted or postponed because the male relatives of one half of the couple were dissatisfied with the other's financial status abound in the papers of colonial families. Occasionally, fathers downplayed the importance of money to a marriage, but their actions commonly belied their words. For example, Benjamin Franklin, who in 1757 remarked to his sister Jane Mecom that economic status was "not very material" to marital plans if the proposed partner were of good character, ten years later predicted "ruinous consequences" if his daughter Sally married Richard Bache, a struggling young printer, before his business was securely established. Angered by the fact that the young people went ahead without his formal consent, Franklin refused to write to his new son-in-law for nearly a year.[35]

Mothers, by contrast, explicitly rejected the notion that marriages should be founded upon economic considerations. Abigail Franks, an outspoken Jewish woman from New York City, wrote typically of a wealthy suitor for the hand of her daughter Richa, "[H]e is such a Stupid wretch that if his fortune was much more and I a begar noe child of Mine Especialy one of Such a good Understanding as Richa Should Never have my Consent." Mothers like Mrs. Franks were more concerned about the possibility that their daughters might marry too soon, for they believed that an early marriage could be disastrous. The Virginian Anne Randolph, who in 1788 discovered that her teenaged daughter Judith was secretly corresponding with the man she eventually married, her second cousin Richard Randolph, explained this line of reasoning most fully. In a letter to St. George Tucker, Richard's stepfather, Mrs. Randolph declared, "[A] Woman's happiness depends entirely on the Husband she is united to," so "it has ever been my wish to keep my Daughters single 'till they were old enough to form a proper judgment of Mankind." Unless a young couple was "so happy as to find in each other a similarity of temper and good qualities enough to excite esteem and Friendship," she asserted, "they must be wretched, without a remedy." [36]

Anne Randolph's comments reflected a mother's fears arising from the general feminine perceptions of marriage. But the difficulties Mrs. Randolph thought would be resolved by ensuring that her daughters were mature before they selected a marital partner were believed by the girls themselves to be surmounted by love. Young women commonly rejected suitors for whom they felt only "esteem," and their friends fully approved of their actions. "I think you did perfectly right to refuse him if you did not feel a greater affection for him then any other person," the New Englander Susan Kittredge told her closest friend, Eliza Waite, in 1792, adding that her mother concurred in the belief that women should not "give their hand where they could not give their heart." Significantly, though, Susan's father continued to press the match upon the reluctant Eliza. In company with other men, he did not believe that love was a necessary prerequisite to a good marriage. Some males, like a wealthy Maryland planter, even argued that the best way to choose a wife was by "not being in love, that is . . . not letting our Passion blind our understanding." [37]

It should not be inferred, however, that eighteenth-century men failed to love their wives or fiancées. Rather, they simply placed less emphasis on the role of affection in matrimony. Young women, for their part, uniformly insisted upon the necessity of love "to make the bands silken" and to make "[you] not wish to throw off the chains . . . but *dance along* without knowing (except from inclination) that you weare them." The feminine consensus was stated concisely in 1768 by one of Sarah Franklin Bache's friends, who, congratulating her upon her wedding, observed that "an union without affection is the most deplorable situation a woman can be in." [38]

Yet, as their choice of words indicated, women recognized that even an affectionate marriage was a form of bondage requiring their subordination and submission. They knew that, once wed, they would have to shoulder the responsibility of preserving the marriage, just as in courtship they had taken on the primary burden of restraint. Their future welfare depended on their ability to satisfy their husbands.

III

The universal message conveyed to brides was that contained in a letter Thomas Jefferson addressed to his newly married daughter, Martha (Patsy) Randolph, in 1790. "The happiness of your life depends now on the continuing to please a single person," he wrote; "to this all other objects must be secondary." The same theme pervaded the advice William Shippen offered Nancy Livingston in 1781 and that which George Lucas tendered to Eliza Pinckney in 1744. Cadwallader Colden's 1737 directive to his daughter, Elizabeth DeLancey, was notable only for its length (eight pages), and for his explicit suggestion that she keep the letter near her so she could refer to it again in the future. "You have been a Dutyfull Child to your Parents Your natural Disposition will in like manner incline you to be Dutyfull & affectionate to your husband & to his Parents," Cadwallader assured Elizabeth. "Let your Dress your Conversation & the whole Business of your life be to please your Husband & to make him happy & you need not fail of being so your self," he declared, inquiring, "can any study be more becoming in a Lady or gain her more Honour?" [39]

Eighteenth-century wives, therefore, could have had little doubt about what was expected of them. The key question is: did they, and their husbands, follow the prescribed line of conduct? Were the marriages of white couples in the latter half of the century commonly founded on feminine submission and masculine superiority?

At the outset, a secondary position for wives was signaled in the way their husbands addressed them. The standard formality of colonial modes of address — which often led husbands and wives of many years to refer to each other as "Mr." and "Mrs." — did not reveal a lack of intimacy, but rather pointed up the nature of marital relationships. James Iredell, for instance, invariably addressed his wife as "my dear Hannah." She, on the other hand, normally employed no salutation — thus perhaps suggesting her confusion as to what she should call him — but consistently referred to him in the text of her letters as "my dear Mr. Iredell." The nature of that particular marital hierarchy was thus as obvious as it was in those cases where husbands addressed their wives "dear child," or where a wife, beginning a letter with "my dearest Husband," a fairly standard opening, hastily added, "[Y]ou will excuse the liberty of addressing you as I have done," expressing her hope that she did not "give offence by this address."[40]

In the letters themselves, the unequal character of many eighteenth-century American marriages is further revealed. Occasionally, husbands separated from their families wrote not of how much they missed their wives, but of how much their wives must be missing them, in the process disclosing their own exalted sense of their relative importance. Moreover, in some sets of correspondence a blatant note of condescension entered a husband's letters. For example, when in 1783 business took George Logan away from Debby Norris, his wife of two years, he wrote her a series of letters as self-consciously didactic as any of those addressed by a parent to a child. "Remember that you are young [she was twenty-one] and have your Manners yet to form," he observed; "on this acct I hope you will always make it your business to associate with your *superiors.*" Advising her to devote several hours each day to reading, he reminded her, "[M]y good opinion . . . depends on the *amiable accomplishment* of your *mind.*" Should he be disappointed in her progress at his return, he threatened, "[I]nstead of embracing you with tenderness & affection, I shall be ready to turn from you & quit you forever." Although he did not address Debby as "dear child," George's later warning to his young son bore a striking resemblance to his earlier admonition to his wife: "Pray be particularly careful of the company you keep I hope you are convinced of the great disadvantage of associating with your inferiors."[41]

George Logan represents an extreme example of the paternally instructive husband. But his condescension was nevertheless of a piece with that of the men who began letters to their wives with "dear child" or those who, like James Iredell, employed Christian names while their spouses did not. Eighteenth-century American white men clearly expected their wives to be submissive, and many wives consciously and deliberately met that expectation.

"One of my first resolutions I made after marriage," wrote Elizabeth Foote Washington in her journal in 1789, "was never to hold disputes with my husband." When families were beset by quarrels, she continued, women were to blame, for "it is their business to give up to their husbands." Mrs. Washington, like that other submissive wife Martha Laurens Ramsay, based her opinion on the Bible: since God had told the sinner Eve that Adam should rule over her, "how dare any of her daughters dispute the point"? As might be anticipated, Elizabeth's journal entries consequently reflected her desire to please Lund and her acceptance of his primacy in their relationship. Some time after their fourth wedding anniversary, she commented, "I think [I] have had the satisfaction of conducting myself much to the approbation of my husband," thereby accepting his approval or disapproval as the proper standard for judging her behavior. Even more revealingly, she went on to state, "I have reason to think that he is perfectly satisfy'd with the choice he has made."[42]

Although at the same time Elizabeth remarked that she had never had reason to regret their union, the bias in her attitude was apparent: Lund Washington's satisfaction with the marriage was what mattered, not her own. Nowhere did she declare in equivalent terms that she was satisfied with him, or that he had conducted himself so as to win her approval. It was simply not her place to judge his behavior in the same way that he judged hers.

Many women who were more secular in their orientation and in their rationale for their actions differed little from Elizabeth Washington in their approach to the marital relationship. Wives submitted to their husbands' decisions about the family's place of residence, their religious affiliation, or their social lives, not without murmuring, to be sure, but nevertheless in explicit recognition of the obedience they owed to the head of the household.[43] Anna Bowen Mitchell demonstrated her awareness of the possible consequences of refusing to conform to this standard when she told her sister in 1792, "I know that the continuance of the first of my blessings — my husbands affection — depends in a great degree on my own conduct. . . . if I lose my hold on his affections I lose all I now have to make my life happy." Again the emphasis was crucial: she had to retain her husband's affections, rather than vice versa; her conduct was the determining factor; and her happiness rested upon the maintenance of their relationship, perhaps in a way that his did not, although she left the latter part unstated. Unsurprisingly, three months later she told her mother, "I never feel inclined to contend any point with him . . . he makes me do just as he pleases — without appearing to controul me in the smallest degree."[44]

To describe such wifely subordination as the ideal is not to argue that all eighteenth-century white women were equally submissive, or even that Anna Bowen Mitchell and Elizabeth Foote Washington were entirely accurate in their characterization of their own behavior. As has already been seen, there was a great deal of marital discord in America at the time, much of it stemming from wives' refusal to follow their husbands' desires. But the point is that women as well as men expected wives to subordinate themselves to their spouses. So, when she received her father's letter directing her to assume a submissive role in her marriage, Eliza Lucas Pinckney assured him, "[T]'is not more my duty than my inclination" to take his advice. "Making it the business of my life to please a man of Mr. Pinckney's merit even in triffles, I esteem a pleasing task," she explained, "and I am well as[s]ured the acting out of my proper province and invading his, would be an inexcusable breach of prudence."[45]

The marriage of Charles and Eliza Pinckney was an extremely happy one, as was that of George and Deborah Norris Logan. The latter's eulogy of her husband concluded with the words, "[W]e had lived together nearly 40 years, and the most tender love and entire confidence had always subsisted between us." The hierarchical organization of such marriages, therefore, did not preclude their being solidly based on mutual affection. "My Love to you is inextinguishable," said a New Hampshire clergyman to his wife in 1772; "[O]ur Hearts have been united from the first, in so firm, so strong, so sweet an Affection, that words are incapable of setting it forth," wrote Sally Logan Fisher in 1777. "I believe there never was married people who liv'd happier than we do," declared Elizabeth Foote Washington; "[E]very day increases the enthusiasm of my tenderness for him," effused Anna Bowen Mitchell; and Mary Norris Dickinson told her husband, John, the prerevolutionary pamphleteer, that she loved him "with an Affection . . . reaching beyond the present Shadows of a short Existence."[46]

Such sentiments were genuine and deeply felt. White American wives had an unambiguously subordinate marital role, but — at least until the very end of the century — there are few or no indications that they resented their secondary status. When the marriage was unhappy, their subordination in law and in fact had severe personal consequences, but under more normal circumstances they saw no reason to challenge or question their position. The "painful reaction" Mary Palmer recorded when she first realized her "total dependence" on her husband, Royall Tyler, after a period in which she had blissfully romanticized "the idea of being his for life, of spending that life in doing everything to make him happy," was unique to her. Most wives would have instead agreed with Abigail Adams, who in 1783 asserted, "Well ordered home is my chief delight, and the affectionate domestick wife with the Relative Duties which accompany that character my highest ambition." [47]

IV

When one turns from a discussion of the marital lives of female whites to a consideration of black women's experiences, difficulties immediately arise. The evidence available for the study of slave marriages in the eighteenth century lacks the variety and richness of that pertinent to whites or to blacks who lived later, during the antebellum years. Furthermore, since all but an infinitesimal number of black women in this period were illiterate, they left no documents comparable to the ones that have been analyzed in the preceding pages. In order to learn about a female slave's marital life, it is accordingly necessary to rely on the letters and papers of white planters and overseers.

Plantation records demonstrate that, although most black women married, matrimony was probably not as universal an experience for them as it was for whites. Thomas Jefferson's periodic censuses of the slaves who lived on his holdings show proportions of single female adults ranging from an anomalous low of 5 percent in 1783, after wartime runaways and deaths had affected the population, to an equally anomalous high of 40 percent in 1810, which was undoubtedly an artifact of Jefferson's record-keeping methods. In more normal times the proportion of single females averaged 22 percent. Although many of these women married at some point during their lives, at no time during the latter part of the eighteenth century was as large a proportion of adult white females unattached to a marital household. The high percentage of single black women on Jefferson's lands, then, implies that a relatively large number of them failed to marry at all.[48]

The cause of this phenomenon rested in the slave system itself. Women who lived on isolated small farms and plantations must have found it difficult to locate satisfactory marital partners, for in some regions the black population was thinly scattered. Where most white families owned only one or two slaves — who were purchased for their work skills, not for their compatibility by age or sex to other nearby blacks — the development of long-term marriages would have been difficult indeed. On larger plantations, despite their sizable populations of slaves, heavily imbalanced sex or age ratios could prevent the formation of families, even leaving aside the question of personal preference. What is striking about the evidence from plantation registers, therefore, is the fact that, against all odds, they show the existence of high proportions of marriages. Of thirty-two women on a Georgia plantation in 1777, thirty were living with their husbands; of twenty-five on another Georgia holding some years later, seventeen had spouses present; of seven on a small South Carolina estate in the late 1790s, four had husbands who shared the same owner, and a fifth appears to have had a husband nearby, for she bore children regularly.[49]

The problems that could confront black couples parted by divergent ownership can be illustrated by reference to the courtship and marriage of Juliet and Jack, who were Massachusetts residents. In 1769, Jack, who belonged to Elizabeth Murray Smith, began to pay court to Juliet, the property of Christian Barnes and her husband, Henry. By December, Jack had had a pair of earrings made for his loved one, and in February 1770 Mrs. Barnes reported, "I believe they have consented to take each other for Better for worse in their own way." Jack, she said, was "an extreem fond Husband" who "could not bear to be long absent from his beloved." Juliet soon became pregnant, and Mrs. Barnes began to consider "how I shall dispose of it." When Juliet's time came, though, she put her to bed "in the Best rome under the Green Curtains," for Jack "would take it ill if she was to be put any where else." Late in November 1770,

Juliet had a baby girl, making Jack "the very Happiest of Mortals." One wonders how Jack and Juliet felt when Mrs. Barnes quickly "disposed of" their daughter by giving her to a woman who lived about three miles away. In any event, five years later Juliet bore a mulatto child, and as a result Mrs. Barnes decided to sell both her and the baby. "If you have any inclination to part with Jack," she told Mrs. Smith, "I beleive it would conduce to both their Happiness to be fellow Travilers his dillicacy does not seem to be much hurt and she has declared that if she could be with Jack she would never have any other Husband." [50]

Slave women who lived on large plantations were not necessarily less vulnerable to sexual exploitation by whites, but at least they could establish more permanent marital relationships than could Juliet and Jack and others similarly separated in both the North and the South. Thomas Jefferson's records make this especially clear. Out of sixty-two marriages noted on his censuses and other slave lists, only one was broken for a reason other than the death of one of the partners. Barnaby (b. 1783) and Lilly (b. 1791), the parents of three children, were last listed as husband and wife in 1812. By 1816, he was married to Milly (b. 1797), by whom he had another child, and Lilly was married to Ben. Other than this sole example, Jefferson's records reveal no marital separations. To a certain extent, this remarkable fact results from the nature of the documents, since Jefferson failed to identify the husbands of some of his female slaves who bore children. In such instances, either the woman had no regular partner or she had married off the plantation, and in neither case can her marital history be traced with precision. But once marriages were established between men and women on Jefferson's holdings, they persisted until broken by death.

Jefferson recognized the value of having couples thus united under his ownership. The policy not only reduced casual absenteeism, it also prevented the trouble that could ensue if another planter decided to sell the spouse of a particularly valuable slave. As a result, although he grumbled about blacks who "imprudently married out of their respective families," he still indicated his willingness "to indulge connections seriously formed by those people, where it can be done reasonably." He lived up to his words on a number of occasions, buying slaves he did not need or selling those he would have preferred to retain in order to keep husbands and wives together. Jefferson never assigned spouses to different quarters, and he also took special steps to encourage marriages within his plantations. In 1815, for example, he scolded an overseer for refusing to allow Phill Hubbard to visit his new wife, Hannah, asserting, "[T]here is nothing I desire so much as that all the young people in the estate should intermarry with one another and stay at home. They are worth a great deal more in that case than when they have husbands and wives abroad." He accordingly ordered the overseer to give Hannah a pot and a bed as a reward for marrying at home, and expressed the hope that "others of the young people [will] follow their example."[51]

Other planters, though, were not as respectful of black marriages as was Thomas Jefferson. Judging by the number of instances in which Robert Carter moved slaves from quarter to quarter in order to reunite divided couples, he was not nearly so careful as Jefferson in the initial determination of living arrangements. Furthermore, what would have been great personal tragedies for the blacks involved were revealed offhandedly when slaveowners casually mentioned buying a young woman "big with her first child" or proposed to sell "[Hanna]hs husband" in another state.[52] In addition to the ever-present threat of sale, enslaved couples had to cope as well with strains unknown to their white masters and mistresses — among them the possibility that the wife might have to submit to a white man's sexual advances. Consequently, it comes as no surprise to find in planters' records accounts of battered wives, rapes, and violent quarrels among young men over marriageable girls.[53]

The conditions of their bondage thus laid heavy burdens upon black husbands and wives. Fortunately, on large plantations, where most slaves lived, marriages did not exist in isolation. Since the settled area of the slaveowning South did not expand substantially during the last half of the eighteenth century, black families were not broken up quite so drastically or so often through widespread movement as they were after 1815, when the fertile Gulf Coast states first opened to large-scale cultivation. Although sales occurred, many transactions were confined to the local area. Accordingly, at least from the standpoint of their female members, enslaved families could well have been more geographically stable than those of free white people.

In contrast to a white woman, who usually left her parental home when she married, a black bride normally did not leave the plantation on which she had been reared in order to join her husband elsewhere. If she married another slave on the same plantation, the young couple simply set up housekeeping near both sets of parents. If she married off the plantation, she still remained where she was, unless her husband's master was willing to buy her. In familial terms, this pattern meant that a black woman in colonial America was far more likely to be surrounded by extended kin than was her white counterpart. And the fact that siblings, grandparents, aunts, and uncles lived in proximity for years gave slave marriages a kind of familial insurance against catastrophe. If marriages or families were broken by sale, close kin almost always remained on the home plantation to care for children or old people.

In 1792, for example, Thomas Jefferson decided to sell eleven slaves from his Bedford estates: two unattached men, two single women (one of whom was only eighteen), the two unmarried uncles of the latter, and a young couple with their children, whom Jefferson directed to be sold "in one lot." The couple, Sam and Dilcy, left behind them a total of nine blood relatives (parents and siblings). Jefferson specifically provided that the buyer of the two brothers, who were both in their twenties, would have to agree to accept their parents, Will and Judy, "for nothing should they chuse to go with their sons." But instead, Will and Judy decided to remain at Bedford with their oldest daughter, Abby, and her husband, Will Smith, the parents of the eighteen-year-old.[54]

The details of this one sale suggest something of the complexity of the kin relationships that developed over time on Jefferson's plantations, but an even better sense of those familial ties can be gained by taking a close look at the people who lived on one Bedford quarter in 1810. After Phill Hubbard married Hannah in 1815, Jefferson moved them from Poplar Forest quarter to Bear Creek, noting, "Phill has been long petitioning me to let him go to Bearcreek to live with his family." The family at Bear Creek Phill wished to join consisted of (in 1810): his mother and father, Cate and Jame Hubbard; his sisters, Eve, Maria, Sarah, and Rachael; Rachael's husband, James; all his sisters' children with the exception of two teenaged boys who lived at Monticello; his foster brother, Armistead; two of his nephews through his sister Hannah, who lived with her husband and family at Poplar Forest; and a son of Hannah's sister-in-law. The only persons at Bear Creek apparently unrelated to the Hubbard clan were a married couple and their five young children. Conversely, the only Hubbards who did not live at Bear Creek were another foster son and those already identified above (that is, Hannah and her family at Poplar Forest and the two boys at Monticello).[55]

Phill Hubbard's persistent campaign to move to Bear Creek to be near his parents and siblings only hints at the emotional bonds that infused black family life. Even whites like Thomas Jefferson understood the strength of those ties, a fact Jefferson confirmed obliquely in 1803, when he sought a means of penalizing Cary, a young man who had seriously injured another plantation resident in a fight. The worst punishment Jefferson could think of was to sell Cary to a slave trader from Georgia, for, he explained to his son-in-law Thomas Mann Randolph, "if he could be sold in any other quarter so distant as never more to be heard of among us, it would to the others be as if he were put out of the way by death. I should regard price but little in comparison with so distant an exile of him as to cut him off compleatly from ever again being heard of."[56] Jefferson's recognition that exile from the plantation family was the equivalent of death speaks eloquently to the force of kin relationships among eighteenth-century blacks.

Chapter Three

FAIR FLOWERS,
IF RIGHTLY CULTIVATED

An EIGHTEENTH-CENTURY AMERICAN WOMAN COULD EXPECT TO BE-
come pregnant within twelve months after her wedding, and to bear
children at roughly two-year intervals during the remainder of her
fertile years. Multiple pregnancies, in other words, were as universal
a female experience as matrimony itself. A woman's total number of
children was thus directly related to her age at marriage: the earlier
she married, the more children she was likely to have. Mature women
spent much of their lives either pregnant or nursing, and so the little
Virginia girls who in 1774 mimicked adulthood by "stuffing rags . . .
under their Gowns just below their Apron-Strings" accurately perceived their future.[1] Because of the way in which births were spread
through her life span, a colonial woman usually had dependent children in her home almost until the day of her death. Child rearing
consequently occupied much of her time and attention, competing
directly with her household chores for her limited resources of energy.

Just as many women enjoyed a satisfying relationship with their
husbands, so too they gained great pleasure from their children.
Endearing terms and expressions of love for their youngsters fill their
diaries and letters. It would be incorrect to assert that there was never
any friction between mother and child, but women's comments on
child rearing stand in sharp contrast to their attitudes toward domestic
work. Their positive feelings about children are especially striking

when viewed against their dread of pregnancy, for female Americans well knew that they could enjoy their maternal role only after they had survived the many hazards of childbirth.

I

Demographic studies of colonial fertility reveal the stark statistics of childbearing in eighteenth-century America. In completed families — that is, those in which the union was not broken by the death of one of the partners before the wife's childbearing years were finished — white women could expect to bear five to seven live children. Since many pregnancies ended in miscarriage, stillbirth, or the early death of the baby, most mature women experienced five to ten pregnancies and had between three and eight surviving children. Abigail Smith Adams, to take a prominent example, had four living children, a stillbirth, and a baby who died in infancy, and Sally Logan Fisher bore five children who survived, had two stillbirths and a miscarriage,. and lost one infant at the age of eleven months.[2]

Among the white population of Hingham, Massachusetts, which has been studied in detail by Daniel Scott Smith, the standard period between births was about twenty-eight months. On average, then, Hingham women became pregnant again only one and a half years after the birth of a previous child. In comparison, the black women who lived on the South Carolina plantations of John Ball bore children at an average thirty-four-month interval, with just 35 percent of them becoming pregnant as early as the Massachusetts whites. On Thomas Jefferson's Virginia holdings, on the other hand, 47 percent of the women had children as frequently as did the average northern woman.

As a result, Jefferson's female slaves on the whole experienced a higher number of live births before the end of their fertile years than did Hingham whites, for they began bearing children sooner. Whereas in Hingham females normally married at twenty-three and bore their first children at the age of twenty-four or twenty-five, women on the Jefferson plantations had usually borne a child before they reached twenty. Therefore, they would have had two or possibly even three children by the age at which whites began childbearing. But the black patterns were not uniform. The Virginians began childbearing earlier, had children at shorter intervals, and ended with larger families than did the women on Ball's plantations. The differences, which are evident in tables 1 and 2, probably resulted from the more stringent physical conditions under which the Carolinians lived rather than from divergent social customs.[3]

Despite such variations, though, the general pattern of a birth every two or three years to each fertile married woman was accepted as a rhythmic part of colonial Americans' everyday existence. Esther Edwards Burr, for example, remarked in March 1757, a year after the birth of her second child, Aaron, that during the coming fall she might not be "in circumstances proppor for Traveling, tho' nothing of that yet," and Americans often commented that shorter-than-normal birth spacing would bring larger-than-usual families.[4] To Thomas Jefferson, the expectation that slave women would give birth regularly was a key component of good plantation management. "I consider a woman who brings a child every two years as more profitable than the best man of the farm," he declared bluntly in 1820. "What she produces is an addition to the capital, while his labors disappear in mere consumption." Jefferson therefore regarded "the labor of a breeding woman as no object," and he ordered his overseers to make certain that women had as much time as they needed for childcare. His solicitude for the preservation of black marriages also probably stemmed partly from the same mercenary motive, although he nowhere explicitly stated as much.[5]

A sense of inevitability pervaded Americans' reflections on fertility. Abigail Adams remarked in 1808, "I have heard some good women say with respect to children that they must have their Number. This doctrine takes away the free agency of Man, but I believe serves as a consolation to those who can fully assent to it." Mrs. Adams's choice of words is instructive. To her mind, women needed "consolation" when they considered their likely fate as childbearers, a consolation gained perhaps through resignation. She herself showed that she could not "fully assent" to that philosophy, for she openly lamented her daughter Nabby's repeated pregnancies, declared that her sister Elizabeth was "foolish" to start "a second crop" of children at

Table 1

AGES OF MOTHERS AT FIRST BIRTH, JEFFERSON AND BALL PLANTATIONS

Age	15	16	17	18	19	20	21	22	23	24	25	26	Total children	Average age of mother
Jefferson:														
all births	4	8	7	18	12	9	8	1	2	1	0	2	72	18.5
post-1774 only	4	8	7	16	6	7	7	1	1	0	0	0	57	18.2
Ball:														
all births	1	1	4	8	6	4	4	2	3	1	0	2	37"	19.9"
post-1780 only	0	1	3	5	1	3	3	2	2	1	0	1	23"	20.3"

" Includes one birth at 28.

NOTE: Birth records improve on the plantations after 1774 and 1780, respectively, so that the second set of figures is probably more accurate, though the sample is smaller.

74

the age of forty, and welcomed the news of a young relative's miscarriage in 1800, believing that "it is sad slavery to have children as fast as she has."[6]

Mrs. Adams was not alone in revealing a negative attitude toward excessive childbearing, for the parents, siblings, and husbands of exceptionally fertile women echoed her sentiments. "My Poor Dr Polly is again in ye way to increase her Family," wrote a Virginia mother in 1791. "I cou'd wish she did not have 'em quite so fast," since "breeding . . . has alter'd her very much." "Poor Soul," said the Marylander Molly Tilghman of her sister Henny in 1788; "she is decidedly *gone* to my great grief, and her own too." To Catherine Vanhorne Read, the New York–born wife of a South Carolinian, her friend Martha Laurens Ramsay was "unconsionable" for declaring that she wanted to bear numerous children. "The act of getting them with the sweet Dr must be very delightful for when you hear people talking of such things you cant help bringing to your mind that situation," Catherine mischievously told her sister, adding, "I do not wish you to fill your nursery too soon."[7]

Relatives regretted a pregnancy principally because of its possible adverse effect upon the mother's health. Yet the few statistical analyses of female life expectancy in eighteenth-century America do not support the once-standard belief that a large proportion of women died in childbirth and that women had significantly lower average longevity than men. Nevertheless, such studies do imply that women ran a greater risk of dying in the prime of life than did their male counterparts.[8] In any event, actual circumstances were less important than perceptions. Like unhappy marriages, childbed deaths were sufficiently familiar to adult Americans to affect their attitudes. Indeed, all white colonists appear to have been acquainted with women who died as a result of childbearing.

Even if one confines the analysis to Americans' accounts of the deaths of close friends and relatives, the evidence is clear. The Reverend Ezra Stiles, whose mother, Kezia, had not long survived his own birth, lost his second daughter, also Kezia, before her first child could be delivered in 1785. The Virginia diarist Frances Baylor Hill observed the death of her sister-in-law from puerperal fever in 1797; Abigail Paine, Robert's sister, had a good friend who died from the

Table 2

HOUSEHOLDS WITH BIRTHS ON JEFFERSON (1755–1823) AND BALL (1740–1815) PLANTATIONS

by Number of Births per Household

Number of Births	0	1	2	3	4	5	6	7	8	9	10	11	12	Total families	Total children	Average number of births
Jefferson:																
all families	9	19	12	13	10	12	6	5	6	3	5	4	1	105	434	4.5[e]
completed families[a]	0	0	1	0	1	3	1[c]	2	4[d]	3	2	3	1	22	166	7.5
Ball:																
all families	[b]	16	17	17	10	8	5	3	6	2	1	1	1	87	331	3.8

[a] On the Jefferson plantations, completed families are those in which first births fall between 1774 and 1800 and in which the woman remained on the plantation throughout her childbearing years. The number of completed families for the Ball plantations cannot be calculated because the only detailed source is a birth register. In the absence of other evidence, it is impossible to know whether women who stopped bearing children remained on the plantation through their fertile years. The lower numbers in the "all families" columns are inflated by the inclusion of young women who had just begun childbearing at the end of the period.

[b] No figures available for nonchildbearing married women on the Ball plantations.

[c] A woman who married twice.

[d] Includes a family in which births begin 1801.

[e] Families with children. If the 9 childless couples are included, the average is 4.1.

same cause; and David Ramsay's first wife, a daughter of the New Jersey educator John Witherspoon, likewise succumbed to fever only five days after the birth of her son in 1784. The experience of the Virginian John Coalter was extraordinary, but it is nonetheless illuminating. Both of his first two wives, Maria Rind and Margaret Davenport, died as a result of their first pregnancies. No special insight is needed to understand the panic that filled him when his third wife, Fanny Tucker, told him of her forebodings on the approaching birth of their own first child, an event he termed "the Crisis of all our hopes & fears."[9]

The cumulative effect of such deaths on the women and men who witnessed them cannot be underestimated. Whatever the statistical probabilities, pregnant women believed they faced a genuine threat of imminent death.

Expectant white women disclosed their own fears when they concealed pregnancies in order to avoid "alarming" their relatives, as did Sarah Livingston Jay in 1783 while she was in Europe with her diplomat husband, John. But they could not hide their apprehensions from themselves. Women referred to childbirth as "the Dreaded apperation," "the greatest of earthly miserys," or "that evel hour I loock forward to with dread." When the newlywed Helen (Nelly) Blair Tredwell suspected she was pregnant in 1790, she told her aunt Hannah Johnston Iredell, "I shall have to exert myself to the utmost to keep from the greatest dejection of spirits & Caprice of Temper."[10] Some women, like Elizabeth Foote Washington in 1784, were convinced that they would die in childbirth; others movingly revealed their reflections upon their perilous circumstances. Thus in 1755 Abigail Paine Greenleaf instructed her brother Robert, "[L]ook upon me as a sister who is traviling on with her life in her hand not Expecting to write much less to see you again before she must be call'd at best to step over the grave for so my approaching hour always appears to me." And, poignantly, a young Pennsylvanian who was to die in childbirth two years later told her mother in 1772, "I am not disheartened the same Good God, that delivered my Dear Mama, I trust will have Mercy on me in my distress, & hear my Prayer."[11]

Knowing what her fears must be, a woman's friends and relatives supplied a constant stream of encouragement during her pregnancy.

"Do not let your spirits get to much depresed for your helth gretly depends on that," a New Yorker told her sister in 1804, echoing the advice that had been offered by Elizabeth Murray Smith to her favorite niece, Dolly Forbes, thirty-five years previously: "[K]eep up your spirits anxiety is bad for health." Thomas Jefferson informed his younger daughter, Polly Eppes, in December 1803 that a friend of her mother's "used to say it was no more than a knock of the elbow," urging her to follow the example of her older sister, who had a month before successfully borne a daughter. But Polly Eppes, who was to die in that childbed, must have recalled her own mother's death after a difficult childbirth, just as Margaret Davenport Coalter, receiving in 1797 from a similarly pregnant acquaintance a brave but nonetheless panicky assurance that "Matrons tell me it is *nothing*," must have reflected on the fate of her close friend and predecessor, Maria Rind, who had died, as she was to do, from the effort of attempting to bear their husband John's first child.[12]

When a woman's time approached, her female relatives would, if at all possible, come to help her prepare for the event. A pregnant woman's most likely attendant would have been a younger, unmarried sister, because if her mother had small children remaining at home, as most women did, she would not have been able to leave her household for an extended period. The oldest unmarried daughter could most easily be spared from the parental home; by serving as chief nurse to her sister she fulfilled yet another of her multitudinous household functions.[13]

In this respect a slave woman was probably more fortunate than her pregnant white counterpart. Although no detailed descriptions of the persons present at a female black's childbed seem to have survived, it is logical to assume that her mother and sisters were at her side, since they commonly lived on the same plantation and perhaps even on the same quarter. When Winney, a 1784 runaway from one of Robert Carter's quarters, surrendered herself to the overseer after an absence of seven months, she may have been seeking just such assistance from her relatives, for she was described as being "forward with Child." In any case, planters' records show that women attended each other at births, even when the relationships among them are obscure.[14]

Immediately before a white woman was brought to bed, her female friends were summoned to her side. The full meaning of such assistance from close acquaintances was revealed by expectant mothers deprived of this aid. Dolly Forbes, facing childbirth in St. Augustine far from her New England family, hastened to assure her worried aunt Elizabeth Murray Smith, "[A]ltho I am in a strange place I meet with great Friendship," especially a "fellow feeling" developed with another young woman similarly pregnant and living away from her relatives. Martha Jefferson Randolph bore her eighth child at the White House in 1806 because her closest Virginia friend would have been unable to help her in childbed, and Sarah Jay attributed her slow recovery from the birth of a daughter in 1783 to the fact that she was in Spain and did not have her "dr mamma or sisters" with her.[15]

Husbands too remained nearby. Although no direct statements place a husband at a birth itself, surviving letters indicate men's deep emotional involvement with their wives' travail. Joseph Reed, the Pennsylvania revolutionary leader, refused to leave his wife Esther's side when she was about to have their first child, and he likewise was present in the house for her next births. A New Englander described himself as "Nursing" his wife following the birth of their daughter, and in 1770 Robert Treat Paine spoke of how Sally had "Endured a Natural Regular uncommonly tedious & painful Travail for 21 hours, the pore Girl endured beyond description." The detailed nature of this passage suggests that Robert was present during at least part of his wife's labor, and a similar indication came from the New Yorker Elizabeth Kent, when she told her lawyer husband, James, in 1807, "I never will bring you a son or daughter again in your absence — my heart is too tender & it suffers too much." In light of statements like these, childbirth in late eighteenth-century America cannot be interpreted as a purely female affair. Although husbands were perhaps not present at the actual moment of birth, neither they nor their wives wished them to be excluded from the process of bringing a child into the world.[16]

Both black and white women were usually attended by midwives as they gave birth. As early as the 1770s, though, whites occasionally consulted doctors during pregnancy.[17] By the later years of the century, they had begun to employ physicians to supervise births when-

79

ever difficulties were anticipated, but relatives and neighbors continued to assist even in such instances. In 1794, for example, Sally Logan Fisher recorded attending a birth at which Dr. William Shippen officiated. Although male doctors had begun to practice obstetrics, in other words, they did not — at least initially — follow the advice of the medical manuals of the day and bar women from helping their friends in childbed.[18]

The way in which all the factors that have been discussed so far — ambivalence about pregnancy, the role of female friends, fears of possible complications, preparations for the event, and reactions to the childbirth deaths of acquaintances — together impinged upon a woman expecting a child can be seen in the experience of one woman, Sally Logan Fisher. Because her diary is both long and complete, her lifetime of childbearing can be examined sequentially in its totality, thereby summing up in a single example the comparable histories of her contemporaries.

Mrs. Fisher's diary begins in the fall of 1776, when she was twenty-five and had been married to her "beloved Tommy" for approximately three years. She already had one child, Joshua, and she was eager to bear another. For several months the entries spoke of her "great dissapointment" when her menstrual period arrived. Then, in mid-March 1777, she wrote, "very sick" and, several days later, "very sick indeed." The pregnancy must have progressed without incident, for she did not refer to her condition again until only a few weeks before her second child, Hannah, was born in November. While she was still nursing Hannah eleven months later, Sally suspected she had again become pregnant and, after consultation with a nurse and a female relative, decided to wean her daughter. But shortly thereafter she suffered a miscarriage, and she had to console herself with the thought that she was "so blessed, in having such a comfortable Home, such a beloved Partner, & two such dear Babies, to sweeten, & releive every Toil."[19]

Once again, in mid-December 1778, an entry marking her menstrual cycle appeared in the diary: "[M]uch dissapointed this evening . . . what would I give, to have [what] I wish accomplished by this Day twelve month." Mrs. Fisher did not have long to wait, for she became pregnant within a month. During this fourth pregnancy matters did not go quite so smoothly, for several times she became worried about her condition and arranged to be bled. She continued to work actively around the house, in spite of her discovery that washing clothes, churning, and whitewashing the walls fatigued her greatly. She wrote in August, "[I am] putting every thing in order, which I love to have done against my confinement if I can, for that generally brings work enough, without having any thing else to do." By early September everything was ready, and her second son, William, was born after "a very hard difficult Labour" on September 21, the exact day she had predicted two months previously.[20]

But less than a year later Sally sadly recorded the death of that "dearest Billy," and on New Year's Eve 1780 she lamented, "[W]hat a loss I have met with since this Day twelvemonth in my sweet Billy, will it be supplied, in another twelve or how will it be." The following day she noted, "[Q]uite give up on a certain matter for the present a great fault somewhere on ytiliba." Yet later that same month (January 1781) the signs of pregnancy appeared again, and in early October she bore another Billy in "a very fine easy Labour" to take the place of the one who had died.[21] Exactly two years later she had a third surviving son, James. During this sixth pregnancy Sally Fisher was much troubled by the deaths of two of her friends in childbed and by the "very dangerous difficult Labour" of a third acquaintance, which, she wrote, "made me very thoughtfull about myself," but the similar death of another friend in January 1784 prompted her most extended reflections on the subject: "[H]ow many accidents & sudden Deaths, particularly among young Married Women, have lately happened, to awaken & arouse us that are yet continued, may it have the proper effect, for we none of us know how soon, how suddenly we may be summoned to the silent Grave."[22]

Despite increasingly poor health and the deaths of two more friends in childbirth — the latter of which brought her comment that it was "an awfull consideration to those who expect to be in that way" — Sally hoped for a fifth child. In July 1785 her prayers for pregnancy were answered, but the following March Dr. Shippen delivered her of a dead girl a month prematurely. It took Mrs. Fisher a long time to recover: four weeks after the stillbirth she noted, "[A]m weak & poorly more so than common, owing to backening my Milk, & feel very lonely without my dear little Baby." Nine days later she observed, "Betty took down my Blue Bed — will it ever go up again or not."[23]

Less than a year after that Sally Logan Fisher's inquiry was answered, as she conceived for the eighth time. She was brought to bed in August 1787, after a pregnancy that had been troubled from its outset. As early as the second month she sensed that something was wrong; by the fourth she feared another premature birth; by the sixth she was having "very restless uneasy Nights" and needed Dr. Shippen's medicine to allow her to sleep. In late June, she wrote, "I much wish to be resigned, but this sometimes is a hard Lesson for Human Nature to learn, & cannot be come at of our selves." A month later a woman friend came to help her make "little Caps" for the expected baby, just as Sally had always prepared "little things" during her previous pregnancies, but this time she remarked disconsolately that she was "uncertain" whether she would need them. This time, too, Sally took great comfort from the regular visits of her female friends and relatives. "Neighbour Evans called in to see me & encouraged me," she noted at the end of July, and on August 10, after a large group of women had come to see her, she commented, "[T]heir kindness & attention to me since my confinement I hope I shall ever remember with Gratitude & Affection & endeavour to return it." But neither Sally nor her friends could do anything to save the baby: on August 19 she was delivered "by force of a very fine Boy which had been Dead some Days." She observed, "This was a close triall to me, greatly retarded my recovery & sunk my Spirits."[24]

In spite of the two successive difficult stillbirths Mrs. Fisher welcomed her ninth, and final, pregnancy the following year. She tired easily while she carried the child, and although she did not experience severe problems her diary entries were filled with a new note of resignation as she expected a death — either her own or the baby's. But this time her worst fears went unrealized, and she bore a second daughter, Hetty, in December. An illness following the birth weakened her considerably, and in May 1789 Susanna Dillwyn described her as looking "the most like a corpse I ever saw a living face." Indeed, Sally Logan Fisher never fully recovered from the rigors of her last three pregnancies, and she died an invalid in 1796 at the early age of forty-five.[25]

After each of her pregnancies Sally Logan Fisher faithfully observed the custom of "lying in," that is, not engaging in strenuous activity, for a month following the birth, regardless of whether the child lived. She and other middling or wealthy wives with servants and the lesser household responsibilities that characterized residence in urban areas were extremely fortunate in this regard. The vast majority of American women — those who lived on farms or lacked household help — could not afford the luxury of sufficient leisure time to recuperate from the rigors of childbed. Sarah Snell Bryant, for example, noted in her diary that she "got up" the day after the birth of her third son, Cyrus, and that she went out visiting only two weeks later.[26]

The potentially tragic consequences of women's immediate resumption of their household duties may be illustrated by reference to the North Carolinian Judith Mordecai. Because of "the Want of Skill in the Phisician" who supervised the birth of her fourth child in 1790, she developed "an Inflamation of the Womb . . . attended With Very Painful and Debilitating Symptoms." Nevertheless, she informed her stepmother, "[T]he attention My family required would not admit of My Useing endulgence tho I found my strength, Daily decrease." Following another pregnancy in 1792, "My disorder returned With redoubled Voilence," and "Nearly brought me to the Brink of the Grave," she wrote in February 1793. She still expressed her belief that "if I am so plesd as to have No farther addition in the small Way, I flatter myself I shall yet be a Hearty woman." But Judith Mordecai's hope was unrealistic, and she died after her next childbirth experience, in early 1796.[27]

Although Mrs. Mordecai's health problems originally stemmed from her doctor's lack of obstetrical skill, they were compounded by the fact that she could not ignore the demands placed on her by her older children and her household tasks. Indeed, even mothers in excellent health found it difficult to cope with their myriad responsibilities. Shortly after the birth of her son Aaron in 1756, Esther Edwards Burr remarked, "[W]hen I had but one Child my hands were tied, but now I am tied hand and foot (how I shall get along when I have got ½ dzn or 10 Children I cant devise)." Older women could have supplied the answer. A Maine mother of six was fond of saying, "[I]f I should now be called it seems as if I had not time to die," and Esther Atlee of Lancaster, Pennsylvania, who had eight children, informed her husband in 1782, "[G]loomyness . . . too frequently comes over me, I think if I had a little more relief in My family affairs by having some careful person to take charge of my little ones, I should be much easier." [28]

A woman like Esther Atlee could acquire necessary household help in several ways. An unmarried female relative (usually the wife's younger sister) could join the household as an assistant, or oldest daughters could be employed in the same capacity. In the summer of 1793, for example, Hannah Fisher, who was then sixteen, took over the care of her baby sister Hetty. "I could not have done at all without her," Sally Fisher wrote in her diary. The South Carolinian Margaret Izard, daughter of Ralph and Alice DeLancey Izard, proclaimed herself "the best of nurses" for the brother who was born in 1785, when she was in her late teens. That such assignments could lead to sibling ties with special overtones was demonstrated in 1786 when the New Jersey poet and intellectual Annis Boudinot Stockton told her brother Elisha, "[Y]ou are the *Brother* of my heart" for whom she felt "maternal fondness," because "I was your nurse and had you always about me in your infancy." [29]

In middling or wealthy households, in addition to using daughters and relatives as needed, mothers usually turned most household chores over to servants or slaves, thereby freeing their own time for childcare. Consequently, there were significant child-rearing differences between poor and better-off households. Only in wealthier homes could mothers devote much attention to children above infancy. In households where older youngsters had to compete with essential household tasks for their mothers' time, the children tended to lose the competition. Accordingly, much of the evidence on which the remainder of this chapter is based comes from wealthier homes, for only they generated documents that mention child rearing. Poor mothers, beset by other problems, could spare little time for supervising their older children's activities. It is thus possible, even probable, that poor parents' attitudes toward their offspring differed considerably from those which are analyzed in the pages that follow. [30]

II

Many eighteenth-century white American parents apparently failed to perceive their newborn infants as human beings invested with individual personalities. Instead, they referred to babies in sexually neutral terms, without identifying or commenting upon specific characteristics. These adults employed three peculiar forms of reference for newborns. First, they continued what must have been their practice during pregnancy by alluding to an infant as "it" instead of designating the child by sex. Second, they sometimes called a new baby "the little stranger." Finally, even after an infant was christened they commonly did not use its name, employing instead "the baby" or "the child." [31]

All these practices taken together imply a failure to see newborn infants as full-fledged individuals. Instead of investing a baby immediately with a name, a sexual identity, and unique characteristics, adults referred to it impersonally and distantly. As John Walzer has perceptively observed, it is as though infants were like "the embryos of marsupials . . . out of the womb, but not really 'born.'" Not until the child began to take on identifiable traits and started to respond to its parents did they consistently begin calling it by name and designating it by sex. Further, the custom of naming newborns after dead siblings, which Tommy and Sally Fisher followed in the case of their second and third sons, indicates, as Daniel Scott Smith has concluded, that parents "did not perceive their children as unique *per se.*" It is accordingly not surprising to find eighteenth-century adults remarking that the birth of a baby "supplies the place, in some measure, of the dear little one we lost," whether or not they christened the new arrival with the same name as its dead sibling. [32]

Smith argues persuasively that "naming reveals the choices a culture presents for individuals to make," and therefore that examinations of general child-naming patterns can disclose some aspects of the nature of familial ties in certain communities. His analysis of the evidence for Hingham demonstrates that the practice of naming for lineal kin, although gradually losing its dominant position, persisted well into the 1800s. The significance of naming children after parents and grandparents, Smith asserts, "lies in the idea of family continuity as the fundamental determinant of procreation. Children are important and valued because they perpetuate the lineage, not because of their significance as autonomous individuals apart from the family." [33] Although Smith cautiously notes that the Hingham patterns may not hold for other American communities, an examination of the naming patterns among the slaves on Thomas Jefferson's plantations yields similar results.

Of the 96 families with children who lived on Jefferson's quarters between 1774 and 1822, 58 (or 60 percent) included at least one child who bore the name of a close relative. Of these, 29 percent included 2 children named for relatives and in 16 percent relatives' names were given to 3 or more offspring, up to a maximum of 7 children named for relatives in each of 2 families. Of a total of 373 children whose families can be traced beyond their parents, 111 (or 30 percent) bore the names of known relatives, and since the kin connections of most of the adults on the 1774 census are obscure, these figures represent absolute minimums. [34]

An analysis of the specific relative whose name the child bore gives intriguing results. Unsurprisingly, 23 first sons or daughters were given the names of their father, mother, grandfather, or grandmother, and 28 other sons and daughters were likewise named for parents or grandparents, these categories together constituting just under half of all children who bore relatives' names. But children were also named frequently for aunts or uncles on both sides of the family; 30 fall into that category, with 2 named for great-uncles. The explicit recognition of multigenerational ties is suggested by the fact that 1 son was named for a great-grandfather and 3 daughters for their great-grandmothers. Sex differentials were also apparent in the naming patterns. Despite the fact that maternal connections are easier to trace than paternal lines in Jefferson's records, and thus that the statistics are biased in favor of the maternal family, sons were more frequently named for recorded fathers than were daughters for mothers. On the other hand, daughters were more likely to be named for grandmothers or aunts than were sons for grandfathers and uncles. But sons and daughters were both named for paternal and maternal kin; neither side of the family seems to have dominated, once one allows for the maternal-line bias that has already been noted.

Although exact comparisons with Smith's Hingham evidence are impossible because he failed to investigate naming for nonlineal kin, it is nonetheless striking that the Virginia black families named their children for grandparents more often than did the white New Englanders. In contrast to the Hingham households, where children named for parents vastly outnumbered children named for grandparents, among the blacks youngsters who bore their grandparents' names held a marked percentage edge over their parentally named siblings (57 percent to 43 percent).[35] This phenomenon implies that the Virginia blacks had a strong sense of lineage, and for two of the families on Jefferson's plantations specific evidence points directly to that conclusion.

In 1816 Bec, whose husband is not identified in Jefferson's records, had a child she called Fleming, a name belonging to no one else on the plantation. Bec was a daughter of Bagwell, who was a son of Ursula — who had, in 1773, been purchased by Jefferson from the estate of a man named Fleming. Bec could not have happened upon that name for her son by chance: it must have been a means of recapturing a part of the earlier history of her family. A similar illuminating instance occurred in 1804, when Flora had a son named Gawen, after her double brother-in-law (she was married to Gawen's brother Austin and her sister Sal was Gawen's wife). At the time Flora's son was born, Sal and Gawen had four daughters, but no sons to bear their father's name. Thus the first male child of that generation was named for an uncle with no sons of his own, a fact that indicates the significance for the family of recognizing a male line of descent.

Despite the close ties of black parents and their children, many slaveholders evidently never thought twice about separating them. For example, a Virginia planter casually told a female relative in 1788, "[P]erhaps, two or three young Negroe Girls may be useful to your dear little Girls, if so, it will be in my power to spare such, and send them to you." Likewise, the John Brown family seemed unconcerned about the fact that in moving from the Bahamas to New Jersey they had separated Kitty and two of her children from her husband, her parents, and another child. Even Thomas Jefferson, who carefully kept married couples together, often separated teenaged children from their parents. Indeed, most of the slaves Jefferson sold over the years were young couples or single teenagers.[36]

Although the practices of eighteenth-century whites and blacks suggest both a sense of family lineage and a failure to perceive new-

Baby in a High Red Chair, by an unknown artist, c. 1800. Courtesy of Abby Aldrich Rockefeller Folk Art Center, Williamsburg, Virginia. This delightful painting, perhaps of Pennsylvania German origin, vividly shows the attitude of loving late-eighteenth-century American parents toward their infants.

borns as unique, it is important to keep in mind that within only a few months parents began to see their babies as individual personalities. Many parental encomiums upon the glories of their still-infant offspring expose the error in speculations that high child mortality led adults to maintain an emotional distance from their youngsters. As Daniel Scott Smith has noted, necronymic practices ceased long before children's chances of survival to maturity increased dramatically. Consequently, changing rates of infant mortality had little or nothing to do with parental perceptions of the individuality of their children. White adults' reactions to infants' deaths demonstrate conclusively that they quickly became deeply attached to their youngsters, in spite of the fact that Protestant clerics encouraged them to "live loose" to their children so that they would be prepared to surrender them to God whenever He so desired.[37]

Parents, to be sure, were usually able to face the death of newborns with more equanimity than they were the demise of older children. A baby lost at birth or even in the first weeks of life did not have the emotional hold on its parents that an older sibling did. Relatives could report such a loss laconically, as did a Virginian when he told his sister, his daughter's baby son had "staid with us just three weeks, when he was again born into a better world," or as did a Bostonian when he informed his father, "Polly has had a Boy since you left us, we had the Mortification to Lose it a few Days after it was Born." Joseph Reed probably summed up the attitude of many colonial parents on the subject in his 1776 statement: "[T]o lose a Child when first brought into Life is very hard but it is a Tax we must pay."[38]

Reed's resignation was not, on the other hand, shared by all his compatriots. Charles and Eliza Lucas Pinckney's second son, George, died at the age of fifteen days in 1747. Describing her feelings to a friend, Mrs. Pinckney wrote, "[Y]oung as it was the pain was sharp we found at parting with it, it was a most lovly infant." Likewise, although John and Sarah Livingston Jay's first daughter, Susannah, died less than a month after her birth in 1780, Sarah told her mother (after whom the girl had been named), "[W]hen I used to look at her every idea less pleasent vanis[h]'d in a moment, scenes of continued & future bliss still rose to view, and while I clasp'd her to my bosom my happiness appear'd compleat."[39]

When children grew older, there could be no parental detachment from their deaths. "Our Dear babey," recorded a Virginian sadly in 1786, "just lived with us long Anuf to make us love him and began to play and be compiny for us and then was takein from us." A northern father similarly wrote of his dead four-month-old son that he "tho' so young 'twas taking a piece of the heart," and James Kent was devastated by the death of his eighteen-month-old daughter in 1793. Six years later he commented, "[N]o Event in my Life had ever before taught me the genuine agonies of Grief. My whole Soul seemed to be buried in my child," adding, "I think of the lovely Babe to this Day." Just as affecting was the New Englander William Palfrey's reaction to the death of his seven-year-old daughter, Polly, in 1772. Palfrey, who was away from home on business when he heard the news, started to write his wife a conventional letter of consolation. "I set down cooly and calmly to reason with you upon our late melancholy and distressing loss," he began, telling her that God must have had "some valuable purpose" for taking their daughter and that they should be pleased she would "escape the troubles & temptations" of the world. But after expressing his concern for his wife, he completely lost his composure: "O my poor dear little Polly — never to see her again! Never to see her dance Nansy Dawson again — I can't bear the thoughts — This Letter you will see is wet with my Tears — I go about crying like a fool whenever I think of her." [40]

Palfrey's palpable grief dramatically reveals the conflict colonial parents felt between their own emotions and traditional teachings of religion. Theological platitudes that assured them their children were better off in heaven, or that urged them to be resigned to their loss because God knew best, could do little to assuage their sorrow at the deaths of beloved children.

The close emotional relationship a mother quickly developed with her infant undoubtedly stemmed, at least in significant part, from colonial mothers' commitment to nursing their own babies. In contrast to the English and European practice of hiring wet nurses, American women — and men as well — assumed that mothers would suckle their infants unless unusual circumstances intervened. As a result, the English child-rearing literature that inveighed against wet nurses merely validated prevailing colonial custom. One of the standard compliments offered to a new mother was the expression of hope that she would "make a good nurse," and women commonly encouraged hesitant members of their sex to adopt the practice, in addition to reassuring doubtful husbands concerned about their wives' health. [41]

Statements made by nursing mothers and the tenacity with which some of them attempted to continue nursing despite painful breast problems testify to their desire to feed their own infants. Nelly Custis Lewis, who told a friend in 1800 that she knew "no delight equal to nursing" her baby daughter, was not alone in her sentiments. Many other mothers similarly commented on the pleasure they derived from nursing their babies, and those who were forced by illness to send their children to wet nurses described themselves as "unfortunate." When in 1793 Sally Logan Fisher's sister-in-law had to hire a wet nurse, Sally observed in her diary, "[T]o me [this] would be a very great triall." Likewise, after a recurring breast ailment prevented the young Pennsylvania Quaker Betsy Rhoads Fisher from nursing any of her three sons, her husband, Samuel, recorded that the "Incapacity" was "a Source of trouble to her delicate Mind, & seemed a greater trial of her fortitude than her own bodily pains." [42]

Significantly, eighteenth-century white southern women appear to have been as dedicated to the notion of nursing their own children as were their northern counterparts. Little evidence suggests that black wet nurses were more widely used in the South than were white ones in the North, or that female slaves would normally nurse the offspring of healthy white mistresses. The Marylander Polly Galloway Ringgold's husband and father both owned many slaves, but she did not employ wet nurses until compelled to do so by extreme pain in her breasts. Eliza Lucas Pinckney stated in 1753 that she had relied upon black wet nurses for her offspring only because her "constitution would not bear" the strain of nursing, and such well-to-do white women as Martha Laurens Ramsay and Mrs. Robert Wormeley Carter (daughter-in-law of Landon Carter) regularly nursed their children, sometimes to the detriment of their own health.[43]

Weaning, which generally occurred when the child was approximately a year old, could accordingly be traumatic for both mothers and their offspring. Few white American children of the period 1760–1810 seem to have been nursed less than ten months or longer than eighteen, unless some unexpected event such as the illness of mother or child, a new pregnancy, or difficulty in weaning intervened to cause either hastening or delay of the process.[44] Scattered comments in letters and diaries make it clear that late eighteenth-century Americans believed twelve months was the optimum age for weaning a child, with six months being too young and eighteen months rather too old.[45]

Mothers and fathers rarely described the precise method of weaning, yet it seems to have varied considerably. In some families, weaning was accomplished abruptly, sometimes by separating the child physically from its mother for a few days. This practice could lead to unhappiness on the part of both and further to physical pain for the mother until her milk ceased to flow. A young New England woman, for instance, told her aunt in 1789 that weaning her son had been "a sorrowful peice of business . . . he Cry'd dreadfully the first night. . . . it seems very odd or rather hard not to give him the breast but let him cry on however the worst is over now."[46]

In other families, especially those living in the first years of the nineteenth century, children were weaned gradually. In 1800 the Philadelphian Gertrude Ogden Meredith described herself as "foolish and irresolute" when she allowed the son she was trying to wean to suckle her at night for a week, but she still asserted, "[I]t is certainly much better to wean the dear little creatures by degrees than to take so great a comfort from them all at once, as I did from my dear little Gertrude." Similarly, three years later the Virginian Lelia Skipwith Tucker advised her stepdaughter Fanny Coalter to wean her daughter "gradually from yourself, and to take every moderate method to lessen your quantity of milk 'till it wastes quite away.'" Mrs. Tucker's proposal was clearly designed to lessen the physical and emotional strain on both mother and child.[47]

The indulgent, affectionate attitude toward small children apparent in the comments on weaning can be discerned as well in parental descriptions of their children's characteristics and development. Wealthy southern mothers and fathers in particular referred to their young offspring in playful, animalistic terminology. Edward "[is] a very lovely, fat, rosy, laughing little donkey," wrote Margaret Izard Manigault of her infant son in 1801; Nelly Custis referred to her nieces as "such sweet toads"; and the correspondence of the Tucker family of Virginia is filled with repeated characterizations of children as monkeys, toads, pugs, pigs, and sluts, the latter being a common form of reference to a child who was not yet toilet trained.[48]

Although nursing probably led mothers to form close emotional ties to their infants sooner than fathers, men quickly came to rival their wives in their interest in, and attachment to, their youngsters. Men separated from their families because of the demands of business, politics, or wartime military service eagerly requested news of their children and declared their love for the "dear little ones." "O how I doat upon them," William Palfrey told his wife, Susannah, in 1776, writing of his daughter, "I love her like my Soul." The following year another Massachusetts husband, Timothy Pickering, peppered his wife, Rebecca, with inquiries about his then only child, John: "[H]ow could you forbear telling me often how fast he grew? Whether he was quiet? and what signs of understanding he discovered?" Timothy asked in August. Four months later he complained that Rebecca had failed to tell him "in every letter what progress he makes in growth & *knowledge*," though he admitted that her last missive had brought news of John's first tooth. September of 1778 found Timothy still lacking sufficient information about his son's development. "How come you to omit telling me what words he could speak?" Pickering inquired somewhat testily, and he expressed his longing "to see the childish amusements of our sweet boy to hear his fond prattle & view his little wanton tricks." [49]

With a child's ability to walk and talk came both greater delights and increased problems for parents, especially for mothers. A South Carolina father wrote that his daughter was "a very diverting chatterbox," but many mothers would have concurred with Frances Randolph Tucker, who said of her child Fanny, "[She] chatters so much that I am fatigued to death with her." Mothers wrote of being "plagued" with children's demands for attention while fathers happily described their "active & sprightly" little ones and gloried in their "sweet little tricks." [50]

Yet mothers, too, enjoyed the children's antics. Nowhere is this made clearer than in the remarkable series of daily letters Margaret Izard Manigault wrote to her husband, Gabriel, in the fall of 1792, describing their children's activities in great detail. One time she noted that the "little sly rogue Henry," sitting beside her, was "begging me to let him do what he ought not," while Elizabeth was simultaneously "worrying me to know what I am saying to you, & amusing me with her conjectures on the occasion." Margaret recounted her conflict with Henry over his desire to own a "vile noisy" toy in addition to the drum upon which he liked to make "a fine racket," and she often commented on the children's love of candy. Late in November Margaret wrote to Gabriel at her son's dictation, and she dispatched two "Caramelles" sent by Elizabeth to her father, despite the fact that they were no longer fresh. "This is her idea I assure you," she informed her husband, "& I could not refuse her." [51]

From these letters and others less detailed one gains a distinct impression of households in which youngsters were indulged and allowed considerable freedom to roam. Parents frequently described their children as running and tumbling about the house or lawn. When Abigail Smith Adams and Harriott Pinckney Horry became concerned about the falls their daughters were taking as they learned to walk, their solution was not to restrain the girls' movements but rather to make soft helmets to protect their heads. [52] Reports of household accidents likewise indicate the high degree of independence and mischievousness displayed by American two-, three-, and four-year-olds. Charley Paine (son of Robert and Sally) was but one of a number of children scalded by boiling liquids pulled off the fire. Others drowned in wells or cisterns, burned or cut themselves badly, or broke limbs in falls.[53]

Such infants and toddlers of both sexes came fully within their mothers' sphere of authority, and they were consistently referred to as "hers" by men and women both.[54] Yet there came a time when children grew old enough to move out from under the maternal wing, when they ceased to be amusing playthings and began to be viewed as future adults who needed to be trained and shaped. In a 1756 letter to her father, Abigail Paine Greenleaf drew a common analogy to the world of plants: "[H]ow the tender buds of reason opening promise fair flowers if rightly Cultivated and Spar'd to a full Growth," she wrote of her children, "but how tender is the Stalk! may it be long e'er they are cut down."[55] Like many other colonists, she and her husband, Joseph, worked hard to achieve the goal of "right cultivation" of their children. In the process they drew heavily on their past experience and on their understanding of the roles their children would play in adult life.

III

One of the best explications of a white man's view of the paternal role came from the Creek Indian Agent Benjamin Hawkins in 1797. Hawkins had been approached by an elderly Creek woman, who wanted him to marry her widowed daughter. During the subsequent negotiations, Hawkins decided that, since Indian women were "in the habit of assuming and exercising absolute rule . . . over their children," he should outline in writing the behavior he would expect from a Creek wife.

"The ways of the white people differ much from those of the red people," he told the old woman, for, contrary to Creek practice, "white men govern their families." Accordingly, he declared, his wife would have to agree to his raising the children (even hers by a previous marriage), "as I please, and no one of her family shall oppose my doing so. The red women should always be proud of their white husbands," he continued, "should always take part with them and obey them, should make the children obey them, and they will be obedient to their parents, and make a happy family." When Hawkins translated the message for his prospective mother-in-law, he recorded, she "could not be prevailed on to acquiesce in the conditions proposed. She would not consent that the women and children should be under the direction of the father." And so the negotiations collapsed.[56]

White women did not have the option of refusing to enter into marriage on the terms proposed by white men. But what Hawkins had described to the old Creek woman was a man's ideal vision rather than an accurate depiction of reality. To be sure, fathers expected to have, and for the most part did wield, final authority over the other members of the family. But the theoretical paternal power was tempered by a maternal presence, especially with respect to daughters. Whereas all infants were assumed to be under their mothers' care, older children were differentiated by sex. Again linguistic custom disclosed the practice: men spoke of "my son" and mothers of "his Boys," at the same time women wrote of "my Girl" and fathers of "your" daughters.[57]

Such formal child-rearing literature as was available to eighteenth-century Americans — most of it published in England — was addressed solely to fathers. The maternal role received no direct consideration, although authors took pains to specify that parents should agree on both the means and the ends of child rearing and that neither parent should undercut the other in any way. When mothers were mentioned, which was seldom, they were usually accused of overindulging their children.[58] Yet family correspondence and the reminiscences of Americans who grew up in the late eighteenth century indicate that mothers were as concerned as fathers about matters of discipline. Consequently, the formal child-rearing literature serves as an inadequate guide to actual practice. Not only did mothers take a more active role in raising their children, especially daughters, than the printed works would indicate, but they also did not behave in the ways the publications predicted.

So a South Carolinian wrote with reference to his wife, "I need not caution her against too much discoverd fondness, she has too much good sence & firmness to spoil her lovely Boy." Sally Logan Fisher likewise vowed "not to improperly indulge my Children, in every thing their little fancys crave, but early to teach them a strict lesson of Obedience, knowing they will in the end be much happier." The same philosophy was also adhered to by such careful mothers as Judith Mordecai, Esther Edwards Burr, and Ann Tasker (Mrs. Robert) Carter.[59] Even grandmothers, who were commonly charged with spoiling their grandchildren, deliberately tried to avoid excessive indulgence. Thus Kitty Livingston assured her brother-in-law, John Jay, whose son Peter was being raised by his grandmother while the Jays were in Europe in the early 1780s, that "her fondness for him never leads her to do any thing to his prejudice," and Deborah Franklin made no move to intervene when her daughter, Sarah Franklin Bache, physically punished her son, Deborah's beloved only grandchild, in 1770.[60]

To point out mothers' and grandmothers' concern with discipline is not to imply that eighteenth-century American mothers never spoiled their children, nor to say that all adults practiced what they preached when it came to raising their offspring. Often strict parents complained that acquaintances did not properly control their youngsters, accordingly making them seem "rigid & severe" by contrast. Yet if Timothy Pickering cautioned his wife, Rebecca, in 1777 *"not to spoil our little son by too much fondness,"* fifteen years later she warned him against falling into the same error of excessive indulgence.[61] In short, little or no evidence suggests that mothers were any more likely to spoil their children than were fathers, and much evidence indicates that mothers and fathers both believed in giving their children a strict upbringing, enforcing obedience to their commands and stressing continued subjection to the parental will.

A single word suffused comments made by all members of the family on parent-child relationships: duty. Parents had a duty to their offspring, and children had even greater obligations to their parents. Adults fulfilled their part of the bargain by raising their children properly, disciplining them when necessary, and watching over them with tender care. The parental role was a "great Duty" indeed — to use Sally Logan Fisher's invariable phrase — yet, as a South Carolina mother told her son in 1783, the responsibility ended when children reached adulthood. "Should we be so unfortunate as to see our Children not prove so good, and be as happy as our fondest and most anxious wishes would make them," she declared, "yet let our conscience acquit us let us have the heartfelt satisfaction to say we have fulfill'd our part that heaven has allotted."[62]

Children's obligations to their elders, on the other hand, were never ending. They were supposed to care for their parents in old age and to remain respectfully subordinate throughout their lives. Sons could discharge these obligations through financial contributions and continued filial deference, but daughters were expected to provide care and service. Their debt was signaled as early as congratulations offered couples on the birth of a female infant: "[M]ay the dear babe Live and grow up and be a comfort to its Parents," wrote the Rhode Islander Sarah Osborn in 1760, in words echoed in messages to new parents of baby girls throughout the late eighteenth century. Daughters fully understood their special duty to mothers and fathers. So the Brookfield, Massachusetts, teenager Pamela Foster told her father, Dwight, earnestly in 1799, "[S]hould I live to see my beloved Parents, aged and infirm, . . . it shall be the first wish of my Heart to soothe their sorrows and make the 'Evening' of their Lives glide smoothly away," and a year later Ann Jay similarly assured her mother, Sarah, "[I]n endeavouring to contribute to the comfort & happiness of my beloved & worthy parents, I cannot fail finding lasting enjoyment myself."[63]

Just as children's duties to their parents were differentiated by sex, so too were parental duties to children. As befitted their dominant position in the family, fathers assumed a highly paternalistic, instructive stance with respect to all their offspring, while mothers, at least until the last years of the century, confined themselves to advising their daughters.

Fathers interested themselves in many aspects of their children's lives, peppering sons and daughters with advice about everything from posture to hairstyles to relations with the opposite sex and the selection of friends. Not confining themselves solely to small points of conduct, they also tried to present their children with general rules of behavior. "Virtue will Lead you to Happiness & Vice will make you miserable dear Billy," a Virginian told his son portentously in 1785; "you Can not, dabble in dirt & be Clean." A Rhode Islander cautioned his daughter "Against Pride": "Concider from Dust We Came & to Dust we must Return Treet all with Decency and Good

Manners."[64] A standard theme in fathers' correspondence with boys was the need to "improve yr Time to the best Advantage," to quote the words Moses Kent employed when he wrote to his son James in 1781. By contrast, girls were more often reminded of the importance of being industrious. In 1777, for example, Alice Lee Shippen advised her schoolgirl daughter Nancy that "industrious[ness] . . . makes so great a part of a female Character."[65]

The distinction between the injunction to boys to "improve their time" and that addressed to girls — to be industrious — is instructive. Although both admonitions were explicitly offered with an eye to aiding the young person's future prospects, that directed to boys carried an implication of development, of bettering oneself, whereas the advice intended for girls contained no such notion of progress. Industry was, in effect, to be its own reward for girls throughout most of the latter half of the century. Only in the last decade of the 1700s did scattered signs of change appear.

So, when in 1779 the North Carolina teenager Nelly Blair, who was both high-spirited and quick-tempered, showed a tendency to "dissipation" and idleness, her relatives pressed upon her the necessity for industry — not because she would thereby gain anything, but because employment was preferable to indolence. "Consider, a whole life is not to be passed in frolic and dissipation," Nelly's uncle James Iredell informed her. "Let your Mind sometimes receive useful and agreeable Instruction, and your hands be employed in the pleasing task of not only serving yourself, but assisting your Mamma, your Brothers and your Sister." Likewise, in 1787 Thomas Jefferson instructed his older daughter, Patsy, that her future happiness depended on her "contracting a habit of industry and activity." "A mind always employed is always happy," he told her on another occasion, and when he asked her to take charge of her younger sister he requested that she teach Polly not only "to be good" and "never to be angry," but also "teach her industry and application to useful pursuits."[66]

The same static sense was conveyed by fathers' standard direction to daughters to "copy after their dear mothers in modesty & industry." Girls were told to "imitate" their mothers, to "try to emulate" and "equal" them. The quite different expectation for boys was best expressed by a New Englander offering an after-dinner toast. "May our sons exceed their fathers, and our daughters be equal to their mothers," he intoned, neatly revealing his belief that the best girls could hope for was to reach the same level of achievement as their female ancestors, whereas boys could anticipate surpassing previous generations' accomplishments.[67]

Thomas Jefferson was a master of a technique often used by fathers, especially, though not exclusively, with daughters, in order to reinforce their instructions: threatening to withhold love if the child did not comply with their wishes. Mothers, incidentally, never seem to have employed this tactic, which placed on the child the onus for any failure of parental affection. Remember "not to go out without your bonnet because it will make you very ugly and then we should not love you so much," Jefferson told his daughter Polly in 1785 with fatherly overkill. Tragically, he tried a variant of the same ploy nineteen years later when she lay on her deathbed: "Maria must . . . resolve to get strong to make us all happy," he declared to Patsy, in what can only be seen as a sadly ineffectual reversion to type as a means of coping with the reality of his beloved daughter's impending death.[68] Other fathers also played a similar game, with perhaps more positive results. "As long as Maria is a good Girl, she will allways be dearly loved by her Papa," John Dickinson informed his younger daughter in 1787; if John "continues a good boy, tell him I shall love him still more," wrote Timothy Pickering to his wife; and a South Carolinian told his daughter, "[C]ontinue my Child to merit the Love of your Friends, and you may be assured of receiving it."[69]

The fact that fathers evidently adopted this approach more frequently when dealing with daughters is significant. There was no stronger weapon in the parental arsenal than to warn of the withdrawal or lessening of love, no method better calculated to keep a child in continued subjection. Yet eighteenth-century adults recognized that sons should eventually become independent of their fathers and mothers. Thus, for example, Mercy Otis Warren, the playwright and historian, explained to John Adams in 1778 that her three older sons were no longer living with her, they "being at an age that makes it proper they should Leave the parental Roof," and Rebecca Stoddert wrote of the "Impropriety of Boys living at home" after they had been away to school. No such comment was ever made about girls. Quite the contrary: young women were expected to live with their parents until they married.[70]

Furthermore, as has already been noted, daughters of whatever age or marital status had a special obligation to their parents in old age. Unless a girl were properly obedient, she might neglect that crucial duty. To ensure their own eventual security late in life, fathers therefore attempted to bind youthful daughters closely to them by using one of the most powerful threats at their command.

Given the broad scope of paternal authority, it might well be asked what role remained for mothers. Colonial women had to confront that problem straightforwardly, for the standard English child-rearing literature gave them no independent function, barely even acknowledging their presence in the family circle. Yet a woman's husband and children were the central facts of her existence, and from them she gained a joy she could not derive from her household tasks. Alice DeLancey Izard declared typically in 1801, "[M]y pleasures are . . . entirely concentrated in my family." Sally Logan Fisher put it slightly differently in 1792: "I daily almost more and more see, . . . that if we do not seek for happiness at home, and endeavour to live in love with our nearest connections, and cultivate it all that we can in our own family, wherever shall we find it."[71] Thus the white women of late eighteenth-century America, understanding the significance of their familial role, began the process of defining that role to their own satisfaction.

IV

"I am resolved to be a good Mother to my children," wrote Eliza Lucas Pinckney in the late 1740s; "to pray for them, to set them good examples, to give them good advice, to be careful both of their souls and bodys, to watch over their tender minds, to carefully root out the first appearing and budings of vice, and to install piety, Virtue and true religion into them; to spair no paines or trouble to do them good; to correct their Errors whatever uneasiness it may give myself;

and never omit to encourage every Virtue I may see dawning in them." [72]

With these words Mrs. Pinckney briefly summed up the white American mother's view of her role, the large number of items on her list of resolutions indicating the broad range of child-rearing responsibilities a mother assumed. Middling and well-to-do women like herself devoted a great deal of thought to the problems and pleasures of raising children. They understood implicitly what the contemporary male writers of prescriptive literature evidently did not: that mothers could, indeed would, have a major impact on their children, especially in their early years, and that women accordingly had to consider carefully and thoughtfully the methods they would use to raise their offspring. As Abigail Paine Greenleaf asserted in 1755, mothers believed that "even we the weaker Sex may be Servicable to the Society where we live and to the world in general by bringing up our Children in Such a manner as to abhor Vice and act Virtuously from a principle early inculcated which is the most likely to be lasting." [73]

Women accordingly began to reflect upon child rearing before they married. In 1785 Nabby Adams wrote in her journal that she had come to realize "the very great importance of early education, and the necessity of forming the first habits with propriety." Years before, and some time prior to her own marriage, Nabby's aunt Elizabeth Smith had reached the same conclusion. "I am sensible much is dependent on Education," she told a male cousin. "The Infant Mind, I beleive[,] is a blank, that eassily receives any impression." Yet, she observed, the same system would not work equally well with different children. "Some dispositions require a more assiduous care than others. . . . The government that is proper for one Child might inevitably ruin another." [74]

After women had married and become mothers, child rearing often developed into a major preoccupation. Take Sally Logan Fisher, for example. Again and again she confided to her diary fears that she was "much unqualified" for the "great task" of raising her children. She observed the methods used by her acquaintances, deciding to adopt some that pleased her; earnestly discussed the characteristics of a good education with older female relatives; paid avid attention to the

101

homilies on motherhood delivered in Quaker women's meetings; and, like Eliza Lucas Pinckney, made a series of resolutions concerning her maternal role. "May I be favored & enabled to improve in my conduct," she wrote characteristically on January 1, 1786, "so that my example may be benificial to my Family & I not altogether like the barren Fig tree of no use."[75]

Once her children had passed infancy, a mother concentrated her attention on her daughters. As was already noted, a boy moved into his father's sphere as he grew older,[76] while a girl remained within her mother's orbit. She was her mother's assistant and pupil as well as her child, but far more than a sharing of work roles was involved in colonial mother-daughter relationships. Although father-son ties superficially appear to parallel those of mother to daughter, in fact they did not. A father's relationship with his son was distant, didactic, and condescending, whereas a mother's relationship with her daughter was characterized by egalitarian friendship. Mothers and daughters each gained from the association; mothers advised their daughters, as fathers instructed sons, but mothers received something in return: companionship. Exploring the meaning of the female connection in 1770, Elizabeth Graeme, who had a close relationship with her own mother, declared that "the tie of a mother to a Daughter was the softest and fondest the Human Heart could experience: For tho' through life Our pride and ambition may be promoted by the figure our Male Conections may make in the world yet daily observation shows that Our Domestic Comfort receives its most balmy sweets from the female branches of our family."[77]

The mother-daughter tie began early, with many women longing for female babies, although few fathers expressed the same wish. Abigail Adams wanted a girl in 1777, but her daughter was stillborn. Thereafter she repeatedly mentioned her preference for female grandchildren and great-nieces. Although she congratulated her niece Betsy Cranch Norton on the birth of a son in 1792, for instance, she went on to add, "I could have wishd it had been a daughter." Many women were resigned to the male preference for sons, but Alice DeLancey Izard had little patience with that attitude. "What nonsense!" she exclaimed to her daughter Margaret Manigault in 1801 as she told of how a male acquaintance was "excessively disappointed" at the birth of a baby girl. "With such a Daughter for an eldest born I am angry when I hear expressions of this sort."[78]

Appropriately, mothers and daughters tended to describe each other as "friend" and "companion." In 1795 a North Carolina girl termed her mother her "best friend"; five years earlier, when Hannah Fisher was thirteen, her mother, Sally, had commented, "[She is] now grown of an Age to be a Companion to me," writing revealingly of "sitting sweetly with my dear Hannah at work in the Piazza." Other mothers too called their daughters "sweet friend and companion," and in 1800 Eliza Southgate likewise reminded her mother, "[Y]ou have always treated me more like a companion than a daughter."[79]

The depth of the anguish felt by mothers and adult daughters at the death of one another points up the special nature of their relationship. When Abigail Adams's mother died in the dysentery epidemic that struck New England in the fall of 1775, Abigail was devastated. She wrote John a series of long letters in an attempt to assuage her grief, but more than a month afterwards she noted that she still spent every evening thinking about her mother, "absorb'd in a flood of tenderness." The first anniversary of her mother's death brought "more than common depression of spirits," she admitted, as "a Train of melancholly Ideas forced themselves upon me and made me very unhappy." But at least Abigail's mother was a mature woman who had lived a full life before her death. Mothers whose adult daughters predeceased them had no such consolation, and their grief was, if anything, even more palpable. In 1798, Abigail's sister Elizabeth Shaw Peabody lost her twenty-year-old daughter Betsy to consumption. "Every thing seems a burden since your dear Sisters death," Elizabeth told her son. "While she was well & smiling by my side, my work was easy — *she* made every burden light, & pleasant. . . . I know I am very wrong & some might say very foolish to shed so many unavailing tears — But I cannot help it."[80]

The Philadelphian Sarah Rhoads's anguished reaction to the death of her older daughter, Mary, in 1788 similarly revealed the closeness of their relationship. In a moving memoir, Mrs. Rhoads recalled how, after her husband died four years earlier, it was her daughter who had saved her from total despair. "I communicated every thing to her, and derived great reliefe from that confidence, by her encouraging and salutary counsel," she observed, lamenting the loss of "a beloved daughter who had shared all my pleasures — Cares, anxieties! to whome as to a second-self I confided my most secret Thoughts." Not surprisingly, the perceptive Debby Norris Logan recognized seven years later when Sarah's younger daughter, Betsy Fisher, lay dying as well that "in case of her being removed what a blank life will be to her poor Mother!"[81]

Fortunately, such obituary comments are not the only evidence of close mother-daughter relationships. Correspondence among a series of mothers and daughters in the DeLancey-Izard family illustrates how these relationships developed over time and were transmitted to subsequent generations. Indeed, the very existence of documentary evidence for the earlier years of the family is itself an indication of close mother-daughter ties and of a deliberate attempt to replicate that experience. The letters from the 1760s are contained in a copybook, transcribed in a girlish hand of the late eighteenth century, with overwritten corrections and occasional notes in mature handwriting. A DeLancey woman (probably Anne, since she seems to be the common denominator in the book) obviously had her daughter copy the letters she had received years before from her own mother, not only as an exercise in writing and spelling but also as a means of introducing her to the nature of female relationships in their family.[82]

The first letters in the book, dating from 1760, are typical maternally instructive notes addressed by Elizabeth Colden DeLancey to her older daughters, Anne and Alice. By the middle of the decade, Elizabeth had come to look upon Anne and Alice as friends as well as daughters, for she told them that although their younger sister, Betsy, was "very serviceable[,] . . . she is not yet arrived at those years of experience and knowledge to be very companionable[.] I feel the want of your society." In 1768, after Alice had married Ralph Izard and Anne had gone to South Carolina to visit her, Betsy in turn informed Anne, "I begin to experience that tender Friendship [with our Mother] which my Sister Izard and you have so long posses'd." Finally, Betsy's own transition from daughter to friend was completed when Elizabeth thanked her for some advice, observing, "I will reverse an employment that has often given me great pleasure by receiving Instructions from my daughters instead of offering it to them."[83]

Alice DeLancey Izard eventually bore fourteen children, the oldest of whom was Margaret Izard Manigault. Their correspondence, especially that from the summer of 1801, when Margaret and her family were visiting relatives in New York City, indicates that their relationship was comparable to that which Alice had enjoyed with Elizabeth. Mother and daughter wrote often — so often, in fact, that Margaret told Alice in late July, "[O]ur friends are astonished at the frequency of our intercourse" — and their letters were filled with expressions of deep affection for one another. At the end of her second long letter in three days in early July, Alice exclaimed, "How I forget myself when I write to you!" In August Alice asserted, "Mr. M. must not be offended at my saying that Maternal love is the strongest of all attachments." For her part, Margaret profusely thanked her mother for so many long letters: "I who know so well the various occupations which employ every moment of your time, can estimate their value." The closing phrase in Alice's October 18 letter concisely summed up their relationship. "I am always yours," she noted, "with as much affection as ever Mother felt."[84]

Living in a world dominated by men, mothers and daughters like the DeLancey-Izard women turned to each other for support and companionship. Along with initiating their daughters into the mysteries of housewifery, mothers also taught them about the possibilities for female friendship, about ties that had little or nothing to do with the fathers, brothers, and husbands who otherwise controlled their existence. Recall Elizabeth Graeme's statement drawing a distinction between what women gained from men — "pride and ambition" based on male status — and what they gained from each other — the "balmy sweets" of "Domestic Comfort." Since so much of a woman's life revolved around her household, it is easy to see why feminine companionship held such attractions for her and why young women developed close ties with their female contemporaries as well as with their mothers. Friendships with other members of their own sex formed a constant backdrop to the otherwise fluctuating rhythms of their existence. A woman's relationships with men changed as she grew older and married, but she often retained throughout life her

Elizabeth Colden DeLancey, by Mat-
thew Pratt. Courtesy of The Metro-
politan Museum of Art, Bequest of
Edith Pratt Maxwell, 1957.

attachments to the same female friends — attachments her relationship with her mother had taught her to cultivate and cherish.

Thus the one time Esther Edwards Burr recorded losing her temper
was when a Princeton tutor declared in her presence that *"he did not*
think women knew what Friendship was, they were hardly capable of
anything so cool and rational as friendship." In her extended journal-
letter to her closest friend, Sarah Prince, Mrs. Burr described her
infuriated reaction: "My Tongue, you know, hangs pretty loose,
thoughts Crouded in — so I sputtered away for dear life . . . I
retorted several severe things upon him before he had time to speek
again." After an hour's argument, she recalled proudly, "I talked
him quite silent." [85]

Esther Burr had good reason to challenge the tutor's "mean
thoughts" about female friendship. Her own affectionate relationship
with Sarah Prince, whom she called "Fidelia," is chronicled in the
document that has been known as her "diary," but which was in fact

Alice DeLancey Izard, by Henry Spicer, 1774. Courtesy of Carolina Art Association, Charleston, South Carolina.

Margaret Izard Manigault, by Walter Robertson. Courtesy of The Metropolitan Museum of Art, Amelia B. Lazarus Fund, 1928.

a continuous letter, written daily and dispatched to Prince in Massachusetts at irregular intervals. After Esther and her husband, Aaron, moved to Princeton in late 1756, she told Sarah that she was making new friends every day, "[B]ut Alas for me I cant find a *Fidelia* amongst em all, nor need I look for it for there is not another Fidelia on the face of the Globe." Not that she desired another: "I dont want to devide my Friendship to two [sic] Many — no you shall have it all." Terming Sarah "the Sister of my Heart," Esther observed appropriately, "*Friendship* does not belong to the *world*. *True Friendship* is first inkindled by a spark from *Heaven*, and heaven will never suffer it to go out, but it will *burn* to all *Eternity*." [86]

Other "diaries" similar to Burr's and reams of correspondence attest to the fact that female friends, often cousins of roughly the same age, kept in close touch even when parted for long periods of time. [87] Such relationships, formed in youth, continued through maturity. The New Jersey woman who observed in 1790, "[T]here has always been a great intimacy between Mrs Parker & my Mother, they were very fond of each other when girls, & their affection seems to suffer no abatement by time," was describing a generalized phenomenon. Nelly Custis Lewis and Elizabeth Bordley Gibson, friends from childhood, corresponded regularly for sixty years. And when in 1792 Peggy Emlen Howell visited her cousin Sally Logan Fisher, Sally's diary entry recalled their closeness as teenagers nearly thirty years before: "I feel a strong Friendship for her, and that affection that united us together in very early Years, still remains at the bottom, tho' circumstances have prevented our being together as much as could be wished." [88]

Even more remarkable than the existence of such deep and long-lasting affection was the fact that eighteenth-century Americans, male and female alike, recognized that friendships were essential to a woman's happiness. On a practical level, women friends assisted each other in time of trouble, [89] but more than pragmatic considerations were involved in their relationships. Grace Growden Galloway wrote about the departure of a close acquaintance in these lines: "No more shall I with Moving Tears reveal / Those things which I to none but you cou'd tell." A woman, then, could say things to her closest female friend that she could say to no other person — not her husband, perhaps not even her sister. After Janette Day Barclay's marriage, she wrote to Elizabeth Murray Smith from England, "[H]appy as I am in the Tenderest of Husbands, ther[e] is still a want, I long to sit with you as formerly and talk without resarve." One New England girl put it this way in a 1791 letter: "Happy should I be, could I be with you sometimes to unbosom myself to you. . . . there has something turn'd up which if you was here you would share and advise me what to do, but as you are not, I must follow my own judgment, and not trust any one, ah Peggy you little know how [hard] I find the want of a sister or some one to whom I could at all times speake with freedome."[90]

A revealing set of letters exchanged by John Coalter, his second wife, Margaret Davenport, and her friend Fanny Currie in 1794 and 1795 gives added insight into the nature of intimate female friendships. Margaret and Fanny's closeness was evidenced by Margaret's statement to Fanny before her marriage: "[M]y heart when addressing itself to a Friend loves not to repress its thoughts, but feels an irresistible propensity to disclose its inmost recesses." In response to the announcement of the forthcoming wedding, Fanny strikingly treated John as a rival for her friend's affections: "How *dare* Mr C think of carrying you away from me so suddenly? and how can *you* be such a coquette as to agree to it, after your *long* engagement to me?" she asked Margaret. Later in the same letter, Fanny referred to her friend's fiancé as "the Usurper of my rights." Even more strikingly, John adopted the same mode of discourse after the wedding. On one occasion he told his wife he was pleased she had heard from her friend, "who perhaps alone could so well supply my place," and on another he joked about Fanny's "intentions in geting us divorcd."[91]

The fact that all three participants in this triangular relationship regarded it as an equilateral affair is extraordinary. Yet John and Margaret Coalter and Fanny Currie were only acknowledging the existence of a female friendship that in its basic characteristics was by no means unique. Ignoring the prescriptive literature, which directed them to center their affections solely on their husbands, eighteenth-century American white women developed close ties with members of their own sex.[92] To their prescribed roles of mother, wife, and mistress they added that of friend. The feminine companionship originating within the home extended its sphere beyond the boundaries of the household.

Chapter Four

ɕ

IN WHAT WOU'D YOU
SHEW YOUR ACTIVITY?

Throughout most of the eighteenth century, male and female Americans alike took woman's domestic role largely for granted. Prior to the redefinition of society prompted by their conversion to republicanism, Americans saw little need to analyze the boundaries of the feminine sphere, for women's inescapable responsibilities to households, husbands, and children confined their experience to the domestic realm more surely than could any abstract ideology. No systematic defense of the broad dimensions of the female role was formulated, since no one challenged the dominant assumption that a woman's destiny was sealed at birth, determined by her sex in a way that a man's fate was not. Females would marry, have children, and direct the work of households: these propositions were so generally accepted they were usually left unstated.[1]

But although the female sphere remained unexamined before the 1780s, feminine behavior did not. English, French, and American authors often analyzed those traits reputed to be peculiarly feminine, developing a consistent view of female nature that rested firmly upon a consensus shared with their readers.[2] Women's diaries and letters make it abundantly clear that to a large extent they acquiesced in the analysis of feminine characteristics promulgated in print. In addition to the physical limitations imposed on their lives by their obligations to home and family, therefore, white women labored as well under a set of mental restrictions that defined the ways they thought about themselves and their sex as a whole. Black women enjoyed a dubious exemption from these limitations, but even poor whites, untouched by the notions of feminine propriety outlined in the published essays, appear to have accepted the basic assertions about femininity. The boundaries that circumscribed the American woman's mental universe were, in short, as palpable as the realities of her domestic role.

I

Uppermost in women's minds was the very fact of their feminine identity. They thought of themselves primarily as women, as possessors of all the attributes their society commonly designated *feminine*. Their acceptance of a specifically female persona was indicated in a variety of ways: by explicit statements to that effect, by patterns of word usage, by implicit assumptions about their own nature, by casual asides in diaries and correspondence. Femininity formed their invariable point of reference. When they compared themselves to an abstract standard, that standard was sexually defined. When they judged themselves by the behavior of others, those others were female.

Thus, when Nabby Adams Smith at the age of twenty-three sought to express confidence in her ability to assess the characters and motives of other persons, she did not state her contention in absolute or sexually neutral terms but declared instead that she was as perceptive "as most *ladies* of my *age* and *experience*." Her fellow countrywomen, too, knew that femininity inexorably shaped their lives; they seemed unable to talk about themselves or their reactions to events without alluding to their sexual identity.[3]

By using the word *female* as a descriptive term in situations that would not seem to require it, women revealed how central to their self-conceptions was a recognition of their sexual nature. A New York girl referred to herself not as "a correspondent," but as "a female Correspondent," though the man she addressed knew perfectly well that she was a woman; others spoke superfluously of a "Female letter" or a "Female Breast"; and a young Virginian rather extraordinarily alluded to "us female Ladies."[4] As their peculiar linguistics suggest, eighteenth-century American white women found the fact of their sexual identity inescapable.

Of what, then, did femininity consist? Women were "much more pure, tender, delicate, irritable, affectionate, flexible, and patient" than men, asserted a widely reprinted article. They were, in addition, modest, chaste, cheerful, sympathetic, affable, and emotional: in brief, they displayed what was commonly termed "native Female softness." This catalogue of qualities was at once descriptive and prescriptive, serving both as a list of goals for feminine behavior and as an enumeration of characteristics exclusively and innately female. Paradoxically, therefore, although women were "soft" by nature, they also had to cultivate that softness deliberately. Dr. John Gregory, the author of *A Father's Legacy to his Daughters* (1765), one of the most popular prescriptive works, implicitly indicated his recognition of the logical difficulty this caused when he told his readers, "I do not want to make you anything: I want to know what Nature has made you, and to perfect you on her plan."[5]

The process of "perfecting" themselves demanded that women work to develop in particular the interconnected virtues of modesty and delicacy. Modesty "adds charms to their beauty, and gives a new softness to their sex," asserted a male essayist in 1789; "when a woman loses her native modesty . . . she loses all her charms, she loses all her virtue, and is undone forever," wrote another a few years later. Indeed, one commentator declared, "[M]odesty is so essential . . . that it must be preserved, even in the very moment appointed for its loss."[6]

Delicacy, defined as "an inward sense of propriety, which regulates and beautifies the whole conduct," was no less important. "So fair and so delicate is the *female character*," said an author in the *Massachusetts Magazine* in 1790, that "the minutest speck upon its surface . . . will . . . appear to obscure almost all its lustre." Among the "specks" that could destroy a woman's delicacy were an "ungraceful" walk, a careless choice of clothing, a "slovenly" hairdo, "injudicious" conversation, or even "an elevated tone of the voice." A woman who maintained her delicacy could look forward to being "respected, protected, caressed" by men, whereas one less fastidious would be shunned by respectable folk. In other words, an essayist told his female readers in 1792, "[W]hile you retain modesty and delicacy, you will be loved, cherished, and esteemed; as you depart from these very amiable companions . . . satiety will give birth to disgust."[7]

Genteel women testified to their adherence to these standards in both word and deed. In their comments on other women, they praised those who displayed the approved feminine qualities and criticized the ones who departed from them. "She is just what a Woman ought to be — Sensible — polite — tender — & sympathizes in the distresses of her friends," said Nancy Shippen Livingston of a new acquaintance in 1783. "I was much pleased with a softness and delicacy in her manners, without any affectation," was the admiring comment a young Pennsylvanian's behavior elicited three years later. On one afternoon in 1766, a New England teenager encountered both "Clarissa," about whose "Modesty & Sweetness" she rhapsodized at length, and the sharply contrasting "Masculina." "Surely she never heard of Female Grace," the girl charged, for "her Voice [was] loud & manlike, her Discourse Rough & indelicate her Dress sluttish, & she strides along, when she Walks, with the Grace of a Cow." Clarissa, then, was her model: "O that I cou'd be like to thee, thou amiable Woman," she prayed, and "never never may I be like Masculina!"[8]

Eliza Southgate undoubtedly spoke for many when she announced in 1801, "I would not intentionally deviate from the laws of female delicacy and propriety." Certainly Elizabeth Smith Shaw agreed with her, for even when she was angrily scolding a niece for her frivolous ways she chose her words carefully. After informing the girl that she "*exceedingly disapprove[d]*" the late hours she kept, Mrs. Shaw added, "[T]he softness of the female Character, will not admit of stronger Terms, *Disapprove* from a Lady, is equal to the strongest expression of *Disgust*, & abhorrence from a Gentleman." If women of the middling and better sorts agreed with the assessment of women's nature promulgated by the New Englander Mary Van Schalkwyck in 1804, it was no wonder they observed such strict rules of behavior. Since a woman was "more delicate, more tender and generous" than a man, she remarked, when "she violates the first principles of her being, when she becomes rapacious, obdurate and icy-souled, she is a monster — a very monster."[9]

Genteel colonial women thus had to walk a fine behavioral line, displaying properly "feminine" characteristics, yet never exaggerating those qualities to the point at which they would seem artificial. They had to avoid adopting "masculine" modes of conduct, for otherwise all would be lost: they would be graceless eccentrics on the fringes of society, unsexed females deprived of the core of their identity.

White women from the lower ranks of society, the wives and widows of poor farmers and urban laborers, could not have been expected to be modest and delicate. But they too accepted a feminine persona as essential to their nature, and like their counterparts of the middling and better sorts, they understood that females shared a series of undesirable traits — those "failings peculiar to our sex," as Peggy Emlen termed them in 1768. If men repeatedly alluded to "womanish fears," "Female absurdities," or "the virulence of female resentments," women just as frequently mentioned "the foolishness of us Women" or "the Natural timidity of our sex." [10]

When women remarked upon the characteristics they presumably shared with others of their sex, they did so apologetically. Men, for their part, turned similar comments into satire. Take, for example, the matter of feminine curiosity. When Abigail Adams asked Mercy Otis Warren for some information in 1775, she asked her friend to "excuse" the "curiosity . . . natural to me as a ———." That same year a Connecticut girl also felt compelled to defend her curiosity, "one of the greatest essentials in a Woman," by observing, "I dont think it any faling." [11] Apologies additionally littered women's comments on their supposed loquacity and love of gossip. "I hope my Dear Brother will Excuse my Dwelling so Long upon one Subject our Sex you men say is given to prolixity & I freely Confess your sister is one instance of it," said a New Englander typically in 1772. A male traveler at mid-century joked about the reputed feminine tendency to talkativeness. After noting one evening that the wife of his host had taken no part in the conversation, he commented in his journal, "[H]er muteness is owing to a defect in her hearing. . . . It is well I have thus accounted for it," he continued, "else such a character in the sex would appear quite out of nature." [12]

Men's frequent allusions to "Female *Caprice*" or "their fickle dispositions" revealed their belief that women were by nature changeable and irrational. A Virginian in 1785 advised his nephew to "captivate" girls by appealing "not to their reason or their interest, but to their fancy." Likewise, when a Maine youth expressed anger at his mother's refusal to allow him to go to sea, he focused his rage on the alleged irrationality of her sex rather than on the decision itself. "What is the reason a Woman will never employ the abilities which God has bestow'd on them, to reason in the right way?" he asked his sister ungrammatically. "They look judge, think and condemn, upon the external appearence; but never trouble themselves to serch [sic] the internal." His ability to transform a private dispute into a sweeping statement on female nature must have found its imitators elsewhere, if Sarah Livingston Jay's sensitivity on the subject is any indication. In 1784, upon learning that Congress had decided to move from Trenton to Philadelphia after meeting in the former location for only a short time, she dryly remarked to her husband, "I think it fortunate for the reputation of the Ladies that there are none of our sex in Congress."[13]

Above all else, though, women's "prevailing passions" were reputed to be "vanity, and the love of admiration." Authors of all descriptions mercilessly excoriated the female sex's "extravagant fondness for flattery, however gross and nauseous," and women themselves admitted that they were "said to be [composed of] only Pride and Vainety." The severest strictures on this tendency in "the sex" came from the pen of Lord Chesterfield, whose letters to his son were widely read in America. "Scarce any flattery is too gross for them to swallow," Chesterfield declared; "he who flatters them most, pleases them best." Eliza Lucas was so accustomed to reading these critiques of feminine vanity that in 1742 she misinterpreted Samuel Richardson's use of the epistolary mode of narration. The fact that Richardson had allowed his heroine Pamela "that disgusting liberty of praising her self, or what is very like it, repeating all the fine speeches made to her by others," she concluded, must have been "designed . . . as a reflection upon the vanity of our sex."[14]

Abigail Adams and Mercy Otis Warren were less inclined than Lucas to accept unquestioningly the belief that females were especially susceptible to flattery. In 1780, Abigail not only acquired an abridged version of Chesterfield's letters but also learned that her friend Mercy had written a long commentary on the volume for one of her sons. Complaining of Chesterfield's "abuse upon our sex," Mrs. Adams told Mrs. Warren testily, "I could prove to his Lordship were he living that there was one woman in the world who could act consequentially more than 24 hours," remarking in passing that Chesterfield had proved himself to be, "with all his elegance and graces, . . . a Hypocritical polished Libertine." Mercy Warren's commentary, which Abigail liked so much that she arranged for its publication in 1781 (it was subsequently reprinted in 1784 and again in 1790), pronounced Chesterfield to be "beneath the resentment of a woman of education and reflection" and accused him of making a series of "trite, vulgar, hackneyed observations" in no way salvaged by his polite style. Strikingly, Mrs. Warren insisted upon the injustice of concentrating on the faults of women alone. Rejecting the contention that women and men had different natural characteristics, she asserted that "the foibles, the passions, the vices and the virtues, appear to spring from the same source," rising to "the same degree of perfection" or falling to "the same stages of depravity," depending on the circumstances involved. Consequently, she implied, it was unfair for Chesterfield and other authors to brand females with "peculiar marks of infamy" for displaying flaws that could equally be perceived in men.[15]

Such iconoclasm was exceedingly rare. In the 1790s, when a few women began to repudiate the conventional wisdom about feminine attributes — a development that will be examined in chapter 8 — Mrs. Warren's essay would have been less unusual but still distinguishable for its boldness. Her impassioned reaction to Chesterfield was also unusual within her own corpus; only on infrequent occasions did she directly confront questions involving woman's status. Abigail Adams was somewhat more willing to address such issues, but in contrast to her friend she accepted the notion that certain traits were peculiarly feminine. Her letters were peppered with references to woman's dependent nature, to "the part allotted to my Sex — patience and submission," and to "the tender Heart of our frail Sex." Once (in the context of a discussion of women's particular susceptibility to "these impressions which create happiness or misiry") she even admitted, "I never wonderd at the philosopher who thanked the Gods that he was created a Man rather than a Woman."[16]

Since so many "feminine" qualities had negative connotations that were neither questioned nor challenged at mid-century, it seems logical to conclude that American white women in all likelihood believed themselves inferior to men. This hypothesis is borne out by an examination of a variety of contemporary sources.

II

Just as women's use of the superfluous modifier "female" reveals the significance of their sexual identity in their self-perceptions, so too the adjectives they employed in descriptions of themselves or their sex show their lack of a positive self-image. "*I am a poor helpless Woman*," a Virginian seeking a favor told Thomas Jefferson in 1790. That same year, when Sarah Jay informed her husband, John, that she became depressed during his frequent absences, she explained her mental state not in purely personal terms, but rather as a consequence of the "weakness" of her sex: "[Y]ou know we (females) are but weaker Vessels." A man in poor health might possibly be termed "weak," but women like Mrs. Jay normally used the word to refer to females as a group, alluding to "the weakness of my Sex" or "so weak & imperfect a creeture as woman." [17]

Even more significantly, "helpless" was specifically sex-typed, never being applied to men. Occasionally, "helpless" was employed to modify "children" or "family" (that is, a man's dependents excluding himself), but no man ever employed it as a self-description. The most systematic evidence of this phenomenon comes from the loyalist claims submitted to the British government after the Revolution. Although refugee women and men were in the same dire financial straits following the loss of all their property in America, only women regularly used that term to describe themselves: "being a Poor helpless Widow," "a helpless woman advanced in life," a "disconsolate, Distressed and helpless Widow." Men, on the other hand, most often deemed themselves "unfortunate," which had entirely different, even contrary, connotations. If one was "helpless," one's condition was inherent and irreversible; if one was "unfortunate," one was simply unlucky and could hope for a better future. [18]

Women's letters and diaries reflect their pervasive sense of inferiority in four other ways. First, women were consistently apologetic about their sex, using femininity as a ready excuse for any failings. Thus when Elizabeth Graeme Fergusson, the Philadelphia poet, petitioned the Pennsylvania executive council during the Revolution, she commented that, if she had made any errors in the form or content of her presentation, she hoped the council members would "impute it to the ignorance of a Female." So, too, a woman loyalist refugee, questioned by the claims commission about the details of her memorial, replied that "as far as a Woman can know, she believes the contents to be true." The same negative attitude made a female Virginian in 1788 assume that Thomas Jefferson would think she had "no abilities and no Industry" because of her sex. And constant exposure to the pejorative connotations of femininity in Anglo-American culture led a female traveling in the West the following year to comment wonderingly upon the fact that in Iroquois society "the greatest compliment you can pay a young hero, is that *he is as wise as an old woman.*"[19]

In the other three types of references to their inferiority, women did not explicitly mention sex, but they nevertheless assumed the burden of negative feminine attributes. So women, widely said to be irrational creatures, frequently complained in their letters and diaries of an inability to reason properly. Betsy Rhoads Fisher, for example, told her husband, Samuel, in 1793, "[M]any are the Ideas that occur to me but alass I cannot find Language to array them in to my mind." Similarly, a Connecticut girl declared in 1782, "[A]t present My Ideas are all lock'd up," and the following year a New Jersey resident admitted, "[T]ho I at times seem to have much to say, when I make the attempt I hardly know how to arrange my thoughts."[20]

Logically enough, given this diffidence about their powers of reasoning, women also constantly belittled their writings, terming their letters "insipid scribbles," "Poor Productions," "stupid," "strange . . . Inconsistent and various," or "a most dolefull heap of Scrawls."[21] As might well be expected from the relative position of the two sexes, such expressions appeared more often and in more exaggerated form in women's letters to men than in missives to members of their own sex. In a unique instance, a middle-aged

Pennsylvania woman even told her youthful nephew that she hesitated to correspond with him because she thought herself "uneaqual to" the task "of writeing to a Man of good Sense and Education." Women often began letters to men (especially learned or prominent ones) with extended apologies for their temerity in presuming to write. That they would do so is not surprising in light of the contents of men's letters to them. "I have been so long disused to female company that I have lost all my small talk, and forgot that fund of nonsense which alone can please a triffling mind," a New Hampshire man told his sister-in-law unthinkingly in 1789 before he hastily apologized for his arrogant condescension.[22]

Only a short distance separated women's diffidence about their writings from the fourth category, a noticeable self-deprecation that went far beyond simple modesty. "My tallent is but small," wrote a Rhode Islander in 1774; Pamela Dwight Sedgwick in 1789 referred to "my own Imbecillity and Weakness"; "my brain is so vacant that it seems to be void of Ideas," said Mary Norris Dickinson in 1791; and the bright, thoughtful Esther Edwards Burr insisted in 1755, "I have a poor judgme[n]t of my own."[23] One of the best indications of women's excessive self-deprecation came from their husbands, who regularly felt it necessary to tell them to have more confidence in themselves. Lund Washington repeatedly lectured his wife, Elizabeth Foote, about her diffidence, and James Iredell chided Hannah Johnston for the same flaw. After the death of his wife, Polly Ambler, John Marshall recalled, "[Her] native timidity . . . so influenced her manners, that I could rarely prevail on her to display in company the talents I knew her to possess," even though her judgment was "so sound & so safe that I have often relied upon it in situations of some perplexity." Likewise the Virginian Augustine Smith, who believed that feminine diffidence was "one of the finest & most engaging traits," still asked his fiancée, Alice Page, "[M]ay not the greatest accomplishments of character degenerate into improprieties, when verging too near to excess?"[24]

But the extreme self-deprecation that men like John Marshall and James Iredell deplored in their wives was nothing other than the ultimate proof that women had internalized the inferior self-image eighteenth-century social norms impressed upon them. They understood their lesser status clearly, perhaps more clearly than the husbands who loved them and who were accordingly prepared to exempt them from its strictures.

A key indicator of women's low standing relative to men was the peculiar form of praise offered a few of their number: a declaration that they were superior to the rest of their sex because they possessed a "masculine" quality of mind. These comments, which originated with both men and women, avoided the dangers inherent in attributing male qualities to a female by invariably emphasizing their subjects' femininity. Thus Benjamin Rush wrote of Anne Keith Graeme, Elizabeth Graeme Fergusson's mother, that she had "a masculine mind, with all those female charms and accomplishments which render a woman alike agreeable to both sexes," and a New England girl quoted an English author when she approvingly assessed a new acquaintance in 1800: "'[T]o more than manly sense she joins the softening influence of more than female tenderness.'" [25] In this way an individual woman's intellectual achievements could be acknowledged without undermining the overall construct of feminine inferiority.

Such plaudits ultimately had the effect of denigrating the female sex as a whole, because of a dual implication. The favorable application of the adjective "masculine" to a woman who otherwise maintained her sexual identity through feminine behavior patterns carried with it the unmistakable message that, at least in the realm of the mind, to be masculine was superior to being feminine. Furthermore, in the process of thus praising specific females, their admirers thereby distinguished them from ordinary representatives of the "fair sex," who suffered by the comparison.

Margaret Davenport Coalter's observation on a friend in 1795 provides an apposite illustration of this phenomenon: she "[is] possess'd of a most excellent well improved understanding and a judgment much sounder than usually falls to the lot of us poor females," Margaret commented revealingly. A letter Elizabeth Smith Shaw addressed to her niece Nabby Adams in 1785 exposed a similar, though more ambivalent, attitude. In the following quotation, the material in brackets was contained in a first draft, which she then altered. "Though I know you as human, liable to *Errors*," Elizabeth informed Nabby, "yet I have ever viewed you in a variety of Instance, as rising above [y]our sex — superior to the weakness, & the Foibles that more generally attend [them] us."[26]

Mrs. Shaw's evident confusion over whether or not to number herself among the weak and foible-prone female sex was significant. She was accustomed to being praised for her "masculine" intellectual abilities, and she at first excluded herself from her negative characterization of women. In the end, though, Elizabeth Shaw accepted a link to the rest of inferior womanhood. Indeed, she had no choice. She could not change her sexual identity.

Abigail Adams, Elizabeth's sister and Nabby's mother, fully understood the negative messages concealed in admiring phrases. She rejoiced when she learned in 1778 that a statue had been erected to honor the English radical Catharine Macaulay, whom she greatly respected, but she nevertheless criticized "the narrow contracted Spirit" evident in the statue's inscription, which read, in part, "[O]nce in every Age I could wish such a Woman to appear, as a proof that Genius is not confined to Sex." Mrs. Adams quickly perceived in that phrase the implications that have been discussed here. It was small-minded, she declared, "to wish that but one woman in an age might excell, and she only for the sake of a prodigy." Why could men only "do justice to one Lady, but at the expence of the whole Sex?" she inquired tellingly.[27]

The Adams family's friend Mercy Otis Warren struggled throughout her long career as a pamphleteer and historian with the discomfort caused by the ambiguity inherent in her status as an intellectual woman. Her husband, James, in typical fashion described her as having a "Masculine Genius" coupled with that "Weakness which is the Consequence of the Exquisite delicacy and softness of her Sex." Mrs. Warren was well aware that women were not supposed to display a satirical wit (a 1768 essayist had written, for instance, "I can never think a satirical woman an amiable character"), yet she had obvious talents in that regard. In order to resolve the conflict between her own inclinations and prescribed feminine behavior, she anxiously asked John Adams in early 1775 if he thought she would be deemed "deficient" in womanly qualities if she allowed herself to express "personal Acrimony" in her planned parodies of Thomas Hutchinson and his political allies. John, who was to be less indulgent of such unfeminine conduct in later years when he himself became the target of Mercy's pointed pen, assured her that he saw nothing reprehensible in her efforts.[28]

Even so, certain curious nuances twice surfaced in the wartime correspondence of the two friends. The first occasion came in September 1775, when Adams commented to Mrs. Warren, seemingly in all innocence, that he did not want to "Stain this Paper with any Thing concerning Politicks or War." Mercy Warren took his statement as an implicit challenge to her ability to discuss political and military questions. In her reply she begged his pardon for introducing the subject of politics, "as I think you gave me a hint in yours not to approach the verge of any thing so far beyond the line of my sex." John's response, addressed to James rather than to Mercy, insisted that she had misinterpreted him, "since I never thought either politicks or War, or any other Art or Science beyond the Line of her Sex." John then declared that in any case Mercy would constitute an obvious exception to such a rule, along with his wife, Abigail. One would be inclined to dismiss this exchange as a peculiar but unimportant misunderstanding had it not been replicated seven years later. In a letter to James from Holland in 1782, Adams expressed his hope that Mrs. Warren would give his "Dutch Negotiation a Place in her History. It is one of the most extraordinary, in all the diplomatic Records." Mercy's reply accused John of displaying "sarcasm" in this phrase, and threatened him with the "little thirst of revenge" he had aroused in her otherwise "Good Naturd" heart. Again Adams protested that he had not intended any slight: "I assure you, Madam, what I said about certain Annals was no Sarcasm," he declared in early 1783.[29]

Whether Mercy Otis Warren was correct in her interpretation of the implications of John Adams's choice of words matters less than the fact that she detected implicit hostility and criticism in his phrases. Her sensitivity to apparent sexual putdowns indicates as nothing else could the force of the pressure she felt as she moved out of the realm of feminine behavior and into the male world of political and historical analysis. The perceptive author of an essay printed in the *American Magazine* in 1788 could well have had her situation in mind when he wrote, in a somewhat different context, that "afraid of an inferiority, a woman of sensibility feels a certain degree of uneasiness in the company of men of high ability and profound learning. Diffident of being able to converse with such men on equal terms, she fancies she is contemned by them."[30]

In Mrs. Warren's case more than "fancy" may have been involved. Her female contemporaries certainly understood that outspoken erudition was not expected of them, for they habitually used such phrases as "all the knowledge of books proper for a woman to know," a degree of learning "which som persons think is enough for a woman," or "the arguments a woman could offer appear frivolous to a man." In his youth, John Adams had arrogantly urged women not to become "pedants" and had referred to their conversation as "little contemptible tittle tattle." In his old age, confronted with Mrs. Warren's criticism of him in her history of the American Revolution, Adams magisterially declared that "history is not the Province of the Ladies."[31] During the intervening years he might well have silently communicated the same attitude to a woman who knew him well and who was familiar with his style of expression.

In any event, it is clear that, like the Maine boy who moved from a personal dispute with his mother to a universal condemnation of women's powers of reasoning, John Adams was unable to treat his conflict with Mercy Warren over the contents of her history as a private disagreement without sexual overtones. For him, as for her, the inescapable fact of her femininity was of decisive importance. Although in 1775 he had formally exempted her from the limits placed on others of her sex, in 1813 he firmly put her back in her place. If she had ever truly been an exception, she was one no longer.

In contrast to Mercy Otis Warren and Abigail Adams, most female Americans were never granted even a temporary exemption from the restrictions of womanhood. In 1789 a young wife demonstrated her understanding of this fact by telling Thomas Jefferson, "I own that we are made but for little things and our employments ought to extend at the furthest to the interiour economy and polacy of the family, and the care of our Children when they are little."[32]

The fullest contemporary explication of the restrictions felt by women came from the pen of a New York teenager in the early 1760s. Anne DeLancey had asked her friend Anne Moore if she enjoyed living in the country, "in such a dull inactive state." "Give me leave to answer this question by another," Moore replied. "In what wou'd you shew your activity?" She then elaborated on the theme: "I dare say when you speak of active life for a Woman you mean something that I dont comprehend." After all, Moore declared, "[O]ur sex can appear truely amiable in no light but the domestic, and in that if every duty is discharg'd she will find room to display every virtue." There was no other outlet for women's talents, she asserted, linking domesticity to feminine inferiority by "joking" explicitly about women's loss of status since the days of the Amazons. Had they lived then they might have chafed at such limitations, but since in their own day, she told her friend, "those selfish creatures Men have put it out of our power to share those honours with them[,] we must be content and endeavour to make it appear by a steady conduct . . . that we have equal abilities with those in former ages, tho custom has put it out of our power to shine with so great advantage."[33]

In a few words Anne Moore had summed up her fellow countrywomen's understanding of their status and role. They could "shine" only in the domestic sphere, where they proved their virtue by discharging "every duty" to husbands, households, and children — tasks her Virginia contemporary, like many others, regarded as "but . . . little things." Once, perhaps, in an ideal past, women had been equal to men, had "share[d] . . . honours" with them, but now "those selfish creatures" had deprived them of that status, and they had to be content. Women could aspire to prove that they possessed abilities equal to their Amazonian forebears, but they had to act upon a much smaller stage. Most important of all, the very notion of "activity" was foreign to womanhood. Anne Moore freely admitted that she did not understand what Anne DeLancey meant when she referred to an "active life for a Woman." The idea was beyond her comprehension, appearing to be a contradiction in terms. The tender, delicate, deferential female simply could not be "active." In what, after all, *would* they show their activity?

A few of Anne Moore's female contemporaries found an answer to that question which differed from hers, and the significance of their experiences outweighed the scantiness of their numbers.

Chapter Five

ॐ

AS INDEPENDENT AS
CIRCUMSTANCES WILL ADMIT

IF ANY QUALITY WAS ANTITHETICAL TO THE COLONIAL NOTION OF femininity, it was autonomy. To eighteenth-century Americans, dependence upon men seemed an inherent attribute of the inferior feminine character. Nevertheless, a noticeable minority of colonial white women either sought independence or had it thrust upon them.

The pervasive acceptance of female subordination in the secular realm did not necessarily imply a similar secondary status in religion. Women were able to rely on the widespread recognition of their spiritual equality to advance to positions of prominence in Quaker meetings and evangelical congregations in particular. Even if a woman was a *feme covert,* a legal dependent of her husband, she could acquire the responsibility and prestige of religious leadership. And if a woman was a *feme sole,* a spinster or widow, she was legally free of male control. Most colonial women did not choose *feme sole* status deliberately; as was pointed out in chapter 2, an unmarried female's life had few attractive qualities. Thus single women constituted a small group in comparison to their married counterparts, and they commonly worked at traditionally feminine tasks, but the autonomy they experienced often led them to develop self-conceptions quite different from those of their housebound female contemporaries.

I

Piety was as characteristic of the ideal colonial woman as was notable housewifery. Innumerable essays, sermons, and tracts outlined a twofold religious role for females: first, they were to guard the state of their own souls through regular church attendance, Bible study, pious conversations, and private meditations; and second, they were expected to instruct their children in moral principles. "Without religion," declared one prescriptive writer, woman would be "raging and monstrous." Many female colonists, it appears, fully agreed with him, for surviving diaries and entire volumes filled with personal reflections attest to the strength of their religious commitment.[1]

Women from various denominations were alike motivated to spend many hours in self-examination. The Quaker Anne Emlen prepared "Some Account of My Religious Progress"; the Anglican Elizabeth Foote Washington filled three manuscript books with drafts of prayers; and Martha Laurens Ramsay, a Presbyterian, kept a religious diary for at least seventeen years, in addition to composing devout exercises on such topics as "A Self Dedication and Solemn Covenant with God" and "Contrition for Mispent [sic] Time, and Resolutions to Improve it in Future."[2] Similarly, colonial women devoted themselves to giving religious instruction to their youngsters. Elizabeth Colden DeLancey, for example, required her children to present her with "some moral sentence written in a fair hand, with a short Note commenting on it" before allowing them to eat breakfast with her. A Virginia woman recalled that her pious Anglican mother (who had been born in 1743) had read the Bible to her children each morning, as well as hearing their prayers and catechizing them daily. In short, it was not only ministers' daughters like Abigail Adams or ministers' wives like Mrs. Ezra Stiles who concerned themselves with the spiritual welfare of their offspring.[3]

The chief message of colonial religion to both women and men was the necessity of resignation to God's will. In an era of high infant mortality and minimal medical knowledge, a belief that God saw and ordered all events for purposes beyond human comprehension provided ready consolation for otherwise inexplicable afflictions. Thus in 1778, in the midst of the war that threatened the lives of her sons and placed her property holdings in jeopardy, Eliza Lucas Pinckney exclaimed to her daughter, "[H]is Sacred Will be done! Wealth and Poverty, Prosperity and adversity are in his disposal, and infinite Wisdom guides the whole." It was generally believed, as the bereaved mother Elizabeth Foote Washington asserted, God "will not afflict us more then he will enable us to bear — he knows when it is necessary to lay the cross upon us." Eighteenth-century Americans knew that every trial inflicted on them had its own purpose, one that was sufficient to accomplish God's mysterious ends. "All he does is for the best," wrote the teenaged Peggy Emlen typically in 1768, "and no one knows so well what is best for us."[4]

Unfortunately, it was easier to preach such a doctrine than to practice it. In the early stages of her final illness, Sally Logan Fisher prayed to attain "a state of full resignation" yet found it "a hard & difficult leasson to learn," even as she asked for God's help in accepting the "low state of Health" to which He had evidently consigned her. Sally's fellow Quaker Elizabeth Sandwith Drinker, like many others, believed resignation to be the source of "the most comfort and consolation" in life, but she too admitted that it was "hard, very hard in many cases to effect."[5]

Despite such acknowledged difficulty in achieving perfect resignation to divine will, contentment with one's lot remained the spiritual ideal throughout the late eighteenth century. Religion pressed upon women a conservative outlook, one that stressed accepting present conditions rather than encouraging attempts at change. Superficially, therefore, it would appear unlikely that religion could offer colonial women a relatively unrestricted outlet for their talents. Yet, because piety was seen as a peculiarly feminine virtue, and because of the universal insistence upon the equality of souls before God, women were occasionally able to pursue active public careers in religion even though they found the road to secular eminence closed against them.

Within the Society of Friends, females had a formally structured role revolving around women's meetings, which were run by and for their members, and which paralleled similar gatherings composed of men. Quaker women also traveled widely in both America and England as "public Friends"; that is, as messengers and ministers to other Quaker meetings. The published memoirs of these women reveal that they often abandoned home and family to take prolonged trips "for truths sake," as one of them put it in 1798, but they were rarely criticized for such "unfeminine" actions. Instead, their courage and religious commitment generally drew praise from all who knew them.[6]

Anne Emlen, who became one of their number in the first years of the nineteenth century, demonstrated her penchant for independent thought as early as 1781, when she was twenty-six. A pious pacifist, she decided to leave home because her mother used Continental currency and paid taxes, thereby contributing to the American war effort. Anne's friends, Sally Logan Fisher and Anna Rawle among them, judged her actions "extroandiary" [sic], believing "she carrys the matter too far," but they nevertheless thought her "a very fine woman." Emlen's reaction to a Methodist meeting she attended in the 1780s shows that she had thought seriously about the status of women in organized religion. She chastised the congregation for not permitting a young woman to speak during the service, "seeing Male & Female are declared to be one in Christ." After the minister explained that church members allowed women to talk in private meetings, but were divided over their proper public role, Anne forcefully tackled the scriptural point. St. Paul's intent in enjoining women to keep silence in church, she argued, was not to halt their "speaking in prophecy, or under divine influence," but only "the indulgence of a restless inquisitive disposition at an improper time."[7]

Clearly the evangelical, or New Light, churches were more ambivalent about women's role than was the Society of Friends. But some congregations did offer women opportunities for full participation in church affairs. In Virginia Baptist churches, for instance, women frequently constituted a majority of the membership, often were allowed to vote, and occasionally served as exhorters. In Newport, Rhode Island, Baptist women had long voted to admit new members and to elect deacons; consequently, "Usage and practiced Principle," thought the Reverend Ezra Stiles in 1771, implied that they could also vote on matters of church business. Significantly, Stiles, whose advice on the subject was sought by a bewildered Baptist deacon, then went on to extend his reasoning to his own Congregational church, where women "often stay with the Brethren & see & hear what is transacted, but dont even speak." Forced to consider the issue for the first time, Stiles reluctantly concluded that "upon the

Principle that there can be no vote unless every Brother consented, the Consent of every Sister may be required."[8]

Women's roles in New Light meetings are further illuminated by the diary of Mary Cooper. In February 1769, dissatisfied with orthodox religion, the Long Island woman joined the local evangelical congregation, and she attended faithfully whenever her domestic obligations allowed. By mid-1772, she had been named to a committee "to talk of some church business"; her diary also reveals that women as well as men regularly spoke in meetings. But in the early fall of 1773 the congregation that meant so much to her was irrevocably split by a dispute between "Peter" and "Sister," its two leaders. Although the cause of the division is obscure, it probably stemmed from a disagreement over the question of whether women could properly become ministers, with Sister defending the practice and Peter attacking it. After a series of bitter confrontations, Peter and his followers walked out. Mary Cooper remained with Sister's group, but her daughter Esther attended Peter's meeting on occasion, thus splitting the family along the same lines as the congregation.[9] The episode is important not only because it shows the Cooper women's religious commitment but also because it demonstrates Sister's willingness to challenge Peter formally on a doctrinal question that had a direct bearing on her own role in the church.

Sister was not alone among eighteenth-century females in insisting upon her right to continue in an established position of religious leadership. Another notable example of this phenomenon is provided by Sarah Haggar Osborn, a member of the First Congregational Church in Newport, Rhode Island.

Although Mrs. Osborn's early life was distinguished by her piety, only after her conversion during the Great Awakening (the revival that swept through the colonies at mid-century) did she begin to assume the mantle of religious leadership. She started in 1741 by agreeing to direct the activities of a young women's prayer society. With the exception of a lengthy hiatus in the 1750s, the group met continuously for the rest of her life, and from it she drew much spiritual comfort. In 1761 she told a regular correspondent, the Reverend Joseph Fish, "[A]ll things are carried on in an orderly secret way we have none that devulges to the world what Passes amongst us that I Ever Heard off [so] that we enjoy the sweetest freedom with each other." Religion, she observed accurately, was "the chief business" of her life, even at a time when, as a widow, she was working in a shop to support herself.[10]

In the spring of 1765, Sarah Osborn unwittingly initiated a revival when she allowed a number of slaves to attend family prayers in her home on Sunday evenings. Before long, she was reporting to the Reverend Mr. Fish that "Little white Lads and Neighbours daughters also press in" to the meetings, and by mid-1766 fully 312 persons, both black and white, were coming to her house each week for religious gatherings. "Who would Ever Have thot that God by such a poor Mean despicable worm would have Gathered Such a Number?" she asked Fish. "Is this not the Lords doings is it not Marvellous in our Eyes what but His Secret Drawing could incline so Many to Send a Listning Ear to serious things?"[11]

Yet despite Mrs. Osborn's undisguised pleasure at her success in spreading God's word, two difficulties had to be surmounted. At the beginning of the revival, she was widely criticized for "keeping a Negro House," since Newport slaveowners feared she was spreading "disturbance or disorder" among their servants. "Such a one is not allow'd to have one intimate friend in the world o the bitters that lurk under the most splendid appearances," she complained to Fish. But within a few months her onetime critics started to applaud her efforts, for they quickly discovered, she claimed, that many formerly recalcitrant slaves had "reform'd" under her influence, instead becoming "diligent and condecending."[12]

The second problem was not so easily handled, being posed inescapably by Sarah Osborn's leadership of the revival. She herself recognized that she was venturing perilously close to the acceptable boundaries of feminine behavior. Consequently, she deliberately took steps, as she said, "to avoid Moving beyond my Line": she did not pray with teenaged boys, she had "no thing" to do with young men, and she did not act as the "Instructor" of married men.[13] In short, she attempted to confine her attention to the women and children whom convention allowed her to lead. Mrs. Osborn even tried to fit her work with the blacks into the same acceptable mold by contending, "[T]he Servants appear to me no otherwise now then children tho for Stature Men and women." But all her efforts were insufficient.

In early 1767 her friend Fish urged her to halt her activities, simultaneously asserting that men were more qualified than she to be spiritual leaders and hinting that she could better devote her time to appropriately "feminine" tasks.

In his letter, Fish reminded Mrs. Osborn of Exodus 18:18–19, wherein Jethro recommended that Moses share with others the burden of judging the Israelites, "for this thing is too heavy for thee." Instead of following Moses' lead and yielding to this advice, however, the Newport woman chose to dispute Fish's interpretation of the text. Jethro's suggestion was "very Good" for Moses, she admitted, "but Here my dear Sir Lies the difference" with her own case: Moses was a leader, whereas she was but an "unworthy and unequal" servant. Who was she to tell God, who had "assignd" her a "great Work," that she could not complete it? Rather, she argued, she should continue with her task as before "until God in his providence point out a way for it to be better done."

Sarah Osborn dealt with Fish's other arguments in equally brisk and uncompromising fashion. He had asked, she recalled, "Have you Strength ability and Time consistent with other Duties to fill a Larger sphere by attending the various Exercises of other Meetings?" "As to Strength Sir it is Evident I gain by Spending," she declared in response. "I always feel stronger when my companies break up then when they come in." As for ability, that was not for her to assess: "I can only say I trust christs Strength is Made perfect in my weakness." And, finally, she decisively rejected Fish's implicit suggestion that more properly feminine "other Duties" should occupy her evenings. Needlework, after a long, tiring day, "overpowers me vastly more than the duties I am Engaged in," Mrs. Osborn explained, and because of the same fatigue she was incapable of prolonged "clost fixt Meditation." As a result, if her evenings were not filled with religious meetings, "they doubtless would be with trancient visiters, and some chat Less to Edification . . . would break in." Moreover, she said, the meetings "seem then to refresh recruit and enliven my Exhausted spirits"; they were truly her "resting reaping times." Her question on another occasion accurately represented her perception of the only alternative to continuing her role in the revival: "Would you advise me to shut up my Mouth and doors and creep into obscurity?"[14]

Behind that inquiry lay a lifetime of drudgery, dutiful wifely sub-mission, and feminine inconsequentiality suddenly transformed by God's miraculous will into a life of leadership, purpose, and social importance. The revival had provided Sarah Osborn with an escape from the confines of deferential womanhood, and she did not intend to relinquish her freedom without a fight.

As late as July 1769 "private praying Societies Male and female" were still meeting regularly at Mrs. Osborn's house, but the religious fervor in Newport inevitably diminished. The end of the revival did not signal the decline of her prominent position in the church, though, for in the spring of 1770 she and "the Sorority of her Meeting" became "violently engaged" in a struggle over the appointment of a new minister. According to Ezra Stiles, Mrs. Osborn exercised such "great Influence" in the selection process that her candidate, the Reverend Samuel Hopkins, won the coveted post over the opposition of at least one-half the congregation and with the strong support of only about a quarter of the total membership.[15] Nothing could more clearly indicate her continuing impact on church affairs than the power she wielded in this crucial instance.

Unlike most of her female contemporaries, Sarah Osborn pushed her role to its outer limits, and in the process she helped to blaze the trail that generations of pious nineteenth-century American women were to follow, as they found an acceptable outlet for their talents and energy in thousands of female religious and charitable organiza-tions. She did not found new sects, as did Jemima Wilkinson and Mother Ann Lee, nor did she achieve the eventual recognition ac-corded to her other countrywoman Saint Elizabeth Bayley Seton; but Sarah Osborn, like them, discovered in religion a realm in which her femininity did not in itself constitute an insurmountable barrier to the exercise of her considerable talents.[16]

II

Although women had to seek religious autonomy actively, secular independence came unbidden to a large proportion of female Amer-icans in the form of widowhood. Given the fact that widows commonly failed to remarry quickly, if at all, historians have estimated that perhaps as many as 10 percent of the adult white women living in America in the latter half of the eighteenth century were widows at any particular time.[17] These women, and their few never-married counterparts, had to forge roles for themselves that extended beyond the boundaries of the standard feminine sphere.

A husband's death thrust a woman abruptly into a world with which she had had little previous contact, precisely at a time when she was ill prepared to adjust to new responsibilities. Recently widowed women described to relatives their depression, their inability to act, their sense of loss. "The *Sun* to me has *set forever*," wrote a Marylander to her father-in-law; "all and every day is alike gloomy to me, *he* is gon[e] and with him all my plans for earthly happiness." A New Englander repeatedly dreamed of trying to release her husband "from the Confinement of the Coffin and Tomb," all the while listening to his vivid complaints that she "wou'd not come to his assistance nor hear his calls for help." Even Eliza Lucas Pinckney, who before and during her marriage had demonstrated an unusual independence, was prostrated with sorrow by her husband's sudden fatal illness. Her daughter Harriott later recalled that Eliza's "heavy affliction . . . obliterated for a long time the remembrance of every thing that had been agreeable," and more than two years after Charles's death Mrs. Pinckney's letters still spoke of how she felt "overwhelmed with meloncholy," describing herself as "a walking Ghost."[18]

Widows were given little time to recover from the shock of their changed status, for a significant percentage of them were made executrices of their husbands' estates.[19] Although a few had been involved in the administration of family property during their husbands' lifetimes, most had had no previous experience with settling accounts, writing business letters, or handling legal questions. They were acutely aware of their ignorance. The Philadelphia widow Juliana Scott declared in 1800, since she was "so little competent to anything of the kind, and so wholly unaccustomed to the forms of Business," she found it "a most unpleasant Task" to have to "think, and determine for myself in affairs of consequence — to write letters of Business to Lawyers where one is afraid, lest each word should commit, or involve one in trouble." Kitty Livingston Ridley, a sister of Sarah Jay, likewise remarked in 1790 that she could depend only on "prudence and judgement" to guide her in the "disagreeable business" of administering her husband's estate. Mrs. Ridley's inexperience soon caused her to err. Two years after her husband's death she realized that she had made a crucial mistake in allowing one of his business associates to retain control of some legal papers. "As I was very innocent, & ignorant in regard to them, it made very little impression on my mind, too little I now think," she explained to her brother-in-law John as she asked his advice on how to gain possession of the papers.[20]

Even so minimal a task as keeping comprehensive records proved to be beyond Elizabeth Foote Washington's capacity. Her husband became blind five years before his death, and so Elizabeth was forced to take over the accounting chores prior to her widowhood. She annotated the records in revealing fashion: "I neglected putting down the Hay as I ought to have done," she wrote in 1791; the following year elicited the comment, "This is also not a proper account, which am sorry for — keeping accounts is a new thing for me." The next year, 1793, was no better: "I hope if my dear Mr. Washington should be so fortunate as to recover his eye sight, he will excuse my neglect." If anything, Lund's death in 1796 increased her difficulties. "This account is kept by far worse then any has been yet," she declared in 1797. "I know not what hay we have made this year — my Nephew being my manager — I am totally at a loss in many respects indeed I scarce know how any thing goes on — or what is made."[21]

Widows often discovered that their husbands' debtors or creditors tried to take advantage of their lack of business expertise. The illiterate Halifax, Nova Scotia, resident Elisabeth Freeman, who had to persuade others to write for her, informed Robert Treat Paine in 1758 that she had taken out letters of administration on her husband's estate, but, she wrote, "Canot Get my Debts in peopl Seems to trifel with me." Better-educated women had identical problems. Juliana Scott complained that an associate of her husband's seemed determined to give her "as much trouble as possible," relying on her "ignorance, and helplessness" to allow him to win his point. Catherine Livingston, a New Yorker, revealed to her daughter her fear: "I shall make trouble by management[.] I have not fortitude enough if a person brings an account tho' I may think [it] false rather than run the risk of being sued I shall pay." Yet the estate records show that

Mrs. Livingston, after first trying to persuade her son-in-law to take over as executor, ultimately did a competent job in handling her late husband's affairs. And within two years of her spouse's death Juliana Scott, who had originally disparaged her business abilities, proudly described herself as "a regular Accomptant," who kept books "in which the price of every purchase is entered" carefully.[22]

The growing self-confidence and familiarity with finances that can be discerned in the papers of widows like Juliana Scott manifested itself in the event of their remarriage. Although no one has systematically surveyed the incidence of antenuptial agreements in America, the impression one gains from studying scattered marriage settlements is that widows were more likely to insist upon them than were women who had never married. Moreover, whereas widows often sought an "active use," which allowed them to continue to control their possessions after remarriage, the few previously unmarried women who entered into antenuptial agreements commonly had only a "passive use," which simply held property in trust for them and any children they might bear.[23]

The distinction between the two uses is crucial. Both protected a woman against the possibility that her husband's economic indiscretions would leave her bereft of support, but the latter permitted her no voice in the management of her property, while the former gave her a significant amount of financial autonomy.

The pattern of active and passive uses resulted from the divergent origins of antenuptial agreements. A contract signed before a first marriage usually reflected the concerns of the bride's male relatives rather than her own fears for her financial future. Men who insisted that their female kin have marriage settlements were motivated by a desire to ensure a bride's economic security during eventual widowhood instead of by a wish to give her control over her finances. Thus in 1808, when Beverly Tucker and Polly Coalter planned to marry, it was primarily at the insistence of St. George Tucker (who was simultaneously father of the groom and related by marriage to the bride) that an antenuptial agreement was arranged. "I rely upon you to see the settlement properly drawn etc *before the marriage*," St. George told his son-in-law John Coalter, "for [I] by no means consent that Polly shall be left to the Vicissitudes of Life, of Virginia Laws, & Virginia Adjudications in Cases of *Widows*." In such instances the girls themselves often saw no need for a premarital contract. Landon Carter's daughter Lucy blithely announced, for example, that "there would be no manner of occasion for such a settlement," although her father expressed concern over the amount of support she could expect from her husband's entailed estate if she were widowed. Likewise, Harriet Hill Scott, a Pennsylvanian who had an antenuptial agreement, told her father in 1755, "[I]ndeed I would as readily have married him without any, and would now give it up if he would hear of such a thing." Only two years later, though, she had changed her mind, and she informed her family that she would hold her husband to the settlement despite the fact that he now believed it to have been a mistake.[24]

Just as experiencing a wife's restricted legal status taught Harriet Scott the value of a marriage settlement, so too the added burden of widowhood convinced other eighteenth-century women of the necessity for such contracts, especially ones providing for active uses. In South Carolina in 1793, a young widow broke off her engagement to a wealthy planter because he would not agree to her request for an antenuptial agreement, and the Boston businesswoman Elizabeth Murray, whose career will be examined in detail later in this chapter, carefully prepared premarital contracts before both her second and third marriages. Lucy Ludwell Paradise, a Virginia heiress married to a drunken wastrel, generalized from her own experience when she pleaded with Thomas Jefferson in 1789: "[I]ntroduce the Marriage Settlemen[t into Virginia law] for to preserve My Sex from want in case of the Bad behaviour of their husbands." If he would help to make such protection a part of regular statutes, she promised, "we poor Women, shall *Immortalize Your Name*." But Jefferson, who arranged antenuptial agreements with passive uses for his daughters, failed to act on Mrs. Paradise's request, demonstrating the same disregard for her complaints about women's legal status that John Adams had displayed in 1776 when his wife chided him on the identical subject.[25]

On the whole, marriage settlements were a device of the wealthy — of fathers concerned about their daughters' welfare, of fairly well-to-do widows whose first marriages and subsequent independence had led them to conclude that they should prevent their property from falling entirely into their new spouses' hands. For ordinary women, another aspect of wives' legal status had more direct implications for their eventual widowhood: their dower right in their husbands' estates.

American statutes, modeled after the English common law, provided that a man had to leave his wife, at a minimum, a life interest in one-third of his real estate plus a set proportion of his personal property. If he did not fulfill this obligation in his will, his widow could challenge it in court; if he died intestate, the courts would see that she received her "thirds." The purpose of this provision was not so much to guarantee a woman's future economic independence as to ensure that she would not become a public charge. As Alexander Keyssar has correctly pointed out, a life interest in part of an estate offered a woman few options. She could not sell or significantly alter the property because it had to be passed on intact to the eventual heirs, usually her children, and if her inheritance was largely in the form of land she would have difficulty cultivating it in the absence of adult sons. Furthermore, a life interest in a third of a small or middling estate, frequently one encumbered by debt, would rarely give a widow financial security. She would continue to be dependent on the men in her family, most likely her oldest sons, and she would have little opportunity of improving her circumstances, even through remarriage, since many husbands provided in their wills that any special arrangements made for the support of their widows would cease upon their taking a second spouse.[26]

Ironically, the inadequate provision for widows' support under the common law sometimes fostered exactly that independence it seemed designed to suppress. Faced with the alternative of subsisting on a tiny income from their husbands' estates, coupled perhaps with humiliating charity, many widows decided to try to support themselves and their children through their own efforts. Such widows were joined as laborers by a few spinsters and some wives of poor men. Since eighteenth-century Americans believed that women normally should remain within the domestic sphere, economic necessity alone could justify their seeking work outside the home. This fact, along with a lack of opportunities for employment, kept the proportion of working women below 10 percent of the female population even in urban areas, where the chances of obtaining paid work were far better than in rural America.[27] The female laboring force was accordingly quite small, but a detailed examination of it can identify the wage-earning options open to American women and can also reveal the effect of their working experiences on their self-perceptions.

III

The occupations of the forty-three loyalist refugee women who noted their work on claims for compensation after the war illustrate the distribution and range of white women's employment. Only three of them — a tavernkeeper, the owner of a small shop, and a housekeeper for a wealthy landowner — came from rural areas. Most of the other forty had lived in cities, along with a few from towns like Wilmington, North Carolina, or Williamsburg, Virginia. The urban exile women, some of whom engaged in multiple enterprises (combining shopkeeping with running a boardinghouse, for example), fell into the following large occupational categories: eighteen owned shops, most of them dry goods, liquor, or grocery stores; ten took lodgers; five ran taverns or inns; four were milliners; and two were mantua makers, that is, fashionable dress and cloak makers. There were, in addition, two prostitutes, a midwife, a seamstress, the owner of a coffeehouse, a teacher, and a printer. A majority of the employed women, therefore, worked at jobs that were extensions of the feminine sphere — sewing, housekeeping, teaching small children, nursing, and selling food or clothing. Those who did not, like the printer, generally took on the task of running businesses first established by deceased husbands. Even the refugee prostitutes, a Boston mother and daughter, earned their living through the performance of a traditional female function. Judging from the strong support given their claim by high-ranking British officers and leading male citizens of Boston, they must have been highly successful.[28]

Prostitution was an occupation that could earn a living for any untrained woman, and diaries kept by male visitors to American cities attest to the fact that more than one eighteenth-century female, like a Rhode Island runaway in the 1790s, decided to "abandon herself to prostitution."[29] But if women with no money and only the traditional domestic skills sought a more respectable way of supporting themselves independently, they could usually find work as nurses, seamstresses, or perhaps teachers.

Since teenaged girls often nursed sick relatives and attended the childbeds of their older sisters and friends, many acquired medical knowledge early in life.[30] Such experience proved to be a definite advantage to women who needed a means of support in later years. Those females who earned an income from medical practice can be divided into three groups, based on their relative degrees of skill, prestige, and potential earnings.

On the lowest rung of the ladder were the urban specialists in infant care who assisted well-to-do mothers after the births of their children. Such women — who were not wet nurses — would live with a new mother for six to ten weeks after a baby's birth, then move on to another house and a similar job elsewhere. These peripatetic nurses might also be employed under other circumstances. A concerned young woman, for example, found a nurse who agreed to assist her mother, a Boston shopkeeper who had fallen and injured herself. "She sas she thought hir Work would pay for hir bord till she Culd git sum business," the daughter reported to her mother; "she sas you may depend On it she shuld not let the Child go into the Shope and the time she was with you she Shuld be wiling to put hir Hand to any Woork you had to do."[31]

At the middle rank of the medical women were those resident nurses who were consulted by friends and neighbors before they sought the assistance of physicians. When illness struck Sally Logan Fisher's family, for instance, she turned first to Nurse Moore or Nurse Evans. Only if the problem was beyond their skill did Mrs. Fisher employ one of the male Philadelphia doctors. Similarly, Mary Palmer Tyler's neighbors in Guilford, Vermont, went to a local "doctress" for medical advice, and so too did the family of Joseph and Abigail Paine Greenleaf.[32]

Although such women were respected for their wide-ranging knowledge, they never acquired the prestige of those who occupied the top rung of the medical ladder: the expert midwives. In November 1774 Ezra Stiles learned from a discussion with Newport's "principal midwife," Mrs. Dennis, that she delivered approximately 350 of the 430 babies born in the town each year, the additional births being handled by three other midwives and a few local doctors. The extent of Mrs. Dennis's practice helps to make the apparently extraordinary claims of Janet Cumming, a loyalist refugee midwife, seem more believable than they otherwise might. Mrs. Cumming, a Charleston widow, told the claims commission that she had earned £400 sterling a year from her profession, an income easily equivalent to that of a merchant, lawyer, or government official. Her supporting witnesses, among them some of the most eminent male residents of Charleston, confirmed her estimate of her standing and earnings. "She was one of the first in her profession in Charles Town," declared one man, who believed her income estimate was conservative; "£40 currency was the usual price paid her for delivery of White Women," he disclosed, "and £10 Currency for Negroes." When Mrs. Cumming decided to leave Charleston in 1777, one woman described her departure as "a great loss to this place, as she is one of the best of that profeshion here." Indeed, she recounted, Cumming "was with [her] Sister with her two last Children." [33]

Few women could earn as much as experienced midwives like Mrs. Cumming and Mrs. Dennis, even those with comparable talents in other fields. This fact was made unmistakably clear by Sarah Osborn's comments on her years as a schoolteacher. Mrs. Osborn (then Wheaten) began teaching after her first husband's death, and she continued to run a school throughout most of her life. Like many other widows, she sought a ready means of support that required little outlay of money and that also enabled her to educate her own children without expense. But she was beset by financial difficulties. In spring 1759 she informed her friend Joseph Fish, whose daughters she had taught, the only "means that Holds up our Heads above water at all is a couple of boarders." Some years later, when she tried to raise her fees in order to improve her income, a furor ensued. The parents were "many o[f] them almost up in arms against me," expressing "many cutting bitter reflections," she told Fish, going on to outline her dilemma. "If tis unreasonable, for me to Keep so Large a School . . . then it is reasonable [I] should be able to Live comfortably by a smaller: and that I know we cannot, without a better Price," she contended logically. Other Newport teachers, she disclosed, had long complained about her charging such low fees, "for tho I could [li]ve by my great one, they could not by theirs[,] . . . but Except I rais'd my fees they [co]u'd not." So when Mrs. Osborn increased her prices, the others followed suit — and she "bore the blame for them all too." In the end, she was forced to rescind the increase, consoling herself with the thought that she was not "indulging in a covetous worldly mind."[34]

Poor women whose training was minimal could always find work sewing. The less skilled seamstresses, like Polly Bancker and her daughters, mended and altered clothes and occasionally made simple shirts and dresses. Such women often worked in the homes of their customers, leading a difficult, transient existence much like that of the urban infant nurses. In 1782, Nancy Tompkins, a young woman who had supported herself for five years "by working at day works in the Country," decided she would be "better satisfied" to live as a domestic servant in the Pickering household. The reason, Rebecca explained to her husband, Timothy, was that, despite the lower wages, "she wishes to have one place that seems like home she is heartily tired of working in diferent familys she finds it very disagreble going out all weathers." In addition, Rebecca noted, Nancy's "continuance with me will prevent her being obliged to sitt so steady at her needle which she finds hurts her health."[35]

Seamstresses of Tompkins's relatively low level of expertise also found it nearly impossible to earn a decent living from their work, as Mary Rhodes Bagnall, a Bostonian whose husband, Robert, deserted her to seek his fortune in Ohio, discovered to her dismay. In happier days, Mary had worked alongside Robert in their shop, but the business failed and so did their marriage. In the spring of 1791 Mrs. Bagnall informed her brother that she had sent two of her four daughters to live with a friend, that the other two were earning some money by spinning, and that she got "a little sewing work some times but it is very hard for poor people to live in Boston at present." By then Mary was also estranged from her younger sister Sally, who had sided with her husband in their marital dispute, but she had once tried to help Sally better herself. If they could obtain sufficient funds, she had told her father in 1784, then Sally "could lern the taylors trade."[36]

The distinction between the "taylors trade," or mantua making, and the ordinary sewing that Mrs. Bagnall did was crucial. Mantua making required a lengthy apprenticeship, but girls who received such training in the art of fashionable dressmaking could hope for a more secure and affluent life. John Adams learned as much when he tried to hire a housemaid just prior to his wedding to Abigail Smith. He informed his fiancée that a highly recommended young woman had refused his offer of a job because she had a "noble aspiring Spirit" and "intends for Boston to become a Mantua Maker." Rebecca Dickinson, the spinster seamstress, declared in 1787, "[T]he trade of goun making . . . has been of unspeakable adventage to me," but another New Englander complained in 1781, "I have Bin Luring a mantare maker Trade Bot to no porpes for I have no work to do at prasent." She attributed her troubles, though, to the fact that "now a Days Times ant as thay youst to Be," and probably her business did improve once the war had ended.[37]

The benefits of knowing what an Englishman termed "the Genteel way of Making up things" are readily apparent from the loyalist claims. The one refugee woman who described herself as a seamstress was desperately poor, whereas the four milliners and two mantua makers all seem to have made "a comfortable livelyhood" or to have had "very tolerable Business," to use the words with which witnesses described their circumstances. Elizabeth Thompson of Charleston told the claims commission that, when she first settled in town, "she was a Mantua maker and afterwards kept a Shop," thereby suggesting just the sort of capital accumulation and upward mobility that girls sought when entering the profession. Experienced dressmakers could both live well and acquire their own stock of dry goods. Margaret Hutchinson, a Philadelphia milliner, estimated her annual income at £78 sterling and listed among her losses such items as 170 yards of "different Coullered Persions" (£17), "Thread Lace" worth £56, assorted ribbons (£22), and "plain, and flowered, Muslins for Aprons, & handkercheif" to the amount of £27. The financial status of such women was far superior to that of Polly Bancker or Mary Bagnall.[38]

Running a dry goods or grocery shop was an option available to any woman who had sufficient resources to lay in a small stock of salable items. Often widows opened shops in their homes, and, like Helena Kortwright's mother, many found that such stores would support themselves and their families "in a very genteel way." Jane Mecom ran a highly successful shop in Boston during the 1760s, for her brother Benjamin Franklin kept her supplied with the latest English fashions in caps, aprons, cloaks, and hats. Anna Rogers Hunter, a loyalist woman who owned a grocery store in Shelburne, Nova Scotia, always had an eye out for profitable opportunities. Send butter, cheese, eggs, pickles, and "a fue Roots of all Cainds . . . likeways onons" from Boston as soon as possible, she told her brother in 1785; "they Bringe Doble here to What they Cost there Likeways Live Stoke poltrey." But still Mrs. Hunter did not prosper. Nine years later she wrote, "My fate has Ben hard . . . I was in Hoopes that I Shold [have] Had Somthing By this time that I mite Have leaft Searveing Streangers But feear that Must Be my porcson." [39]

That opening a shop may have required more initiative and knowledge than many women possessed is suggested by a comment made by Christian Barnes in 1770, when she was temporarily left in charge of her absent husband's store in Marlborough, Massachusetts. "To one gentleman I write for insureance to another to secure freight to a third to purchase Bills and all this is done in such a Mercantile Strain that I beleive many of them think me a Woman of great capacity," she told her friend Elizabeth Murray Smith. But, she continued, she was in fact only trying "to keep up appearences and if Possible not to discover [i.e., reveal] my Ignorance." Mrs. Barnes then admitted, "[T]he other Day I had like to have made a great Mistake by not knowing what was meant by Bills being at nine & a quarter but I am now set right in that perticular and for the futer shall be very cautious how I enter upon any subject of Business that I don't clearly understand." [40]

Mrs. Barnes's admission that she did not understand the basis of colonial commercial transactions — the current value of bills of exchange — not only tends to confirm the contention that female Americans led largely domestic lives but also indicates why shopkeeping as an occupation might fail to appeal to them. In order to run a store successfully a woman had to venture into the unfamiliar world of credit transactions, accounting, and relatively large-scale purchasing. Doubts about their ability to cope with such procedures may well have led many women with some financial resources to select another means of supporting themselves. Often the easiest method was to take in paying guests, either by running an inn for the accommodation of transients, or by seeking genteel long-term boarders.

Travelers' accounts reveal that women often ran roadside inns in the colonies. Not all these female tavernkeepers were widows, although many of them undoubtedly had once worked alongside their husbands, handling what a traveler called "the female part of the business." Of the five loyalist women innkeepers, two had assisted their husbands, while three (a widow and two army wives) had run their enterprises independently. Travelers were surprised when they encountered single women in this role. In 1805, a New Yorker en route to Philadelphia stayed at a tavern owned by a young woman. "I think it would be the last thing that a young Girl of any creadit ought to do for a liveing however we were very well entertaind and that was all I ought to expect," she told her sister. Another traveler described the youthful female operators of a New Jersey tavern as a pair of "*amazoons*" who "swore & flew about 'like *witches*'" but who nonetheless seemed to be "obliging & good natur'd."[41]

Perhaps the girls who ran such inns were the orphaned daughters of the previous owners. Certainly that was the case with the Archbald sisters of Boston, who operated one of the best boardinghouses in the city in the early years of the nineteenth century. Lodging houses like theirs were both more respectable and potentially more lucrative than the inns that catered to transients. In such homes boarders were accommodated "very genteely," to use William Palfrey's description of his 1779 Philadelphia lodgings. A later resident of a similar establishment in the same city commented, the owner "[is] a very fashionable fine woman"; "tho' the house is hers and we her boarders, we have no connexion with her only as we meet her at table as we should any other Lady." Mary Palmer's mother, who opened a Boston boardinghouse after the family met with financial reverses, learned the hard way that gentility and good business practices were not necessarily compatible. Mary later recalled that her mother, who had been "born and brought up in the lap of plenty" and "nursed in the abode of hospitality," evidently never thought of "economizing upon those who were paying for their board." The result was that Mrs. Palmer soon became deeply mired in debt and was saved from jail only by the generosity of one of her boarders — Royall Tyler, who years later was to marry her daughter.[42]

Despite the potential pitfalls, a woman could make a comfortable living from taking in lodgers, a fact evident from the loyalist claims. Witnesses and the owners of boardinghouses testified repeatedly that their houses were "well furnished" and that they had lost large stocks of foodstuffs, linen, and other supplies. Particularly revealing was the case of Mary Cloudsdall, a Philadelphian who moved to New York City during the war. She and her husband, who had been a merchant's clerk, used their small monetary reserves to set up a boardinghouse for soldiers in a rented building. During the next few years, she told the claims commission, "they made so much Money at New York that they were enabled to buy the House." Admittedly, the heavy demand for housing in the city helped to increase their profits, but still the experience of the Cloudsdalls, who had been (as the commission noted) "in a very obscure Situation" in Philadelphia, demonstrates the possible profitability of this line of work.[43]

Considering both their past experience and the resources available to them, the widows best provided for were those who inherited large southern plantations. Unlike the widows of small farmers, they did not have to worry about acquiring the necessary labor force to cultivate crops, since slaves were a part of their legacy. Moreover, because of their previous involvement with the internal administration of the estate, they were familiar with more aspects of their family's property than were most widows. Accordingly, one finds in travelers' accounts and plantation records evidence of women like Mary Willing Byrd, widow of William Byrd III, who personally and very successfully ran the family estates. The best known of all such women is Eliza Lucas Pinckney, who before her marriage had managed three plantations for her father. But even though she had had such extensive prior experience, she still wrote after two years of widowhood, "I find it requires great care, attention and activity to attend properly to a Carolina Estate, tho' but a moderate one, to do ones duty and make it turn to account, that I find I have as much business as I can go through of one sort or other."[44]

Perhaps the heavy demands on one's time alluded to by Mrs. Pinckney were what led a number of other wealthy southern widows to decide not to handle their husbands' plantations themselves, in spite of their knowledge of estate affairs. After all, managing the property meant adding the administrative duties formerly performed by their spouses to their own responsibilities for food and clothing distribution and domestic personnel supervision. Consequently, some southern widows asked male relatives to take over the management of their dead husbands' estates, usually in exchange for a fee. Others rented the property to a neighbor or hired their slaves to nearby planters. Any of these options was more likely to ensure them a set income than would an attempt to handle the estate themselves, with all the uncertainties that entailed.[45]

On the other hand, relying wholly on others had its disadvantages as well, as the Marylander Anna Maria Ringgold discovered. Mrs. Ringgold entrusted the care of the estate she had inherited from her husband to her son Thomas in exchange for an annual annuity of £600, but with only an oral agreement to that effect. After Thomas's early and unexpected death in 1776, his widow, Polly, decided to renounce the will (which formally continued the annuity) in order to claim dower right in the estate instead of the income he had left her. The resulting legal tangles were immense, embroiling mother- and daughter-in-law and their respective families in an acrimonious dispute that lasted for years. Martha Washington may have foreseen a situation similar to Mrs. Ringgold's when she advised her widowed niece Fanny to try to handle the affairs of her plantation herself. "Thare are few people that can mannage more than their one [own] business," she told Fanny; "I very sincearly wish you would exert your self so as to keep all your matters in order your self without depending upon others as that is the only way to be happy to have all your business in your one hands." Strikingly, Mrs. Washington, who was not known in her day (or ours) as an advocate of feminine autonomy, declared she wanted Fanny to be "as independent as your circumstances will admit . . . : a dependance is I think a wrached state and you will have enough if you will mannage it right."[46]

In so counseling her niece, Martha Dandridge Custis Washington was obviously drawing upon her own recollections of two years of widowhood following the death of her first husband. She was not the only eighteenth-century widow or working woman who had learned to appreciate autonomy: "Dependence, surely, is one of the capital evils, inflicted on the human species," a Virginia widow told her daughter in 1789. In 1800, Polly Bancker declared her personal independence; she was determined, she told her father-in-law, "never to look to a Child [for support] while I am able to provaid my self with what I want." The Nova Scotia storekeeper Anna Hunter likewise rejected her brother's invitation to join him in Boston because she feared that same "capital evil." "Shold not lick to Com till I see My way Clear to Live And not Be Beholden to won and A Nother as I was When ther Last," she told him in 1793; "I Dow Get My Self A living Hear But I should Not lick to Com theair And Goo out to Live." [47]

The experience of widowhood and independent wage earning could thus leave an indelible mark upon an eighteenth-century American woman's perception of herself and her role. Females who spent part of their lives outside the confines of male-dominated households and the traditional domestic sphere often proved reluctant to surrender their autonomy and regarded dependence, the supposed hallmark of the feminine character, with overt distaste. For most women, of course, such independent periods came only in middle or old age, when their financial resources were limited and when they had little opportunity to act upon whatever new conclusions they might have reached about themselves. But a detailed examination of a woman who achieved independence in her youth shows how that experience shaped her attitudes and guided her plans for the rest of her life.

In 1749, at the age of twenty-three, the Scottish immigrant Elizabeth Murray established herself in a small dry goods shop in Boston with funds supplied by her older brother James. Murray prospered because she quickly learned the benefits of judiciously timed sales, buying trips to England, regular bookkeeping methods, and careful watching of her finances. In 1754, when another woman merchant in town was forced to sell her stock of goods at a loss in order to pay off her creditors, Elizabeth told James, "[S]uch things make me double my diligence & endeavour to keep my self as clear [from debt] as is possible." [48]

When she married for the first time, in 1755, Elizabeth Murray evidently did not sign an antenuptial agreement with her intended husband, Thomas Campbell, who was another Boston merchant of Scottish descent. She seems not to have pursued her business during

Elizabeth Murray Smith (Inman), by John Singleton Copley, 1769. Courtesy of Museum of Fine Arts, Boston, Gift of Mary and Joseph Rogers.

their brief union, which implies the absence of a marriage settlement. But her behavior upon contracting for matrimony a second time was quite different. In the spring of 1760, the widowed Elizabeth Campbell married James Smith, a seventy-year-old distiller who was one of the wealthiest men in Boston. Then thirty-four, she could obviously expect to outlive her husband, but she nevertheless insisted upon a marriage settlement with an active use that not only gave her control over her own property and the right to make a will disposing of it but that also guaranteed her £10,000 at Smith's death. The scope of this settlement was highly revealing. Although Mrs. Smith never explicitly stated her motives, she had unquestionably drawn the same conclusion from her union with Campbell that other eighteenth-century widows who drafted antenuptial agreements had also reached: she recognized the necessity of preserving her property intact and retaining her right to do with it what she wished.[49]

Even though Smith's resources were so much greater than hers, she resumed her shopkeeping during their marriage. At his death in 1769 she was enabled, as she said, "to live & act as I please" through his generosity — his will left her even more than the marriage settlement had required — and she abandoned her own business when she found herself responsible for managing his large estate. Several years later, though, Elizabeth Murray Smith suffered the one lapse from a commitment to independence evident in her life: after a prolonged visit to English and Scottish relatives to assuage the grief caused by her second widowhood, she returned to America to find her affairs in disarray. In her absence, she reported to her brother John, the estate left her by Smith had been reduced in value by £1000, and "I found things in a Situation that was very disagreeable to me." Accordingly, she decided to marry for a third time, "an honest generous Man, who will render a faithful Account [of his] Stewardship," instead of continuing to administer Smith's businesses herself.[50]

Elizabeth's antenuptial settlement with her third husband, Ralph Inman, a Cambridge merchant and farmer, was, if anything, more tightly drawn than the one she had arranged with Smith. In it she preserved for herself and her heirs the considerable real and personal property she had accumulated through her own efforts and from her inheritance. Ralph was to receive the income from the real estate during their marriage, but he agreed to pay her £200 annually for her "separate use and benefit," and she could ultimately decide to sell any of the real estate at any time. Her personal property was to remain entirely within her control. Furthermore, she was granted the right to make a will during her marriage and, if she died intestate, the settlement provided that her property would be distributed as though she had been "sole and unmarried."[51]

Elizabeth Smith had, in short, provided herself with an ironclad guarantee of security and autonomy in her third marriage. Although she apparently had little confidence in her ability to manage her late husband's large estate, she obviously approached her third wedding with great self-assurance. She knew how to protect herself, and she drew upon that knowledge to make a match on her own terms. Shortly after the wedding she accurately told an English relative, "[N]o one has more of their own Will & few so much as I have" in marriage.[52] The experienced businesswoman had driven a hard bargain indeed.

Elizabeth Murray applied the lessons she had learned as a shopkeeper not only to herself but also to younger women. As early as the mid-1750s, when she was married to Thomas Campbell, she encouraged other females, among them the five nieces who were her surrogate daughters, to support themselves by engaging in business enterprises. In recommending a "very Industers" needlework teacher to the attention of her brother James in 1756, Elizabeth reported, she "ded as I would have liked to have been done by" when she assisted the girl in acquiring the necessary skills of her trade. In subsequent years Mrs. Smith helped the destitute unwed mother Janette Day open a sewing school, financed a shop that supported the orphaned sisters Anne and Betsy Cuming, and invested heavily in a millinery business run jointly by two of her nieces and Janette Day's daughter Jackie. Above all, Mrs. Smith told Christian Barnes in 1770, she did not like the idea of "young people being brought up in idleness and entering the world with all its gaietys, triffling away the most active part of their life or marrying imprudently." Every young woman, she wrote, should adopt "some scheme to improve her mind time & fortune," an activity that would "rouse her facultys and make her industrious." "I prefer an usefull member of society to all the fine delicate creatures of the age," she forthrightly told another friend that same year.[53]

In 1783, two years before her death, Elizabeth Murray Inman observed revealingly to her brother John, "I rejoice that the spirit of Independence caused such exertions as to place me in a setuation that I am content to pass the remainder of my days in, untaught as I was I am surprised & my heart overflowes with gratitude at the success I have met with."[54] Murray was, undeniably, a woman unique in her commitment to an independent existence. By consistently rejecting the conventional feminine role and repeatedly urging younger women to follow her example, Elizabeth Murray showed that she recognized the benefits that could accrue from the maintenance of "as much independence as circumstances will admit." In the decades before the American Revolution, women with such an autonomous outlook on life were exceedingly rare, but the years of conflict disrupted normal patterns of society and brought to large numbers of female Americans the experience of independence that had previously been confined to a few. The effect of the new independence on women's collective consciousness was extraordinary, and it is the subject of the second section of this book.

Part Two

THE CHANGING PATTERNS
OF WOMEN'S LIVES

Chapter Six

♋

WE COMMENCED
PERFECT STATESMEN

THE DECADE OF TURBULENCE THAT PRECEDED THE REVOLUTION touched the lives of colonial women as well as men. Public demonstrations against British policy and its supporters, celebrations of the repeal of hated parliamentary acts, days of fast or thanksgiving proclaimed by colonial governments, and incidents of mob action necessarily impinged upon the consciousness of women who had previously left public affairs entirely to their husbands, fathers, and brothers. Still more important, when American leaders decided to use economic boycotts in their struggle against Great Britain, women's domestic roles took on political significance. The chosen tactics could succeed only if white housewives and their daughters refused to purchase imported goods and simultaneously increased their production of homespun. Even the work assignments of female slaves would have to be changed if the colonial policy was to be fully effective. Thus the attention of male political leaders had to focus on the realm of the household, and the public recognition accorded the female role irreversibly altered its inferior status. Although traditional denigrating attitudes would continue to be voiced as late as the 1790s, the reevaluation of domesticity that began during the revolutionary years would eventually culminate in nineteenth-century culture's glorification of woman's household role.

In addition, during the revolutionary decades the boundaries of the feminine sphere itself began to change. White women, who in the mid-1760s offered profuse apologies whenever they dared to discuss politics, were by the 1780s reading widely in political literature, publishing their own sentiments, engaging in heated debates over public policy, and avidly supporting the war effort in a variety of ways. Indeed, some females were so unstinting in their activism that disagreements over politics during the war led to broken marriages and friendships. Moreover, their commitment to the Revolution caused a number of Philadelphia women to attempt to establish the first nationwide female organization. Even though they had only limited success, the very fact that women embarked upon such an ambitious, unprecedented venture revealed the extent to which their lives had been reshaped during the preceding years.

I

Women could hardly have remained aloof from the events of the 1760s and early 1770s even had they so desired, for, like male Americans, they witnessed the escalating violence of the prerevolutionary decade. Into their letters and diary entries — which had previously been devoted exclusively to private affairs — crept descriptions of Stamp Act riots and "Rejoicings" at the law's repeal, accounts of solemn fast-day observances, and reports of crowd actions aimed at silencing dissidents. The young Boston shopkeeper Betsy Cuming, for instance, was visiting a sick friend one day in 1769 when she heard "a voilint Skreeming Kill him Kill him" and looked out the window to see John Mein, a printer whose publications had enraged the radicals, being chased by a large crowd armed with sticks and guns. Later that evening Betsy watched "ful a thousand Man & boys" dragging around the city "a Kart [on which] a Man was Exibited as . . . in a Gore of Blod." At first Betsy believed Mein had been caught, but she then learned that the victim was an unfortunate customs informer who had fallen into the crowd's hands after Mein made a successful escape.[1]

Betsy herself confronted an angry group of Bostonians only a few weeks later. She and her sister Anne had just unpacked a new shipment of English goods when "the Comitey wated" on them, accusing them of violating the nonimportation agreement. "I told them we have never antred into eney agreement not to import for it was verry trifling owr Business," Betsy explained to her friend and financial backer Elizabeth Murray Smith. She charged the committeemen with trying "to inger two industrious Girls who ware Striving in an honest way to Git there Bread," resolutely ignoring their threat to publish her name in the newspaper as an enemy to America. In the end, Betsy and Anne discovered, the publicity "Spirits up our Friends to Purchess from us," and they informed Mrs. Smith that they ended the year with "mor custom then before." [2]

Despite their bravado the Cuming sisters had learned an important political lesson: persons with their conservative beliefs were no longer welcome in Massachusetts. As a result, they emigrated to Nova Scotia when the British army evacuated Boston in 1776. Patriot women, too, learned lessons of partisanship. Instead of being the targets of crowds, they actively participated in them. They marched in ritual processions, harassed female loyalists, and, during the war, seized essential supplies from merchants whom they believed to be monopolistic hoarders. [3] In addition, they prepared food for militia musters and, in the early days of September 1774 — when the New England militia gathered in Cambridge in response to a false rumor that British troops were mounting an attack on the populace — they were reported by one observer to have "surpassed the Men for Eagerness & Spirit in the Defence of Liberty by Arms." As he rode along the road to Boston, he recounted later, he saw "at every house Women & Children making Cartridges, running Bullets, making Wallets, baking Biscuit, crying & bemoaning & at the same time animating their Husbands & Sons to fight for their Liberties, tho' not knowing whether they should ever see them again." [4]

The activism of female patriots found particular expression in their support of the colonial boycott of tea and other items taxed by the Townshend Act of 1767. Male leaders recognized that they needed women's cooperation to ensure that Americans would comply with the request to forgo the use of tea and luxury goods until the act was

January, 1770
_1773(1)_

WILLIAM JACKSON,

an *IMPORTER*; at the

BRAZEN HEAD,

North Side of the TOWN-HOUSE,

and *Opposite the* Town-Pump, *in*

Corn-hill, BOSTON.

It is desired that the SONS and
DAUGHTERS of *LIBERTY*,
would not buy any one thing of
him, for in so doing they will bring
Disgrace upon *themselves*, and their
Posterity, for *ever* and *ever*, AMEN.

A Revolutionary Broadside. Courtesy of Library of Congress Prints Division.

repealed. Accordingly, newspaper essays urged women to participate in the boycott, and American editors frequently praised those females who refused to drink foreign Bohea tea, substituting instead coffee or local herbal teas. A gathering of New Hampshire women, for example, won applause for having "made their Breakfast upon Rye Coffee," and it was reported that in Newport a group of ladies "most judiciously rejected the poisonous Bohea, and unanimously, to their great honour, preferred the balsamic Hyperion."[5]

The South Carolina Presbyterian William Tennent III directed an emotionally charged appeal on the subject of the tea boycott to the women of his province in August 1774. Calling upon his readers to help save America "from the Dagger of Tyranny," Tennent emphasized the "trivial Pleasure" derived from drinking imported tea and contrasted that "trifling . . . Amusement" to the advantages of abandoning the "darling Tea-Dish Ceremony." "Yes Ladies," he asserted, "You have it in your power more than all your committees and Congresses, to strike the Stroke, and make the Hills and Plains of America clap their hands." If women stopped drinking tea, he said, their action would convince the British "that American patriotism extends even to the Fair Sex, and discourage any future Attempts to enslave us." Tea purchased by housewives would "be paid for by the Blood of your Sons," Tennent warned, but if they instead avoided its use, "your Country will rise and called you blessed."[6]

To the female readers of this and other similar patriotic calls to action, the stress upon the vital significance of their participation must have been novel and refreshing. For women to be told, even in an obvious hyperbole, that their activities could be more important to America's future than the efforts of male committees and congresses, represented an extraordinary departure from the past American devaluation of the feminine role. Consequently, one can understand the possible psychological as well as political motivations for women's abstention from the use of tea.

In their verses, female poets demonstrated a clear comprehension of the political implications of the nonconsumption movement. "Farewell the Tea Board, with its gaudy Equipage," wrote one whose words were published in the *Virginia Gazette* in early 1774, "because I'm taught (and I believe it true) / Its use will fasten slavish Chains upon my country." Hannah Griffitts, a Pennsylvania Quaker who later became a loyalist, called upon her fellow countrywomen in similar terms:

> *Then — for the sake of Freedom's Name,*
> *Since British Wisdom scorns repealing,*
> *Come — sacrifice to Patriot fame,*
> *And give up Tea — by way of healing.*

Still another woman, effectively using maternal imagery, accused men of being "kept by a Sugar-Plumb . . . Supinely asleep" and trumpeted,

> *Let the Daughters of Liberty, nobly arise,*
> *And tho' we've no Voice, but a negative here,*
> *The use of the Taxables, let us forbear.*

She urged her female compatriots: "Stand firmly resolved and bid Grenville to see / That rather than Freedom, we'll part with our Tea." And she had another purpose as well: "Thus acting — we point out their Duty to men." To her, then, American women were leading the struggle against parliamentary policy; although men might be "strip'd of their Freedom, and rob'd of their Right," women would never surrender to British tyranny.[7]

Many female Americans responded enthusiastically to these powerful appeals to their patriotism. One night in early July 1774 John Adams's landlady would not serve him tea, even though he requested some that had been "honestly smuggled, or paid no Duties." A sick woman in Salem, Massachusetts, refused on principle to drink tea, despite the fact that local committees readily granted exemptions from the boycott to those who were ill. And Pamela Dwight's mother, Abigail, all of whose friends would take "not a Drop of Tea," attributed her indisposition in June 1769 to the novel practice of "Drinking strong Coffee in the Afternoon" on social visits.[8]

In a marked departure from the tradition of feminine noninvolvement in public affairs, women occasionally formalized their agreements not to purchase or consume imported tea. Most notably, the *Boston Evening Post* reported in February 1770 that more than three hundred "Mistresses of Families" had promised to "totally abstain" from the use of tea, "Sickness excepted." Their statement showed that they understood the meaning of their acts: the women spoke of their desire to "save this abused Country from Ruin and Slavery" at a time when their "invaluable Rights and Privileges are attacked in an unconstitutional and most alarming Manner." In the South, groups of women went even further by associating themselves generally with nonimportation policies, not confining their attention to the tea issue alone. The meeting satirized in the famous British cartoon of the so-called Edenton Ladies' Tea Party fell into this category. The agreement signed in October 1774 by fifty-one female North Carolinians — among them two sisters and a cousin of Hannah Johnston Iredell — did not mention tea. Instead, the women declared their "sincere adherence" to the resolves of the provincial congress and proclaimed it their "duty" to do "every thing as far as lies in our power" to support the "publick good."[9]

This apparently simple statement had unprecedented implications. The Edenton women were not only asserting their right to acquiesce in political measures, but they were also taking upon themselves a "duty" to work for the common good. Never before had female Americans formally shouldered the responsibility of a public role, never before had they claimed a voice — even a compliant one — in public policy. Accordingly, the Edenton statement marked an important turning point in American women's political perceptions, signaling the start of a process through which they would eventually come to regard themselves as participants in the polity rather than as females with purely private concerns.

Yet the North Carolina meeting and the change it embodied aroused amusement among men. The same tongue-in-cheek attitude evident in the satirical drawing of the grotesque "Ladies" was voiced by the Englishman Arthur Iredell in a letter to his emigrant brother James. He had read about the Edenton agreement in the newspapers, Arthur wrote, inquiring whether his sister-in-law Hannah's relatives were involved in the protest. "Is there a Female Congress at Edenton too?" he continued. "I hope not," for "Ladies . . . have ever, since the Amazonian Era, been esteemed the most formidable Enemies." If they choose to attack men, "each wound They give is Mortal. . . . The more we strive to conquer them, the more are Conquerd!"[10]

A SOCIETY of PATRIOTIC LADIES.

The Edenton Ladies' Tea Party, as viewed by a British cartoonist. Courtesy of Library of Congress Prints Division.

Iredell thus transformed a serious political gesture that must have been full of meaning for the participants into an occasion for a traditional reference to women's covert power over men. Like many of his male contemporaries, he dismissed the first stirrings of political awareness among American women as a joke, refusing to recognize the ways in which their concept of their role was changing. In an Englishman, such blindness was understandable, but the similar failure of perception among American men must be attributed to a resolute insistence that females remain in their proper place. The male leaders of the boycott movement needed feminine cooperation, but they wanted to set the limits of women's activism. They did not expect, or approve, signs of feminine autonomy.

Nowhere was this made clearer than in a well-known exchange between Abigail and John Adams. As was noted in chapter 2, Abigail asked her husband in March 1776 to ensure that the new nation's legal code included protection for wives against the "Naturally Tyrannical" tendencies of their spouses. In reply John declared, "I cannot but laugh" at "your extraordinary Code of Laws." Falling back upon the same cliché employed by Arthur Iredell, he commented, "[O]ur Masculine systems . . . are little more than Theory. . . . In Practice you know We are the subjects. We have only the Name of Masters."[11] Adams, like Iredell, failed to come to terms with the implications of the issues raised by the growing interest in politics among colonial women. He could deal with his wife's display of independent thought only by refusing to take it seriously.

American men's inability to perceive the alterations that were occurring in their womenfolk's self-conceptions was undoubtedly heightened by the superficially conventional character of feminine contributions to the protest movement. Women participating in the boycott simply made different decisions about what items to purchase and consume; they did not move beyond the boundaries of the feminine sphere. Likewise, when colonial leaders began to emphasize the importance of producing homespun as a substitute for English cloth, they did not ask women to take on an "unfeminine" task: quite the contrary, for spinning was the very role symbolic of femininity itself. But once the context had changed, so too did women's understanding of the meaning of their traditional tasks.

Because the pattern of home manufactures in the colonies showed considerable regional variation, differences also appeared in Americans' responses to calls for expanded domestic cloth production. In the plantation South, which had long been heavily dependent on imported cloth, home manufactures did not readily take hold. Planters were reluctant to reassign female slaves from field work to spinning and weaving, believing both that the change would be expensive and that, as a North Carolinian declared during a 1775 congressional debate on nonimportation, the women were "best employed about Tobacco." Consequently, it was not until late 1774 and early 1775 that planters acquiesced in the inevitable and began to establish large-scale cloth manufactories on their lands.[12]

The beginnings of the new era were noted by John Harrower, the tutor indentured to the Daingerfield family in Virginia, when he recorded in his journal in October 1775 that slaves had started to process the first crop of flax grown on the plantation in order to make "coarse linnen for Shirts to the Nigers. . . . Before this year," he continued, "there has been little or no linnen made in the Colony." The accuracy of Harrower's observation is confirmed by the contents of Robert Carter's daybooks and letterbooks. Carter decided in the fall of 1774 that the nonimportation agreement would require "all people here, who have slaves & plantations, to make clouthing for their Negroes & Families." He accordingly purchased large quantities of hemp and flax seed, made extensive notes on the manufacture of thread and cloth (including estimating the amount of work that reasonably could be expected from spinners and weavers), and began to buy the equipment his slaves would need — spinning wheels, woolen cards, hatchels for flax and hemp.[13] In early 1775 Carter directed his overseers to "sett a part, Ten black Females the most Expert spinners belonging to me — they to be Employed in Spinning, solely" in renovated tobacco storage sheds. Only a year later the planter had already discovered that this work force was insufficient, and so he ordered that another six girls be taught to spin. At the end of the war Carter was employing ten weavers, four of them women, and twelve female spinners at the "Linnen and Woolen Factory" on his Aries quarter.[14]

The shift to home manufacturing in the South was undeniably successful. In 1778, a Virginia merchant reported that his neighbors were "manufactoring so much of the necessary wear that the demand will be but triffling till a change of times & Measures," and a year later a visitor noted that in Virginia spinning was now "the chief employment of the female negroes." Planters in the Carolinas and Georgia likewise made an extensive commitment to the domestic production of cloth.[15] After the war, white southerners continued to use skilled black female spinners and weavers until machine-made American textiles became available following the War of 1812. In the words of Rolla Tryon, the scholar who has studied the subject most fully, "The Revolution changed the South from a region depending almost wholly upon the outside world for manufactured commodities to one in which many of such commodities were made by the people in their homes or in their plantations."[16]

One can only speculate about the effect of this change on female slaves, for no records of their reactions to the new circumstances have been located. But assignments to spinning and weaving factories must have been coveted, if only because the work was less physically demanding than field labor. Furthermore, the manufactories afforded women the opportunity to learn demanding skills comparable to those of male artisans. Planters soon discovered that not all women could spin equally well, and they came to place the same special value on the more practiced female spinners and weavers that they did on experienced blacksmiths and carpenters. In a study of Virginia runaways, Gerald Mullin has argued persuasively that the acquisition of artisan skills led to the development of greater independence and self-confidence among male slaves. Although he does not apply his theory to women, the same reasoning would seem pertinent. It is highly unlikely that the approximately forty-year period during which large numbers of black women had the chance to become skilled workers was without impact on their individual and collective consciousness.[17]

Farther north, home manufactures had to be increased by persuasion, not by giving orders to slaves. Political leaders had to convince individual adult white women, and especially their daughters, of the importance of producing more homespun. In the process the men were forced to reevaluate the importance of a crucial component of the feminine domestic role. One of the most common, and indeed most tedious, household tasks took on a high social and political value for the first time. Again, men did not anticipate the consequences.

Initially, the authors of newspaper articles recommending an expansion of home manufactures did not single out women for special attention. Instead, the calls for domestic industry published between 1766 and 1768 emphasized the achievements of households or cited the examples of entire towns. Thus a Newport resident was praised for the 369½ yards of cloth and the 300 skeins of yarn that were "spun in his own house" during a thirty-month period, and a New Jersey man was applauded for the fact that he "has within the year past manufactured in his own family 580 yards of linen and woollen cloth." In neither case, nor in many other such notices, was there any mention of the fact that all of the spinning and weaving in question would have been done by women.[18]

But this neglect did not continue beyond the end of 1768, for, as a writer in the *Providence Gazette* had noted late the previous year, "[W]e must after all our efforts depend greatly upon the female sex for the introduction of oeconomy among us." The first months of 1769 brought an explosion in the newspaper coverage of women's activities, especially in New England. Stories about spinning bees, which had been both rare and relegated to back pages, suddenly became numerous and prominently featured. The *Boston Evening Post*, which carried only one previous account of female domestic industry, printed twenty-eight articles on the subject between May and December 1769, and devoted most of its front page on May 29 to an enumeration of these examples of female patriotism. The editor prefaced his extensive treatment of women's endeavors with an enthusiastic assessment of their significance: "[T]he industry and frugality of American ladies must exalt their character in the Eyes of the World and serve to show how greatly they are contributing to bring about the political salvation of a whole Continent."[19]

It is impossible to know whether the increased coverage of spinning bees in 1769 indicated that women's activities expanded at precisely that time, or whether the more lengthy, detailed, and numerous stories merely represented the printers' new interest in such efforts. But one fact is unquestionable: the ritualized gatherings attended by women often termed Daughters of Liberty carried vital symbolic meaning both to the participants and to the editors who reported their accomplishments.

The meetings, or at least the descriptions of them, fell into a uniform pattern. Early in the morning, a group of eminently respectable young ladies (sometimes as many as one hundred, but normally twenty to forty), all of them dressed in homespun, would meet at the home of the local minister. There they would spend the day at their wheels, all the while engaging in enlightening conversation. When they stopped to eat, they had "American produce prepared which was more agreeable to them than any foreign Dainties and Delicacies," and, of course, they drank local herbal tea. At nightfall, they would present their output to the clergyman, who might then deliver a sermon on an appropriate theme. For example, the Reverend Jedidiah Jewell, of Rowley, Massachusetts, preached from Romans 12:2, "Not slothful in business, fervent in spirit, serving the Lord," and the Reverend John Cleaveland of Ipswich told the seventy-seven spinners gathered at his house, "[T]he women might recover to this country the full and free enjoyment of all our rights, properties and privileges (which is more than the men have been able to do)" by consuming only American produce and manufacturing their own clothes.[20]

The entire community became involved in the women's activities. Large numbers of spectators — Ezra Stiles estimated that six hundred persons watched the bee held at his house in 1769 — encouraged the spinners in their work, supplied them with appropriate American foodstuffs, and sometimes provided entertainment. The occasional adoption of a match format, in which the women competed against each other in quality and quantity, must have further spurred their industry. And they must have gloried in being the center of attention, if only for the day. In reporting a Long Island spinning bee, the *Boston Evening Post* captured the spirit of the occasion with an expression of hope that "the ladies, while they vie with each other in skill and industry in their profitable employment, may vie with the men in contributing to the preservation and prosperity of their country and equally share in the honor of it."[21]

"Equally share in the honor of it": the idea must have been exceedingly attractive to any eighteenth-century American woman raised in an environment that had previously devalued both her and her domestic sphere. Those involved in the home manufacture movement therefore took great pride in their newfound status, demonstrating that fact unequivocably when satirical essayists cast aspersions on their character.

Late in 1767, "Mr. Squibo" of Boston joked that the spinners were so patriotic they consumed only "New-England Rum . . . the principal and almost only manufacture of this country." Shortly thereafter, "A Young American" hinted that women discussed only "such triffling subjects as Dress, Scandal and Detraction" during their spinning bees. Three female Bostonians responded angrily to both letters, which they declared had "scandalously insulted" American women. Denying that gossip engrossed their thoughts or that rum filled their glasses, they pronounced themselves so committed to the patriot cause that they would even endure the unmerited ridicule of "the little wits and foplings of the present day" in order to continue their efforts. "Inferior in abusive sarcasm, in personal invective, in low wit, we glory to be," they concluded; "but inferior in veracity, honesty, sincerity, love of virtue, of liberty and of our country, we would not willingly be to any." Significantly, the Bostonians made a special point of noting that women had been "addressed as persons of consequence, in the present oeconomical regulations." They thereby revealed the novelty and importance of that designation in their own minds. Having become established as "persons of consequence" in American society, women would not relinquish that position without a fight.[22]

The formal spinning groups had a value more symbolic than real. They do not seem to have met regularly, and in most cases their output appears to have been donated to the clergyman for his personal use. The women might not even have consistently called themselves Daughters of Liberty, for many newspaper accounts did not employ that phrase at all. But if the actual production of homespun did not motivate the meetings, they were nonetheless purposeful. The public attention focused on organized spinning bees helped to dramatize the pleas for industry and frugality in colonial households, making a political statement comparable to men's ostentatious wearing of homespun on public occasions during the same years. The spinning bees were ideological showcases: they were intended to convince American women that they could render essential contributions to the struggle against Britain, and to encourage them to engage in increased cloth production in the privacy of their own homes. Sometimes the newspaper accounts made this instructional function quite explicit. The fact that many of the participants came from "as *good families* as any in town," one editor remarked, showed that "it was no longer a disgrace for one of our fair sex to be catched at a spinning wheel." [23] Women's private papers provide confirmations of the success of the campaign.

"The plan laid down for our education was entirely broken in upon by the War," the Virginian Betsy Ambler Brent recalled late in life. "Instead of Morning Lessons, we were to knit Stockings, instead of embroidering to make up home spun garments." Betsy's contemporary, the eleven-year-old Boston resident Anna Winslow, learned to spin, termed herself "a daughter of liberty," and declared, "I chuse to wear as much of our own manufactory as pocible." Sukey DeLancey, the youngest of the well-to-do New York sisters, also began to spin, and Betsy Foote, the Connecticut farm girl whose ordinary chores included spinning and weaving, found her tasks invested with new significance. In October 1775 she proudly recorded in her diary that she had carded all day, then spun ten knots of wool in the evening, "& felt Nationly into the bargain." [24]

Charity Clarke, a New York City teenager who eagerly knitted "stockens" from homespun yarn supplied by a friend, showed in letters to an English cousin that she too "felt Nationly." Warning him that, although "Heroines may not distinguish themselves at the head of an Army," women could still contribute to the defense of colonial liberties, she set forth her vision of a "new arcadia." There "a fighting army of amazones . . . armed with spinning wheels" would be attended by men "who shall all learn to weave, & keep sheep." Together, she said, the Americans would "retire beyond the reach of arbitrary power, cloathed with the work of our own hands, & feeding on what the country affords." If Britons like himself believed that the colonies were dependent on imported goods, she declared, they were badly mistaken. In 1774 Clarke asserted staunchly, "[Y]ou cannot deprive us [of our property], the arms that supports my family shall defend it, though this body is not clad with silken garments, these limbs are armed with strength, the Soul is fortified by Virtue, and the Love of Liberty is cherished within this bosom." [25]

But despite her political fervor, Charity Clarke worried about how her cousin would react to her words. Perhaps they would change "the Idea you should have of female softness in me," she told him worriedly in late 1769. Politics as a subject was "out of my province," she admitted, and so she felt uneasy about expressing her opinions, though, she asserted, "I cannot help them, nor can I by any means think them seditious."[26] In her hesitancy Clarke resembled her female compatriots. Like her, they discovered by the late 1760s that the new role they had assumed brought them into conflict with one of the primary limitations on the feminine sphere: their exclusion from the world of politics. In the chaos of the revolutionary period they accordingly began the process of developing an innovative conception of their relationship to the public realm.

II

Before the mid-1760s, most men and women accepted without question the standard dictum that political discussion, like direct political participation, fell outside the feminine sphere. As Esther Burr observed in 1755, "[T]he Men say . . . that Women have no business to concern themselves about em [politics] but trust to those that know better." Accordingly, when such issues became (in the words of Sally Logan Fisher) "the prevaling topic of Conversation," women found themselves in a quandary. They all agreed that political discussion was "not our province," yet at the same time, Sarah Franklin told her father in the fall of 1765, "[N]othing else is talked of, the Dutch talk of the stompt ack the Negroes of the tamp, in short every body has something to say." Were women to deny themselves the ability to comment on what a New Englander called "the most animating Subject," one that "Concerns us all"?[27]

In 1777, Anne Emlen addressed precisely that question in a reflective essay in her commonplace book. "How shall I impose a silence upon myself when the subject is so very interesting, so much engrossing Conversation — & what every Member of the Community is more or less concerned in?" she inquired rhetorically, admitting that at times she felt an overwhelming desire to express her opinion on public affairs. In the end, she asked God "[for] prudence, divine prudence, which may prove a stay to my mind & a bridle to my tongue." Other women developed different resolutions of the same conflict. Some, like a Virginia loyalist, indulged in political analysis while simultaneously denying that they did so. "Dont think I am engaging in politics," Elizabeth Feilde wrote in 1776 in the midst of an astute conservative commentary on current events. "No; I assure you its a subject for which I have not either Talents or Inclination to enter upon." More commonly, women simply punctuated their political discussions with apologies. Anne Clark Hooper, a niece of Elizabeth Murray Inman who lived in North Carolina, declared in 1768 that she included politics in her letters only because "its being so much talked of here." And Annis Boudinot Stockton likewise explained her fascination with public affairs: "[T]ho a female I was born a patriot and cant help it If I would."[28]

As the years passed and women more frequently engaged in political discourse, the apologies tended to disappear. Simultaneously, men began to change their minds about women's political capacities. The transition can be seen clearly in the correspondence of Samuel Adams and his wife, Betsy. Early in 1776 Samuel "for once" included a "political anecdote" in a letter to her. Later that same year, prefacing his remarks with the accurate observation, "it has not been usual for me to write to you of War or Politicks," Samuel nevertheless transmitted the most recent political and military news because he knew, he said, "how deeply you have always interested your self in the Welfare of our Country." Although in 1780 he was still wondering whether he should "trouble" her with his reflections on public affairs, the following year he formally challenged the conventional outlines of the feminine sphere by declaring, "I see no Reason why a Man may not communicate his political opinions to his wife, if he pleases."[29]

By 1783, wartime circumstances had created a generation of women who, like the North Carolinian Elizabeth Steele, described themselves as "great politician[s]." Several years after the event, Eliza Wilkinson, a resident of the South Carolina sea islands, recalled that during the British invasion of her state in 1780 "none were greater politicians than the several knots of ladies, who met together. All trifling discourse of fashions, and such low chat was thrown by, and we commenced perfect statesmen." Women read newspapers and pamphlets as eagerly as their male counterparts, repeatedly asked their husbands to keep them supplied with accurate information on military affairs, and followed the progress of war and diplomacy throughout the world, not just on the American continent.[30] Even girls were affected. Nelly Blair and Anna Winslow learned to differentiate between Whigs and Tories; before she reached the age of ten Betsy Ambler had decided that Lord Dunmore, Virginia's last royal governor, was "despicable"; and over the course of a six-month period in 1774 Jemima Condict advanced from a belief that the dispute with Britain was a "trifling" one over tea to the conviction that the English were bent on "our destruction." Young women's correspondence, previously filled solely with social chitchat, began to contain political commentary, just like the letters written by their older female relatives.[31]

Interest in public affairs and partisan commitments were not confined to women of the middling and better sorts. In 1774, a Boston seamstress firmly aligned herself with the "libe[r]ty boys" against what she called the "tyranny [that] rides in our harbour and insults us in our fields and streets." Travelers regularly encountered politically committed landladies, and British prisoners of war found themselves verbally and sometimes physically assaulted by female Americans. The Baroness Frederica von Riedesel, wife of one of the Hessian officers who served with Burgoyne, recorded in the journal of her travels with the captured troops vivid portrayals of poor patriot women who only grudgingly (if at all) gave food and shelter to "the royalist dogs." At one house, a mother insisted upon combing the lice out of her children's hair while the von Riedesels were eating; at another, they were refused even the slaves' cornmeal, being told by the mistress, "[I]f you die of hunger, so much the better"; at a third, a teenaged girl proclaimed that she would like to tear out George III's heart, "fry it over these coals, and eat it."[32]

Loyalist women from all social ranks were no less firmly committed to their political position. The letters Christian Barnes wrote to her friend Elizabeth Murray Smith in the late 1760s and early 1770s not only showed her fidelity to Great Britain but also revealed the unpleasant consequences of her political views. In late 1769 she told Smith, who was then in England, "[T]hese dareing Sons of Libberty are now at the tip top of their Power and to transact any thing contrary to their Sentiments or even to speak disrespectfully of the well disposed, is a Crime equal to high Treason." Christian's husband, Henry, nevertheless resisted all efforts to force him to comply with the nonimportation agreement. As a result, the Barnes's coach was vandalized, he was twice hanged in effigy, a wagonload of merchandise destined for their store was attacked, and they were sent an "incendiary" threatening letter. Yet the persecution did not cause Christian Barnes to retreat from her opposition to "such a set of wretches whose only aim is to delude the multitude by false representations." She and other women steadfastly retained their loyalty to Great Britain, despite having their property plundered and enduring insults and physical abuse.[33]

That political allegiance had come to be of major importance to American women was demonstrated by the large number of friendships broken by divergent beliefs. Mrs. Barnes learned in the summer of 1768 that one of her close friends had "become a violent advocate in the Cause of Libberty." For a time, Christian managed to avoid "warm disputes" by remaining closemouthed about her own opinions, but by the summer of 1770 the split between them was irrevocable. The same pattern repeated itself throughout the colonies. In New York City, Helena Kortwright Brasher recalled in later years, the "most intimate friends became the most inveterate enemies." In St. Augustine, a woman reported in 1774, "[T]he Party work that has prevailed here for some time, has almost put an end to what Society was among the few Ladys that remained here." Two years earlier, a lack of partisan divisions in Boston was so unusual even on social occasions that Elizabeth Murray Smith made a special point of telling an English relative that, at her marriage to Ralph Inman, "their [sic] was neither Whig nor torry but every one joind to make the day & evening compleatly agreeable."[34]

Marriages, too, broke under the strain of political differences. That of Elizabeth Graeme, the wealthy Philadelphia heiress, and Henry Hugh Fergusson, a penniless Scottish immigrant fourteen years her junior, might have seemed ill-fated from its outset in 1772, especially because her father's opposition forced them to marry in secret. Nevertheless, according to contemporary observers, their marital problems "arose originally from the Difference of Political Opinion." The loyalist Henry left Philadelphia for his homeland in 1775. When he returned two years later with the occupying British troops, the Fergussons made an abortive attempt at reconciliation, but each remained politically adamant. In the 1780s, although he asked her to join him in England (since the United States would not allow him to return), she refused on the grounds that both her "Principles and Interest is on the Side of America." Elizabeth's bitterness was magnified by the fact that her property had been confiscated by the government of Pennsylvania because of her husband's loyalism. Only after years of effort did she and her friends persuade the legislature to adopt a private bill reversing the confiscation. Mrs. Fergusson spent her last decades sorrowfully reflecting on her situation, expressing herself through poetic criticism of those who

> *Deem Woman made alone for mans Control,*
> *Like* Mahomets *fair ones void of noble Soul*
> *As Birds or Insects for a Boy to please*
> *They torturd Subjects made [for] their Lords to teize.*[35]

The same partisanship that led to broken marriages and friendships also caused women to take active roles in the conflict. Camp followers like the woman called Molly Pitcher are today the most famous of the female activists, yet it is impossible to know whether those wives who followed their spouses to the armies of both sides were merely deprived of alternative means of support by their husbands' enlistments, or whether their participation in the war may be attributed to their own political beliefs. When women acted independently, on the other hand, one can be fairly certain they did so out of political conviction. Innumerable anecdotes recount the exploits of such female patriots as Deborah Sampson, who disguised herself as a man to fight in the revolutionary army; Nancy Hart, the Georgian who single-handedly captured a group of Tories; Patience Wright, Lydia Darragh, and other spies; and teenaged messengers like Emily Gieger and Deborah Champion.[36] Such well-known tales dramatically reveal a few women's intense commitment, but they provide no basis for estimating the extent of female partisan activity. By studying the 468 claims submitted by loyalist refugee women, though, one can gain a better idea of the proportion of activists and of the ways in which they contributed to their chosen side.

Paul Smith has argued persuasively that about 15 percent of adult white male loyalists took up arms for the British cause. The percentage of activist women was significantly smaller: only twenty-six, or 5.5 percent, of the female refugees said that they had directly assisted the British. Of these, some of whom contributed in more than one way, six aided loyalists, nine helped British soldiers (including those being held as prisoners of war), six carried letters through the lines, and eight served as spies. In addition, two women from upstate New York worked to prevent the Iroquois from allying themselves with the rebels.[37]

Although their numbers were limited, the women's participation required a strong sense of commitment. Unlike men, they could not be drafted into service or forced to take an active role through peer pressure. Their work was both entirely voluntary and extremely dangerous, since it was almost always performed behind the American lines. The most accurate comparison to them would be the percentage of men who had engaged in clandestine activities, but that figure is obviously unobtainable.

Three examples will illustrate the types of contributions made by female loyalists. In Philadelphia, the milliner Margaret Hutchinson "Releive'd at her own Exspence [sic], Severall English prisoners" who were jailed in the city early in the war. During the British occupation of 1777–1778, since her business often required her to leave the city, she was employed by Sir William Howe's aide-de-camp to carry letters to and from British spies among the rebel forces. She also brought back "Verbal Intelligence, of what, she had seen, of their different Movements." The Charleston shopkeeper Elizabeth Thompson likewise began by aiding prisoners, but she later became as bold as Mrs. Hutchinson. On one occasion she traveled through the American camp at night to carry letters to the redcoats, and on another she drove her chaise past the rebel lines, with a disguised British officer as a passenger, so he could "View their works in order to inform the British Commander." The New Yorker Lorenda Holmes, whose aunt also worked on behalf of the British, carried messages to and from the invading royal forces in the summer of 1776. Caught by some rebel committeemen and denounced as "the Damned Tory the penny Post," she was stripped naked and exposed to the mob but, she noted, "received no wounds or bruises from them only shame and horror of the mind." Some months later, though, after she had helped a group of loyalists slip through the lines into New York City, a rebel troop retaliated by holding her right foot on some hot coals until it was badly burned.[38]

To argue that the politicization and partisanship which led to the fervor of Lorenda Holmes, Elizabeth Thompson, and others was common among women is not to contend that it was universal. After all, the vast majority of female loyalist claimants gave no indication that they had taken positive steps on behalf of the British cause. To be sure, many of them fled their homes at an early stage of the conflict and so could not have contributed actively to the war effort, but some evidence suggests that for many women home and family remained the sole concern throughout the period of the war.

Such a conclusion emerges from an examination of the pension petitions submitted in the 1830s and 1840s by the elderly widows of Revolutionary War soldiers. In order to receive their stipends, the women had to present proof of their husbands' service in the American army. Since most of them had long since lost whatever documentary evidence they might once have possessed, they were forced to rely heavily on their memories. And how did they date their husbands' military careers? Not by reference to the great events of the Revolution, but rather by their familial circumstances at the time. The former Connecticut resident Nancy Davis recalled in 1841 that her first husband, Abner Lee, had enlisted in the army when their son was about six months old; a Rhode Islander who had been married in late 1780 declared that her husband was called up for militia service eleven months later, "which she remembers on account of her confinement which took place at that time"; and Anna Lawson, who "states she is no schollar and can not keep the date and is now governed by the time of her marriage," estimated that her husband, John, first served in the army six years after their 1775 wedding, because she then had three children.[39]

The same domestic flavor permeated the recollections of Helena Kortwright Brasher. When she described the prewar years in private memoirs prepared for her children, Helena disclosed her resentment of her husband's revolutionary activism, even though her "politicks were the same as his." Their father had often said, "[M]y country first and then my family," Helena explained, but "in this we differed.

I thought a mans family should and ought to be his first object." She then admitted, "[I] frequently, perhaps peevishly, complained of his neglecting me and our children." The situation was even worse because "he had formerly been a most domestick man," with the family as "his sole care and pleasure in which all his happiness centered." By the early 1770s, though, "he was forever out or had his house surrounded with gentlemen conversing on politicks; every evening out at some meeting or other haranguing his fellow citizens, writing for the publick prints."[40]

Mrs. Brasher's memoirs reveal her alienation from the political world that so captivated the attention of some of her contemporaries, both such girls as Charity Clarke and such mature women as Eliza Wilkinson. There must have been many others like her, women who had no desire to assume public roles and who stressed private values even in the midst of revolution. But those who adhered wholly to the traditional domestic realm were anomalous. The change in women's political perceptions wrought by revolutionary circumstances was truly momentous. For the first time, women became active — if not equal — participants in discourse on public affairs and in endeavors that carried political significance. As they discussed politics with men and among themselves during the twenty years from the mid-1760s to the mid-1780s, they gained both sophistication in political analysis and a new sense of their own role — one they expressed most fully in the summer of 1780 when they attempted to form a nationwide organization.

III

Charleston, South Carolina, fell to besieging British forces on May 12, 1780, striking a heavy blow to American hopes for an end to the war in the foreseeable future. Galvanized into action by the disaster, Philadelphia merchants and government officials took steps to support the inflated Pennsylvania currency and began soliciting funds for enlistment bounties to pay new army recruits. In this time of crisis their wives and daughters too adopted "public spirited measures," to use the words of the *Pennsylvania Gazette*: they signaled their intention to found the first large-scale women's association in American history.[41]

In the eleven years since the peak of the activities of the Daughters of Liberty, female Americans had not engaged in organized support of the war effort. Some women had published their opinions on revolutionary events, but these had all been individual endeavors. Even when "Clarissa" described her "Vision of the Paradise of Female Patriotism" in the *United States Magazine* in 1779, she wrote only of a "delicious garden" in which American women strolled beside the heroines of the past rather than of a world in which her contemporaries contributed as energetically to the welfare of their country as had the women she cited as exemplars — Deborah, Miriam, Portia (the wife of Brutus), Boadicea, and Joan of Arc.[42] The activism displayed by the Philadelphia women just over a year later was of a different order of magnitude altogether. Recognizing that the American soldiers were suffering from a serious loss of morale in the aftermath of the fall of Charleston, the women proposed a nationwide relief effort to aid the hard-pressed troops.

The campaign began on June 10, 1780, with the publication of a broadside, *The Sentiments of an American Woman*. The broadside was composed by the thirty-three-year-old Esther DeBerdt Reed, who was to become president of the Ladies Association. The daughter of a prominent English supporter of America, Esther had lived in Pennsylvania only since her 1770 marriage to Joseph Reed, but she was nonetheless a staunch patriot. Her *Sentiments* asserted forcefully that American women were determined to do more than offer "barren wishes" for the success of the army: they wanted to be "really useful," like "those heroines of antiquity, who have rendered their sex illustrious." Recognizing that in proposing an active political role for women she was challenging the boundaries of the feminine sphere, Mrs. Reed built her case carefully.

She began by reviewing the history of women's patriotic activity, referring to female monarchs, Roman matrons, and Old Testament women. Linking herself explicitly to such foremothers, she declared, "I glory in all which my sex has done great and commendable. I call to mind with enthusiasm and with admiration, all those acts of courage, of constancy and patriotism, which history has transmitted to us." Mrs. Reed especially held up Joan of Arc as an appropriate model, for she had driven from France "the ancestors of these same British, whose odious yoke we have just shaken off, and whom it is necessary that we drive from this Continent."

Esther Reed then addressed the question of propriety. Some men might perhaps "disapprove" women's activity, she admitted. But in the current dismal state of public affairs anyone who raised this objection would not be "a good citizen." Any man who truly understood the soldiers' needs, she wrote, could only "applaud our efforts for the relief of the armies which defend our lives, our possessions, our liberty." By thus hinting that critics of her scheme would be unpatriotic, Mrs. Reed cleverly defused possible traditionalist objections even before they could be advanced.

Finally, she outlined her plan. Recalling the contributions women had made to the nonimportation and home manufacture movements, Esther Reed recommended that female Americans renounce "vain ornaments," donating the money they would no longer spend on extravagant clothing and elaborate hairstyles to the patriot troops as *"the offering of the Ladies."* [43]

Her appeal drew an immediate response. Three days after the publication of the broadside, thirty-six Philadelphia women met to decide how to implement its suggestions. The results of their deliberations were printed as an appendix to *Sentiments* when it appeared in the June 21 issue of the *Pennsylvania Gazette.* Entitled "Ideas, relative to the manner of forwarding to the American Soldiers, the Presents of the American Women," the plan proposed the mobilization of the entire female population. Contributions would be accepted from any woman, in any amount. A "Treasuress" appointed in each county would oversee the collection of money, keeping careful records of all sums received. Heading each state's county treasuresses would be the wife of its governor, who would serve as "Treasuress-General." Ultimately, all contributions would be sent to Martha Washington to be used for the benefit of the troops. Only one restriction was placed on the employment of the contributions: "It is an extraordinary bounty intended to render the condition of the soldier more pleasant, and not to hold place of the things which they ought to receive from the Congress, or from the States." [44]

The Philadelphians set to work collecting funds even before the publication of their "Ideas." Dividing the city into ten equal districts, they assigned between two and five of their number to each area. Traveling in pairs, the canvassers visited every house, requesting contributions from "each woman and girl without any distinction." Among the collectors in the fifth ward, Market to Chestnut Streets, were Sarah Franklin Bache and Anne Willing (Mrs. Tench) Francis, sister of Elizabeth Willing Powel; Julia Stockton (Mrs. Benjamin) Rush worked in district six; and in the eighth ward, Spruce to Pine Streets, the canvassers included Alice Lee Shippen, Mrs. Robert Morris, and Sally McKean, wife of the Pennsylvania chief justice. The fact that women of such social standing undertook the very unfeminine task of soliciting contributions not only from friends and neighbors but also from strangers, poor people, and servants supports the contention of one of the Philadelphians that they "considered it as a great honour" to be invited to serve as canvassers. In a letter to a friend in Annapolis, an anonymous participant declared that "those who were in the country returned without delay to the city to fulfil their duty. Others put off their departure; those whose state of health was the most delicate, found strength in their patriotism." When a nursing mother (who may have been Esther Reed herself) was reluctant to leave her baby, this witness recorded, a friend volunteered to nurse the child along with her own.[45]

Accounts of the women's reception differ. The anonymous letter writer claimed that "as the cause of their visit was known, they were received with all the respect due to so honourable a commission." She explained that no house was omitted, not even those inhabited by Quakers, and that even there the subscription met with success, for "nothing is more easy than to reconcile a beneficient scheme with a beneficient religion." But Anna Rawle's description of the canvass of Quaker homes painted a different picture. "Of all absurdities the Ladies going about for money exceeded everything," she told her mother, Rebecca Shoemaker, whose second husband, Samuel, was a loyalist exile. Sarah Bache had come to their door, Anna reported, but had turned away, saying that "she did not chuse to face Mrs. S. or her daughters." Anna characterized the collectors as "so extremely importunate that people were obliged to give them something to get rid of them." Even "the meanest ale house" did not escape their net, and men were harassed until they contributed in the name of their wives or sweethearts. "I fancy they raised a considerable sum by this extorted contribution," Anna concluded, but in her opinion the requests were "carried to such an excess of meanness as the nobleness of no cause whatsoever could excuse."[46]

Whether the letter writer's examples of women proudly and voluntarily giving to the cause or Anna Rawle's account of reluctant contributors is more accurate is impossible to determine. But by the time the Philadelphia canvass was completed in early July, more than $300,000 continental dollars had been collected from over 1600 persons. Because of inflation, this amount when converted to specie equaled only about $7500, but even that represented a considerable sum. In financial terms, the city canvass was a smashing success.[47]

It was a success in other ways as well, for the Philadelphia women sought and achieved symbolic goals that went far beyond the collection of money. As the anonymous participant put it, the canvassers hoped that the "general beneficient" subscription would "produce the happy effect of destroying *intestine discords*, even to the very last seeds." That endeavor was particularly appropriate for Philadelphia women, because some of their number had become notorious for openly consorting with enemy troops during the British occupation in 1777–1778. The author of the 1780 letter alluded delicately to that questionable conduct when she explained that the canvassers wanted to "give some of our female fellow citizens an opportunity of relinquishing former errors and of avowing a change of sentiments by their contributions to the general cause of liberty and their country."[48]

But the symbolism of the fund drive was national as well as local. The anonymous participant stressed that through their gifts American women would "greatly promote the public cause, and blast the hopes of the enemies of this country" by demonstrating the populace's unanimous support of the war. That others also viewed the women's efforts in this light is evident from newspaper comments on the Ladies Association. As early as June 27, a laudatory essay signed "Song of Debora" appeared in the *Pennsylvania Packet*. "It must strike the enemy as with an apoplexy, to be informed, that the women of America are attentive to the wants of the Soldiery," the author declared, arguing, "[I]t is not the quantity of the money that may be collected, but the idea of favour and affection discovered in this exertion, that will principally give life to our cause, and restore our affairs." Urging other women to copy the Philadelphians' example, she predicted that "the women will reinspire the war; and ensure, finally, victory and peace."[49]

In July, newspapers throughout the country reprinted *Sentiments*, usually accompanied by the detailed collection plan, and editors occasionally added exhortations of their own to the women's call for action. Thus the *Continental Journal* of Boston declared on July 13, "[I]f ever an Army deserved every Encouragement from the Country it protects, it is that of America: And nothing could make a deeper Impression on the Minds of those brave men, . . . than such a Mark of Gratitude, and Regard, as is proposed from the FAIRER HALF of the United States." Praising the Philadelphians, the editor went on to assert confidently that "it cannot be doubted that the Ladies of New-England will exhibit the same amiable Disposition, and an equal alacrity in promoting the cause of their Country." The symbolic importance of the subscription was likewise conveyed to the nation by a frequently reprinted "Letter from an Officer at Camp, dated June 29, 1780." The patriotism of Philadelphia women "is a subject of conversation with the army," the officer wrote. "We do not suppose that these contributions can be any stable support to the campaign for any length of time; but, as it is a mark of respect to the army, it has given particular satisfaction, and it may be a great temporary service," for the soldiers had felt themselves "neglected" and forgotten by their fellow citizens.[50]

Successful as this publicity was in spreading the news of the Philadelphians' plan, Esther Reed and her fellow organizers did not rely solely upon print as they sought to involve other women in their association. The anonymous participant told her Annapolis friend that after they completed the city collections the women decided to write circular letters to their acquaintances in other counties and towns: "[W]e have it in charge to keep up this correspondence until the whole subscription shall be completed." Despite their inexperience, the Philadelphians demonstrated considerable organizational expertise by taking explicit steps to avoid having more than one member contact persons in the same area and by providing for meticulous record keeping. Sarah Franklin Bache, for example, was given the responsibility for correspondence with Bethlehem, Germantown, and Lancaster, Pennsylvania. Esther Reed's task, as befitted her position, was to write to the wives of the governors. Explaining that the purpose of the group was to reward the soldiers "for their Hardships & their Virtue," she enclosed a copy of the plan with her circular letter to the governors' wives, "not doubting your Interest & Influence to carry it into execution through your State."[51]

The women of Trenton, New Jersey, were the first to copy the Philadelphians' lead. As early as June 28 they began to organize their own subscription campaign, and on July 4 at a general meeting they outlined plans for a statewide association. As the "Ideas" had suggested, they appointed a treasuress and they also named Mary Dagworthy as corresponding secretary. Ambitiously, they proposed to establish coordinating committees in each county, and when they announced their scheme in the newspapers they published "Sentiments of a Lady in New Jersey" in deliberate imitation of the Philadelphians. "Let us animate one another to contribute from our purses in proportion to our circumstances towards the support and comfort of the brave men who are fighting and suffering for us on the field," the author exhorted her female compatriots. Although the final accounts of the New Jersey campaign have evidently failed to survive, in mid-July Dagworthy forwarded nearly $15,500 to George Washington as an initial contribution to the fund.[52]

Maryland women also responded quickly to the Philadelphians' request. Mrs. Thomas Sim Lee, the wife of the governor, wrote to friends in each county to ask them to serve as treasuresses, and by July 14 the organization was actively soliciting money in Annapolis. In that city alone, even though many residents had left town for the summer, more than $16,000 in currency was collected, with additional sums in specie. In Baltimore, the merchant and revolutionary leader Samuel Purviance welcomed the formation of the association, since, he told a friend, "[I] have for 3 years past been engaged in a continual Warfare against the exhorbitant Follies of my Fair Countrywomen." Samuel's wife, Katherine, was initially selected as local treasuress of what he termed "this Amazonian Society," but she declined the post, largely because, her husband explained, "her health [is] such as will prevent her taking the Field this Camp[aig]n." Some months later, writing with particular reference to the Marylanders, the editor of the

Pennsylvania Packet rhapsodized that "the women of every part of the globe are under obligations to those of America, for having shown that females are capable of the highest political virtue."[53]

Only for one other state, Virginia, is there evidence of successful activity connected with the Ladies Association. Martha Wayles Jefferson, whose husband, Thomas, was then the governor, received a copy of the Philadelphians' plan directly from Martha Washington. Since she was in poor health, Mrs. Jefferson decided to encourage her friends to take part but not to assume an active role herself. Interestingly enough, the letter she wrote on August 8 to Eleanor Madison, a copy of which also made its way into the hands of Frances Bland Tucker, is the sole piece of her correspondence extant today. In it she asserted, "I undertake with chearfulness the duty of furnishing to my countrywomen an opportunity of proving that they also participate of those virtuous feelings" of patriotism. The following day a public announcement of the campaign appeared in the *Virginia Gazette*. Given the diffuse pattern of settlement in the state, a house-to-house solicitation would have been impossible, so the plan specified that collections would be made in the churches. Only fragmentary records have ever been located, but they indicate that county treasuresses gathered total currency contributions ranging from £1,560 (Albemarle) to $7,506 (Prince William). Among the donors was Rebecca Burwell Ambler, mother of Betsy Ambler Brent and Polly Ambler Marshall.[54]

The association's organizing efforts in other states seem to have failed not because of lack of will or interest but because of lack of financial resources. That, at least, was the message conveyed to the Philadelphians by some of their out-of-state correspondents. Hannah Lee Corbin, a Virginia widow, told her sister, Alice Shippen, "The scheme of raising money for the Soldiers would be good — if we had it in our power to do it." But she was already "so heavily Laded" that she was having to sell her property just to obtain "common support," Hannah explained, and so she could not afford to contribute. Catharine Littlefield (Mrs. Nathanael) Greene, replying to Esther Reed's circular letter, told a similar story. "The distressed exhausted State of this little Government [Rhode Island] prevents us from gratifying our warmest Inclinations," she declared, because one-fifth of its territory, including Newport, was still in British hands. "The

Women of this State are Animated with the liveliest Sentiments of Liberty" and wish to offer relief to "our brave and patient Soldiery," she exclaimed, "but alass! the peculiar circumstances of this State renders this impracticable."[55]

Although the women's association found active participants only in Pennsylvania, New Jersey, Maryland, and Virginia, still it collected substantial sums of money. Its organizers next had to decide how to disburse the funds in accordance with their original aim, which was to present the American soldiers with "some extraordinary and unexpected relief, . . . *the offering of the Ladies.*" Since Martha Washington had returned to Virginia by the time the collection was completed, the association's leaders agreed to leave the disposition of the funds to her husband. There was only one problem: George Washington had plans for the money that differed sharply from theirs. "Altho' the terms of the association seem in some measure to preclude the purchase of any article, which the public is bound to find," General Washington told Joseph Reed in late June, "I would, nevertheless, recommend a provision of shirts in preference to any thing else."[56] Esther Reed's much revised, amended, and overwritten draft of her reply to the general, with all its tactful phrasing, suggests something of the consternation this proposal caused in the ranks of the canvassers who had worked so hard and so long to collect the money.

On July 31, Mrs. Reed listed the reasons for her hesitancy in complying with the general's request for shirts. She had not only found it difficult to locate linen, she reported, but she had also learned that Pennsylvania was planning to send two thousand shirts to its troops and that a large shipment of clothing had recently arrived from France. "These Circumstances togather with an Idea which prevails that the Soldiers might not consider it in the Light," she began, then crossed out the words following "Soldiers," and continued, "Soldiers woud not be so much gratified by bestowing an article to which they look upon themselves entitled from the public as in some other method which woud convey more fully the Idea of a reward for past Services & an incitement to future Duty." There she ended the sentence, having been so involved in her intricate prose that she failed to realize she had composed a fragment without a verb. Undaunted, she forged breathlessly ahead. "Some who are of this Opinion propose turning the whole of the Money into hard Dollars & giving each Soldier 2 at his own disposal." Having made her point, Mrs. Reed then attempted to soften the fact that she was daring to dispute the judgment of the commander in chief of the American army. "This method I hint only," she added, "but would not by any means wish to adopt that or any other without your full approbation." To further lessen her apostasy, she also assured Washington that if shirts were still needed after the "fresh supplies" had been distributed, a portion of the money could be applied to that use.[57]

Washington's response was, as Mrs. Reed later told her husband, "a little formal as if he was hurt by our asking his Opinion a second time & our not following his Directions after desiring him to give them." In his letter the general suggested, "A taste of hard money may be productive of much discontent as we have none but depreciated paper for their pay." He also predicted that some soldiers' taste for drink would lead them "into irregularities and disorders" and that therefore the proposed two-dollar bounty "will be the means of bringing punishment" on them. No, he insisted; if the ladies wanted to employ their "benevolent donation" well, the money should be used for shirts — which they should make to save the cost of hiring seamstresses. Faced with Washington's adamant stance, Esther Reed retreated. "I shall now endeavour to get the Shirts made as soon as possible," she told Joseph, and he agreed with her decision. "The General is so decided that you have no Choice left so that the sooner you finish the Business the better," he wrote on August 26, reminding her, "[I]t will be necessary for you to render a publick Account of your Stewardship in this Business & tho you will receive no thanks if you do it well, you will bear much Blame should it be otherwise."[58]

Unfortunately, however, Esther DeBerdt Reed had no chance to "finish the Business" she had so ably begun, for she died the following month as a result of a dysentery epidemic. The leadership of the association was assumed by Sarah Franklin Bache, with the assistance of Anne Willing Francis and three other women. They took control of the funds that had been in Mrs. Reed's possession, overseeing the purchase of linen and the shirtmaking process. By early December, when the Marquis de Chastellux visited Sarah Bache's home, more than two thousand shirts had been completed. He recorded that "on each shirt was the name of the married or unmarried lady who made it." Late that same month, the women gave the shirts to the Deputy Quartermaster General in Philadelphia, and Mrs. Bache told General Washington, "We wish them to be worn with as much pleasure as they were made."[59]

In February 1781 Washington offered profuse thanks to the members of the committee that had succeeded Esther Reed as leaders of the Ladies Association. The organization's contributions, he declared, entitled its participants "to an equal place with any who have preceded them in the walk of female patriotism. It embellishes the American character with a new trait; by proving that the love of country is blended with those softer domestic virtues, which have always been allowed to be more peculiarly *your own*."[60]

Washington's gratitude was genuine, and the army certainly needed the shirts, but the fact remains that the members of the association, who had embarked on a very unfeminine enterprise, were ultimately deflected into a traditional domestic role. The general's encomium on their contributions made this explicit by its references to "female patriotism" and "those softer domestic virtues," which presumably included the ability to sew. Ironically and symbolically, the Philadelphia women of 1780, who had tried to chart an independent course for themselves and to establish an unprecedented nationwide female organization, ended up as what one amused historian has termed "General Washington's Sewing Circle."

The amusement has not been confined to subsequent generations, for male revolutionary leaders, too, regarded the women's efforts with droll condescension. Benjamin Rush and John Adams exchanged wry comments on the association, with Adams proclaiming, "The Ladies having undertaken to support American Independence, settles the point." Women, on the other hand, saw nothing to smile at in the affair. Kitty Livingston, whose mother was a participant in the New Jersey group, sent a copy of *The Sentiments of an American Woman* to her sister Sarah Jay, then in Spain. "I am prouder than ever of my charming countrywomen," Sarah told her husband in forwarding the broadside to him, and she later repeated that message to Kitty when she thanked her for the information. Abigail Adams had a similar reaction, one that stands in sharp contrast to her husband's. Mrs. Adams took the association as a sign that "virtue exists, and publick spirit lives — lives in the Bosoms of the Fair Daughters of America, who blushing for the Languid Spirit, and halting Step, unite their Efforts to reward the patriotick, to stimulate the Brave, to alleviate the burden of War, and to shew that they are not dismayed by defeats or misfortunes." To her, the women's activities proved that "America will not wear chains while her daughters are virtuous." Not for Abigail were any references to "female patriotism" or "softer virtues." She saw female Americans as equal participants in the war effort.[61]

The anonymous Philadelphian expressed an identical point of view in her correspondence with her Annapolis friend. "Some persons have amused themselves with the importance which we have given it," she remarked, alluding to what must have been widespread male condescension. "I confess we have made it a serious business," she declared, but "with great reason; an object so interesting was certainly worthy an extraordinary attention." She and her fellow canvassers had, she wrote, "consecrated every moment we could spare from our domestic concerns, to the public good," enduring "with pleasure, the fatigues and inconveniences inseparable from such a task," because they could reflect proudly on the fact that "whilst our friends were exposed to the hardships and dangers of the fields of war for our protection, we were exerting at home our little labours to administer to their comfort and alleviate their toil."[62]

The proud sense of involvement in public affairs evident in these comments and in women's observations on their private contributions to the war effort carried over into the postwar years, for the return of peace did not bring with it a retreat from politics on the part of American women. Quite the contrary; their interest in the affairs of state continued unabated.

IV

In 1782, Eliza Wilkinson took up the cudgel on behalf of her sex. "The men say we have no business with them [politics], it is not in our sphere!" she told a friend angrily. "I won't have it thought that because we are the weaker sex as to *bodily* strength, my dear, we are capable of nothing more than minding the dairy, visiting the poultry-house, and all such domestic concerns. . . . They won't even allow us the liberty of thought, and that is all I want. . . . Surely we may have sense enough to give our opinions to commend or discommend such actions as we may approve or disapprove; without being reminded of our spinning and household affairs as the only matters we are capable of thinking or speaking of with justness and propriety." [63]

The serious interest in politics that lay behind Mrs. Wilkinson's tirade was not hers alone. In the late 1780s and 1790s women whose appetite for public affairs had been whetted by the events of the Revolution kept themselves abreast of political happenings through newspapers, conversations, and correspondence. "I am turned a great Politician," Margaret Manigault typically told her husband, Gabriel, in 1792; "I read the papers, & talk learnedly about them all." Similar statements may be found in the diaries or correspondence of nearly every white woman in late eighteenth-century America. In the spring of 1789, for example, Susanna Dillwyn reported that "a general subject of conversation at present" among herself and her female friends was "the newly elected president of the united States" and his recent inaugural address. Five years later, Alice DeLancey Izard turned a journey from Philadelphia to South Carolina into an opportunity to take soundings on the current political situation for her husband, Ralph, then a senator, sending him detailed accounts of her conversations with innkeepers and ferryboat operators. [64] From the French traveler who in 1791 encountered two young Virginia women eagerly taking part in political debates, to the New England girl who at a 1788 dance proudly pronounced herself a "politician" to a youth wishing to discuss the new Constitution, to Debby Logan, who in 1799 found it notable that during a visit to Philadelphia she had "scarsly spoke a Political Sentence," the indications are unanimous: after the Revolution women no longer regarded politics as falling outside their sphere. As Abigail Adams put it in 1799, "If a woman does not hold the reigns [sic] of Government, I see no reason for her not judging how they are conducted." [65]

Mrs. Adams was perhaps the foremost female expert at that task of judging government. John Adams's travels as a diplomat and his long career in public service, concluding with his presidency at the end of the century, necessarily brought his intelligent wife more directly into contact with the political world than any of her female contemporaries. Abigail, as her daughter Nabby once remarked, loved her "dish of politics," and from the beginning of John's involvement with the revolutionary cause she took an avid interest in public affairs. Hundreds of letters to her husband (in the 1770s and early 1780s) and to her sisters (in the late 1780s and the 1790s) testify to her unique political acumen. In November 1775, for example, she recognized the need for a "Code of Laws" at a time when America had been governed for some months by a de facto combination of committees and congresses. "Can any government be free which is not adminstred by general stated Laws?" she asked her husband. "Tis true your Resolutions as a Body have heithertoo had the force of Laws. But will they continue to have?" she inquired, accurately identifying the shaky legal ground upon which the American government would continue to rest until the adoption of the Articles of Confederation. She demonstrated similar perception when she predicted to her uncle in 1786 that Great Britain would not make concessions to the United States until "every legal impediment to the recovery of British debts" had been removed from state statute books. For Abigail Adams, political commentary not only was as natural as breathing (which was what she said to a granddaughter in 1812), but it was also an endeavor for which she showed remarkable talent.[66]

But Mrs. Adams believed that a woman should express her political opinions only in private, rather than by taking part in public debates. Others of her female contemporaries were less traditionally minded. Letitia Cunningham, a Philadelphia widow who had bought government bonds during the war, published in 1783 a closely reasoned, well-researched pamphlet, *The Case of the Whigs Who Loaned their Money on the Public Faith Fairly Stated*, arguing on behalf of herself and other investors — but especially widows — that they were entitled to full interest payments on the loans. Likewise, Anne Willing Bingham, a niece of Elizabeth Willing Powel, openly challenged Thomas Jefferson's belief that American women should be "too wise to wrinkle their foreheads with politics." To Jefferson, the ideal feminine role was "to soothe and calm the minds of their husbands returning ruffled from political debate," and he criticized French women for meddling publicly in political affairs. Mrs. Bingham saw the matter quite differently. "The Women of France interfere in the politics of the Country, and often give a decided Turn to the Fate of Empires," she told Jefferson in 1787. As a result, "they have obtained that Rank of Consideration in society, which the Sex are intitled to, and which they in vain contend for in other countries." Female Americans, she concluded, "are therefore bound in Gratitude to admire and revere them, for asserting our Privileges," rather than finding reason to shun their example, as Jefferson had suggested.[67]

Although many American men were willing to allow women private political influence of the sort advocated and exercised by Abigail Adams, only in one state did the postrevolutionary era bring a real, if temporary, recognition of women's potential public role. In 1790, New Jersey adopted an election law that explicitly referred to voters as "he or she," thereby instituting a formal experiment with woman suffrage more than a century prior to the adoption of the Nineteenth Amendment to the Constitution.[68]

The origins of the New Jersey law are obscure. The state constitution of 1776 neither specifically disfranchised women nor enfranchised them, defining voters vaguely as "all free inhabitants" meeting property and residence requirements. Although this broad wording could conceivably have been intended to encompass eligible widows and spinsters as well as free black males, the constitution's phraseology probably represented a simple oversight on the part of its framers, as the opponents of woman and black suffrage later claimed. The electoral clause aroused no special comment at the constitutional convention; if deliberate, such a novel extension of the suffrage would surely have elicited considerable debate. Even so, the state constitution's lack of specificity allowed the newly politicized property-holding women of New Jersey to seize the initiative, and they successfully claimed the right to vote in local elections during the 1780s. The 1790 statute, and similarly worded election laws passed later that same decade, thus simply acknowledged and legitimized extant practice. By 1800, woman suffrage was so well established in the state that the legislature rejected an amendment providing for female voting in congressional races on the grounds that it was unnecessary. As one legislator said, "Our Constitution gives this right to maids or widows *black or white*."[69]

One well-documented election in which women played a prominent role was the heated contest in 1797 over the seat for the town of

191

Elizabeth in the legislature. Reportedly, seventy-five female Federalists appeared at the polls to vote against the Democratic-Republican candidate, John Condict. Although Condict won, Federalist newspapers celebrated the women's activism, declaring their party's intention to "not only preach the 'Rights of Woman' but boldly push it into practice." The Newark *Centinel of Freedom* published a poem proclaiming,

> *Let Democrats with senseless prate,*
> *maintain the softer Sex, Sir,*
> *Should ne'er with politics of State*
> *their gentle minds perplex Sir:*
> *Such vulgar prejudice we scorn;*
> *their sex is no objection. . . .*
> *While woman's bound, man can't be free,*
> *nor have a fair election.*[70]

Yet not all male New Jerseyites greeted woman suffrage with such exuberant glee. In his 1798 commentary on the state constitution William Griffith remarked that he found it a "mockery," even "perfectly disgusting," to watch female voters casting their ballots. "It is evident, that women, generally, are neither, by nature, nor habit, nor education, nor by their necessary condition in society, fitted to perform this duty with credit to themselves, or advantage to the public," he asserted. Griffith's words were echoed four years later by "Friend to the Ladies," who described women as "timid and pliant, unskilled in politics, unacquainted with all the real merits of the several candidates," and subject to the direction of their male relatives. "How will an obedient daughter dare to vote against the sentiments of her father and how can a fair one refuse her lover?" he asked. Assuring his female readers that he did not wish to deprive them of their rights, he suggested, "Let them rather consider that female reserve and delicacy are incompatible with the duties of a free elector, [and] that a female politician is often [the] subject of ridicule."[71]

In 1807, relying on the persistence of such traditional attitudes among his colleagues in the legislature, John Condict had his revenge for his near-defeat at the hands of female voters ten years earlier: he introduced the bill that successfully disfranchised both women and blacks. A fraudulent referendum supplied the immediate impetus for the law. The citizens of Newark and Elizabeth, vying over the location of the new Essex County Court House, evidently voted early and often. Whereas previous county elections had drawn a maximum of 4,500 votes, more than 14,000 ballots were cast in the 1807 referendum. In the wake of the contest, female and black voters became the scapegoats because they were believed to be easily manipulable. Even though white men undoubtedly composed most of the offenders, just as they made up the vast majority of voters, the legislature responded to the obvious corruption by disfranchising blacks and women, in order to restore "the safety, quiet, good order and dignity of the state."[72]

New Jersey men had never displayed a strong commitment to the principle of woman suffrage; they had merely left a loophole in their constitution that allowed the boldest among their female fellow citizens to express directly a new sense of public responsibility. That the experiment was formalized at all was a tribute to the wartime politicization of the state's female population, and, indeed, illustrated the possible long-term consequences of that politicization. But even though the women of the revolutionary generation enthusiastically exercised their newfound public role, there are indications that many of their daughters and granddaughters reverted to a more traditional understanding of woman's place.

Take, for example, some suggestive evidence from nineteenth-century memoirs. Eliza Perkins Cabot, who was born in Boston in 1791, recalled as a novelty that in her youth women had been interested in politics. Her description of how her mother, aunts, and mother-in-law had "discuss[ed] political questions a great deal" makes it clear that to her such conversations were alien. A descendant's detailed memories of the political pursuits of Mary Anna Boardman, who had been born in 1767, convey a similar impression. "She felt, throughout life, those pulsations which, when she was a little child, she had felt, while rocked in the cradle of the Revolution," he wrote, finding it necessary to explain why she had been "careful to obtain accurate information" on "the various leading topics of the times" and to "intelligently mark the progress of our political affairs" as late as the 1840s.[73]

Appropriately, then, in 1801 a new reference to sex in relationship to politics appeared in a letter written by a girl too young to remember the Revolution. Cautioned by her congressman father "not to converse much on political subjects," the fifteen-year-old North Carolinian Ann Steele drafted a reassuring reply. "I make it an invariable rule to be silent on political subjects. In my opinion they are altogether out of a ladys sphere." In spite of superficial appearances, all had not come full circle, for Ann admitted in the same letter, "I like to hear how the wheels of Government move," and, when she joined her father in Washington the following year, she regularly attended congressional debates.[74]

Ann Steele, the patriotic daughter of a republican congressman, had accordingly become politically aware much earlier in life than her grandmother Elizabeth — the very woman who in 1780 had termed herself a "great politician" — or her mother, Polly. She grew up in a world very different from the colonial one that had shaped them, and her sensibilities likewise diverged from theirs. She may not have believed with them that a "lady" could regularly comment on politics, but she believed in keeping herself well informed about public affairs. Such matters were a part of her youth, whereas they had not been an element of the early lives of her mother and grandmother, whose youthful experiences had been entirely confined to the domestic realm. That fact alone meant that for her and the other members of the postwar female generation political discussion and even activism was never to be as alien as it had been to women born before 1760. Nineteenth-century women took pride in the contributions that members of their sex had made to the winning of independence. The existence of such public-spirited models showed them that women could take active roles in politics without losing their feminine identity. It was not by chance, in other words, that in 1848 the organizers of the first women's rights convention at Seneca Falls, New York, chose to use the Declaration of Independence as the basis for their calls for reform in women's status. They understood the relevance of the revolutionary era to their own endeavors.[75]

Chapter Seven

NECESSITY TAUGHT US

MOST NARRATIVES OF THE REVOLUTIONARY WAR CONCENTRATE UPON describing a series of pitched battles between uniformed armies. Yet the impact of the conflict can more accurately be assessed if it is interpreted as a civil war with profound consequences for the entire population.[1] Every movement of troops through the American countryside brought a corresponding flight of refugees, an invasion of epidemic disease, the expropriation of foodstuffs, firewood, and livestock, widespread plundering or destruction of personal property, and occasional incidents of rape. In addition to bearing these common burdens of warfare, Americans who remained loyal to the Crown had to contend with persecution, property confiscation, and forced exile, as did patriots who lived in areas controlled by the British, although for them such reverses were only temporary.

The disruption of normal patterns of life that resulted from all these seldom-studied aspects of the conflict had an especially noticeable effect upon women, whose prewar experiences had been confined largely to the domestic realm. With their menfolk away serving in the armies for varying lengths of time, white female Americans had to venture into new fields of endeavor. In the midst of wartime trials, they alone had to make crucial decisions involving not only household and family but also the "outdoor affairs" from which they had formerly been excluded. After initially expressing hesitation about their ability to assume these new responsibilities, many white women gained a new appreciation of their own capacity and of the capability of their sex in general as they learned to handle unfamiliar tasks.

For black women, too, the war brought changes. Most notably, the British policy of offering freedom to runaway slaves encouraged a significant percentage of them to abandon their home plantations in order to seek refuge with the redcoats. In times of peace, the vast majority of runaways were youthful males, but ready access to the British army in the South during the later years of the war enabled even mothers encumbered with many children to take advantage of the opportunity to win freedom for themselves and their offspring. Of the many ironies of black-white relations in the revolutionary era, one of the most striking was the fact that while American whites were struggling against British attempts to "enslave" them, American blacks correctly regarded those same redcoats as liberators.

I

White women's experiences with wartime disruptions varied according to the region in which they lived, for the war did not affect all Americans equally at all times. New Englanders had to cope with turmoil first, but after the British evacuated Boston in 1776, the northern section of the country was relatively free of armed conflict, with the exception of coastal areas, which remained continually open to attack from the sea. In the middle states, by contrast, the continuing presence of the British army in New York City and environs from July 1776 to November 1783 and the redcoats' brief occupation of Philadelphia in 1777–1778 meant that many families had no respite from the dangers of warfare for a period of years. Although the South, on the other hand, was little touched by the war before 1778, subsequent British army movements and the internecine guerrilla conflict that raged incessantly through the backcountry had a devastating impact on the economy and society. Each of these regional patterns had different consequences for the female population.

Yet there was also similarity among women's experiences. Northerners and southerners responded alike to such stimuli as the looming threat of invasion by enemy troops, the incidence of disease, or the opportunity to accompany their husbands to the army. Since the residents of Massachusetts were the first Americans who confronted these problems, an analysis of their reactions to warfare may serve as an introduction to a discussion of their compatriots' behavior.

When news of the British sortie from Boston spread rapidly through New England towns on April 19, 1775, panic struck a civilian population awakened from "benign Slumbers" by the "beat of drum and ringing of Bell." Sixty-seven years later, Susan Mason Smith, who was thirteen in 1775, still vividly remembered that night of terror. Although her family decided not to leave their Salem home because they did not know where to find safety, she did not remove her shoes for several days thereafter, afraid to be unprepared for the next alarm. Many other families made the opposite choice, for on the morning of April 20 an observer found the roads around Boston "filld with frighted women and children, some in carts with their tattered furniture, others on foot fleeing into the woods." In the months that followed such scenes became commonplace in New England. After the battle of Bunker Hill, during which much of Charlestown was destroyed by fire, James Warren reported from Watertown that "it is Impossible to describe the Confusion in this place, Women and Children flying into the Country, armed Men Going to the field, and wounded Men returning from there fill the Streets." [2]

Even though no other major clashes occurred in the area, life did not soon return to normal, especially for those who resided near the coast. "We live in continual Expectation of Hostilities," Abigail Adams told her husband shortly after the destruction of Charlestown. A month earlier four British ships had dropped anchor nearby in search of forage, creating another panic. "People women children from the Iron Works flocking down this Way — every woman and child above or from below my Fathers," she wrote then, conveying a sense of distraction even in her prose. "My Fathers family flying, the Drs. in great distress, . . . my Aunt had her Bed thrown into a cart, into which she got herself, and orderd the boy to drive her of[f]." [3]

The same images of disorder reverberated through later descriptions of similar scenes. "I arrived here late last night and found people in the utmost confusion, Familys, Women, Children, & Luggage all

The Battle of Bunker Hill. Courtesy of Library of Congress Prints Division. This view

along the road as I came, mooving different ways," reported a Georgian in 1776 after an Indian raid. Rumors that the British were sailing up the Chesapeake that same year elicited an identical reaction in Annapolis, "what with the darkness of the night, thunder, lightning, and rain, cries of women and children, people hurrying their effects into the country, drums beating to arms, etc." Many of the refugees must have felt like Helena Kortwright Brasher, who, when she and her family fled from the British attack on Esopus, New York, asked, "Where God can we fly from danger? All places appear equally precarious," or like Ann Eliza Bleecker of Tomhanick, New York, whose friends and relatives "scattered like a flock of frighted birds" before the "hurricane" of Burgoyne's invasion in the fall of 1777. Mrs. Bleecker, who never recovered her emotional equilibrium after the death of her baby daughter on that wild flight, wrote of how she and her children had wandered "solitary through the dark woods, expecting every moment to meet the bloody ally of *Britain* [the Indians]," before reaching the safety of Albany. Over two years later Mrs. Bleecker told a friend, "Alas! the wilderness is within: I muse so long on the dead until I am unfit for the company of the living." The eighty-six-year-old widow of a revolutionary soldier obviously spoke for many when she observed in 1840, "There was so much Suffering, and so many alarms in our neighborhood in those hard times, that it has always been painful for me to dwell upon them."[4]

Faced with the uncertain dangers of flight, some, like the Mason family of Salem before them, decided to remain where they were. In 1777 a Pennsylvanian told John Adams resolutely that "if the two opposite Armys were to come here alternately ten times, she would stand by her Property untill she should be kill'd. If she must be a Beggar, it should be where she was known." Hannah Iredell's sister Jean Blair made the same choice in 1781 when the redcoats neared her North Carolina home. "The English are certainly at Halifax but I suppose they will be every where & I will fix myself here it is as safe as any where else & I can be no longer tossed about," she declared. The Philadelphian Elizabeth Farmar also decided to stay in her house, despite the fact that it lay between the lines during the occupation of the city in 1777–1778. As a result, she, her husband, and their daughter were endangered by frequent gunfire, had difficulty obtaining adequate food supplies, and suffered "manny cold days" that winter because the British confiscated their firewood. "Notwithstanding we thought ourselves well of[f] in comparison to some," she remarked in 1783. "Most of the houses near us have been either burnt or pulled down as would have been the case with us if we had not stayd in it even at the hasard of our lives."[5]

But not many families were as determined to protect their property. Greater numbers of Americans preferred, like the Amblers of Virginia, to go "scampering" when they learned that the enemy was nearby, seeking shelter with friends and relatives in more secure parts of the countryside. After twenty such unexpected guests descended on Jean Blair one day in May 1781, she commented, "I hardly ever knew the trouble of house keeping before, a large family and continual confusion and not any thing to eat but salt meat and hoe cake and no conveniences to dress them."[6] Sally Cobb Paine likewise felt compelled to offer refuge to her husband Robert's sisters when they fled south to Taunton after the alarms of April 19, 1775, but housing simultaneously both the spinster Eunice Paine and the six-member Greenleaf clan proved to be difficult. In mid-May the pregnant Sally reported to her congressman husband, "I have my house full and hands too." She expressed her hope "[that] they will Live by themselves before Long for it is most too hard for me to have the Care of so Large a family at present." As it turned out, though, the Greenleafs found "but very few willing to contribute to the oppressed," and so they remained in the crowded Paine household until the evacuation of Boston, although Eunice did return to her lodgings in Germantown, near Braintree.[7]

Even after the redcoats' long-awaited departure, Boston, said one resident, was not "that agreable place it once was — Almost every thing here, appears Gloomy & Mallancholy." One of the chief reasons for the Bostonians' gloom was the presence of epidemic disease in their midst. The unhealthy conditions in the besieged city had helped to incubate both smallpox and dysentery, and an epidemic of the latter had already swept the Massachusetts countryside the preceding fall, killing Abigail Adams's mother and niece, among many others. "The desolation of War is not so distressing as the Havock made by the pestilence," Abigail remarked then. She could do nothing to prevent the deaths from dysentery, but smallpox was another matter. After it became clear that the disease would probably spread across New England, carried by soldiers returning from the army that had invaded Canada as well as by Bostonians, she began making arrangements to have herself and her children inoculated.[8]

Abigail Adams and other eighteenth-century Americans could not reach such a decision lightly, for inoculation required being deliberately infected with the disease. Waiting to take smallpox "in the natural way" was to court death, yet no parents wanted to place their children knowingly into mortal danger or to risk their serious disfigurement. Accordingly, adults usually postponed inoculation for themselves and their offspring as long as possible. The war forced them to face the issue directly, since smallpox followed the armies so inevitably that some Americans charged the British with the "hellish Pollicy" of intentionally spreading the disease. Therefore, whenever a large number of soldiers from either side arrived in a given area, parents had to make life-or-death decisions. Indeed, like Abigail Adams, many wives were forced to reach those decisions on their own in the absence of their husbands.[9]

In January 1777, the choice was Sally Logan Fisher's, with "the infection being so much about" in Philadelphia among the patriot troops who had come to town after the New Jersey campaign. Terming herself "very anxious, about my little Boy what to do for the best, whether to Inoculate him or not," Mrs. Fisher decided to follow her doctor's advice and arrange for the inoculation. Two years later, when another smallpox outbreak hit the city, she made the same choice for her daughter Hannah. That such decisions could cause deep anguish is demonstrated by the correspondence between Henry Knox, the revolutionary general, and his wife, Lucy Flucker. "Altho the Smallpox is disrob'd of the greatest part of its terrors by innoculation," he wrote after she and their baby daughter had entered a Boston smallpox hospital in April 1777, "yet my heart palpitates at the thought of my dearest Lucy being in the least danger[. M]ay God preserve and carry you and our dear babe safe through it, it will be at least disarming death of one of his Shafts." Abigail Adams was obviously relieved to be able to report to her husband as she prepared to leave the inoculation hospital, "[A]ll my treasure of children have passed thro one of the most terible Diseases to which humane Nature is subject, and not one of us is wanting." [10]

In addition to carrying smallpox, the armies brought a specific terror to American women: the fear of rape. The only female New Englanders who personally confronted this problem on a large scale were residents of Fairfield and New Haven, the Connecticut towns raided by English and Hessian troops in early July 1779. Shortly after the raid, the Continental Congress collected depositions from women who had been attacked by the redcoats. Two local residents declared that they had fought off sexual assaults with the help of passersby, but Christiana Gatter was not so fortunate. Her husband, who had been severely beaten by the British earlier in the day, ran away when a group of soldiers broke into their home at half past two in the morning. "Two of them laid hold of me and threw me on the Bed and swore if I made any noise or Resistance they would kill me in a moment," Mrs. Gatter testified, so "I was obligded to Submit" to each of them in turn. [11] Her fate was hardly enviable, yet far worse were the circumstances of girls living on Staten Island and in New Jersey, who during the fall and winter of 1776 were subjected to repeated rapes by British troops stationed in the area. Whereas the Connecticut incidents and other similar occurrences took place in the context of brief excursions in search of plunder, the 1776 rapes were both systematic and especially brutal.

That series of attacks on American women may have been prompted by the redcoats' frustration at Washington's successful escape into New Jersey and then Pennsylvania after the fall of Manhattan, an accomplishment which forced the continuation of the war instead of allowing the quick end to the fighting they had anticipated. In any event, the soldiers went on a rampage of rape, and their officers did little to stop them. Lord Rawdon, a cavalry commander, may not have been typical, but he described such incidents light-heartedly. "The fair nymphs of this isle [Staten Island] are in wonderful tribulation," he told his uncle; "a girl cannot step into the bushes to pluck a rose without running the most imminent risk of being ravished," and as a result "we have the most entertaining courts-martial every day." The residents of the region understandably saw the epidemic of rape in a very different light. A Princetonian recognized one of the worst aspects of the crime, observing, "[A]gainst

both Justice and Reason We Despise these poor Innocent Sufferers";
consequently, "many honest virtuous women have suffered in this
Manner and kept it Secret for fear of making their lives misserable."
Nevertheless, the stories surfaced, though anonymously: sixteen girls
from Hopewell, New Jersey, held captive for days in the British camp
and repeatedly raped; a farmer's daughter "Ravisht" twice in her
father's barn; a thirteen-year-old raped by six soldiers; and, in Newark, groups of officers going "about the town by night, entering into
houses and openly inquiring for women." [12]

Depositions collected by the Continental Congress give the most
vivid accounts of the experiences of women in New Jersey in late
1776. Particularly revealing are those that pertain to a series of incidents at the home of Edmund Palmer, an elderly Hunterdon County
farmer. One December day, a number of British soldiers from a
nearby camp came to the house. One of them dragged Palmer's
thirteen-year-old granddaughter, Abigail, into a back room. She
"Scream'd & beged of him to let her alone, but some of Said
Soldiers said they wou'd knock her Eyes out if she did not hold her
Tongue." Over the ineffectual pleas of her grandfather and her aunt
Mary Phillips, Abigail was raped three times. Abigail testified that
"for three Days successively, Divers Soldiers wou'd come to the
House & Treat her in the Same manner." On one of those days, her
aunt Mary was raped in the barn and her friend Sarah Cain, who had
come to comfort her, was also assaulted. Finally, on the evening of
the third day two soldiers demanded that Abigail and Sarah's younger
sister Elisabeth, who was fifteen, accompany them to their camp.
"One of them Said he had come for his Girl, & Swore he wou'd have
her, & Seiz'd hold of her Hand & told her to Bundle up her Cloaths
for she shou'd go with them," Abigail recounted. She and Elisabeth
were then forced into another room despite the efforts of Edmund
Palmer and Elisabeth's father, Thomas. Elisabeth recalled that "the
said Soldiers Ravished them both and then took them away to their
Camp, where they was both Treated by some others of the Soldiers
in the same cruel manner," until they were rescued by an officer.
After spending the night at a nearby farmhouse, the girls went home
— not to Palmer's, but to Thomas Cain's. And there they were
evidently safe, for they told the investigators of no further
attacks. [13]

203

Such incidents could occur only in areas where troops were stationed for long periods of time, since only then did they have the opportunity to sexually exploit the local female population in systematic fashion. This was what saved the women of New England and, to a certain extent, southern women as well from the fate visited upon their counterparts in the middle states. Not all the contacts between British regulars and American women were as unpleasant as the ones just described, but the constant proximity of troops — rebel as well as redcoat — made the experiences of middle state women differ in a number of ways from those of their female compatriots to the north or south.

In all occupied areas, women often had to quarter troops in their homes. The results varied according to whether the soldiers were from the side the woman herself supported, but the consequent disruption of household affairs was universal. Elizabeth Drinker discovered as much during the British occupation of Philadelphia. Pressured to take an officer into her home, Mrs. Drinker, whose husband was then being held by the rebels in Virginia, resisted the request as long as possible, on the grounds that her household of "lone women" feared "the malbehavior of British officers." But in the face of tales of how officers had retaliated violently against persons who refused them lodgings, she at last consented to quarter a Major Crammond, who seemed to be "a thoughtful, sober young man." Unfortunately, Mrs. Drinker soon discovered her error. Crammond commandeered the stable for his stock, stayed out late at night, and gave noisy dinner parties. Furthermore, shortly after he arrived he moved into both the front parlors, plus an upstairs room and part of the kitchen. Not until the British evacuation in June 1778 was order fully restored to the Drinker household.[14]

The journal of Lydia Mintern Post, a patriotic Long Island housewife, also reveals the disruptive impact of quartering. Along with many of her rebel neighbors, she was forced to house Hessian troops after the redcoats had taken New York City. The soldiers, she wrote, "take the fence rails to burn, so that the fields are all left open, and the cattle stray away and are often lost; burn fires all night on the ground, and to replenish them, go into the woods and cut down all the young saplings, thereby destroying the growth of ages." Even worse was the effect on her household. The Hessians lived in her kitchen (with the door to the rest of the house nailed shut), and when they received their monthly ration of rum, she recorded, "we have trying and grievous scenes to go through; fighting, brawls, drumming and fifing, and dancing the night long; card and dice playing, and every abomination going on under our very roofs." Most threatening of all, though, was the relationship of the homesick Hessians and her children. The soldiers taught her son German and made baskets for her daughters, telling the youngsters "of their own little ones at home." "The children are fond of them," she noted, but "I fear lest they should contract evil." Her words detailed her dilemma: she was powerless to prevent her children from being attracted to an alien way of life promulgated by persons who were enemies to her country, for they were residents of her own home.[15]

Continued contact with British soldiers (including one who was quartered with her) during the occupation of Philadelphia caused Sally Logan Fisher to have a major change of heart about politics. At the outset of the Revolution she was an open partisan of the British, repeatedly expressing the hope that the redcoats would subdue the Americans' "rebellious spirit." In the early months of 1777 Sally referred to Sir William Howe as "our beloved General," and she described British rule as a "mild & gentle Government which breathes with Liberty & Peace." Accordingly, she welcomed the arrival of British regulars in September 1777, "an event I had so long wished to take place."

Just three months later, disillusionment had set in. She commented in her diary on the "poor protection" given loyalists by the redcoats, who plundered all Americans indiscriminately, and in March 1778 she recorded the "very bad accounts of the licentiousness of the English Officers in deluding young Girls." When she learned of the planned British evacuation, Mrs. Fisher disclosed her fear of "again coming under the arbit[r]ary power of the Congress," but she also observed that she did not want "to put too much confidence in Armies." Indeed, after December 1777 she forsook partisan statements altogether. Sally Logan Fisher did not come to support the Revolution, but she grew distrustful of the redcoats. After she had lived with a British officer in her home for some months, she no longer wrote of "the noble fire of Loyal Britons" but rather of the "wanton destruction" of Philadelphians' property by the occupying

troops. In 1783, she declared her "great satisfaction" that peace —
and the independence she had once abhorred — had at last been
achieved.[16]

When the occupying troops were French or American instead of
British, patriotic teenaged girls openly rejoiced. To many of them the
trials of war appeared remote, while the presence of dashing young
officers promised romance and an active social life. In 1785, a Newport belle lightly told a foreign traveler that "she wishes there was to
be [more war] if it were not for the shedding blood. 'They had a little
fighting, to be sure, in the summer, but when the winter came they
forgot all the calamities of war and drowned their cares in assemblies,
concerts, card parties, etc.'" with "'the flower of the French army,
some very elegant young men'" as constant escorts. Betsy Ambler's
recollections of the winter of 1777–1778, which she and her sister
Polly spent in Winchester, Virginia, were of a piece with the Newport
girl's memories. "Here was a fine field open for a romantic girl to
exhibit in; and here I could tell you many pretty stories of sighing
swains, tender billets, love inspiring sonnets etc.," she told her sister
Nancy many years later, but reflected soberly in retrospect that "a
girl of 13 left without an advisor; of a gay and frivolous temper,
fancying herself a Woman, stands on a precipice that trembles beneath
her." When she wrote those words, of course, the mature Betsy was
thinking about the fate of her friend Rachel, who had become too
deeply involved with one of those elegant French officers at Yorktown
in 1781. Yet even so the Revolution remained in her memory not
simply as a time of trouble and disruption but also as an era of novelty
and romance.[17]

Only girls like Betsy could take such a lighthearted view of the
Revolution in the South. She herself recognized that her family's
repeated moves, which to her were exciting, had greatly "afflicted"
her mother, Rebecca Burwell Ambler. What distinguished the war in
Virginia, Georgia, and the Carolinas from that in the North was its
length and ferocious intensity. From the invasion of Georgia in 1778
to the ratification of the peace treaty in 1783, the South was the main
theater of war, and there battles were not confined to the formal
clashes between armies that had characterized the northern phase of
the conflict. A prolonged guerrilla war, coupled with sporadic non-
partisan plundering and the wanderings of the British army through

Veluti in Speculum. Courtesy of Library of Congress Prints Division. In 1779, a British cartoonist invited Americans tired of war to look at his drawing "as if in a mirror." Note the way the children echo their mother's words.

North Carolina and Virginia in 1780–1781, left much of the South devastated. David Ramsay's assessment of South Carolina can accurately be applied to the entire region: "[T]here was scarcely an inhabitant of the State, however obscure in character or remote in situation, whether he remained firm to one party or changed with the times, who did not partake of the general distress."[18]

Thus Georgians and South Carolinians universally complained of the "Banditti" who raided, pillaged, and looted through their states. "Property of every kind has been taken from its Inhabitants, their Negros, Horses & Cattle drove & carried away," declared a Georgian in 1779. That same year a South Carolinian commented that the "Havoc" caused by the robbers "is not to be described. Great Numbers of Women and Children have been left without a 2nd Shift of Clothes. The furniture which they could not carry off they wantonly broke, burnt, and destroyed." Fifteen months later Eliza Lucas Pinckney observed that "the plantations have been some quite, some nearly ruind and all with very few exceptions great sufferers[. T]heir Crops, stock, boats, Carts etc. all gone taken or destroyd and the Crops made this year must be very small by the desertion of the Negroes in planting and hoeing time." Virginia was not so seriously affected as its neighboring states to the south, but there too the distress was great in the months before the American victory at Yorktown.[19]

Eliza Wilkinson's account of her life in the South Carolina sea islands during the 1780 British invasion dramatically conveys the sense of fear and uncertainty she felt. The area was completely at the mercy of the redcoats, she noted, with "nothing but women, a few aged gentlemen, and (shame to tell) some skulking varlets" to oppose them. On one "day of terror" in early June, she recounted, a British troop accompanied by armed blacks robbed her home of clothes and jewelry, using "the most abusive language imaginable, while making as if to hew us to pieces with their swords." After the looters had left, "I trembled so with terror, that I could not support myself," she wrote two years later, recalling that she had "indulged in the most melancholy reflections. The whole world appeared to me as a theatre, where nothing was acted but cruelty, bloodshed, and oppression; where neither age nor sex escaped the horrors of injustice and violence; where the lives and property of the innocent and inoffensive were in continual danger, and the lawless power ranged at large." In the aftermath of the attack, Mrs. Wilkinson revealed, "[W]e could neither eat, drink, nor sleep in peace; for as we lay in our clothes every night, we could not enjoy the little sleep we got. . . . Our nights were wearisome and painful; our days spent in anxiety and melancholy." [20]

But what to Eliza Wilkinson and her fellow whites was a time of trouble and distress was for their slaves a period of unprecedented opportunity. The continuing presence of the British army in the South held out to black men and women alike the prospect of winning their freedom from bondage, for in an attempt to disrupt the Americans' labor supply and acquire additional manpower, British commanders offered liberty to slaves who would flock to the royal standard. No sex or age restrictions limited the offer to adult men alone, and so women fled to the redcoat encampments, often taking their children with them. [21]

The detailed plantation records kept by Thomas Jefferson and John Ball make it possible to identify the family relationships of runaways from their lands. Among the twenty-three slaves who abandoned Jefferson's Virginia holdings were ten adult women and three girls. Of the five female adults who can be traced with certainty, two left with their husbands, one of them accompanied by children as well; another fled with three of her four offspring; and the remaining two, one of whom was married, ventured forth by themselves. The fifty-three blacks who fled John Ball's plantations in 1780 included eighteen women, among them eight mothers with children, some of the latter still infants. Charlotte, a childless woman whose family connections are unknown, probably led a mass escape from Ball's Kensington quarter. She originally left the plantation on May 10, in company with Bessy and her three children, but she was soon recaptured. A week later she ran away again, this time along with (and perhaps as a guide for) what Ball termed "Pino's gang." This fifteen-member group, which escaped via Ball's flatboat, was composed of Pino, his wife, their youngest daughter, and one of their two grand-daughters; their daughter, Jewel, her husband, Dicky, and son, Little Pino; Dicky's sister, her husband, and their daughter; and Eleanor Lawrence, her husband, Brutus, and their two daughters. Although it is not clear whether Eleanor was related to the Pino clan, her sister

209

Flora had also absconded to the British, along with an infant son, two weeks previously.[22]

The impressions one receives from such fragmentary evidence — both of large numbers of female runaways and of families leaving together — are confirmed by an examination of records kept at the evacuation of New York City. Each time the British left an American port in the later years of the war, they carried large numbers of former slaves away with them, approximately ten thousand from Savannah and Charleston alone. Because the preliminary peace terms accepted in November 1782 included a clause requiring the British to return slaves to American owners, Sir Guy Carleton, the British commander, ordered the enumeration of all blacks who claimed the protection of the army. Crude biographical details were obtained from former slaves then within the lines in order to ascertain whether they should be allowed to embark with the troops for England and Nova Scotia. Blacks who had belonged to loyalists were excluded from the promise of freedom offered by the British during the war, as were any who had joined the British after November 1782. But Carleton believed himself obliged to ensure the liberty of all the others.[23]

Of the 2,863 persons whose sex is specified on the surviving embarkation lists (119 small children were not differentiated by sex), 1,211 (or 42.3 percent) were female and 1,652 (57.7 percent) were male. The substantial proportion of female runaways reflects the ease with which even a woman with children could seek freedom when the British army was encamped only a few miles from her home. Further, the analysis of the age structure of those on the New York City lists indicates that women often brought children with them into the lines. Nearly 17 percent of the refugees were nine years of age or younger, and fully 32 percent were under twenty. Slightly more than a quarter of the mature women were explicitly identified as being accompanied by children, and the addition of other likely cases brings that proportion to 40 percent. Disregarding the 96 children who had been born free in British-held territory, each mature woman who joined the royal forces had an average of 1.6 children at her side.[24]

An examination of familial relationships from the standpoint of the 605 children (503 of them nine years old or under) listed on the embarkation rolls shows that 3 percent were accompanied solely by fathers, 17 percent were with both parents, 56.2 percent with mothers alone, and 24.3 percent with other relatives, some of whom may have been parents but who are not explicitly noted as such on the occasionally incomplete records. These families included such groups as Prince Princes, aged fifty-three, his forty-year-old wife, Margaret, their twenty-year-old daughter, Elizabeth, with her "small child," and their son, Erick, who was eleven; "Jane Thompson 70 worn out wt a grand child 5 y[r] old"; and Hannah Whitten, thirty, with her five children, ages eight, seven, six, five, and one. The five-member Sawyer clan of Norfolk, Virginia, evidently used the opportunity to seek freedom with the British as a means of reuniting. Before they all ran away in 1776, the family was divided among three owners: the mother and a child in one location, two children in another, and the father in a third. In all, despite the preponderance among the refugees of young, single adults, 40 percent of the total, like the Sawyers and the others just noted, appear to have been accompanied by relatives of some kind.[25]

To arrive at New York City, the blacks listed on the British records had had to survive many dangers and hardships, not the least of which was the prevalence of epidemic diseases in the encampments to which they had fled.[26] Yet they were not entirely safe even in British-occupied Manhattan. The minutes of the joint Anglo-American board established to adjudicate claims under the peace treaty reveal liberty lost on legal technicalities important to the presiding officers but of little meaning to the blacks involved. Mercy and her three children were returned to her master because, as a resident of Westchester County, New York, she had not lived outside the British lines and so could not have come within them voluntarily to earn the protection of the freedom proclamation. Elizabeth Truant remained the property of a New Jerseyite because she had not joined the British until April 1783, after the signing of the preliminary peace terms. And, tragically, Samuel Doson, who in 1778 had kidnapped his two children from the house of their owner in order to bring them with him into New York, lost them to that same man in 1783, after he and his youngsters had already boarded a ship bound for Nova Scotia. He himself was likewise reclaimed by his loyalist master.[27]

When enslaved men and women decided whether to run away they could not see into the future and understand the full implications of British policy for their ultimate fate. But many undoubtedly heard the tales of disease in the refugee camps, and others (like some belonging to Eliza Lucas Pinckney) were undoubtedly so "attatched to their homes and the little they have there [that they] have refused to remove." Indeed, amid the chaos of war, plantation life sometimes bore little resemblance to that of peacetime. Remaining at home in a known environment, surrounded by friends and relatives, could seem an attractive alternative to an uncertain future as a refugee, especially when white owners and overseers could no longer control the situation. For her part, Mrs. Pinckney simply surrendered to the inevitable. Speaking of her slaves, she observed to her son Thomas in the spring of 1779 that "they all do now what they please every where." The blacks on Thomas's Ashepoo plantation were no less troublesome. They "pay no Attention" to the overseer's orders, he told his mother; and the pregnant women and small children were "now perfectly free & live upon the best produce of the Plantation."[28]

If black women chose to run away to the redcoats, they risked their lives and those of their children, but they gained the possibility of freedom in Canada, the United States, or even Africa as a reward.[29] If they decided to stay at home, they continued in bondage but kept all their family ties intact. It must have been a wrenching decision, regardless of which choice they made. The Revolutionary War brought blacks a full share of heartbreak and pain, even as it provided them with an unprecedented opportunity to free themselves from servitude.

II

The experiences of white women during the Revolutionary War were affected by the extent of their husbands' political activism as well as by the region in which their families lived. Wives of ardent patriots and loyalists alike were left alone for varying lengths of time while their spouses served in the army or, in the case of loyalists, took refuge behind the British lines. Although women could stay with their soldier husbands and earn their own keep by serving as army cooks, nurses, or laundresses, most did not find this an attractive alternative. Life in the military camps was hard, and army commanders, while recognizing that female laborers did essential work, tended to regard them as a hindrance rather than an asset. Only in rare cases — such as the time when the laundresses attached to General Anthony Wayne's regiment staged a strike in order to ensure that they would be adequately paid — were camp followers able to ameliorate their living and working conditions. Consequently, most women who joined the army probably did so from necessity, lacking any other means of support during their husbands' absence.[30]

At least, though, patriot women had a choice. For the most part, loyalists were not so fortunate. From the day they and their spouses revealed their loyalty to the Crown, their fate was sealed. Like other eighteenth-century women, their lives had focused on their homes, but because of their political beliefs they lost not only those homes but also most of their possessions, and they had to flee to alien lands as well. Understandably, they often had difficulty coping with their problems. Only those women who had had some experience beyond the household prior to the war were able to manage their affairs in exile in England, Canada, or the West Indies with more than a modicum of success.[31]

Female loyalists' claims petitions are particularly notable because the women frequently commented on their lack of a network of friends and relatives. The laments convey a sense of an entire familiar world that had been irretrievably lost. Many women submitted claims after the deadline, each giving a similar reason in her request for special consideration: there had been "no person to advise her how to proceed," she "was destitute of advice and Assistance," or "she had nobody to advise with & that she did not know how to do it." Even when some of a woman loyalist's friends were also exiles her situation was little better; as one southerner pointed out to the claims commission, "[T]hose Friends and Acquaintances to whom under other circumstances she could look up to for comfort and Assistance are equally involved in the Calamities which overwhelm" her.[32]

As a result, a number of the exiled women reached the same conclusion expressed privately by a southerner in 1782: "[I]t is not like Virginia, Poverty there would have been much more tolarable to us, we sincerely wish we had never left that Country." A North Carolinian who was permitted to stay in the United States despite her loyalist sympathies complained to the claims commission about the

"Humiliating" experience of having to rely on "the Charity of Friends." "I have no prospect of returning it but by my Gratitude, I am as much distressed with it as with my Misfortune." Yet she was fortunate in her access to such friends, a fact underscored by one of the most poignant letters preserved in the claims files. James Deas, a hairdresser from New York City, left his family in Scotland in 1787 while he went to London to press his claim against the British government. In November his wife, Elizabeth, wrote to him of her fear that his efforts would not be successful. "I dread this Winter much more than when you was in Goal [i.e., jail] at New York," she told him. "There I was amongst my Friends where I could work and help to maintain you. But here I am a Stranger and can get nothing to do, and no money comeing in." Every day she expected their few remaining goods to be seized as payment for debt, Mrs. Deas disclosed, "and the Children round about me wish:ng we was home again to North America. Dear Jamie," she concluded, "if you have any regard for your distressed Wife and your Dear Children do let me hear the worst of it and if you are well and what you are doing so Long in London." The news Deas must have transmitted to his wife was indeed "the worst of it": his request for government assistance was denied, and there is no further record of what happened to the family.[33]

The importance of friendship networks and a familiar environment for women left alone is further confirmed when the focus shifts from widowed loyalists to the patriots who called themselves temporary widows — those women whose husbands had joined the American army. In contrast to the distressed, disconsolate refugee loyalists, who often complained of their inability to deal effectively with their difficulties, patriot women who managed the family property in the absence of their menfolk tended to find the experience a positive one. Although they had to shoulder a myriad of new responsibilities, they did so within a well-known and fully understood context: that of their own households. Accordingly, aided by friends and relatives, they gained a new sense of confidence in themselves and their abilities as they learned to handle aspects of the family affairs that had previously fallen solely within their husbands' purview. And the men, in turn, developed a new appreciation of their wives' contributions to the family's welfare.

Numerous accounts of civilian life during the war reveal the reorientation of standard work roles that occurred as a direct consequence of wartime disruption. Women who had never previously earned money were forced to find ways of supplementing their families' incomes, especially during the period of severe inflation in the late 1770s.[34] But of greater significance was the fact that women had to undertake tasks normally performed by men. Thus, after her oldest son had died of smallpox during the 1775 Canadian invasion and two other sons had also enlisted in the army, the wife of a New Hampshire farmer — and her daughters, too — had to help with the cornhusking in the fall of 1776. That same year in Lyme, Connecticut, "so many [of the men] were gone" to the army at harvest time, a soldier's widow testified in 1836, "that she, her aged Father in Law Smith (who married her mother and was about the only man at home in their neighborhood) and such little children as could be had, dug the potatoes and husked the corn." Another Connecticut woman, Azubah Norton, similarly declared that after Burgoyne's defeat her husband, Benjamin, "was out more or less during the remainder of the war, so much so as to be unable to do anything on our farm. What was done, was done by myself."[35]

The effects of such long-term absences were especially pronounced in the South, where the war raged for the longest period. As early as 1778 William Hooper, Anne Clark's husband and a signer of the Declaration of Independence, lamented the heavy demands placed on North Carolina for troops. "A Soldier made is a farmer lost," he complained to his friend James Iredell. Husbands were being "torn from their wives and Children," fields were being "robbed of their husbandmen, our Towns of our Manufacturers." After years of what one woman described as "continuous service against the British and their more dreaded allies the Tories," southern men and their families eventually reached the end of their tether. When the Virginia government, under the leadership of Governor Thomas Jefferson, tried to muster its militia in the spring of 1781 to counter the anticipated invasion by Cornwallis's forces, it met with serious difficulties. Recruiting officers across the state reported to Jefferson on the "spirit of disquietude" among the men — not from any "Coolness in the Cause," one assured him, but rather because their families faced "inevitable Ruin" since they would be unable to plant spring crops.

Although Jefferson pointed out that "it will be vain for them to sow or plant and leave the enemy to reap," the unrest continued, and in some areas the draft was resisted "in a Roiatous manner."[36]

However reluctant they were, though, northern and southern men found it difficult to avoid service in the militia or the Continental Army. They accordingly had to leave their wives behind to take charge of their affairs for months or years at a time. Most sets of wartime correspondence that survive today come from the families of officers or congressmen — in other words, from those patriots of some wealth or prominence who also tended to experience the longest separations — but the scattered evidence available for couples of lesser standing suggests that the same process was at work in poor, middling, and well-to-do households alike. As the months and years passed, women became more expert in their handling of business matters and their husbands simultaneously more accustomed to relying on their judgment.[37]

A standard pattern emerges from the sequences of letters, some of which will shortly be examined in greater detail. Initially, the absent husband instructed his wife to depend upon male friends and relatives for advice and assistance. In 1776, for example, Edward Hand, a Pennsylvania officer, told his wife, Kitty, to have one neighbor invest money for her and to ask another to estimate the value of two horses he had sent home for sale. Women, for their part, hesitated to venture into new areas. "In some particulars I have been really puzzled how to act," a South Carolinian informed her spouse, a private soldier; and in 1777 Esther Reed, asking Joseph whether she should plant some flax, explained, "[A]s I am not famous for making good Bargains in things out of my Sphere I shall put it off as long as possible, in hopes you may be at home before it is too late."[38]

But as time went on, women learned more about the family's finances while at the same time their husbands' knowledge became increasingly outdated and remote. Accordingly, whereas men's letters early in the war were filled with specific orders, later correspondence typically contained statements like these: "I Can't give any Other Directions About Home more than what I have Done but must Leave all to your good Management" (1779); "Apply [the money] to such as you think proper" (1780); draw on a neighbor for "any Sums you may choose, for providing things necessary & comfortable for yourself

& the little Folks & Family for the approaching Season, in doing which I am sure you will use the greatest discretion" (1779). By the same token, women's letters showed their increasing familiarity with business and their willingness to act independently of their husbands' directions.[39]

The women who found it easiest to adjust to their new circumstances were those few who had previously engaged in business. Elizabeth Murray Smith Inman provides a case in point. She and her third husband, Ralph, were separated by the unexpected start of the war, for he was paying a visit to friends in Boston on April 19. With him trapped in the besieged city, Elizabeth set to work managing their farms, dismissing her anxiety "with a laugh," telling friends, "[W]e could die but once, and I was a predestinarian, therefore had no personal fear." It was consequently with astonishment and anger that she learned Ralph had panicked and intended to depart alone for London, without leaving her a power of attorney so she could act on his behalf in his absence. Is this a proper return "for the many anxious and fatigueing days I have had"? she asked him bitterly. "Believe me, Mr. Inman, I am not anxious about a mentinence [sic]," Elizabeth declared self-assuredly. "Experience has taught me, water-gruel and salt for supper and breakfast, with a bit of meat, a few greens or roots, are enough for me." Indeed, experience had taught her more than that: one of the reasons she was reluctant to leave Cambridge was the fact that she had just harvested a good crop of hay, a commodity much in demand by the rebel army, and she anticipated sizable profits. In the end, Ralph Inman did not emigrate, but his wife never forgave him for his cowardice. As one of her female friends commented, Elizabeth Murray Inman was "above the little fears and weaknesses which are the inseparable companions of most of our sex," and she had no patience with those who did not meet her high standards. Ten years later, when she wrote her will, she left Ralph only a tiny proportion of her large fortune.[40]

Another loyalist woman who had little difficulty in adjusting to her spouse's absence was Grace Growden Galloway, but for very different reasons. The unhappily married Mrs. Galloway found that she welcomed Joseph's exile. "Ye Liberty of doing as I please Makes even poverty more agreeable than any time I ever spent since I married," she wrote in her diary five months after his departure; "his Unkind treatment makes me easey Nay happy not to be with him & if he is safe I want not to be kept so like a slave as he allways Made Me in preventing every wish of my heart." As a result, she resisted his attempts to persuade her to join him and their daughter Betsy in England, partly because she wanted to try to preserve the property she had inherited from her father for Betsy, but also because she distrusted Joseph, having realized that he had mismanaged that same property. With unusual insight into her own psyche, she confided to her journal in August 1779 that her frequent tirades against the British were in fact aimed at her husband: "as his ill conduct has ruin'd me & as I cannot tell ye world I abuse the English Army for their base & treacherous conduct," she disclosed.[41]

Most women, of course, did not feel such relief when their husbands left home during the war. Quite the contrary: like a New Englander, they discovered that "every trouble however triffling I feel with double weight in your absence."[42] Nevertheless, as time passed they learned to rely increasingly on their own judgment and ability, for they had no alternative. Sally Logan Fisher provides an especially illuminating example of this process, because of the detail of her diary entries.

Thomas Fisher was among the Quakers arrested and sent into exile in Virginia by the patriots just prior to the British conquest of Philadelphia in September 1777. Then nearly eight months pregnant with her daughter Hannah, Sally at first found "this fiery triall" almost more than she could bear. Nine days after the men had been forcibly carried off, she commented, "I feel forlorn & desolate, & the World appears like a dreary Desart, almost without any visible protecting Hand to gaurd us from the ravenous Wolves & Lions that prowl about for prey." Sally became so depressed that she failed to write in her diary for several weeks, and when she resumed her daily entries in mid-October she observed, "[N]o future Days however calm & tranquil they may prove, can ever make me forget my misery at this time."[43]

Soon thereafter, though, Mrs. Fisher became too busy to be able to allow herself the luxury of debilitating depression. A long entry on November 1 reflected her changed role in its detailed attention to household financial affairs and at the same time signaled the end of her period of incapacitating despair. "I have to think & provide every thing for my Family, at a time when it is so difficult to provide anything, at almost any price, & cares of many kinds to engage my attention," she wrote revealingly. After Hannah's birth six days later Sally remarked, "[I have] been enabled to bear up thro' every triall & difficulty far beyond what I could have expected." Although in succeeding months she continued to lament Tommy's absence, her later reflections differed significantly from her first reaction to her situation. Instead of dwelling upon her despondency, Sally wrote of "the fond, the delightfull Hope" that her husband would return to love her as before. "Oh my beloved, how Ardently, how tenderly how Affectionately, I feel myself thine," she effused in February 1778, describing "the anxiety I feel for thee, the longing desire to be with thee, & the impatience I feel to tell thee I am all thy own" — but not indicating any sense of an inability to cope with problems in his absence. When Tommy returned in late April 1778, she welcomed him gladly, but she did not revert completely to her former role of ignorance about monetary matters. Her diary subsequently noted several consultations with him about household finances, a subject they had not discussed before his exile.[44]

Although Mary Bartlett, the wife of a New Hampshire congressman, left no similar record of her feelings about her husband's extended stays in Philadelphia during the war, she nevertheless subtly disclosed the fact that her role had undergone a comparable change. When Josiah Bartlett first went to Congress in the fall of 1775, he told Mary he hoped she would have "no Great trouble about my out Door affairs," and he continued to write to her about "my farming Business." In 1776 she accepted his terminology, reporting on "Your farming business," but during Josiah's second stint in Congress in 1778 that phrase became "our farming business" in her letters. No longer was the farm simply "his": she had now invested too much effort in it for that. The distinction between male and female spheres she had once accepted without question had been blurred by her own experience.[45]

Although Josiah Bartlett's persistent use of "my farm" implies that he did not recognize the way in which his wife's role had altered, other patriot men separated from their spouses for long periods revealed changing attitudes toward their womenfolk in their correspondence. The differences are especially apparent in the cases of two

219

New Englanders, William Palfrey and Timothy Pickering, because they both began with a severely limited conception of their wives' capabilities.

Palfrey was one of the very few eighteenth-century American men who showed an inclination to take a hand in household management. In the first months after he joined the Continental Army as paymaster general, he sent his wife, Susannah, detailed instructions about both domestic and outdoor affairs, attempting to exert continued control over the household despite his absence. When Susannah, tired of living in rural Marlborough, wanted to move to Boston in 1778, William not only vetoed the idea but also expressed anger that she would think of going against his wishes. "Can you suppose that I can possibly have an Interest seperate from yours?" he inquired. "My thoughts are constantly employed in consulting ways and means to promote your happiness and Welfare." William left no doubt of the fact that he expected Susannah to follow his lead obediently and to accept his assessment of what was preferable for her and the children when he told her some months later, "[Y]ou cannot possibly be a Judge" of the family's best interests.[46]

Nevertheless, wartime circumstances impinged inexorably on the Palfreys. The turning point came in June 1779, after Susannah had achieved her long-sought move to Boston. Adopting his usual practice, William designated a male proxy (his brother-in-law) to receive some money due him, but then he had second thoughts. A postscript to his letter read, "I have altered my mind & made the Bills payable to you, for fear Mr. Cole should be out of the way." By the end of the summer he was regularly using her as his financial agent, and his subsequent letters kept her well informed of his business dealings. The following fall she began to act on her own (albeit with a certain hesitancy), and William suggested that she teach their daughter Sukey to do the bookkeeping. "I am sorry you have so much trouble with my affairs," he told Susannah in October 1780, "but as Providence and an early affection has destined you to be my help meet you must assist me a little." Before William embarked on what was to be a fatal voyage to France six weeks later, he carefully informed Susannah of the arrangements he had made concerning his estate. By thus breaking with the standard pattern of keeping his wife ignorant of familial finances, William Palfrey demonstrated how much his thinking had changed over the preceding two years.[47]

Timothy Pickering, even more than Palfrey, adopted a patronizing tone in his early letters to his wife, Rebecca White. In November 1775, before their marriage, he told her he wanted to "instruct" her and went on to quote the same poem other Americans cited in discussions of children's education: "'Tis a 'Delightful task to rear the tender thought, / To teach the fair idea how to shoot.'" Like a father teaching a daughter, he encouraged her to write to him, saying, "[F]requent writing will improve your hand." Unremarkably, Pickering's condescension continued during the early years of their marriage, after he had joined the Continental Army's quartermaster corps. When he sent home a lame horse in June 1777, he told her to consult male friends "for advice and direction" in caring for it, then apologized for asking her to undertake a task that was "entirely out of [her] sphere." Even his praise contained an evident patronizing note. "Your conduct in domestic affairs gives me the highest satisfaction," he told her in July 1778, spoiling it by adding, "even if you had done wrong I could not find fault; because I know in every action you aim at the best good of our little family: and knowing this: it would be cruel and unreasonable to blame you." In other words, he was telling her she would be judged on the basis of her intentions, not her actual performance, because he feared she could not meet the higher standard.[48]

For the Pickerings matters changed in October 1780 after Rebecca acted as Timothy's agent in a complex arrangement for the repayment of a debt. "I am very glad you made me fully acquainted with it," she told him. "It is a satisfaction to me to pa[r]take of any thing that gives you Concern. I know my Dear you would make me happy in telling me any thing that had a tendency to make you so." After the successful resolution of the debt problem and her verbalization of her desire to assist him with their financial affairs, Timothy began to rely more heavily upon her. When the family rented a farm in 1782, she ably shouldered the responsibility for managing it despite her fears of "not being acquainted with farming business." Five years later, after they had moved to the frontier community of Wilkes-Barre, Pennsylvania, and Timothy's post required him to be in Philadelphia, she not only supervised the building of their new house but also oversaw the harvest, all the while nursing their newest baby. Timothy continued to apologize for the burdens he was placing on her (as well he should have), but he no longer mentioned her "sphere." Rebecca Pickering, like Mary Bartlett before her, began to speak in her letters of "our business" and "our crops." Timothy had already revealed his new attitude as early as August 1783: "This war which has so often & long seperated us, has taught me how to value you," he told her then.[49]

After months and sometimes years of controlling their own affairs, women tended to reply testily when their husbands persisted in assuming their subservience. In the summer of 1776, for instance, Sally Cobb Paine — who had been on her own since the fall of 1774 — chided her husband, Robert, for not giving her adequate directions about what she should do with some legal papers. She ignored the financial arrangements he had made for her support and informed him flatly, "[W]e have sow'd our oats as you desired had I been master I should have planted it to Corn." Finally, she decided to pursue a court case against his express wishes. "[I]f it had been Let alone till your return their [sic] would have been nothing Left for us."[50] Mrs. Paine had clearly become accustomed to making her own decisions, and if her husband gave orders contrary to her inclinations, she either ignored him or let him know that she disagreed with his judgment.

The Charleston resident Anne Hart reacted in similar fashion when her Baptist minister husband, Oliver, asked her to move to his new parish in Hopewell, New Jersey, in the summer of 1781. Oliver had left her in British-occupied South Carolina some months before, and Anne made no secret of her bitterness at being abandoned. "Such thots as these fill'd my painfull breast," she told him frankly; "Vizt — If my *once* loving Husband had not lost some of that Affection he once had for me, he Cou'd not, he wou'd not leave me Circumstanc'd as I am." Mrs. Hart, who had been operating a small school in her husband's absence, described her reluctance to leave her home and her son by her first marriage. "They tell me its duty to go," she admitted, presumably referring to those friends of Oliver's who, she recorded, had said "many keen things" to her about her failure to join him. Even so, foreseeing trouble no matter what she decided, Anne Hart continued to procrastinate, in effect declaring her own independence from her wifely responsibilities because of her emotional attachment to Charleston and her disappointment at Oliver's having deserted her.[51]

Lucy Flucker Knox did not have such a deep-seated grievance against her husband, Henry, but she found reason to complain of his excessive solicitousness. Lucy, who had been separated from her husband for much of 1775, spent the early summer of 1776 with him in New York City. She and the other wives of high-ranking American officers were then evacuated from Manhattan after General William Howe landed his troops on Long Island. The dispute between the Knoxes arose when Lucy failed to follow Henry's instructions to take refuge in Fairfield, Connecticut, and instead sought shelter in New Haven. To use his word, Henry "scolded" her repeatedly for acting on her own, implying in mid-July that she was no better than most of her sex, whom he characterized as "trifling insignificant Animals." This was too much for the sharp-tongued Lucy, who responded in kind. "You are pleased frequently in your letters to remind me of my incapacity of judging for myself — I now assure you — that I have a deep sense of my own weakness and ignorance and a very high opinion of the abilities of him — in whose eyes mine are so contemptable." Sensing that he had gone too far, Henry Knox diplomatically retreated, pronouncing himself "griev'd and vex'd" that he had ever written "severely" to his beloved Lucy.[52]

But Henry had not yet learned his lesson completely, and it took an exchange over business affairs the following year to make him fully aware of his wife's new conception of her role. In March 1777 Henry directed her to have his brother Billy sell some horses for him. Although Lucy did as she was told, she — like Sally Cobb Paine — insisted she could have done a better job. The horses had gone for only £75, she informed Henry in June, "owing to your not entrusting me with the sale of them." Asking why he did not employ her as "your future agent," she described herself proudly as "quite a woman of business." Two months later, speculating about Henry's return to civilian life after the war, Lucy voiced the expectation that the change in their relationship would be permanent. "I hope you will not consider yourself as commander in chief of your own house — but be convinced . . . that there is such a thing as equal command," she declared pointedly.[53]

A final example of women's newfound confidence in themselves and their willingness to question their husbands' judgment is contained in a 1779 outburst from Sally McKean, the wife of the chief justice of Pennsylvania. Mrs. McKean, who the following year was to take a leading role in the Philadelphia Ladies Association, was visiting relatives in Delaware when her husband, Thomas, summarily informed her that he intended to sell all his real estate and planned to buy a country estate with the proceeds. A week later Thomas wrote with the news that the only land he had sold so far was "your lot at Christiana Bridge," which he had let go for "too cheap" a price. Sally's reply has not survived, but it must have been a scorcher, for his next letter hastily assured her, "I am to get the full value of the lott at the Bridge, and more than I believe any other person will ever offer for it." Thomas pronounced himself "contented" with the deal, although, he noted, "[Y]ou appear to be otherwise." Sally evidently also complained about his unilateral decision to move them to the country, for he commented rather plaintively, "I thought you loved a Country life, but you seem now to prefer the Town — agreed; we will continue in one." Although the fault had clearly been his, he could not resist a snide remark about feminine irrationality. "The general character of the Lad[ies] is, that they are fickle, ever changing, & never satisfied," he observed smugly, "but I flattered myself you were an exception." Exception or not, when the McKeans a few months later had the opportunity to move to a different house in Philadelphia, Thomas made certain that it was Sally who made the decision, not himself.[54]

Previous colonial wars and the obligations of business, religion, or politics had occasionally separated some American couples in the nearly two centuries that preceded the Revolution. But those separations had been sporadic and isolated, the experiences of individuals rather than of an entire society. By contrast, the disruptions of the revolutionary years affected all Americans, to a greater or lesser degree. The cumulative result was the partial breakdown and reinterpretation of the gender roles that had hitherto remained unexamined.

III

"Imitate your husbands fortitude, it is as much a female, as a masculine virtue, and we stand in as much need of it to act our part properly," Eliza Lucas Pinckney instructed her daughter-in-law in 1780. The following year William Hooper proudly proclaimed that his wife, Anne, had shown "a masculine patriotism and virtue." Thomas Cushing, a Massachusetts congressman, described to his wife, Deborah, how John Dickinson, seeing the "patriotic, calm & undaunted spirit" displayed in her letters, declared that "if it was customary to choose Women into the Assembly, he should be heartily for choosing you Speaker of the House." In short, as a New Englander remarked with respect to the wives of American diplomats, both men and women came to realize that female patriots "deserve as much reputation as their husbands and posterity will thicken laurels on their monuments."[55]

The war, in other words, dissolved some of the distinctions between masculine and feminine traits. Women who would previously have risked criticism if they abandoned their "natural" feminine timidity now found themselves praised for doing just that. The line between male and female behavior, once apparently so impenetrable, became less well defined. It by no means disappeared, but requisite adjustments to wartime conditions brought a new recognition of the fact that traditional sex roles did not provide adequate guidelines for conduct under all circumstances. When Betsy Ambler Brent looked back on her youth from the perspective of 1810, she observed, "[N]ecessity taught us to use exertions which our girls of the present day know nothing of. We Were forced to industry to appear genteely, to study Manners to supply the place of Education, and to endeavor by amiable and agreeable conduct to make amends for the loss of fortune."[56]

The realization that they had been equally affected by the war led some women to expect equal treatment thereafter and, on occasion, to apply to their own circumstances the general principles promulgated by the revolutionaries. "I have Don as much to Carrey on the warr as meney that Sett Now at ye healm of goverment & No Notice taken of me," complained the New Jersey widow Rachel Wells as she protested to the Continental Congress in 1786 about a technicality that deprived her of interest payments on the money she had invested in state bonds during the war. "If she did not fight She throw in all her mite which bought ye Sogers food & Clothing & Let them have Blankets," she explained, asking only for the "justice"due her. "Others gits their Intrust & why then a poor old widow be put of[f]?" Mrs. Wells asked. "Now gentelmen is this Liberty?"[57]

Mary Willing Byrd's social standing was much higher than that of Rachel Wells, but she advanced a similar argument when she contended in 1781 that Virginia had treated her unfairly. She claimed the right to redress of grievances "as a female, as the parent of eight children, as a virtuous citizen, as a friend to my Country, and as a person, who never violated the laws of her Country." Byrd's recital of her qualifications was peculiarly feminine in its attention to her sex and her role as a parent (no man would have included such items on a list describing himself), but it was also sexless in its references to her patriotism and her character as a "virtuous citizen." In developing the implications of the latter term, Byrd arrived at her most important point. "I have paid my taxes and have not been Personally, or Virtually represented," she observed. "My property is taken from me and I have no redress."[58]

The echoes of revolutionary ideology were deliberate. Mary Byrd wanted the men she addressed to think about the issue of her status as a woman, and she adopted the revolutionaries' own language in order to make her point. The same tactic was employed by Abigail Adams in her most famous exchange with her husband.

In March 1776, after admonishing John to "Remember the Ladies" and to offer them legal protection from "the unlimited power" of their husbands, Abigail issued a warning in terms that John must have found exceedingly familiar. "If perticular care and attention is not paid to the Laidies," Abigail declared, "we are determined to foment a Rebelion, and will not hold ourselves bound by any Laws in which we have no voice, or Representation."[59] On one level, she was speaking tongue-in-cheek; she did not mean her husband to take the threat seriously. Yet she chose to make a significant observation about women's inferior legal status by putting a standard argument to new use and by applying to the position of women striking phraseology previously employed only in the male world of politics. Like

226

Mary Willing Byrd, Abigail Adams thus demonstrated an unusual sensitivity to the possible egalitarian resonances of revolutionary ideology and showed an awareness of implications that seem to have escaped the notice of American men.

In 1782, Mrs. Adams once again directed her attention to the role of women in the American polity. This time she made no semihumorous comments but instead considered seriously the ramifications of her sex's inferior status. "Patriotism in the female Sex is the most disinterested of all virtues," she contended, because women are "excluded from honours and from offices." Their property is controlled by their husbands, "to whom the Laws have given a sovereign Authority," and they are "deprived of a voice in Legislation, obliged to submit to those Laws which are imposed upon [them]." No levity softened the sincerity of the point she made for the second time. To Abigail, the fact that women demonstrated "patriotick virtue" despite being discriminated against validated their claims to "heroick" stature.[60]

Yet was that sufficient? If John Adams and the other leaders of the Revolution rejected — as they did — the few hesitant complaints women raised about their status, what role were women to play in the republican United States? The war had disrupted normal patterns of existence; afterward, new issues had to be faced. Would familial relationships fully revert to traditional patterns? Would the ideology of woman's place and feminine inferiority persist intact into the postwar world? Or would women find in the republic the sociopolitical role they had not had in the colonies? The answers to those questions emerged in the last decades of the century, and they are the subject of the last two chapters.

Chapter Eight

§

A REVERENCE OF SELF

THE POSTWAR PERIOD WITNESSED ACCELERATING CHANGES IN AMER-ican white women's lives, for their wartime experiences and the developing ideology of republicanism combined to alter both society's view of them and their own self-conceptions. Women who had competently managed the family estates during the Revolution despite severe hardships no longer accepted unquestioningly the standard belief in feminine weakness, delicacy, and incapacity. Their daughters, who had watched their mothers cope independently with a variety of difficulties, felt no pressing compulsion to marry quickly; some decided not to marry at all and others chose to limit the size of their families. And republican theorists, concerned about the future of the nation, invested new meaning in the traditional cliché that women were the source of virtue in a society. Since they thought that republics depended for their survival upon a virtuous citizenry, Americans in the 1780s and 1790s necessarily focused their attention upon women to an unprecedented extent. In short, in the wake of the war both men and women in America began to rethink the hitherto unchallenged negative characterizations of woman's nature and role.[1]

Moreover, although in the postwar decades many families persisted in following the patriarchal patterns outlined in chapters 1–3, some households altered their practices, displaying more nearly egalitarian marital relationships, willingness to relinquish the parental veto over children's selection of marital partners, and less authoritarian approaches to child rearing in general. The old ways were by no means entirely displaced, but increasing numbers of American families no longer conformed to the previously dominant patriarchal style.

I

In 1790, when Thomas Jefferson informed a French acquaintance about his older daughter Patsy's wedding to Thomas Mann Randolph, the young man who would have been his "own first choice" for her, he explained, "[A]ccording to the usage of my country, I scrupulously suppressed my wishes, that my daughter might indulge her own sentiments freely." With Jefferson's history of manipulative fatherhood, one wonders if he did indeed "scrupulously" avoid giving Patsy his opinion of the match, but his statement nevertheless illustrates the attitude of republican parents toward their children's marriages. Eschewing even the right of veto they had formerly claimed, some American parents in the postwar period allowed their offspring complete freedom of choice as to marital partners. "In a matter of such importance," a New Englander declared in 1784, a young woman "ought to be left intirely to herself." [2]

Accordingly, the Virginian John Page told his daughter Alice's impoverished suitor, Augustine Smith, that "she is capable of judging for herself" when the young man fearfully asked for Alice's hand in marriage while simultaneously admitting that he would have difficulty supporting her in the style to which she was accustomed. So, too, the Philadelphian Elizabeth Meredith chronicled her daughter Mary's rejection of a prominent suitor she herself favored with the words, "I am determin'd to avoid any influence in persuading her to place her affections where she has objections." Mrs. Meredith's puzzled reference to the girl's "rather inexplicable . . . Love Matters" revealed her belief that the response to a courtship was wholly Mary's affair.

229

"What she intends to do with herself I know not," Elizabeth observed in bewilderment in 1795.[3]

Parents' readiness to grant their daughters greater freedom in the selection of a spouse found acceptance in republican prescriptive literature. "Were the ladies left to choose for themselves, I am satisfied they would, generally speaking, make better choices, than are generally made for them," asserted "A. B." in the *American Museum* in 1791. "It is she, and not you," A. B. warned mothers, "that must spend her days with the man that she marries." The following year Judith Sargent Murray, the forthright Gloucester, Massachusetts, woman who contributed to the *Massachusetts Magazine* under the title of "The Gleaner," confronted her fictional ideal parents, Mr. and Mrs. Vigilius, with the dilemma of having their beloved foster daughter, Margaretta Melworth, fall in love with a man they knew to be a fortune hunter. The worried couple selected the proper republican solution to their problem, refusing to exercise a veto. "We were determined, if we could not bend her to our wishes, to follow her through all the vicissitudes her unfortunate preference might involve," Mr. Vigilius explained. "We abhorred constraint, and we regarded persuasion . . . as no better than a specious form of tyranny."[4]

Children consequently began to expect the right to decide for themselves in marital matters if they so desired. Many girls, of course, continued to seek their parents' and friends' assessments of potential spouses. Yet when Anna Rawle wanted to marry John Clifford in 1783, she simply informed her mother of her plans, asking her opinion only about the timing of the wedding, and then she rejected even that limited advice. Three years later an English visitor commented that Anna had "a reputation for wearing the breeches" in the Clifford household, but added that she and her husband "are esteemed by some the Superior Male and Female for understanding in the city." Another Philadelphia couple that won the plaudits of visitors was Elizabeth Willing and Samuel Powel. According to the Marquis de Chastellux, they lived in a condition of "perfect equality . . . as two friends, unusually well matched in understanding, taste, and knowledge."[5] In such descriptions as these one can identify relationships openly at variance with older sensibilities. That the Cliffords, Powels,

and other northern couples were not alone in exploring marital egalitarianism can be demonstrated by an analysis of the correspondence
of the Virginian John Coalter and his first two wives.

Coalter, St. George Tucker's legal protégé and the tutor of Tucker's
children by his marriage to Frances Bland Randolph, had fallen in
love with Maria Rind, an orphaned dependent in the Tucker household in Williamsburg. Maria had no money, and John had very little:
that was the barrier that impeded their marriage for over a year. In
his letters from Staunton, where he was trying to establish a legal
practice, John repeatedly urged his fiancée to have "*patience*" and
soulfully lamented the "cruel Poverty" that separated them. In the
1760s, any girl would have replied in kind, waiting resignedly for her
loved one to take the initiative. Not so Maria Rind in 1791. "Let
your Maria go and Share with you at once the poverty you have so
long painted to me," she told him in May, observing that she would
find it not poverty but riches to acquire a family of parents and
siblings. Declaring her willingness "to take in any work that she can
get to do in Staunton," she reminded him that he had seen her
"toiling night & Day for four years" and asserted that she would not
be worth marrying if she was not prepared to endure necessary hardships. Maria aggressively exerted pressure on her fiancé throughout
the summer of 1791, arguing persuasively, "[P]eople . . . as poor as
we are being Mar[r]ied every week down here," and assuring him
that she realized that they could not "expect to begin the World
without a grate number of Difficulties." At last her campaign succeeded, and John agreed to a fall wedding. Thus ended a courtship
notable for its new display of feminine independence. Regrettably,
Maria Rind died in childbirth within a year.[6]

Obviously, little evidence remains to reveal her marital relationship
with John, but in all likelihood Maria would have agreed with the
"marriage articles" outlined for him by her close friend Margaret
Davenport, who was her successor as Mrs. Coalter. In May 1795,
after criticizing a Mr. P. who "rules [his home] with the most arbitrary sway," Margaret decided to tell John how he might "best please
and make me happy." Even if she had gone no further, Margaret
Coalter had already broken strikingly with the tradition that made it
the wife's unilateral duty to please her husband. By merely suggesting

231

that John should try to fulfill her wishes, Margaret had deserted the standard adhered to by Elizabeth Foote Washington, Sally Logan Fisher, and others of her older contemporaries.

Margaret Coalter's requirements for a husband centered on her desire to be treated with respect, as an equal and as a partner. "I do not always require a *lover's* attention," she informed him realistically. Above all, she sought open and candid communication: if she did something of which he disapproved, he should tell her so immediately, not "brood over it in *silent* dissatisfaction." If she "put a serious question" to him, "never answer me carelessly as if what I asked was a matter of no consequence[.] Give me a *decisive* reply if in yr power, if not, 'tell me the reason why.'" Margaret, in other words, asked John never to condescend to her in the manner common to husbands earlier in the century. She viewed herself, her needs and opinions, as matters of consequence, and she insisted upon John's acknowledgment of her importance.[7]

One of the ways in which the new egalitarianism evident in Margaret Coalter's letters manifested itself in other marriages was through the cooperation of husband and wife in the prevention of pregnancy. White colonial Americans frequently lamented the debilitation women suffered as a result of repeated pregnancies, yet prior to the 1780s few couples appear to have employed contraceptive methods regularly. Their failure to do so did not stem from ignorance, for they were well aware of at least one means of preventing birth: prolonged nursing of a previous child. But as long as women remained subordinate within the home, they had little say in the determination of their childbearing futures, and men who were accustomed to wielding autocratic domestic authority had no reason to accede to their wives' desire to bear fewer children. Many mothers undoubtedly agreed with the New Orleans resident Mary Morgan, who wrote in 1779, after she had borne four children (two of whom had died), "I hope I shall have no more for indeed I get very weakly with nursing and bearing Children," but few husbands responded to such wishes before the 1780s. The increasing use of contraception in the last two decades of the century, then, can be seen as a reflection of women's improved status within marriage.[8]

The earliest reference to the collaboration of husband and wife in this manner comes from Esther Atlee in 1778. Her husband had invited her along on a short trip, a suggestion she greeted with enthusiasm. In her response she outlined the arrangements she had made for the care of their "troublesome little folks" during her absence, but, she added, "our little het [the baby she was then nursing] must go where I go, as the leaving her behind might be a means of more trouble." Esther's openness on the subject indicated that she and her husband had discussed it previously. Eight years later another exchange between spouses alluded to a similar mutual decision to avoid pregnancy if possible. In 1786, Theodore Sedgwick wrote his wife, Pamela, from New York that he was sorry to learn she was still nursing their son, not only because he thought it was detrimental to her health, but also because he believed that "a certain reason why he was not earlier weaned ceased when I came from home."[9]

Additional commentaries on the contraceptive effects of lactation were contained in maternal advice to daughters who had just given birth. Consoling her thirty-nine-year-old daughter, Sally Downing, who had just borne a sixth child, Elizabeth Drinker in 1799 told her "that this might possiably be the last trial of this sort, if she could suckle her baby for 2 years to come, as she had several times done heretofore." The fact that Sally had already employed this means of contraception "several times" identified her as a true daughter of her mother. As a young wife, Elizabeth Drinker had borne five children in less than eight years, nursing them for the standard year to eighteen months each. But that fifth child (born in 1769) she nursed for more than two years, successfully postponing a sixth pregnancy until 1773, and she subsequently followed the same procedure with her last two babies. Her diary gives no hint of whether Henry Drinker participated in the decision to limit her fertility. But in later years many other women deliberately selected a similar course of action, presumably with the acquiescence of their husbands. "According to my old principle," Margaret Izard Manigault told a married daughter in 1809, "I think it less fatiguing to the constitution to nurse this one, then to bring forth another. This is not generally taken into consideration as the natural consequence of weaning."[10]

Whether prolonged lactation or the use of other methods of contraception (such as the "certain small contrivances," probably syringes, sold in Philadelphia in the 1790s) was the cause, reduced family size was the result. In studies of Hingham, Massachusetts, and middle colony Quaker families, respectively, Daniel Scott Smith and Robert V. Wells have each observed a decline in fertility in the late eighteenth century. Among the New Englanders, Smith found that women whose childbearing years ended before 1765 had the largest family sizes, whereas women marrying after 1780 and particularly after 1800 exhibited significantly reduced marital fertility. Wells's evidence, too, locates a dramatic drop in family size at the end of the century. Although approximately 40 percent of the Quaker women who married before 1770 bore nine or more children, less than 14 percent of the women who married after that date experienced as many births. Even more striking, nearly 12 percent of the wives whose weddings occurred after 1790 had no children at all.[11]

If recourse to family limitation suggests a somewhat more egalitarian approach to marriage than was prevalent in prerevolutionary years, so do postwar patterns of divorce. Nancy Cott's study of Massachusetts records has demonstrated that increasing numbers of people, including notably larger proportions of women, sought legal separations from their spouses after 1764. She attributes the change to women's rising expectations about marriage and to their new willingness to assert themselves in the event of dissatisfaction. An examination of Connecticut divorce petitions has revealed a comparable pattern in that state. There, too, the revolutionary period was marked by more numerous requests for divorce (although not by an increased percentage of female applicants), with petitions rising from an average of fewer than fourteen annually prior to 1774 to a peak of forty-five in 1795.[12] Although such limited analyses cannot be deemed conclusive evidence of a general trend throughout the United States, when they are considered in conjunction with the attitudes Americans expressed privately and with the new tone evident in prescriptive literature on marriage, they imply that in the aftermath of the Revolution, American families began to abandon their hierarchical character.

If one word could be said to epitomize the republican conception of matrimony, that word would be "mutual." Judith Sargent Murray employed it repeatedly in her discussions of marriage in *The Gleaner*. "Mutual esteem, mutual friendship, mutual confidence, *begirt about by mutual forbearance"* was how Mr. Vigilius described the ideal "matrimonial career" to Margaretta just prior to her wedding. The same phraseology characterized other authors' comments on the topic. "Wherein does the happiness of the married state consist?" one writer in the *Gentleman and Lady's Town and Country Magazine* asked himself in 1784. His reply: "In a mutual affection, a similarity of tempers, a reciprocal endeavour to please, and an invariable aim to each other's comfort." [13] Indicative of the new approach was the fact that marital advice was no longer directed almost solely at the wife. Instead, men were instructed to treat their wives as "reasonable creatures" or were given homilies on the "Character of a Good Husband." A few essayists carried the reciprocal emphasis so far that they failed to designate their audience by sex, addressing both members of a couple simultaneously. "Where there is a necessary union of persons, of cares and of interests, there a union of hearts and affections is indispensable," declared "The Philanthropist" in 1790; "this shows that the exercise of judgment and deliberation is requisite to matrimonial and domestick happiness." [14]

Of course, the traditional attitude toward marriage did not disappear overnight. The same magazines that printed these articles calling for mutuality and reciprocity in matrimony also published essays advocating female subordination and male dominance in marital relationships, evidently without recognizing or ascribing significance to the inherent contradiction. [15] But more important than the persistence of older ideas was the development of such new ones as those expressed by a female "Matrimonial Republican" in the *Lady's Magazine* for July 1792. "I object to the word 'obey' in the marriage-service," she began, "because it is a general word, without limitations or definition." By making such a promise, a woman became, in effect, her husband's *"slave."* "The obedience between man and wife, I conceive, is, or ought to be mutual," she contended. "Marriage ought never to be considered as a contract between a superior and an inferior, but a reciprocal union of interest, an implied partnership of interests, where all differences are accommodated by conference; and where the decision admits of no retrospect." [16]

The same egalitarian spirit that prompted the shift in matrimonial relationships also had an impact upon American child-rearing practices. In 1788, the elderly congressman Paine Wingate of New Hampshire encountered the new style during a working sojourn in New York City, then the capital of the United States. In separate letters to his adult daughters, Wingate described his displeasure at seeing "parents & children . . . as familiar as brothers & sisters." "Fathers, mothers, sons & daughters, young & old, all mix together, & talk & joke alike so that you cannot discover any distinction made or any respect shewn to one more than to another. I am not for keeping up a great distance between Parents & Children," he concluded, "but there is a difference between staring & stark mad."[17]

Such unprecedented familiarity was accompanied by a new attitude toward parental instruction. William Palfrey early epitomized this approach when he suggested to his wife, Susannah, in 1777 that she persuade their son Billy to stop eating green fruit "by Reason and Argument." She "should represent to him the ill Effect it has upon his Health, at the Expence of which he ought never to indulge his appetite." The theory behind Palfrey's advice was also that which informed Mary Smith Cranch's method of raising her own Billy. In 1783 she reminded him, "[Y]ou was treated like a rational creature" from an early age. "When any thing was demanded of you the reason was given why it ought to be done." Precisely this procedure was recommended by "A Friend to Family Government" in the *American Museum* in 1791. Parents should regard their youngsters as "beings possessed of some degree of reason," he asserted; adults had "no right to act the part of tyrants towards their children," because "the imbecility of youth and infancy does not take away their natural rights." A Philadelphia woman who believed that parents should not be tyrannical even took it upon herself to address an anonymous letter to a despotic father. Accusing him of having established a "*domestic bastille,*" she predicted that his "misplaced rigor" would cause his daughters to marry badly simply in order to escape his authority. "Constraint is an oppression at which every independent mind revolts," she declared, summoning up images of the revolutionary struggle in an attempt to make her point and justify her intrusion into another family's affairs.[18]

An integral part of the emphasis on the rational governance of children was a stress on teaching them by example rather than by

Judith Sargent Stevens (Murray), by John Singleton Copley, c. 1770. Private Collection, New York. Courtesy of Frick Art Reference Library.

precept alone. Earlier authors had urged parents to instill piety in their offspring by exhibiting that quality themselves, but they had carried the point no further. In the 1780s and 1790s, by contrast, adults were admonished to pay close attention to all aspects of their secular behavior, for, as the schoolmaster Augustine Smith declared, "[T]he force of example is, confessedly, superior to every other mode of instruction." After listening to several homilies on the subject in the women's meeting, Sally Logan Fisher vowed in 1790, "[M]y dear Children may I be enabled to set you an example, that is worthy in any small degree for you to follow." Pamela Foster assured her father in 1802, "I will try to imitate the virtues of my Parents"; she was, in effect, informing him that he and his wife had been successful in their adoption of republican child-rearing techniques.[19]

One can thus discern a host of new elements in American familial relationships in the 1780s and 1790s. Not all households were affected by the egalitarian trend, to be sure; many white families continued to be organized along traditional lines. But the changes were most evident among younger people, in families formed after the mid-1770s. Dwight and Rebecca Foster, who raised their daughter Pamela to imitate their virtues, were married in the early 1780s; Timothy Pickering, who came to depend heavily on his wife, Rebecca, and who maintained a deep interest in the rearing of his children, married in 1775; Anna Rawle and John Clifford, Maria Rind and John Coalter, Margaret Izard and Gabriel Manigault, Pamela Dwight and Theodore Sedgwick all courted and married during the postwar years. These were the couples who took as their watchword the mutual obligations of which Judith Sargent Murray wrote so compellingly.

Murray herself, born in 1751, married first to a sea captain in 1769, widowed in 1786, and remarried two years later to John Murray, the founder of Universalism in America, was an appropriate commentator upon the new modes of family life. Although her first published essay did not appear until 1784 and the bulk of her work was printed after 1792, she later declared that the American Revolution had initially stimulated her to consider systematically the status of women, child-rearing methods, and marital relationships. In the 1780s and 1790s, Murray was the chief theorist of republican womanhood, and her work will be discussed in detail in the pages that follow.[20]

II

In the years after the war American women grew increasingly willing to challenge the conventional wisdom about feminine faults. Whereas in the 1760s and early 1770s criticisms of women's "natural" tendencies and failings had for the most part gone unanswered, during and after the Revolution women were less inclined to allow such remarks to pass without comment. They noted appropriate counterarguments in their diaries and letters and responded publicly when republican magazines published essays they deemed offensive. Their reactions took two forms: a charge that men were equally guilty of the error in question or a contention that the detrimental quality women supposedly possessed had positive attributes.

Both approaches were utilized when female curiosity was at issue. In 1778, Debby Norris adopted the first when she remarked that "the sons of Adam, have full as much curiosity in their composition, as any of the daughters of good Mother Eve." Judith Sargent Murray, writing as Constantia in the *Massachusetts Magazine* in 1794, chose the second tack. Curiosity, which "is said to predominate in a superior degree in the female bosom," is regarded as a "reprehensible excrescence," yet had humans been "wholly incurious, . . . in what profound ignorance would mankind have been wrapped," she noted. Curiosity was, after all, "the origin of every mental acquisition. Let then curiosity, *female curiosity*, cease to be considered a term of reproach," she concluded triumphantly, "and let the levellers of female abilities, take more certain aim at that worth, which they essay to prostrate."[21]

Few contended that vanity could be a praiseworthy characteristic, but many were quick to observe that men, too, fell prey to its allures. "The men have often endeavoured to prove that this folly or vice is most common among the females yet daily observation & chat with both sexes will prove to the contrary," a Massachusetts girl told a close friend in 1808. "Were the *Vanity* of both sexes weighed in a scale of justice the balance of the males would be so much in favour of them that the female part of the world would be bankrupts at once." Essayists commonly asserted that feminine vanity could be traced ultimately to male flatterers, and therefore that men were more culpable than women. "Let *them* once resume their wisdom, and the dignity of the female character will again be rememb[e]red; let *them* cease to *mislead* our *judgments*, and *impose* on our *senses*, and we shall be found as *we were originally intended by heaven*, the companions the friends of your sex," the writer who signed herself "Amelia" argued in 1779.[22]

A key part of the reassessment of standard clichés was women's new willingness to challenge the sexual double standard. Those who did so, in public and in private, made two points: first, that it was unfair for women to bear all the opprobrium connected with illicit sexual activities, since men were equally involved; and second, that other women, instead of condemning erring members of their sex, should sympathize with and assist them. In her "Sentiments on Libertinism," published in the *Boston Magazine* in 1784, "Daphne" advanced both these arguments. "Women are said to be the weaker vessel," she observed, "yet is the uprightness and rectitude of angels expected from them." A single mistake would "forever deprive them of all that renders life valuable," but at the same time "the base betrayer is suffered to triumph in the success of his unmanly arts, and to pass unpunished even by a frown." The idea that vice is "less odious" in a man is "nothing but an unjust custom," Daphne asserted. Women, she declared, must "stand by and support the dignity of our own sex," for although men claim to admire and respect women, they "take more pains to debase, or at least detract from our honour and right, than to guard or exalt either." Daphne accordingly told her "sister Americans" that they had to protect each other's reputations by refusing to gossip, and she called upon them to ostracize seducers, a tactic also recommended by other commentators.[23]

In this atmosphere of questioning the old ways, women also started to dispute, in tentative fashion, perhaps the most basic assumption of all: the idea that marriage was every woman's destiny. Nothing had happened to expand the limited economic opportunities open to single women in America, yet in the 1780s and 1790s girls began to speak of "the honourable appellation of *old maid*" and to comment that "it is a situation that may be supported with great dignity." "It is not marriage or celibacy, gives merit or demerit to a person," declared Anne Emlen, "but a life ordered in the fear of The Lord." Others gave a more secular cast to their words, though the message was the same. "I Beleve we are as well of[f] as a grate many that is marred," said a Massachusetts woman of herself and her two sisters. "Thare is none without thar trobles as I Se Marred or not married." [24]

In part, the new attitude toward spinsterhood reflected the changing sex ratio in the United States. As early as 1790, women outnumbered men in parts of New England, giving rise to frequent complaints about the scarcity of beaux. But the hypothesis that positive descriptions of the single life represented nothing more than a reaction to demographic change is belied by the fact that identical sentiments were expressed by young women in regions with a more favorable sex ratio. "It is much better to remain single than to be badly matched," asserted a South Carolinian, who remarked on a visit to Pennsylvania, "I know no other reason why so many accomplished girls should be getting old maids except the young men are not worthy of them. . . . The young ladies are like ours very willing to be old maids." [25]

In the last years of the century, then, a number of young women chose deliberately to postpone or forgo matrimony. "I keep my name still," Pamela Dwight Sedgwick's close friend Betsy Mayhew informed her resolutely in 1782. "I think it a good one and am determined not to chang[e] it without a prospect of some great Advantage." Betsy, to whom Pamela attributed a "Love of Independence," eventually married, but only very late in life. A never-wed contemporary of hers was Elizabeth Parker, of Perth Amboy, New Jersey, termed a "sensible and engaging," even "very superior" woman by her acquaintances, who reportedly had "many offers" of marriage but refused them all. In 1808, when she was forty-three years old, Elizabeth lamented the marriage of another spinster. "I heard with concern the other day of one of the sisterhood's falling off," she commented. "She was a sister who promised to be a rising member, an upright vestal who had seen her seventh lustre and demeaned herself with strict propriety." But, unfortunately, she had fallen in love with an actor, "to the utter dismay of her fraternity." [26]

These individual decisions noticeably affected general demographic trends. In their separate studies of Massachusetts and Quaker families, Daniel Scott Smith and Robert V. Wells have noted that the proportion of never-married women in the population increased significantly during the postwar decades. Thus in 1800 the forthright Maine girl Eliza Southgate was speaking for the other female members of her generation when she declared, "I do not esteem marriage absolutely essential to happiness." The way she phrased a subsequent question forecast her answer: "[W]hich is the most despicable — she who marries a man she scarcely thinks *well* of — to avoid the reputation of an old maid — or she, who with more delicacy, than marry one she could not highly esteem, preferred to live single all her life?" Eliza proudly numbered herself among those who would remain unmarried, "if I never find one I can love."[27]

A poem published in the *Massachusetts Magazine* in 1794 suggests in its striking imagery the revolutionary origins of women's motives for not marrying.

> *No ties shall perplex me, no fetters shall bind,*
> *That innocent freedom that dwells in my mind.*
> *At liberty's spring such draughts I've imbib'd,*
> *That I hate all the doctrines by wedlock prescrib'd,*

its author proclaimed, terming herself a "republic," who "abhors . . . tyrannical systems and modes" and "[i]nquires why women consent to be tools, / And calmly conform to such rigorous rules." And so, she concluded, "[R]ound freedom's fair standard I've rallied and paid, / A Vow of allegiance to die an old maid."[28]

The fact that this poet drew such an extended analogy between herself and the American republic is itself significant, demonstrating once again the extent to which women had adopted political rhetoric as a commonplace of their existence. But the analogy also highlights the connection between republican ideology and the conception of femininity that developed after the Revolution. Women's autonomous approach to courtship, marriage, and spinsterhood in the 1780s and 1790s found its rationale in the republicanism that also formed the basis for the new American government. The innovative style of white Americans' private lives was given full blessing by republican theory.

III

"Virtue, Virtue alone . . . is the basis of a republic," declared Benjamin Rush in 1778, expressing the consensus among his compatriots. Indeed, the revolutionaries' one unassailable assumption was that the United States could survive only if its citizens displayed virtue in both public and private life. Virtue must be not only "the national characteristic" but also "the regulator of the conduct of each individual" in the republic, a Harvard student asserted in 1785; "to be destitute of virtue, is to cease to be a citizen." By their adherence to strict moral standards, then, American households ensured the preservation of the whole. Conversely, if too many families strayed from the practice of what David Ramsay termed "industry, frugality, temperance, moderation, and the whole lovely train of republican virtues," the nation itself would be placed in jeopardy.[29]

This train of thought had significant implications for the status of women in the American republic. The domestic realm, which had hitherto been regarded as peripheral to public welfare, now acquired major importance. With the new stress on the household as the source of virtue and stability in government, attention necessarily focused on women, the traditional directors of household activities. The transition was startling in its swiftness and intensity. Before the war, females had been viewed as having little connection with the public sphere. In private, perhaps, they might influence their husbands' or suitors' conduct, but such actions had no general social or political relevance. In the 1780s and 1790s, by contrast, numerous authors proclaimed the importance of America's female citizens. At times it even seemed as though republican theorists believed that the fate of the republic rested squarely, perhaps solely, upon the shoulders of its womenfolk.

Such a belief stemmed in part from the traditional link between women and virtue, which had a long history in European thought. Over the preceding century, prescriptive writers had frequently asserted that men would be virtuous only if women were, that the morals of the female members of a society automatically determined the morals of their male counterparts. If women were vice-ridden, so, too, would men be; but if women adhered to high standards of behavior, they would cause men to adopt similar standards. Nothing could have been more clichéd than this line of argument, but in a republican context such commonplace ideas took on novel resonance. Because the nation would not survive unless its citizens were virtuous, and man's virtue was traditionally linked to woman's, it then followed

243

that feminine influence would play a special role in the United States.[30]

As a result, American magazines of the period were filled with essays exploring "The Happy Influence of Female Society" or "The Advantages to be Derived by Young Men from the Society of Virtuous Women." "We shall always be, what women please to make us," "W. J." insisted in 1784. "It is in their power to give either a good or a bad turn to society, and to make men take whatever shape they think proper to impose." Alphonzo's "Address to the Ladies" made the same point four years later. "You have not only an interest in being good for your *own* sakes," he told his female readers, "but *society* is interested in your goodness — you polish our manners — correct our vices — and inspire our hearts with a love of virtue."[31]

This stress on the need for women to behave virtuously helped to generate the extraordinary amount of attention devoted to the issue of feminine dress in the postwar years. Women's clothing had long been an object of satire, but the theme was infused with new meaning in the republic, for ostentatious female dress appeared to be a visible manifestation of private vice and luxury. Once, women had been warned against frivolous fashions simply because such styles did damage to their reputations; in the 1780s and 1790s, on the other hand, they were told that their extravagance raised questions about the continued independence and survival of the nation.[32]

Well-to-do women who had endured years of deprivation had understandably reacted to the war's end by eagerly adopting the latest European fashions, and they mercilessly criticized those who failed to conform to the new standards of dress.[33] Prior to the Revolution, such inordinate concern with clothing and hairstyles would have prompted only some wry comments about feminine vanity. But during the postwar years the subject was fraught with too much significance to dismiss so easily. In 1790, Elizabeth Graeme Fergusson assumed the guise of a bemused Chinese observer of strange American customs in order to suggest that the United States could not be truly independent as long as its women continued to allow female Britons to set standards of taste. The same theme was developed by other authors as well. "A fundamental mistake of the Americans has been, that they considered the revolution as completed, when it was but just begun," asserted an essayist in the *American Museum* in 1789.

Since the United States was still "totally dependent in manners, which are the basis of government," its independence was a mere facade. To achieve autonomy the Americans had to alter their "principles and manners," which were the responsibilities of the ladies. American women should "exercise the right of their sex, and say, 'we will give the laws of fashion to our own nation, instead of receiving them from another; we will perform our part of the revolution.'" In other words, he declared, they should return to the homespun simplicity of earlier times.[34]

Some women responded to these appeals in the spirit of their predecessors, the Daughters of Liberty of the 1760s. In November 1786 more than one hundred female residents of Hartford formed a "Patriotic and Economical Association," promising to dress "in the plainest manner; and encourage industry, frugality, and neatness" while their husbands were devising "other, and more extensive, plans of policy" to reform the nation's political structure. The parallelism of their approach should be underscored. They saw their efforts as complementary to their husbands', believing that the "strict attention to domestic economy and frugality" they advocated would assist in "effecting the same desirable purpose" their menfolk sought in politics. The Hartford women thereby demonstrated their awareness of the connection between public and private spheres in the new republic, envisaging themselves as active contributors to the public welfare through their domestic roles.[35]

Men, too, recognized that women acting in a domestic capacity could have a beneficial effect upon the republic. In 1790, James Tilton, the president of the Delaware Society of the Cincinnati (an organization of former Revolutionary War officers), indicated as much in a July Fourth oration. "The men possess the more ostensible powers of making and executing the laws," he declared; but "the women, in every free country, have an absolute control of manners: and it is confessed, that in a republic, manners are of equal importance with laws." Such a statement — giving women an equal, if different, role in preserving public well-being — was unprecedented in America. Just as significantly, Tilton went on to stress the other crucial component of the republican view of women: their maternal function. "From the most savage to the most enlightened people," he asserted ahistorically, "the female parent is considered of greatest importance

245

to their descendants, by stamping their manners and sentiments in the early periods of childhood and youth."[36] When coupled with a simultaneous reevaluation of housewifery, the emphasis on motherhood was to lead to a broad reassessment of women's status in the United States.

In the forefront of the new approach to women were the many short-lived magazines published in the early years of the republic. Such self-styled arbiters of literary taste as Matthew Carey, editor of the *Columbian Magazine*; Noah Webster, of the *American Magazine*; or Hugh Henry Brackenridge, of the *United States Magazine*, explicitly addressed their journals to women as well as to men, acknowledging the presence of a female readership not only in formal statements of purpose but also in their selection of articles. When *The Christian's, Scholar's, and Farmer's Magazine* began publication in 1789, its editors noted, "[C]onscious we are of the dignity, importance, and merit of the fair daughters of our country; and, with chearfulness, we shall devote some portion of this work to their peculiar advantage and amusement." The preface to the *Lady and Gentleman's Pocket Magazine of Literature and Polite Amusement* disclosed a similar aim in 1796. "Persons of discernment perceive nothing of higher importance to a nation, than the Education, the Habits, and the Amusements of the Fair Sex," the publisher remarked, explaining that "to distinguish works offered in part to the Fair, by making them trifling and insignificant, however sanctioned by custom, would, in our opinion, at this period, be inexcusable."[37]

Consequently, editors rejected articles that contained "undeserved satire upon the *Fair*" or that constituted "a Libel on the Sex." "S. L's piece we have received," the *Lady's Magazine* noted in 1792, "but must assure him that, while he employs his pen in no other manner than in degrading ideas of female learning, he will be viewed by us as an object of contempt." At the same time, editors appear to have sought pieces that lauded women's accomplishments. Along with the ubiquitous sentimental fiction and prescriptive literature, they printed innumerable admiring biographies of great women. Both the *Massachusetts Magazine* and the *Columbian Magazine* published David Ramsay's lavish paean of praise to the patriotism of South Carolina women during the Revolution, and the *American Museum* reported upon the wartime exploits of Deborah Sampson Gannett, the Massachusetts woman who had disguised herself as a man in order to enlist in the rebel army.[38]

The pages of these journals constituted the single most important public forum for the voicing of radical opinions on women's status and role. There male and female authors alike addressed directly the same issues that confronted them privately in their daily lives. There they began to go beyond the traditional view, which judged women's importance by the influence they exerted upon adult men, and started to see them more as actors in their own right — as expert domestic managers, as mothers, even as independent individuals.

Certainly Judith Sargent Murray's ideal republican woman fitted that mold. She was an active, equal participant in family life, efficiently directing household affairs and concerning herself with raising her children. In the "well ordered" family whose characteristics Murray described at length, "the various duties of humanity are punctually discharged, and the hours of leisure are uniformly devoted to the cultivation of the minds of those children, whom they design . . . as useful and ornamental members of the *community*." Murray consistently referred to parents (in the plural) and particularly stressed the role of the mother.[39] Her break with the past conventions of child-rearing literature was not unique, for other republican theorists, too, focused their attention on mothers and invested the maternal function with political and social significance.

For example, "Sidney's" list of "Maxims for Republics," first printed in 1779 and republished eight years later, included among its aphorisms the assertion that "it is of the utmost importance, that the women should be well instructed in the principles of liberty in a republic. Some of the first patriots of antient times, were formed by their mothers." Republican magazines printed stories entitled, "The Good Mother — an American Tale," and poems like "Stanzas, Addressed to the Ladies, on Maternal Duty." In the introduction to his course of law lectures, delivered to a sexually mixed audience in 1790, the distinguished attorney James Wilson even felt compelled to discuss the maternal role, under circumstances that had never before seemed to call for commentary on women. In 1796, John Adams appropriately explained to his daughter Nabby, then a matron of thirty, "[T]here is a youth, I mean a young generation, coming up in America. . . . You, my dear daughter, will be responsible for a great share of the duty and opportunity of educating a rising family, from whom much will be expected."[40]

The message was umistakable. Women had a major influence upon their children, and they should use that influence to imbue their youngsters with principles of morality and patriotism. As Sarah Pierce, the founder of a female academy in Litchfield, Connecticut, told her pupils, despite the fact that few females were "called to act a conspicuous part on the grand Theatre of life, . . . [their] influence in the community is notwithstanding of immense importance" because only mothers could "plant the seeds of vice or virtue" in their offspring. Eliza Southgate, who was educated at Susanna Rowson's academy in Medford, Massachusetts, learned the identical lesson from her instructors. "The first rudiments of education are always received from them [mothers]," she wrote in her journal in 1802; "at that early period of life . . . the mind is open to every new impression and ready to receive the seeds which must form the future principles of the character. At that time how important is it to be judicious in your conduct towards them!"[41]

The stress upon women's ability to inspire their children with patriotic sentiments helped to lead to a significant shift in emphasis in familial relationships. In the republican context, mothers' influence on their sons was highlighted, and the traditional mother-daughter relationship receded into the background. For the first time, women began to assume a didactic function with respect to their older male children, self-consciously instructing them to prepare for a future of service to the republic. "In our happy America, every Station of Dignity & eminence may be looked up to by any of her citizens," Deborah Logan informed her son Albanus in 1803, expressing the hope that he and his brother would be *fitted for Public Men.*" Likewise, when the South Carolinian John Gibbes entered Princeton in 1783, his mother, Sarah, wanted him to become, she emphasized, not only "a credit to your Family; but also an honor to your Country; that you may when yr Country calls in the hour of exigency rise up in her behalf."[42] Such messages as these, which pervade women's letters to their sons in the postwar decades, demonstrate that the stress on republican motherhood in the published literature was matched by women's private commitments to the identical ideal.

The Reverend Enos Hitchcock of Rhode Island codified the new theories in his *Memoirs of the Bloomsgrove Family*, published in Boston in 1790. As an imitation of Rousseau, the book was an artistic failure, but as an epitome of American thinking on maternity and child rearing it was a resounding success. Elizabeth Willing Powel attested to the fact that Hitchcock had accurately summarized contemporary enlightened opinion when she thanked him for sending her a copy of his book and agreed with him that "upon the Mother the first Impressions chiefly, if not intirely, depend." Commending Hitchcock for being "highly sensible of the important Duties assigned for her [the mother] by the Author of our Existence," she returned the compliment by sending him a copy of Benjamin Rush's recently published *Thoughts upon Female Education*, which, as shall be seen in chapter 9, advocated improvements in the education then available to girls.[43]

That the positive reevaluation of the maternal role had a major impact on women's self-assessments was demonstrated by the remarkable essay "On the Supposed Superiority of the Masculine Understanding," written by "A Lady," which appeared in the *Columbian Magazine* in July 1791. Men, the author argued, assumed they were superior to women, resting their claim "on the vain presumption of their being assigned the most important duties of life." Yet, she contended, God had clearly given the preference to females, because it was to them He had "assigned the care of making the first impressions on the infant minds of the whole human race, a trust of more importance than the government of provinces, and the marshalling of armies." Women, to be sure, could not compare to men in bodily strength, but, she wrote, "this may be chiefly attributed to the exercise permitted and encouraged in their youth; but forbidden to us." Accusing men of attempting to keep women in a submissive, subordinate position, she proclaimed forcefully, "Let them withdraw their injuries, and we shall easily spare their protection."[44]

Female Americans who, like this "Lady," sought to improve the status of their sex in the postwar decades did not wish to abandon their specifically feminine character. Quite the contrary: their claims rested in large part on a newly positive view of their domestic and maternal roles. Even so, they wanted their sphere to achieve equality with man's. "I will never consent to have our sex considered in an inferiour point of light," Abigail Adams told her sister Elizabeth Smith Peabody in 1799. "Let each planet shine in their own orbit. God and nature designd it so — if man is Lord, woman is *Lordess* — that is what I contend for." Adams's younger New England contemporary Mary Van Schalkwyck concurred. "Not to discuss a long-disputed point, the natural equality of man and woman, education alone is calculated to give a decided superiority of strength to the former," she told a male correspondent in 1803, yet to another friend the following year she also emphasized that "the woman who rightly understands her interest, will indeed cultivate her mind as highly as possible, . . . but she will not forget she is still *woman*, that the duties prescribed her by the God of Nature, are essentially different from those of *man*." [45]

Eliza Southgate adopted the same approach, stressing woman's intellectual equality while recognizing differences in gender roles. "I never was of opinion that the pursuits of the sexes ought to be the same," she assured a male cousin in 1801. "I have ever thought it necessary that each should have a separate sphere of action." Nevertheless, she insisted, "to cultivate the qualities with which we are endowed can never be called infringing the prerogatives of man. . . . Do you suppose the mind of woman the only work of God that was 'made in vain'?" [46]

At this point, almost all the republican commentators on the status and role of women stopped — with the upgrading of the feminine sphere to a position of equality, with an emphasis on women's equal intellectual ability, with a recognition of the political and social contributions made by women even when they acted in a private capacity, with an appreciation of the importance of motherhood. None of the orthodox republican thinkers formally challenged the basic assumption that woman's destiny was to marry and bear children, and that girls should be trained solely for that goal. They continued to view women largely within the context of household and family. Accordingly, when 1792 witnessed the publication of a book that insisted upon seeing women as individuals — even if they were still to be primarily wives and mothers — their immediate reaction was overwhelmingly negative.

IV

A Vindication of the Rights of Woman, written by the English radical Mary Wollstonecraft, was widely read in America and almost as widely criticized. Wollstonecraft said little that was not already being said by the more outspoken republican women, but her forceful, unvarnished prose and disreputable personal life — she twice became pregnant out of wedlock — combined to make it practically mandatory for American women to formally reject her ideas. "Upon the whole her life is the best comment on her writings," declared Eliza Southgate in 1801, since "should any one adopt her principles, they would conduct [themselves] in the same manner." That same year Alice DeLanccy Izard informed her daughter Margaret Manigault that she was reading the book aloud to her husband, Ralph, or rather, she said, "as much of it as I could read, for I was often obliged to stop, & pass over, & frequently to cough & stammer etc. He is as much disgusted with the book as I am," Alice revealed, "& calls the Author a vulgar, impudent Hussy."[47]

Yet after offering this negative opinion, Mrs. Izard explained that her disagreement with Wollstonecraft lay not in the Englishwoman's promotion of sexual equality but instead in her apparent denigration of femininity. "It is not by being educated with Boys, or imitating the manners of Men that we shall become more worthy beings," Alice told Margaret. "The great author of Nature has stamped a different character on each sex, that character ought to be cultivated in a distinct manner to make each equally useful, & equally amiable." Other female Americans likewise modified the requisite criticism of Wollstonecraft. Eliza Southgate softened her condemnation by admitting the English author had "said many things of which I cannot but approve. . . . Prejudice set aside, I confess I admire many of her sentiments," and Elizabeth Sandwith Drinker remarked, "[I]n very many of her sentiments, she, as some of our friends say, *speaks my mind*."[48] Similarly attracted by the force of Wollstonecraft's arguments were Elizabeth Graeme Fergusson, Abigail Adams (whose husband termed her a "Disciple of Wolstoncraft" in 1794), Elizabeth Willing Powel, and even such a conventional housewife as Mary Orne Tucker, who in 1802 called the English radical "our Great champion."[49]

In 1803, Mary Van Schalkwyck summed up the common attitude. Wollstonecraft was "held in general abhorrence," and Van Schalkwyck "detest[ed]" some of the maligned Englishwoman's ideas; nevertheless, she observed, "I do not think she has been, by her writings, more injurious to her sex, than those good people have, who, so long, have impressed themselves and us with the belief that we were meant as the mere baubles of an hour, neither capable of being the companion and friend of man, nor the instructress and guide of youth." She favorably contrasted the "dignity and energy" of Wollstonecraft to "all that class of writers, who degrade Woman to infancy, and allow her scarcely any real virtue, except *Humility*."[50]

In Judith Sargent Murray in particular, Mary Wollstonecraft found a sympathetic audience. The Gloucester woman wanted to establish a base upon which a new type of American woman could stand, and she — like Wollstonecraft — clearly understood that the only way to accomplish a break with the past was to reform women's education.

Murray began to develop this theme in her 1779 essay "On the Equality of the Sexes," which was not published until 1790. She compared male and female mental abilities in four areas: imagination, in which women were superior; memory, in which they were equal to men; and reason and judgment, in which they were inferior — but only because of their inadequate training. "We can only reason from what we know," she argued, "and if an opportunity of acquiring knowledge hath been denied us, the inferiority of our sex cannot fairly be deduced from thence." No one would contend that a little boy had better judgment than his sister, yet as they grow up "the one is taught to aspire, and the other is early confined and limited." No wonder, then, that as adults they displayed such different capacities. If girls had the same educational opportunities as boys, they too could develop their rational faculties. Moreover, since "every requisite in female economy is easily attained," and domestic skills "require no further *mental attention*" once learned, mature women would have the time for reflection "worthy of rational beings" if the proper foundation had been laid in their youth.[51]

The foundation Murray had in mind went beyond factual knowledge. Her "Desultory Thoughts upon the Utility of Encouraging a Degree of Self-Complacency, Especially in Female Bosoms," which appeared in the *Gentleman and Lady's Town and Country Magazine* in

Frontispiece, Lady's Magazine, *vol. 1, no. 1, 1792. Library of Congress Rare Books Division. The frontispiece of the first issue of the* Lady's Magazine, *Philadelphia, reflects the impact of Mary Wollstonecraft.*

1784, stressed that an ideal education should "teach young minds to aspire." Girls should be assured that "every thing in the compass of mortality, was placed within their grasp." From her earliest days, a daughter should be addressed as a "rational being," for a girl who did not learn to value herself would likely "throw herself away" on the first man who proposed to her. Summing up her plan for the education of a daughter, Murray declared, "I would early impress under proper regulations, a reverence of self; I would endeavour to rear to worth, and a consciousness thereof: I would be solicitous to inspire the glow of virtue, with that elevation of soul, that dignity, which is ever attendant upon self-approbation, arising from the genuine source of innate rectitude."[52]

By the time she composed the "Gleaner" series for the *Massachusetts Magazine* in the early 1790s, Murray's thinking had advanced still further. Instead of resting her case for investing girls with self-confidence on their need to make an intelligent choice of a marital partner, she stressed rather the preparation for their own independent future. Rejecting the notion — put forward by Enos Hitchcock, among others — that a girl's early life should be aimed at one object, "an establishment by marriage," she argued that to daughters "marriage should not be presented as their *sumum bonum*, or as a certain, or even necessary event; they should learn to respect a single life, and even regard it as the *most eligible*, except a warm, mutual and judicious attachment had gained the ascendancy in the bosom." Young women, she asserted, should be "qualified to administer by their *own efforts to their own wants*"; "independence should be placed within their grasp." In a passage striking for its contrast to traditional linguistic usage, Murray defined her goal for women. If proper methods of female education were adopted, "the term, *helpless widow*, might be rendered as unfrequent and inapplicable as that of *helpless widower*."[53]

Yet for all her iconoclasm Murray recognized that most women would marry and have children, and so she also stressed the importance of better education in preparing girls for their traditional roles. In this she was like both Wollstonecraft — who made the proper training of "affectionate wives and rational mothers" one of her most important themes — and more conservative writers, who visualized improved female education primarily as a means of producing pliable women who could make their husbands "virtuous and happy" and could "instruct their sons in the principles of liberty and government."[54] All the reformers agreed, in other words, that the key to creating — or, more accurately, to perpetuating — the republican woman of late eighteenth-century America lay in changing the course of female education. Thus one must look to the many female academies founded in the latter years of the century in order to discover the enduring effects of the revolutionary redefinition of woman's place.

Chapter Nine

ᵹ

VINDICATING THE EQUALITY
OF FEMALE INTELLECT

Pʀɪoʀ ᴛᴏ ᴛʜᴇ ʀᴇᴠoʟᴜᴛɪoɴ, ᴀᴍᴇʀɪᴄᴀɴs ʜᴀᴅ ᴘᴀɪᴅ ʟɪᴛᴛʟᴇ ᴀᴛᴛᴇɴᴛɪoɴ to the formal education of women. If a girl knew the rudiments of learning, that was thought to be more than sufficient for her limited needs. The education of all colonial children was haphazard at best, depending upon local and familial circumstances, but even less care was taken with girls than with boys.[1] In the new republic, by contrast, the importance of female education was repeatedly emphasized. The Americans' vision of the ideal woman — an independent thinker and patriot, a virtuous wife, competent household manager, and knowledgeable mother — required formal instruction in a way that the earlier paragon, the notable housewife, did not. Moreover, Americans' wartime experiences convinced them that women needed broader training to prepare them for unforeseen contingencies.

These motives combined to lead to widespread changes in the education of white American girls during the postwar decades. Public education at the elementary level was opened to female as well as male children, and private academies founded in the 1780s and 1790s greatly expanded the curriculum previously offered to girls. Whereas their mothers, if they were fortunate, had had advanced training only in such ornamental accomplishments as music, dancing, French, and fancy needlework, republican girls from middling and well-to-do families could attend schools at which they were taught grammar, rhetoric, history, geography, mathematics, and some of the natural sciences. These women composed the first generation of educated female Americans; among them were teachers, missionaries, authors, and the early leaders of such nineteenth-century reform movements as abolitionism and women's rights.

I

The education of American children began at home. In addition to teaching youngsters behavior and manners, literate parents or older siblings instructed them in basic reading and writing. The firstborn children in any family were usually taught by their mother or perhaps by another resident adult. Later-born children often, though not always, learned the rudiments from their siblings. In neither case was the instruction entirely satisfactory; those who were cast in the role of teacher frequently complained of their inadequacies. Thus, for example, Nelly Custis Lewis remarked in 1806 that she was "not well calculated for an instructress" and that she did not know the best method of teaching her daughter to read and write. But Mrs. Lewis and other parents had no alternatives: even such primary schools as existed (both public and private) would not admit pupils who did not already know the basics.[2]

Mary Palmer Tyler's account of the educational history of her family illustrates the changes that would occur in instructional patterns over the course of a family's life cycle. Mary herself was taught to read by an unmarried aunt, but her mother heard her recite lessons in later years. When she and her sister Betsy were teenagers, they did the housework so their mother could instruct the smaller children. But Sophia, the baby of the family, was born while the senior Palmers were "so harassed with trials and afflictions they could not train their little ones as they wished to," so Mary and Betsy undertook to instruct her. Yet Mary revealed, "[W]e . . . had not been properly taught ourselves," and their efforts were not very successful. Eventually, the cycle began again after Mary's wedding to Royall Tyler, for her younger sister Amelia came to live with her in order to teach the Tyler youngsters to read.[3]

In some households instruction began very early. At the age of twenty-two months Charles Cotesworth Pinckney, Eliza's son, could "tell all his letters in any book without hesitation and begins to spell." The farm wife Sarah Snell Bryant taught her sons Austin and Cullen to read when they were only two. Austin, who was born in April 1793, "began to read in words of two syllables" in early February 1796 and started the Bible only six weeks later. Before his third birthday, he had "read Genesis through," and by the time he was four he had completed both Old and New Testaments. Cullen, in turn, knew his alphabet at the age of sixteen months. Yet other parents were less certain that encouraging such precocity was wise. A Georgian informed her husband in 1784 that she did not plan to begin teaching their three-year-old son to read for another year. "Many sensible people will tell you," she wrote, "'tis not right to stuff a child with learning before his mind has had time to expand." And as an adult Charles Cotesworth Pinckney urged friends not to follow his parents' example, declaring that the elder Pinckneys' "over anxiety to make him a clever fellow" had nearly been ruinous.[4]

Reading was taught first, then writing. Whereas the children of literate households generally knew how to read by the time they were five or six, instruction in writing did not begin until they had reached at least seven or eight. Thus, when Philip Vickers Fithian became the tutor of Robert Carter's children in 1773, he discovered that the seven-year-old was learning to spell, the ten-year-old was reading, and the thirteen-year-old was starting to write. But all three were female, and Carter may well have wanted his sons to acquire literacy skills somewhat sooner. In any event, five years later Carter himself began to teach his youngest son to write when the boy was only six and a half.[5]

In rare instances black children learned to read and write. Both Eliza Lucas Pinckney and Elizabeth Foote Washington instructed some of their slaves in the rudiments of literacy. Thomas Jefferson's house servant Hannah, a member of the large Hubbard clan, could write with some facility, although it is not clear how she acquired that skill. But when in the 1760s Dr. Bray's Associates, an English missionary organization, attempted to open schools in Virginia and North Carolina for the instruction of black children, especially girls, they met with both indifference and resistance from the children's masters and mistresses. One discouraged emissary of the group reported in 1767 that he could attract no more than eight or nine pupils to a school he had planned for a minimum of fifteen. "I had agreed with the Mistress to teach the girls to Sew, knit and Mark, thinking that wou'd excite people to send young negroe girls, but I find they wou'd rather their Slaves shou'd remain Ignorant as brutes," he explained to his superiors in London.[6]

As an alternative or supplement to home education, white children who lived in towns or cities could be sent to dame schools. Such schools, as was noted in chapter 4, were usually established by women who needed a means of support. Few instructors were as well qualified as Sarah Osborn, who had briefly attended a female academy in England before her parents emigrated to the colonies. In fact, many of the so-called schools seem to have been little more than baby-sitting establishments. Certainly some mothers used them that way: a Nova Scotian explained, for instance, that she sent her young son to school "merely that he may be kept from Mischief, for he has no idea of learning as yet." Similarly, Mary and Betsy Palmer first attended dame school on a day when company was coming to dinner and their mother wanted them out of the house. A Virginian who attended such an establishment in Norfolk in the 1750s described her teacher, "a poor old dame by the name of Mrs. Drudge, and, to be sure, she did drudge to teach me my letters — spelling and reading after a fashion."[7]

A girl in prerevolutionary America could progress beyond these bare rudiments only through some combination of her own initiative, the inclination of her parents, and the proximity of one of the "adventure schools" that, before the 1780s, constituted the sole means through which girls could gain access to advanced training. Boys could attend private or public grammar schools and eventually colleges like Harvard, Yale, William and Mary, or Princeton, but their sisters' formal education was effectively halted at the primary level. Like dame schools, adventure schools catering to girls were usually run by women or perhaps by married couples. Located in the homes of the instructors, they were short-lived, with no staff other than the owners, and their course of study stressed ornamental accomplishments. By the 1760s, adventure schools teaching music, dancing, drawing and painting, fancy needlework, and handicrafts flourished in every colonial city along with other similar establishments offering some instruction in advanced writing, grammar, and arithmetic. But as late as 1782 a New Englander complained about Boston: "[W]e don't pretend to teach ye female part of ye town anything more than dancing, or a little music perhaps. . . . I will venture to say that a lady is a rarity among us who can write a page of commonplace sentiment, the words being well spelt, & ye style & language kept up with purity & elegance." [8]

One of the best known of these schools, and perhaps the one with the most rigorous curriculum, was that founded in Philadelphia by Anthony Benezet. First established in 1754, it continued for some years under his direction. Among Benezet's pupils was Elizabeth Sandwith Drinker, whose diary entries in the 1780s and 1790s recalling her school days testify to his lasting impact on his students. But Benezet's school was clearly anomalous, even in forward-looking Philadelphia. More common were the several establishments like those attended by the Philadelphian Sally Powel between 1759 and 1766. The accounts for her education detail outlays for crewel work, "fraims Glasses, & Matirials for wax Work & painting," a French language teacher, prints to be copied with "several sorts of paint Gum & Brushes," and a "Master for Learning Artificial Fruits." [9]

Girls would often attend a number of such establishments simultaneously. In 1771–1772, for example, the Bostonian Anna Winslow went to one school for sewing and another for writing. Elizabeth Murray, who herself had taught needlework, sent her niece Dolly to separate schools for sewing, dancing, writing, reading, and fancywork. "I tried her to sew att home," Elizabeth told Dolly's father in 1756, "but people coming out & in so much to the shop took her of[f] so much she made nothing of it." During the winter Dolly received instruction only in reading and sewing, for, Elizabeth explained, "she cannot attend so many schools in the cold wether to advantage." The chance for even such a limited education as this was denied to northern farm girls, though, for the schools rarely made provisions for boarding their pupils. Only wealthy or middling urban residents could attend them. [10]

In the plantation South the pattern differed considerably, since well-to-do girls were taught by tutors hired chiefly for their brothers, and poor girls had no instructors other than members of their own families. The Carter sisters, pupils of Philip Fithian, learned basic reading, writing, and arithmetic from him while their brothers were being taught advanced grammar, Latin, and Greek. Fithian's attempts to keep his female charges at their studies were continually frustrated by frequent interruptions for music lessons, dancing schools, and visits to neighbors with their mother. Both the Carters and their daughters, in other words, saw academic instruction as less important to the girls than training in ornamental skills. Judging by wealthy southerners' lack of attention to their daughters' advancement in learning — as distinct from domestic accomplishments and musical training — southern girls were even less likely to receive an advanced education than were their northern counterparts.[11]

A notable exception was Eliza Lucas, whose father sent her to school in England because he believed that a stress on education in needlework alone left girls' minds "vacant and uninformed." Eliza early established a habit of reading voraciously in French as well as English, and just before her marriage to Charles Pinckney she thanked her father "[for] the pains and mony you laid out in my Education which I esteem a more valuable fortune then any you could now have given me." The contrast to John Hunt, a Harvard graduate, could not have been sharper. According to his granddaughter Mary Palmer Tyler, Hunt adhered "tenaciously" to the principle that boys should go to college, "but girls knew quite enough if they could make a shirt and a pudding." Mary further recalled that her grandmother Hunt "often lectured me and others on our waste of time because we would read while tending baby brothers and sisters," for she thought they should be sewing instead. Thus Mary's mother, Betsy Hunt, had to be educated largely by her husband, Joseph Palmer, who systematically introduced her to literature, history, geography, and arithmetic, as well as overseeing her practice in writing. Betsy's sister Catharine was not so fortunate: because she never learned to write, she was unable to respond when an infatuated suitor began to court her by mail.[12]

Since most colonial parents resembled the Hunts rather than George Lucas, much depended on a girl's own initiative. Accounts of prominent women who reached adulthood before the Revolution uniformly stress their precocity and love of learning. Sarah Franklin Bache insisted on studying French, although her mother "had no desire of her larning that Language." Ann Eliza Bleecker, the poet from upstate New York, was so "passionately fond of books" as a child that she had already read many "long before the time that children in common pass their Spelling-Books." Elizabeth Graeme Fergusson, according to her admirer Benjamin Rush, "discovered, in early life, signs of uncommon talents and virtues." And Harriott Pinckney Horry, whose mother Eliza had early noted and "indulge[d]" her fondness for learning, studied Latin as a girl, in later years teaching herself algebra and geometry by using textbooks borrowed from her younger brother.[13]

Women with less initiative keenly felt their lack of education when they reached adulthood. For the most part, their distress centered upon their inability to spell, write, and "indite" (compose) letters properly. In the eighteenth century the ability to write a good letter was the mark of an educated person. "To be greatly deficient in this matter is almost inexcusable in one of our Sex" who has any social standing, Eliza Lucas Pinckney once explained. Consequently, colonial women referred repeatedly in their letters to their shame at their lack of writing skills. Those who had reached maturity by the middle years of the century, and who had therefore been educated much earlier, were especially sensitive on the subject. "Pray excuse my bat riting and inditing," wrote Abiah Franklin, mother of Jane and Benjamin, in 1751. Thirteen years later Joseph Reed's embarrassed grandmother told him, "I have but one ours warning to rite this in and you will i am sur mack alowins for the shortnis of time and bad riting and wors spalling." The next generation of female Americans labored under the same handicap, and a number of them confessed to being "very avers" to writing. "Nothing would have induced me to set pen to paper but righting to so Dear a friend who I know will Excuse all Erors in righting & Endighing," said Deborah Cushing of Massachusetts to her husband in 1774.[14]

For such women, writing even a "few lins" was "a great undertaken," as a Virginian told a male relative in 1801. "The employment of the pen is of all others the most fatiguing to me," the elderly New Yorker Joyce Myers disclosed to her daughter Rebecca Mordecai, as she explained why she did not write more frequently. A common lament of these older women was the fact that they had had little writing practice in girlhood. Consequently, they repeatedly urged their younger female relatives to improve their handwriting. "Tho I write a bad hand yours shou'd be better," Grace Galloway informed her daughter Betsy in 1780; five years later Abigail Adams acknowledged the deficiencies of her own untutored writing, then revealed to a niece, "[I]t is from feeling the disadvantages of it myself, that I am the more solicitous that my young acquaintance should excel me." [15]

Mrs. Adams's keen sense of deprivation led her to criticize the "trifling narrow contracted Education of the Females" in America during her wartime correspondence with her husband. "If you complain of neglect of Education in sons, What shall I say with regard to daughters?" she asked him rhetorically in 1776. Yet it was to John's protégé John Thaxter that Abigail Adams spoke most vehemently on the subject. It is "mortifying," she told him in early 1778, to see "the difference of Education between the male and female Sex, even in those families where Education is attended too." Perhaps, she hypothesized darkly, men sought to deprive their "companions and associates" of schooling because of "an ungenerous jealo[u]sy of rivals near the Throne." [16]

Apart from Mrs. Adams's letters, there is little evidence that American women before the 1780s perceived their lack of educational opportunity as a circumstance that called for a societal remedy. By failing to complain about the poor instruction they received in other than personal terms, female colonists demonstrated how restricted were their self-conceptions and aspirations. The very idea that their access to education could (or should) be improved was so alien that it never occurred to them. They may have decried their rudimentary literacy, but few of them took the further step of suggesting that the situation could be corrected. [17] Only during the postwar years did American women begin to argue systematically that members of their sex should be better educated.

II

Reformers seeking to improve female education in the United States during the 1780s and 1790s had to confront a major problem: the traditional argument that excessive learning would "unsex" women.

Since it was commonly contended that men and women had different natures, corresponding to their divergent roles in life, most persons believed that woman's intellect, though equal to man's, had quite different qualities. "Nature appears to have formed the faculties of your sex for the most part with less vigour than those of ours," the Reverend James Fordyce told his female readers, pointing out women's "defect in point of depth and force," a failing offset by their "sentiment" and "uncommon penetration in what relates to characters." He recommended that women concentrate on "refined" rather than "profound" subjects, and that they avoid studies irrelevant to the "milder modes of life." The Reverend John Bennet, another popular English author, revealed the reason why females should shun such topics as "politics, philosophy, mathematics, or metaphysics": "They would render you unwomanly indeed. They would damp that vivacity, and destroy that disengaged ease and softness, which are the very essence of your graces." [18]

An improper education, in short, could threaten woman's sexual identity itself. So Dr. Bennet suggested, "[L]et your knowledge be feminine, as well as your person," and Alphonzo, the American essayist, proclaimed in 1788, "[T]o be *lovely* then you must be content to be *women*; to be mild, social and sentimental — to be acquainted with all that belongs to your department — and leave the masculine virtues, and the profound researches of study to the province of the other sex." Neither Bennet nor Alphonzo proposed to deny all education to women; quite the contrary, Alphonzo wrote, "[L]earning or an acquaintance with books may be a very agreeable . . . accomplishment" in a woman. The difficulty was caused when a female tried to go beyond the knowledge appropriate to her sex, for then she risked becoming that universal object of ridicule and reproach, a "learned lady," a "female pedant." An American poet put it this way: if women felt advanced learning's "strict embrace,"

> *Farewell to ev'ry winning grace;*
> *Farewell to ev'ry pleasing art,*
> *That binds in chains the yielding heart; . . .*
> *At her approach the roses fade,*
> *Each charm forsakes th' astonish'd maid;*

And o'er her face, of sickly pale,
Thought slowly draws its loathsome veil.[19]

The educational reformers had to find an effective means of countering such conservative arguments. They fervently believed that the United States had to improve the academic training available to its female citizens, for the survival of the republic required it, yet traditional attitudes seemed to place an insurmountable barrier in their path. In order to circumvent the conventional objections to advanced education for women, then, the reformers developed three separate but intertwined arguments. The first insisted that education would not "unsex" women but would instead make them better wives, mothers, and mistresses of households. The second stressed the "feminine" nature of the instruction proposed for girls by carefully delineating the curriculum and emphasizing the cultivation of proper behavior. Neither of these first two contentions challenged the traditional ends of female education, but the third, which was based upon the novel circumstances of the republic, turned the requirements of republican citizenship into a justification for changing educational goals. In the hands of the conservative Benjamin Rush, the latter tack led to an emphasis on a strictly utilitarian course of study; in the hands of the more radical Judith Sargent Murray, it implied a sharp break with the past and an attempt to give women an education truly comparable to men's.

Eliza Southgate adopted the first approach in 1801, when a male cousin berated her for advocating improved academic training for women. "You ask if this plan of education will render one a more dutiful child, a more affectionate wife, etc, etc, surely it will," she asserted. "A sense of duty, and a mind sufficiently strengthened not to yield implicitly to every impulse, will give a degree of uniformity, of stability to the female character, which it evidently at present does not possess." Abigail Adams, too, found this argument persuasive. "It is very certain, that a well-informed woman, conscious of her nature and dignity, is more capable of performing the relative duties of life, and of engaging and retaining the affections of a man of understanding, than one whose intellectual endowments rise not above the common level," she declared in 1814.[20]

But simple assertions that a broader education for girls would not create the despised "learned ladies" were obviously insufficient to convince the doubtful, and so, paradoxically, the reformers stressed the need to restrict female education at the same time they were arguing for its expansion. By emphasizing the behavioral goals they sought, they downplayed the importance of purely intellectual accomplishments, and by devising their curriculum solely on the basis of its utility for future wives and mothers, they eliminated its more threatening aspects.

Thus Noah Webster, for instance, defined a good education as that which "renders the ladies correct in their manners, respectable in their families, and agreeable in society," making no mention of fostering their intellectual development. A woman's "real merit," he declared, lay in her "domestic worth." Other republican authors echoed the same themes. In 1793, a contributor to the *Lady's Magazine* proclaimed, "[L]et them be taught that domestic usefulness is before modern refinement, and that to manage a family with economy, is far beyond touching a harpsichord." It was not that women should be trained only in domestic occupations, for that was the stance the reformers rejected; rather, the goals of female education were viewed as behavioral and utilitarian instead of intellectual or ornamental. "Lavinia" made this clear in an essay printed in Caleb Bingham's *American Preceptor*. No woman should pursue a subject to the point at which it would "interrupt or supersede domestic employments," she observed, "for these require attention in a greater or less degree from every woman; and unless she understand and discharge them according to her circumstances, she is contemptible and useless." [21]

The dilemma confronting these educators is nowhere more fully apparent than in the Reverend Penuel Bowen's "Upon Virtue in general, and female Education & manners in particular," the address he delivered on November 26, 1786, as he opened his "English Academy for young Ladies & Misses" in Savannah, Georgia. The New England cleric stressed the equality of the sexes, while still pointing out that woman has "her proper station, & her part to act; partly common w[i]th man, & partly peculiar to herself." He went on to discuss female virtue in great detail, embarking upon a series of complex philosophical digressions that must have mystified his audience of prospective pupils and their parents. At least Bowen's conclusion was unambiguous: "[T]he great polar object of female education" was "to nurture & fix the principles of virtue; the Virtues especially proper to the sex: such as are best calculated to render you most accomplished for your department in life."

No goal could have been more traditional, but Bowen, like other reformers, proposed to achieve his end by improving the curriculum. He accordingly told his students, "[Y]our ideas should not be compressed, or shut up within a small circle or particular place, but so open & expanded to comprehend more general & generous sentiments & opinions." Nevertheless, he observed, "[T]o become *much* learned is not an essential requisite in a female. The professions are not proper to the sex, it is not looked for in you to be doctresses, teachers of the arts & sciences, politicks or laws." Yet Bowen had the honesty to admit, "[I]t strikes me as wrongly timeing & placing *here*, anything against Books & reading," because if there was a problem with female learning in America, particularly in the South, it was a "deficiency" rather than a "superabundance." After such intricate waffling, Bowen ultimately resolved his confusion conventionally, by arguing that girls should receive a basic, practical education which attended to their moral development as well as to their academic achievement.[22]

Penuel Bowen's contradictory statements starkly exposed the conceptual problems that lay behind the more conservative reformers' position on female education. They understood that the instruction of girls had to be improved, that keeping the female population in ignorance of higher learning could no longer be justified, yet on the other hand they did not want to change the end product. The better-educated woman was to resemble her ideal predecessor in all important respects. What then could be the rationale for altering the mode of female education, and, in particular, altering it in the manner they proposed, by increasing the academic content of the curriculum? Bowen's floundering was ultimately caused by the fact that he was in effect prescribing an irrelevant remedy for a disease he did not believe existed.

Benjamin Rush avoided these difficulties through the use of a more consistently utilitarian framework in his "Thoughts upon Female Education," an address delivered to the Philadelphia Young Ladies Academy — which he had helped to found — in 1787. Rush's proposed curriculum was based upon his assumption that "female education should be accommodated to the state of society, manners, and government" in the United States. Therefore, he said, it had to be "conducted upon principles very different from what it is in Great Britain, and in some respects different from what it was when we were part of a monarchical empire." American women, he declared, should be trained in bookkeeping and writing so they could assist their husbands or eventually administer their estates; should be acquainted with history, geography, natural philosophy, and religion so they could teach their children more effectively; and should not concentrate their attention on such frivolous and distracting accomplishments as drawing, French, and instrumental music. He did, on the other hand, find vocal music and dancing acceptable, because singing would enable a woman "to soothe the cares of a domestic life" and dancing "promotes health and renders the figure and motions of the body easy and agreeable." [23]

Rush's formula constituted a genuine step forward. By justifying his suggested reforms through reference to the demands of a republican society, he linked women's private development to political imperatives. His emphasis on utility led him to make a much stronger case for the improvement of female education than had the Reverend Mr. Bowen, who was mired in traditional ways of thinking. Unlike Bowen, Rush did want to change the end product; he did want to create a new type of American woman. Yet even so his conception was severely limited. The shortcomings of his approach — and of that taken by the other educators connected with the Philadelphia Young Ladies Academy — can be seen in the contrast between two addresses by the Reverend Samuel Magaw, one to the academy in 1787 and the other at the University of Pennsylvania five years earlier.

At the Young Ladies Academy Magaw was careful to note that he did not advocate "excessive refinement, or deep erudition" for young women, nor was it necessary for a female to have "a classical education, even with respect to her own tongue." He stressed that "all should be formed to the habits of obedience, and a placid graceful attention to whatever duty they may be concerned in." Although he then outlined a broad course of study, Magaw's aim was conservative: the creation of "sensible, virtuous, sweet-tempered women." The contrast to his prescription for the education of the girls' male contemporaries was remarkable. To them he recommended the perusal of Latin and Greek "with critical exactness," because a superficial knowledge would be insufficient. To them he spoke of the "higher exercise of the mind," the development of speculative and rational powers, the study of metaphysics, logic, and rhetoric, in addition to the history, geography, and other topics also suggested for girls. At the university, Magaw described the need "to trim and brighten the golden lamp of learning"; at the academy, he talked of the need to protect the young ladies' "innocence and delicacy."[24]

Magaw and Rush accordingly took a restricted view of even a reformed female education, but some of their republican contemporaries adopted a more enlightened approach. A few men and a larger number of women were convinced that domestic excellence alone was not an adequate goal for females; that women should be able to participate in all areas of study; and that, above all else, like their male counterparts, women students should learn how to reason. Together, these authors advocated a radical departure from past practice.

"Reflections on What is Called Amiable Weakness in Woman," an anonymous essay that appeared in the *Lady and Gentleman's Pocket Magazine of Literature and Polite Amusement* in 1796, stressed the first of these three contentions. Significantly, the author declared that girls should aspire to be more than "*mere* notable women." He would have agreed with the "American Lady" who published "A Second Vindication of the Rights of Women" five years later that "a good kitchen woman, very seldom makes a desirable wife, to a man of any refinement." Can a woman believe that "she was only made to submit to man, her equal?" he inquired. "Can she be content to be occupied merely to please him . . . ? And can she rest supinely dependent on man for reason, when she ought to mount with him the arduous steeps of knowledge?" The "American Lady" concurred. Although females should acquire domestic skills, she argued, yet ought they "therefore to be necessarily excluded from a participation in those improvements that tend to dignify human nature"? The "greatest and most exalted prerogative" of man, "granted from his Creator," was "*freedom of thought, will, and action*. Woman is indisputably included in this grant." But females could not fully realize their potential, she observed, as long as men compelled them "to act inconsistently with their better knowledge and experience, to effect ignorance for fear of giving offence by evincing a superior judgement," or made them "believe that they can best please by prattling incoherent smalltalk." Men had to accept women as equals, and to afford them equal access to knowledge, in order to complete "women's emancipation from injustice and oppression."[25]

Those who believed with this "American Lady" that the key to progress lay in opening learning of all sorts to women refused to accept the sorts of curricular limitations outlined by more conservative thinkers. "Since we have the same natural abilities as themselves," asked a female author in the *New York Magazine* in 1794, "why should we not have the same opportunity of polishing and displaying them by the principles of an independent and virtuous education?" Drawing an intriguing, if inexact, analogy between women's quest for learning and the male rebels' fight for independence, she declared, "[S]ince the Americans have bravely established their liberties, (notwithstanding the vain efforts of tyranny) we hope their modesty will keep them from exercising that despotism over us, which they so openly despised in their masters." She then expressed the hope that men would soon place "the fair sex on an equal footing with themselves, enjoying all the blessings of freedom." Two essayists in the *Massachusetts Magazine* in 1789 developed similar themes. "The Speculator" urged his readers, "[L]et merit and not sex, be the criterion by which we shall determine the most proper subjects [i.e., pupils] for the culturing hand of science to polish," and "Sophronia," in recounting the address delivered by the preceptress general of the mythical Massachusetts Publick Female Academy, stated her belief that men and women should have equivalent educational opportunities.[26]

The final step in this chain of reasoning was taken only by a few. More persons were willing to criticize the restricted schooling offered to women and to advocate its improvement in general terms than wished to hold out to them the identical educational goal ultimately placed before men: training in the exercise of their rational faculties. One of the rare males to do so was one of the Harvard students who contributed to "The Competitor" series in the *Boston Magazine*. "Anaximander" complained that the education currently available to girls was "highly derogatory to their dignity." He accordingly outlined a curriculum that included the study not only of music and geography but also of the sciences, especially astronomy. Rejecting contentions that well-educated women would be "self sufficient, vain and pedantic," he declared unhesitatingly that "the great aim in all their pursuits, should be to obtain, upon a liberal, unbiassed plan, the art of thinking." Sarah Pierce, the Litchfield, Connecticut, educator, adopted this as her primary goal. In an address to her students at the close of the 1818 school year, she revealed the aims her academy had sought since its inception in 1792. In order to "vindicate the equality of female intellect," she had tried to cultivate three faculties of the mind in particular: memory, imagination, and reason. The latter was by far the most important, she noted, for formal instruction would simply place students "on the threshold of improvement." Thereafter, they would have to rely upon "the acuteness of excellent reasoning" to guide them through life.[27]

Judith Sargent Murray, in accord with her innovative approach to women's status and role in the early republic, also placed great stress upon rational thinking as the chief aim of female education. Girls should be taught "to reason, investigate, and compare, and to invigorate their understandings by a comprehension, and a consequent adoption of those arguments which result from sound sense, and are recognized by truth," she asserted. And so she described for the readers of *The Gleaner* her vision of the ideal female: "a sensible and informed woman — companionable and serious — possessing also a facility of temper, and united to a congenial mind — blest with competency — and rearing to maturity a promising family of children."[28]

Although they differed significantly among themselves, Murray, Rush, Pierce, and the other republican reformers all advocated educational opportunities for American girls more advanced than those available to their English and European contemporaries. In Britain the last decades of the eighteenth century witnessed no comparable upsurge in reformist impulses concerning female education, no vast expansion in the number of female academies. The most advanced thinkers of the day in England — Hannah More, Erasmus Darwin, and Thomas Gisborne — continued to emphasize ornamental accomplishments rather than the practical necessities of domesticity and motherhood. They were even more concerned about inculcating properly feminine behavior than were Webster, Bowen, and Rush, and they failed to stress the cultivation of woman's intellectual powers

271

with the same fervor that moved Murray. Darwin, perhaps the most radical of all (with the notable exception of Mary Wollstonecraft), sounded more like American conservatives than like Judith Sargent Murray or Sarah Pierce, writing in 1797 of the necessity for women to be "pliant," to display "the mild and retiring virtues," and to avoid demonstrating "great apparent strength of character," lest men be alarmed. The more advanced American thinkers had long since abandoned such restrictive modes of discourse.[29]

The fact that the English approach to female education diverged so sharply from that taken in the United States underscores the revolutionary origins of American ideas. To their developing national ideology, American girls owed the stress in their education on domesticity and motherhood; to wartime disruptions, the emphasis on the creation of independent, rational female adults. Neither concern was evident in the thinking of foreign educational theorists.

The aims of the Americans were thus distinctive for their time. But most of the founders of academies sought the limited goals outlined by Rush and Webster rather than the more radical ones promulgated by Judith Sargent Murray and Sarah Pierce. Were the new republican academies, then, little more than a continuation of the adventure-school tradition, albeit with a new emphasis on practical achievement, or were they indeed a new creation? What sort of training did their pupils receive, and what eventually became of those students? No examination of postwar education would be complete without attention to these questions.[30]

III

As the Reverend Ezra Stiles observed in 1786, during the postwar years "the Spirit for Academy making" was "vigorous." The event that elicited Stiles's comment was Timothy Dwight's announcement that he had opened his school in Greenfield Hill, Connecticut, to girls as well as boys, "promis[in]g to carry them thro' a Course of belles Lettres, Geography, Philosophy, & Astronomy." In addition to institutions like Dwight's, once restricted to boys but now encompassing girls, a number of academies were founded solely for the instruction of females. In Philadelphia, there was John Poor's school and its successor, the Young Ladies Academy, and in New York City Isabella Graham, a Scottish immigrant, established a school with the assistance of her daughter, Joanna Bethune. During the same decade Caleb Bingham and Jedidiah Morse started girls' schools in Boston and New Haven, respectively; and William Woodbridge, who later claimed the distinction of having run "the first female school . . . that ever was attempted in New England, above the district schools" because he had taught evening classes to a group of girls while he was a Yale undergraduate in 1779, opened his academy for young ladies in Medford, Massachusetts. The 1790s brought the founding of Susanna Rowson's academy, also in Medford, and Sarah Pierce's school in Litchfield. These were but the best known of a large number of similar establishments that, within the space of two decades, suddenly made higher education available to young American women from middling and well-to-do families.[31]

The academies shared four characteristics that distinguished them from the adventure schools of the colonial years. Although they usually offered instruction in some ornamental accomplishments, needlework, music, and dancing played a relatively small role in their overall curricula. At the same time, they stressed the study of such academic subjects as composition, history, and geography, thus helping to close the gap that had traditionally separated the education of girls from that of their brothers. Further, instead of being concentrated in major cities and serving only urban residents, many of the academies were located in small towns and drew boarding pupils from throughout the nation. Among the students at Sarah Pierce's school in 1802, for example, were thirteen from Litchfield, nine from other Connecticut towns, six from Georgia, five from New York, two from Massachusetts, two from New Hampshire, and three from the West Indies. Third, the academies often developed more of an institutional base than had the adventure schools, which had normally been run by a single woman. They acquired permanent buildings, hired additional teachers as their student bodies increased, and relied upon financial support from the communities in which they were based. Consequently, they exhibited a fourth attribute that differentiated them from their predecessors: they tended to be longer lived. Whereas the adventure schools rarely continued for more than two or three years at most, some of the academies survived well into the nineteenth century and a few even have lineal descendants in operation today.[32]

Significantly, the South lagged behind the North in the founding of such academies, and so planter families who wanted their daughters to receive advanced instruction had to send them to northern institutions. In 1785, Judith Randolph, envious of Patsy Jefferson's experiences in a French convent school, lamented to her future sister-in-law, "[M]y prospect for a tolerable education, is but a bad one, which in my opinion is one of the greatest disadvantages which the Virginia Girls, are attended with." As late as 1801, Sarah Pierce's nephew Timothy found the situation no better. On a visit to South Carolina, he recorded his disappointment that "little attention is paid to the cultivation of the mind" of Charleston girls.[33]

The reasons for the South's belated conversion to the cause of advanced female education — its first school on the northern model was that founded by Jacob Mordecai in Warrenton, North Carolina, in 1809 — lay in what one foreign visitor in 1799 termed "the baleful effects of the revolutionary war." The South in general suffered far greater wartime losses than did the North, and those losses were concentrated in the later years of the conflict. By the mid-1780s Philadelphia, Boston, and even New York City had largely recovered from the impact of the war, but the same was not true of the South. When the Reverend Penuel Bowen arrived in Savannah in 1786, for instance, he found the public buildings "going to rack & ruin." The Georgians "were distressed & torn to pieces by the war in this place & neighborhood," he told a relative; "the common observation among them is, they have not had time yet to gain the ground they lost." Other visitors to the South from the mid-1780s to the mid-1790s likewise noted seeing "the ravages of war wherever [they] went" or described in detail "the many charred ruins that still remain." As late as 1790, a Georgian predicted that few planters "can expect to live long enough to see them[selves] recover their former Situation."[34]

Under such circumstances, David Ramsay later wrote, "[T]o reproduce a state of things favorable to social happiness, required all the energies of the well disposed inhabitants." Instead of devoting their resources to such frills as better education for their daughters (and sons), white southerners, recalled a Carolina boy born in 1785, strained "every nerve . . . to repair the broken fortunes of the Planters by the severest thrift and patient industry." To that end, all the money they could spare was allocated to the purchase of slaves to replace those lost during the war. In early 1784, a Georgia merchant commented accurately, "[T]he Negro business is a great object with us. . . . The Planter will as far as in his power sacrifice every thing to attain Negroes." So the Carolinian observed that in his youth "schools, churches, with all the requisites of refinements and amenities of life were sadly neglected." [35]

If southern girls were to acquire an advanced education during the immediate postwar decades, then, they had to be sent far from home. Indeed, the same could have been said of northern girls as well, for they too had to leave their families in order to attend school, unless they were fortunate enough to reside in one of the towns that also housed an academy. Since female whites had usually lived at home until marriage, those enrolled at boarding schools constituted the first generation of well-to-do American girls who lived away from home and relatives for lengthy periods. The novelty of the experience seems to have made the pain of parting especially intense. Indeed, the sense of loss evident in the correspondence of students and their families makes it clear that only the strongest of motives could have prompted their separation. In 1807, after a conversation with her daughter Bess, a boarding-school pupil, the New Yorker Elizabeth Kent told her husband, James, "I almost regret we ever agreed to send her, she takes it so very hard, she Cries very much & says she shall never be reconciled to live there a year — she likes the school & likes her Boarding place exceedingly but the being away from home almost kills her." The only thing that sustained parents and their daughters through such difficult times was a recognition of the significance of the enterprise upon which they had embarked. [36]

The contents of their letters reveal the extent of the change that had occurred in Americans' attitude toward female education. "I consider it a duty I owe you to send you from me and trust you will improve much more then you would at Home," a New Yorker told her daughter in 1806. Admitting ruefully that she had "burst into tears" from homesickness when she first arrived at Wyman's academy in Medford, Eliza Southgate promised her parents in 1797 "[to] think of the duty that now attends me, to think that here I may drink freely of the fountain of knowledge." [37]

In the republic, in short, the education of girls had become a "duty" — a duty their parents owed them, a duty they owed themselves. Whereas parents had once referred only to the need for their daughters to acquire good work habits, they now spoke of improvement, advancement, emulation. Their words conveyed a very different message from the common colonial injunction to girls to be industrious and simultaneously exposed a major shift in attitudes. For the first time, American daughters as well as sons were being told that they could "improve."

"Let your Studies call your first Attention they will lay the Ground Work for Pleasures hereafter," a Rhode Islander instructed her daughter in 1786, when the girl was in school in Boston; "[N]ow is your Goalden Age for the Acquirement of the best and Most Sellibrated Education of the Sex, pray let me Intreet your best Exertions," her father added. In 1801, a Virginia woman reminded her daughter, "[Y]ou know how anxious I am, that you shou'd be Clever as well as good," urging, "be studious, & . . . take every advantage to improve your mind that falls in your way." Significantly, parents urged their daughters to learn to think for themselves, to study subjects in depth, and to prepare for future usefulness. A New Yorker in 1794 advised, "[W]hatever you learn remember that you will receive no Benefit from it without making yourself Mistress of it." Studying with "a great deal of reflection," he explained, "will enable you to form sentiments of your own which is more useful than those you borrow." That same year Sarah Jay told her oldest daughter, Maria, then a student at the Moravian Seminary for Young Ladies in Bethlehem, Pennsylvania, "[I]f you reflect that on your present endeavors, may hereafter depend the satisfaction of rearing a family agreeably to your wishes, it will I'm sure stimulate you to improve every advantage." [38]

Mothers' remarks on their daughters' education occasionally contained special overtones. In Atkinson, New Hampshire, Elizabeth Smith Peabody, who had long complained, "[M]y Sex have been cruelly injured, in the unjust niggardly distructive mode of Education," took great pains to ensure that her daughter could attend a nearby academy and expressed her delight at the fact that a woman was no longer "considered a Pheonix" if she could merely "write intelligbly." "Oh my sister," she exclaimed to Mary Cranch, "what an advantage the youth of the present day have, compared with

Eliza Southgate Bowne, by Malbone. Frontispiece, A Girl's Life Eighty Years Ago, ed. Clarence Cook (London, 1888).

Maria Jay, a profile by Saint Mémin. Courtesy of National Portrait Gallery, Smithsonian Institution.

former times." Similarly, a Virginian whose mother had refused to allow her to attend an adventure school in the 1760s saw to it that her daughter went to a boarding school twenty years later. And when in the 1820s Cornelia Boardman, the daughter of Mary Anna Whiting Boardman, expressed the hope that her school days would soon be over, her mother decisively rebuked her. Mary Anna had been educated at Jedidiah Morse's New Haven school in the mid-1780s, and so she had had better academic training than many of the women of her generation. She valued that education, yet still regretted that she had not had the opportunities her daughter now did. "I am covetous of your school-days," she told Cornelia, "and I do not like you to lose *one* of them." Obviously recalling her own experience, Mary Anna asked her, "[W]hy do you speak with exultation of leaving school? I am much mistaken, if you do not say, twenty years hence, if you live so long, that your school days were the happiest of your life." Her chief fear was, she revealed, "[Y]ou do not improve as fast as you might, because you do not love study as you ought." [39]

But if Cornelia Boardman did not in fact "love study," she appears to have been an exception. Many republican girls hardly needed parental injunctions to encourage them to be studious. Like Eliza Southgate, young women understood that they had the chance for a better education than that available to any previous generation of female Americans, and they were determined to take full advantage of their favored position.

Nelly Custis Lewis's daughter Parke, for example, attended a Philadelphia school at her own "earnest wish," though her mother (who had been a pupil of Isabella Graham) had vowed not to send her away from home to an academy. Kitty Duane, another of Graham's students, worked "to the utmost of her capacity, making the most of her time & opportunities" in 1795–1796. Describing Kitty as "indefatigable," Mrs. Graham reported to her father, James Duane, the New York politician, that the girl had decided to forgo instruction in drawing and embroidery, "finding all her time necessary to accomplish that degree of perfection in her studies that she wished, & has chosen those branches which are likely to give her most enjoyment through life," namely reading, grammar, and geography. Eliza Southgate likewise informed her family in the summer of 1797, "I fear that the time allotted for my stay here will be too short for me to go so far

> Medford May 12 1797
>
> Honour'd parents
>
> with pleasure I sit down to the best of parents, to inform them of my Situation as doubtless they are anxious to hear. permit me to tell something of [my] foolish heart; When I first came here I gave myself to reflection but not pleasing reflections —
>
> [When] Mr Boyd left me I burst into tears and in[stead] of trying to calm my feelings I tried to feel worse. I begin to feel happier and will now gather up all my philosophy and thinky of the duty that now attends me to think that here I may drink freely of the fountain of Knowledge but I will not dwell any longer on this subject. I am first at doing anything but Writing Reading & Cyphering there is a french Master coming next monday

> Medford Sept. 30th 1797
>
> Dear Mother,
>
> You mentioned in yours, of the 16 Ins[t]. that it was a long time since you had recieved a letter from me; but it was owing to my studies which took up the greater part of my time, for I have been busy in my Arithmetic but I finished it yesterday, and expect now to begin my large Manuscript Arithmetic. You say that you "Shall regret so long an absence"; not more certainly than I shall; but a strong desire to possess more useful knowledge than I at present do, I can dispense with the pleasure a little longer of beholding my friends and I hope I shall be better prepared to meet my good Parents towards whom my heart overflows with gratitude You mentioned in your letter about my Winter clothes of which I will make out a memorandum. I shall want a coat and you may send it up for me to make or you may make it your—

The Benefits of an Academy Education. The improvement of Eliza Southgate's handwriting during the summer of 1797, shown in two letters to her parents, Bedinger-Dandridge Family Papers, Duke University Library.

as I wish" in arithmetic. She accordingly asked to remain in school for several additional months, explaining, "[Because of] a strong desire to possess more useful knowledge than I at present do, I can dispense with the pleasure a little longer of beholding my friends." [40]

The same desire to learn also infected girls who were unable to attend the academies, or who had graduated from them but wished to continue their education. Patty Hitchcock, a tavernkeeper's daughter from Brookfield, Massachusetts, felt "mortified" that since she was necessarily "a slave to business" she had "very inferior" chances "for cultivating both mind & manners." Consequently, her brother sought the advice of their uncle Enos, the child-rearing theorist, as to how she could educate herself. Some years later another New Englander took a similar action. "[I] am not satisfied with remaining ignorant as I am of much important knowledge," she told her schoolteacher brother-in-law, asking him to recommend a "future course of reading." In North Carolina, Anne Iredell "entankled [her]self in a course of modern history" and also read the works of Lord Kames, through which she was introduced to Aristotle's logic. In Massachusetts, Ann Jean Robbins, a great-niece of Elizabeth Murray Inman, read a number of leading works in the fields of metaphysics and ethics in the four years after she left school. [41]

The examples could be multiplied endlessly, but the point has been made: advanced learning, so long forbidden to women in America, had become a goal to which they could legitimately aspire. Indeed, as William Woodbridge later remarked, "[T]he love of reading and habits of application became fashionable; and *fashion* we know is the mistress of the world." Part of that new fashion was evident in women's comments on the intellectual capacities of the other females they encountered. Whereas they had once remarked solely upon the "softness" and "delicacy" of new acquaintances, they now began to assess their friends' mental abilities: she "posses[ses] a mind naturely strong, which is intirely improved and cultivated"; she is (or is not) "well informed"; she has "an excellent understanding, a cultivated mind, & a lively imagination." When Gertrude Ogden Meredith, a Philadelphia intellectual and author, visited Baltimore in 1804, she complained to her husband, "I really never have viewed my own sex with so little interest as in this place, they possess not the most common information, less reflexion, and very little understanding."

Clearly, times had changed: the criteria upon which women judged each other now encompassed the qualities of the mind as well as beauty and personality.[42]

As a means of illustrating the remarkable nature of the transition, it is useful to compare the instruction received by Elizabeth Murray Inman's nieces in the 1750s and 1760s with that given to two of her grandnieces in the 1790s. Mrs. Inman had educated her nieces Dolly and Betsy Murray and Anne Clark to the best of her ability. She had sent them to adventure schools and had herself supervised their training in business methods. Consequently, they were among the best-educated American women of their generation, and the many admiring comments they elicited indicated as much.[43] Yet the contrast to the education of Harriet and Anne Eliza Clark, the daughters of Anne's brother John, could not have been sharper. Because their mother, Lydia, was ill for an extended period, the girls were placed in a boarding school earlier than usual, at the ages of six and nine. In other respects, the Clarks' experience was similar to that of other daughters of middling and well-to-do republican families.

The girls spent the years from 1788 to 1791 at Mr. and Mrs. Usher's school in Bristol, Rhode Island. There Harriet learned to write, practiced reading, and began the study of grammar, while Eliza worked on grammar and arithmetic, read such books as *The Ladies Library*, and sewed extensively for her family. Both girls had their "babies" with them and reported to their parents on the dolls' activities. "I have the pleasure to tell you my babies are all recover'd of their illness," Harriet told her mother in 1791, "but are in want of clothes, having but one suit, must certainly lie in bed all day, when those are wash'd." Mrs. Usher paid close attention to the girls' behavior, preparing rules of conduct for Harriet in June 1789 and assuring the elder Clarks that same month that their daughters' "spiritual duties" were being attended to. When the Ushers began to teach male pupils in the fall of 1789, Eliza informed her parents, "Mrs. Usher will take the utmost care tha[t] they [*sic*] [will] be no indecencies acted or spoke in the house that we shall be by ourselves and the boys by themselves except in Schooltime and meal times."[44]

The Clark girls left the Ushers' school in the spring of 1791. The following fall Anne Eliza was enrolled in William Woodbridge's academy in Medford, while Harriet was placed in a day school near her parents' home in Providence. Early in 1792 Eliza described her daily routine for her sister. She arose about half an hour before dawn, washing, participating in prayers, and reciting a geography lesson before breakfast. After the meal and some chores, she wrote, "we then go to school spell two pages write & copy read in the bible and then read in another book and if we have any time we work [i.e., sew]." After dinner,the schedule was repeated, and following tea they studied geography until 8:30. "We then read some novel aloud," Eliza recounted; "we are now reading Evelina." Bedtime was 9:45 or 10 P.M. In other letters she carefully explained to her mother that her schoolwork was so demanding she could no longer do as much sewing for the family. Among Eliza's fellow students at Woodbridge's academy that year were her cousin Julia Bowen, whom she cheerfully described as a *"numskull"* because "she cannot learn her grammer well nor has not learnt a piece perfect since she has been here," and Penuel Bowen's daughter Frances.[45]

After a two-year break in Eliza's boarding-school education, she was next enrolled in Mehetabel Higginson's academy in Salem, Massachusetts. Then fifteen, she had advanced to the study of French and history in addition to geography. She worked hard at her writing and arithmetic, informing her mother in November 1794, "I have kept a constant account of my expences since I have been here and shall forward them to you once in a while[.] I know it is extremely necessary to be acquainted with accounts I shall therefore pay great attention to my cyphering." She purchased Hester Chapone's *Letters on the Improvement of the Mind* on Mrs. Higginson's recommendation, and she asked her parents to send her a copy of Madame de Sévigné's letters in French. Eliza explained to her parents that she liked Mrs. Higginson's school because she "attends to the health and morals of her scholars which is . . . more than any one else does at least there are but few." The Clarks must have been satisfied with Mehetabel Higginson's efforts with Eliza, for the following year Harriet followed her older sister to the Salem school. She too studied French, in addition to writing, arithmetic (including geometry), geography, and even astronomy.[46]

When John Clark visited his sister Anne and brother-in-law William Hooper in North Carolina in late 1792, he informed his wife that their relatives had made "many inquiries" about Harriet and Eliza, "about their abelities and accomplishments, all expecting from the opportunities they have had, to hear of their being something extraordinary." Certainly the Clark girls had had an unusually good education, but even so their parents had explicitly decided not to send them to the largest and best-known of the republican academies, the Moravian Young Ladies Seminary in Bethlehem, Pennsylvania.[47] Since the daughters of many prominent families were educated there, it is important to take a close look at that preeminent republican institution.

From its founding in 1742 until 1785, the Moravian Seminary served only the daughters of members of the small German sect. But congressmen and army officers who visited the school during the Revolution were impressed by what they saw, and they asked the seminary's trustees to open it to non-Moravians. When the trustees complied in 1785, they announced that they would teach girls "reading and writing in both the German and English languages, also arithmetic, sewing, knitting, and other feminine crafts. Likewise they will be instructed in history, geography, and music, with great care and faithfulness."[48]

The leading families of the young republic eagerly took advantage of the opportunity to send their daughters to the Moravian Seminary. The North Carolina congressman John Steele explained to his daughter Ann in mid 1799 that he had enrolled her at the academy because he was "really of opinion that Bethlehem is unrivalled in the United States as a place for female education." When he sent his eleven-year-old daughter Fanny to the school two years earlier, Ephraim Kirby of Connecticut stressed that he wanted her "to be made perfect" in the academic subjects, while the acquisition of ornamental accomplishments was of "secondary" importance. But he also wanted Fanny to learn "the government of the passions" and to develop "habits of industry, oeconomy and neatness." Undoubtedly, the belief that the Moravians would foster moral growth and self-discipline in addition to intellectual development was what led such Americans as Nathanael and Catherine Greene, John and Sarah Jay, and Helena Kortwright Brasher to enroll their daughters at the Bethlehem, Pennsylvania, institution.[49]

In the case of Maria Jay, it is evident that she herself made the decision to attend the highly regarded seminary. Maria's mother,

Sarah, had carefully supervised her early education and had entered her in Isabella Graham's school in 1791. Yet in October 1794 Maria surprised her mother by telling her that she "wished to make a greater proficiency in her studies than in her present situation she was able" and that she had "a long time had a great inclination to go to Bethlehem." Mrs. Jay understandably hesitated to accede to Maria's request, since her daughter was only twelve and the school was hundreds of miles away from their New York City home. But relatives who were traveling west offered to escort her, and, Sarah later commented, "[H]er little heart was so much engaged in it that I could not resolve to disappoint her." Less than a month later the academy had accepted Maria's application and she was on her way, her display of independence having gained her "great eclat" among her schoolmates while it simultaneously earned the disapproval of their mothers.[50]

But although Sarah Jay's friends might not have concurred in her decision to allow Maria to choose her own school, they could hardly have objected to the course of instruction at the Moravian academy. Everyone connected with the school — parents, students, and teachers alike — expressed satisfaction with the education girls received there. Elizabeth Chester, whose daughter Elizabeth attended the seminary in 1789, is a case in point. In response to a question from Lydia Bowen Clark, Mrs. Chester gave the school an enthusiastic recommendation in late 1790. "The people of the Society appear very amiable in their manners; an honest simplicity, void of affectation characterizes them. The government is a government of persuasion, calculated more to attach the affections than pain the body." Mrs. Chester emphasized that the site of the academy was "*very* pleasant & healthy," that the "Tuteresses are well bred & educated," and that girls did not acquire "any rusticity" during their stay. "As to the morals of a Child," she added, "the Parent may repose entire confidence in the directors, who pay the strictest attention to check every deviation from delicacy & decorum." In short, Mrs. Chester concluded, "I wish all my daughters might have the advantage of that school for one or two years," and she acted accordingly by enrolling another of them at Bethlehem in 1793.[51]

The students appeared equally pleased with their experiences at the seminary. In a letter published in the *American Magazine* in 1788, a Baltimore girl, probably Amelia Blakely, described her daily schedule and then observed, "I could not be more happily situated than I am. — I have every possible attention paid both to my person and education." Three years later, upon leaving the academy, a young woman (again probably Amelia) gratefully thanked her teachers for providing her with "such examples of domestic economy, purity of morals, and reverence for religion." Speaking directly to her fellow pupils, she declared, "[W]e are not here prepared to ride the whirlwind of thoughtless dissipation: but in these calm retreats, we are taught lessons which dignify the character of our sex — entitle us to respect in society — and, if duly attended to, will have a happy influence in rendering us accomplished and agreeable companions."[52]

Private comments coincided with the published ones. In 1790 Mary Anna Boardman told a friend that her sister Fanny Whiting, then a student at Bethlehem, was "too happy in her situation, to feel the least inclination to leave it." On a visit to the school in July 1797 Ephraim Kirby found his daughter Fanny to be "apparently very happy." For her part, Ann Steele left Bethlehem reluctantly after having studied there less than a year, simply because her mother wanted her to return home. Maria Jay told her family in late 1794, "I felt a little strange at first but now I like it much," and before her exams the following spring she wrote, "I hope I shall be able to give satisfaction to my dear tutoresses who take much pains with me[.] I shall indeed try all in my power to improve myself in all my studies while I am here[. I] hope when I return again to my beloved parents that they may not be disappointed in my improvements."[53]

Given the breadth of the seminary's curriculum and the rigor of its requirements, it is unlikely that, upon her return home, the Jays were disappointed with Maria's "improvements." On a typical day in 1788, for example, classes began at eight o'clock (after prayers and breakfast) with ciphering, followed by German reading and English grammar before lunch. Afterwards the pupils turned their attention to history and geography, and late in the afternoon they could learn music, drawing, painting, or tambour (a type of needlework) if they and their parents wished. In 1796, in the midst of preparing for the annual examinations, the New Yorker Margaretta Akerly wrote distractedly to her older sister Catherine, who had also been a student at Bethlehem, "I have so much to learn I dont know what to do with

285

Cymbeline, a Needlework Picture from Mrs. Rowson's Academy, by Ann Trask, 1812. The embroidery is in silk on silk with watercolor details. Courtesy of Old Sturbridge Village.

myself I hardly know what I write I think of nothing only what I have to learn; this morning I was up at 4 oClock sitting by the Lamp studying & every night I have 3 or 4 books under my head."[54]

Detailed records of the year-end public examinations reveal why Margaretta was so worried. In 1791, for instance, the examination took five days. On the first morning, the girls were tested on their knowledge of the Bible. That afternoon the subject was German. The following day they were examined in grammar and arithmetic, and on the third the topic was history, with afternoon recitations of memorized pieces. The fourth day was devoted to geography and astronomy in the morning, French in the afternoon. On the final day the students demonstrated their musical ability and showed the audience examples of their writing, drawing, painting, embroidery, and tambour work.[55]

The fact that even the Moravian Seminary, which stressed simplicity, offered instruction in ornamental skills suggests that it is important not to accept unquestioningly the utilitarian reformers' negative judgment of such accomplishments. Jane Nylander, who has studied the paintings and needlework done by young women in this period, has accurately observed that only through such work could girls gain proficiency in the fine arts. Some of the instruction in the republican academies was excellent, and the better teachers did much to develop the artistic talents of their students. Like boys who studied painting, the girls copied well-known prints, often reproducing them in stitchery. Surviving examples of their handiwork show the exquisite care with which they worked and sometimes demonstrate great talent and sensitivity. Most of the students must have learned enough to help them decorate their homes after marriage, and a few became artists of some renown.[56]

The founders of the academies sought to train republican wives and mothers, and this task they unquestionably accomplished. The graduates of the Moravian Seminary, the Philadelphia Young Ladies Academy, Miss Pierce's school, and other similar institutions were well qualified to instruct their sons in the principles of patriotism, to make their homes well-run havens of efficiency, to converse knowledgeably with their husbands on a variety of subjects, and to understand familial finances. But an academy education had unanticipated consequences as well, for some of the graduates of such schools showed in their adulthood a desire to go beyond the standard roles of wife and mother and to widen the boundaries of the feminine sphere.

IV

An excellent source for measuring the impact of educational reform during the era of the early republic is the biographical compendium *Notable American Women*. Although the academies were small and cost enough to put them out of reach of the majority of American families, a survey of the level of education achieved by the 222 biographees born before 1810 shows a dramatic shift in the availability of higher academic training for those women born in the decade 1770–1779 — those who, in other words, were of school age when the first republican academies were founded in the mid-1780s. Table 3 demonstrates that the percentage of American women who received advanced instruction, after remaining roughly constant at about 22 percent through the first three-quarters of the century, more than doubled to 46 percent for girls born in the 1770s, climbed steeply to 63 percent for those born in the next decade, and leveled off at an astonishing 74 percent for the group born in the first ten years of the nineteenth century. Although a large percentage of women born during the colonial period had educational experiences that proved impossible to trace, girls with no formal schooling probably fell into that category more often than ones who had been well educated.[57]

The persons included in *Notable American Women* are, of course, exceptional, and the evidence revealing that an average of 65 percent of biographees born between 1770 and 1809 had advanced education by no means represents the norm for all of American society. Nevertheless, that extraordinary figure indicates that the republican academies and the reform climate of which they were the chief manifestation had a significant effect on the lives of American women. One need not argue that the increasing availability of higher education to female Americans helped to make more of them "notable" in twentieth-century terms, although the absolute number of biographees increased just as dramatically in this period as did the percentage of those with advanced academic training; rather, it is only necessary to acknowledge the trend and to recognize its implications for the lives of specific women and for the collective experience of female Americans. Many individual graduates of the republican academies achieved fame in the nineteenth century. Among them were such early missionaries as Harriet Newell, Cynthia Farrar, and Ann Hasseltine Judson; writers like Margaret Bayard Smith, Lydia Huntley Sigourney, Catharine Sedgwick, and Caroline Gilman; such leaders of the abolitionist and women's rights movements as Lydia Maria Child, Prudence Crandall, Martha Coffin Wright, and her better-known sister Lucretia Coffin Mott; and the early educators Zilpah Grant, Mary Lyon, Emma Hart Willard, and Catharine Beecher.[58]

Table 3
EDUCATIONAL BACKGROUNDS OF *Notable American Women*

Birthdate	Elementary education (home or school)		Advanced education (school or tutor)		Unknown		Total
	%	No.	%	No.	%	No.	
17th century	20	(6)	1	(3)	70	(21)	(30)
1700–1739	34	(11)	19	(6)	47	(15)	(32)
1740–1749	25	(2)	25	(2)	50	(4)	(8)
1750–1759	37	(7)	21	(4)	42	(8)	(19)
1760–1769	33	(6)	22	(4)	44	(8)	(18)
1770–1779	31	(4)	46	(6)	23	(3)	(13)
1780–1789	5	(1)	63	(12)	32	(6)	(19)
1790–1799	15	(5)	61	(20)	24	(8)	(33)
1800–1809	20	(10)	74	(37)	6	(3)	(50)
to 1769	30	(32)	18	(19)	52	(56)	(107)
1770–1809	17	(20)	65	(75)	17	(20)	(115)

It would therefore be possible to trace the continuing influence of the postrevolutionary educational reforms in many areas of American life. But the most direct connection can be made in the field of education itself, for the improved training originally accessible only to the daughters of the republican elite eventually dispersed through a wider population because many of the academy graduates themselves became teachers. Mary Lyon and Catharine Beecher founded colleges; Emma Willard opened a seminary; but more important in numerical terms were the hundreds, perhaps thousands, of former academy students who taught at the elementary level.

The movement for the reform of primary education began at approximately the same time as the first academies were being founded. One of the first calls for the improvement of girls' early education came from the New Hampshire clergyman and historian Jeremy Belknap. Writing as "Civis" in the *Boston Evening Post* in 1782, he suggested that "the FEMALE mind might enjoy some of the benefits of public education, and be dignified with principles of wisdom and virtue." Three years later in the *Massachusetts Centinel* "Humanus" took up the cudgel for the cause, complaining that in Boston the town fathers had neglected the instruction of girls. Why was an "insidious distinction" made between sons and daughters? he inquired. "Is the female part of the inhabitants unworthy of attention? Does ignorance advance their happiness or promote their usefulness?" His ally, the outspoken Daphne, who had attacked the sexual double standard a year earlier, discoursed on the same theme, listing her own questions: "Why must they be denied those advantages that are essentially necessary? Why are all but those whose affluent fortunes will allow an uncommon expense, debarred from attaining any degree of refinement?" Such criticisms of the failure to appropriate public funds for the education of girls became common in New England in the 1780s and 1790s. In consequence, Kathryn Kish Sklar has discovered, Massachusetts towns increasingly began to use tax money to support basic instruction for all children.[59]

The same impetus brought citizens of the middle states to set up charity schools for children of both sexes. In 1796, a school for girls opened in Philadelphia under the auspices of the Society for the Free Instruction of Female Children, a Quaker women's group. The course of study consisted of reading, writing, spelling, memorization of passages from the Bible and other "profitable" books, ciphering, and sewing. In New York City as well charity schools established in the 1790s educated the daughters of artisans and unskilled laborers.[60]

The persons who ran the new town or charity schools, or the groups of parents who sought instructors for their children, soon began to turn to young academy graduates in preference to the untrained widows who had previously served as educators of American youngsters. The women who ran dame schools had had no particular qualifications for the job; they merely needed a means of support. Now, though, the academies were producing relatively large numbers of formally trained young women, and at the same time republican educational theorists continually emphasized the importance of hiring good teachers. "We are under no necessity of making schoolmasters of those who are unqualified, merely to keep them out of idleness," declared a New England cleric in 1801. "If we have any regard to the interest of virtue, of our posterity and our country, let us never suffer the first principles of our children to be formed by those who live in the habitual exercise of vice." The result was inevitable: young women were hired to teach in local primary schools — in such numbers, indeed, that two historians have estimated that fully 25 percent of native-born female New Englanders alive in the antebellum years taught school at some time during their lives.[61]

If those who selected teachers were therefore searching for "young women of good larn'en" (as was the farmer who asked Mary Palmer to teach his and his neighbors' children for three months in the early summer of 1793), the girls themselves probably accepted the jobs from a variety of motives. To some, the pay, though small, must have been welcome. To others, the opportunity to live away from home and family for a few months must have proved attractive. Yet in her diary the young Leicester woman Ruth Henshaw, who kept school during the summers of 1791, 1792, and 1796, made no mention of her reasons for doing so. Neither did Elizabeth Bancroft, another New Englander, who repeatedly complained of her "tiresome tasks" and who welcomed "the sweets of liberty" when she had completed a school season, but who also in September 1794 "engaged to take another school" only two days after she had written, "I finishd my Schools and glad am I."[62]

Others of the early teachers left more detailed accounts of their motivations. In 1778, when she decided to assist in a charity school, Anne Emlen explained in her diary, "[H]aving experienced the benefit of School education, I have earnestly wished it might be more generally extended to poor as well as rich." She observed, "[I]f individuals were to embrace the occupation of School keeping from choice and a Sense of duty, who were under no temporal necessity of doing it; I believe it might have a tendency, in shewing respect to a profession that ought in policy to be considered one of the first offices in life."[63]

Her comment proved remarkably prescient. Once school teaching had ceased to be an occupation engaged in solely by persons who had no alternative and had come to be seen as an acceptable voluntary employment for young women prior to marriage, the profession gained in prestige. According to "Bessie," a minister's daughter who taught in New England district schools for several years at the beginning of the nineteenth century, "the office of school teacher was considered not only respectable, but honorable; and she who could preside with dignity in the school room, commanded respect elsewhere." No wonder, then, that William Woodbridge described republican girls as being "ambitious to qualify themselves for school-keeping," or that when the Palmer household broke up after Mary moved to Vermont with her husband, Royall Tyler, she recorded that her younger sister Betsy "made up her mind to become a teacher in some female academy as soon as possible." Betsy eventually achieved her goal, establishing her own school in Salem after her marriage to Nathaniel Peabody. Perhaps even more importantly, Betsy's daughters Mary Peabody Mann (wife and collaborator of the influential educator Horace Mann), Sophia Peabody Hawthorne (wife of Nathaniel Hawthorne), and Elizabeth Palmer Peabody, the never-married pioneer of the kindergarten movement in the United States, carried on their mother's and aunt's intellectual tradition and commitment to education until their deaths in the later years of the nineteenth century.[64]

A few members of the first generation of American female educators commented on their work. "It is pleasant to reflect at night that we have spent the day in a manner that was improving to ourselves, and useful to others," one young New England teacher remarked to a similarly employed friend in 1807. Another instructor, who had initially complained about having to cope with "thirty six of the little wretches and the oldest not ten," and who had told her sister that she "hate[d] this new Business" expressed quite different feelings when her school closed after two years. "I wouldn't have believed it possible I could have felt so bad," she revealed. "I shall miss their Noise, their Mischief, their bright wits, their Stupidity and their *dear* little Gingerbread — and Molasses — Kisses which made it necessary to wash my Face at *least* a dozen times a Day. Oh, I could cry when I think how soon they will all be grown up."[65]

The fullest account has been left by Rachel Mordecai, the North Carolinian who was her father's chief assistant at the first major southern female academy. Jacob Mordecai had long been interested in female education and had seen to it that Rachel and her younger sister Ellen received the best training available in Richmond in the late 1790s. The Mordecai Academy formally opened in January 1809, and Rachel, who had long expressed "dissatisfaction . . . at occupying uselessly a space on this planet," soon happily reported to her older brother Samuel, "[T]he improvement of those under our care is already manifest," assuring him, "neither papa nor myself find the task an irksome one, fortunately we have several, whose minds, tho totally uncultivated, are capable of recieving instruction, and on these we find peculiar satisfaction in bestowing it." Rachel's younger sister Ellen felt envious of her successful contribution to the family's educational enterprise. "It is *now* more then ever I regret my inferiority to *her*," she disclosed to Samuel, "for what is more humiliating, than the idea of being of *no use* and if you were gone of not being *missed*?" Ellen's question neatly pointed up the attraction of teaching for girls like the Mordecais, who wanted to employ their education in a meaningful way.[66]

Two years later, as the term began, Rachel told Samuel, "I can truly say that I hail the recommencement of my duties with something approaching a sensation of pleasure." Later that same year she explained why. "People really give *me* a great deal more credit than I deserve, they speak of the sacrifice I make in confining myself and giving up every thing like (what they call amusement); little thinking that to me, thinking and feeling as I do, nothing could be more irksome than to be often engaged in such scenes." Rachel went on to declare that she believed in "using hours to greater advantage" than she would if she were "trifling" them away in leisure.[67]

In teaching, Rachel Mordecai had found what other members of her generation, and eventually many younger women, would also discover: a satisfying way of life, if not yet precisely a career. Teaching was the first profession opened to women on a regular basis, and as such it attracted, albeit for only a few years of their lives, a large number of intellectually aware young women, many of them products of the republican academies. As time passed, the participation of women in school teaching came to be seen, not as "very singular" — as Mary Norris had said in 1786 — but rather as a logical extension of the maternal function. Paradoxically, in other words, the first major breach in the conventional feminine role was justified by reference to that role itself. Thus the concern with female education fostered by the Revolution and by republican ideology led to the first significant change in the options open to American women. Judith Sargent Murray alone among the reformers would have welcomed enthusiastically the ultimate implications of that change, but just as it proved impossible for her more conservative counterparts to ensure that the academy graduates would confine themselves to traditional female functions, so too it eventually proved impossible to contain the intellectual aspirations of women within the restrictive boundaries of school teaching alone.[68]

Conclusion

ॐ

A NEW ERA OF
FEMALE HISTORY

In 1798, JUDITH SARGENT MURRAY CONFIDENTLY PREDICTED THE dawn of "a new era of female history." "The partial distribution of advantages which has too long obtained, is, in this enlightened age, rapidly giving place to a more uniform system of information," she asserted. Women were at last "emerging from the clouds which have hitherto enveloped them, and *the revolution of events is advancing in that half of the human species, which hath hitherto been involved in the night of darkness, toward the irradiating sun of science.*" [1]

Most of Murray's contemporaries were less optimistic. The "American Lady" who wrote the "Second Vindication of the Rights of Women" in 1801 pointed out that, although men "do professedly condescend to acknowledge an equality which is evidently founded in nature; yet, they are by no means willing to ab[b]reviate their pretences to superiority." As a result, she observed accurately, woman's improvement could at present "answer no particular purpose in life." [2] Seen in this perspective, an educated woman in 1800 had only a modicum more control over her destiny than her uneducated grandmother had had in 1750: she could, if she wished, teach school for a few years before marriage, decide not to marry at all, choose a husband without consulting her parents, or raise her children in accordance with republican principles. But she could not, realistically, aspire to leave the feminine sphere altogether.

No persons understood this better than the students at the female academies. In her perceptive account of the Philadelphia Young Ladies Academy, Ann D. Gordon has noted the "striking and pathetic" fact that the girls' commencement addresses lacked any vision of a future. Instead of outlining their plans for employing their education after they had left school, the young women recalled the happy days spent with their classmates and then "leapt from academic achievements to immortality, as if nothing lay between their youth and their death." One of the few students at the Philadelphia academy who escaped these constraints was Priscilla Mason, whose salutatory address in 1793 suggested that soon "the Church, the Bar, and the Senate" would open to female participation. Yet even her wide-ranging view of the future was tempered by her notion of femininity: the only task she proposed for the new senators was prescribing a proper mode of dress for republican women.[3]

Like her, Eliza Southgate realized that her sexual identity necessarily limited her aspirations. In 1802, she disclosed, "I have often thought what profession I should choose were I a man" and expressed a preference for the law. But, she admitted, she knew that to be a "respected and admired" attorney was beyond the realm of possibility for her or any other female. After sarcastically observing that since she was "*born* a woman" she had only to wait "till some clever fellow shall take a fancy" to her and then resign herself to whatever marital circumstances ensued, she remarked revealingly, "I should not be content with mediocrity in any thing, but as a woman I am equal to the generality of my sex, and I do not feel that great desire of fame I think I should if I was a man." Even after nearly two centuries the sense of sadness and resignation with which she penned that inherently contradictory passage comes through clearly. Southgate belonged to the first generation of female Americans who could even think about entering male professions, but the thought, as she well knew, did not make the reality.[4]

Yet if the white women who lived in early nineteenth-century America could not escape the constraints of femininity, the precise nature of those constraints differed subtly, but significantly, from the limits that had governed their colonial grandmothers. As the nature of American government and society had changed during the half-century that witnessed the Revolution, so too had American notions of womanhood. Not the least of those changes was the very attempt to place the feminine role in the context of society as a whole. Prior to the Revolution, when the private realm of the household was seen as having little connection with the public world of politics and economics, woman's secular role was viewed solely in its domestic setting. That individual women could have a positive — or negative — effect on their husbands, suitors, or perhaps children, was widely recognized, but no one, male or female, wrote or thought about the possibility that women might affect the wider secular society through their individual or collective behavior. In theory, their sexual identity was a barrier that separated them from the public world. Femininity, it was believed, placed them one step removed from the imperatives and obligations that ruled the white male population.

The war necessarily broke down the barrier which seemed to insulate women from the realm of politics, for they, no less than men, were caught up in the turmoil that enveloped the entire populace. Although some Americans tried to maintain the traditional fiction that a woman was "consequently no party in the present war" or that, in one woman's words, "as a Woman I cannot or at least I will not be a Traytor to either side," most understood that the old notions had to be discarded. Abigail Adams is a case in point. In June 1776, she still adhered to the conventional formula, telling John, "I can serve my partner, my family and myself, and injoy the Satisfaction of your serving your Country," thereby indicating that she believed her contributions to the patriots' cause had to be filtered through the medium of her husband. But less than two years later, in February 1778, she described her "satisfaction in the Consciousness of having discharged *my* duty to the publick." Like others of her contemporaries, she no longer drew a sharp dividing line between the feminine sphere and the masculine realm of public responsibilities.[5]

But to recognize that women had a role to fulfill in the wider society was not to declare that male and female roles were, or should be, the same. Not even Judith Sargent Murray conceived of an androgynous world; men's and women's functions were to be equal and complementary, not identical. And so the citizens of the republic set out to discover and define woman's public role. They found it not in the notion that women should directly participate in politics, New Jersey's brief experiment with woman suffrage to the contrary. Rather, they located woman's public role in her domestic responsibilities, in her obligation to create a supportive home life for her husband, and particularly in her duty to raise republican sons who would love their country and preserve its virtuous character.

The ironies of this formulation were manifest. On the one hand, society had at last formally recognized women's work as valuable. No longer was domesticity denigrated; no longer was the feminine sphere subordinated to the masculine, nor were women regarded as inferior. The white women of nineteenth-century America could take pride in their sex in a way their female ancestors could not. The importance of motherhood was admitted by all, and women could glory in the special role laid out for them in the copious literature that rhapsodized about beneficent feminine influences both inside and outside the home.

But, on the other hand, the republican definition of womanhood, which began as a marked step forward, grew ever more restrictive as the decades passed. Woman's domestic and maternal role came to be seen as so important that it was believed women sacrificed their femininity if they attempted to be more (or other) than wives and mothers. Accordingly, the women who were most successful in winning society's acceptance of their extradomestic activities were those who — like teachers, missionaries, or charitable workers — managed to conceal their flouting of convention by subsuming their actions within the confines of an orthodox, if somewhat broadened, conception of womanhood and its proper functions.

In the prerevolutionary world, no one had bothered to define domesticity: the private realm seemed unimportant, and besides, women could not escape their inevitable destiny. In the postrevolutionary world, the social significance of household and family was recognized, and simultaneously women began to be able to choose different ways of conducting their lives. As a direct result, a definition of domesticity was at last required. The process of defining woman's proper role may well have stiffened the constraints that had always encircled female lives, but that definition also — by its very existence — signaled American society's growing comprehension of woman's importance within a sphere far wider than a private household or a marital relationship.

The legacy of the American Revolution for women was thus ambiguous. Republican womanhood eventually became Victorian womanhood, but at the same time the egalitarian rhetoric of the Revolution provided the women's rights movement with its earliest vocabulary, and the republican academies produced its first leaders. Few historical events can ever be assessed in absolute terms. With respect to its impact on women, the American Revolution is no exception.

ABBREVIATIONS APPEARING
IN THE SOURCES AND REFERENCES

AAS:	American Antiquarian Society, Worcester, Mass.
ALUV:	Alderman Library, University of Virginia, Charlottesville.
AO:	Audit Office series, Public Record Office, London.
APSL:	American Philosophical Society Library, Philadelphia.
CHS:	Connecticut Historical Society, Hartford.
CU:	Rare Book and Manuscript Library, Columbia University, New York City.
CW:	Research Archives, Colonial Williamsburg Foundation, Williamsburg, Va.
DU:	Duke University Library, Durham, N.C.
EAL:	*Early American Literature*.
EGS:	Earl Gregg Swem Library, College of William and Mary, Williamsburg, Va.
EI:	Essex Institute, Salem, Mass.
EIHC:	*Essex Institute Historical Collections*.
GHS:	Georgia Historical Society, Savannah.
HCA:	High Court of the Admiralty series, Public Record Office, London.
HL:	Houghton Library, Harvard University, Cambridge, Mass.
HSP:	Historical Society of Pennsylvania, Philadelphia.
JIH:	*Journal of Interdisciplinary History*.
JMF:	*Journal of Marriage and the Family*.
LCMD:	Library of Congress Manuscript Division, Washington, D.C.
LCP/HSP:	Library Company of Philadelphia, housed at HSP.
MCNY:	Museum of the City of New York.
MHM:	*Maryland Historical Magazine*.

MHS: Massachusetts Historical Society, Boston.
NA: National Archives, Washington, D.C.
NCDAH: North Carolina Division of Archives and History, Raleigh.
NEHGR: *New England Historical and Genealogical Register.*
NHHS: New Hampshire Historical Society, Concord.
NYHS: New-York Historical Society, New York City.
NYPL: Manuscripts and Archives Division, New York Public Library; Astor, Tilden, and Lenox Foundations.
PMHB: *Pennsylvania Magazine of History and Biography.*
RIHS: Rhode Island Historical Society, Providence.
SCHGM: *South Carolina Historical and Genealogical Magazine.*
SCHS: South Carolina Historical Society, Charleston.
SCL: South Caroliniana Library, University of South Carolina, Columbia.
SHC/UNC: Southern Historical Collections, University of North Carolina, Chapel Hill.
SLRC: Arthur and Elizabeth Schlesinger Library, Radcliffe College, Cambridge, Mass.
VHS: Virginia Historical Society, Richmond.
VMHB: *Virginia Magazine of History and Biography.*
WMQ: *William and Mary Quarterly.*
YL: Beinecke Library, Yale University, New Haven, Ct.

GLOSSARY OF MAJOR
FAMILIES AND SOURCES

Bowen/Clark (R.I. and S.C.) The sisters Lydia Bowen (Mrs. John Innes) Clark, Eliza Bowen, and Anna Bowen Mitchell; the Clarks' daughters, Anne Eliza and Harriet; John's sister, Anne Clark Hooper (see *Murray*) (John Clark Papers, RIHS).

Coalter/Tucker/Randolph (Va.) The three wives of John Coalter: Maria Rind, Margaret Davenport, and Fanny Tucker; Fanny's mother, Frances Bland Randolph (Mrs. St. George) Tucker; Fanny's stepmother, Lelia Skipwith Tucker; Fanny's sister-in-law Judith (Mrs. Richard) Randolph (Brown-Coalter-Tucker Papers, Tucker-Coleman Papers, both EGS).

DeLancey/Izard/Manigault (N.Y. and S.C.) Elizabeth Colden DeLancey; her daughters, Anne, Sukey, Betsy DeLancey, and Alice DeLancey (Mrs. Ralph) Izard; Alice's daughter, Margaret Izard (Mrs. Gabriel) Manigault (Manigault Papers, SCL, SCHS; Ralph Izard Papers, SCL, LCMD; DeLancey Family Papers, MCNY; Louis Manigault Papers, DU).

Fisher/Norris/Logan (Pa.) Sally Logan (Mrs. Thomas) Fisher; her cousin Peggy Emlen; her sister-in-law Deborah Norris (Mrs. George) Logan; Deborah's mother, Mary Norris; Mary's cousin Mary Norris (Mrs. John) Dickinson, and her daughter Maria; the Norrises' cousin Hannah Griffitts (Loudoun Papers, Logan Papers, Maria Dickinson Logan Papers, Logan-Fisher-Fox Papers, Sally Logan Fisher Diary, Norris Family of Fairhill Papers, all HSP).

Johnston/Iredell/Blair (N.C.) Hannah Johnston (Mrs. James) Iredell; her daughter Anne; her sister Jean Johnston Blair; Jean's daughter Helen (Nelly) Blair Tredwell (James Iredell Jr. and Sr. Papers, DU; Charles Johnson Collection, NCDAH; Hayes Collection, SHC/UNC).

Lee/Shippen (Va. and Pa.) The sisters Alice Lee (Mrs. William) Shippen and Hannah Lee Corbin; Alice's daughter, Nancy Shippen (Mrs. Henry) Livingston (Lee Family Papers, VHS; Shippen Family Papers, LCMD).

Mordecai (N.C.) The two wives of Jacob Mordecai, the half-sisters Judith Myers and Rebecca Myers; Judith's daughters Rachel and Ellen; Rebecca's mother, Joyce Myers, of N.Y. (Jacob Mordecai Papers, DU; Pattie Mordecai Papers, NCDAH; Mordecai Family Papers, SHC/UNC).

Murray (Mass. and N.C.) Elizabeth Murray Smith Inman; her nieces Betsy Murray (Robbins), Dolly Murray (Forbes), and Anne Clark (Mrs. William) Hooper (see *Bowen/Clark*); her great-niece Anne Jean Robbins (James M. Robbins Papers, MHS; Murray Family Papers, NYHS).

Smith/Adams (Mass.) The sisters Mary Smith (Mrs. Richard) Cranch, Elizabeth Smith (first Mrs. John Shaw, then Mrs. Stephen Peabody), and Abigail Smith Adams; Mrs. Adams's daughter Nabby Adams (Mrs. William) Smith (Shaw Family Papers, Cranch Family Papers, LCMD; Adams Papers, MHS).

Willing (Pa.) The sisters Mary Willing (Mrs. William III) Byrd, Anne Willing (Mrs. Tench) Francis, and Elizabeth Willing (Mrs. Samuel) Powel; their niece, Anne Willing Bingham (Byrd Family Papers, VHS; Powel Collection, HSP).

ESSAY ON SOURCES

The following survey is by no means comprehensive. It is intended to serve as a brief guide for persons interested in the history of the American women, white and black, who lived in the latter half of the eighteenth century. This essay concentrates upon the writings of women themselves, but researchers should always be aware that much information can also be obtained from men's diaries and letters. The notes should be consulted for references on specific topics, since the sources will be described here in general terms.

SECONDARY SOURCES

Studies of colonial women fall into three groups: compilations of anecdotes; early attempts at serious scholarship produced in the middle years of the twentieth century; and recent articles and books, which draw upon both family history and the interdisciplinary field of women's studies.

The distinguishing feature of works in the first category is their lack of theoretical structure. Individual volumes can be useful sources of information, but all fail to provide a conceptual framework within which the many separate stories can be analyzed and understood. The earliest such books were Elizabeth Ellet's *The Women of the American Revolution* (3 vols., New York, 1848, 1850) and her *Domestic History of the American Revolution* (New York, 1850). Direct descendants of Ellet are still being published today; Sally Smith Booth, *The Women of '76* (New York, 1973), and Paul Engle, *Women in the American Revolution* (Chicago, 1976), are but two recent examples of this persistent genre. Among the best are those written by Alice Morse

Earle around the turn of the century; see especially her *Child Life in Colonial Days* (New York, 1899); *Home Life in Colonial Days* (New York, 1898); and *Colonial Dames and Good Wives* (Boston, 1895).

In the 1920s and 1930s authors at last began to transcend the limitations of the anecdotal approach and to try to examine hypotheses about colonial women's lives. The influential volumes by Elisabeth Anthony Dexter, *Colonial Women of Affairs* (Boston, 1924; rev. ed., 1931) and *Career Women of America 1776-1840* (Francestown, N.H., 1950), were transitional. Unabashedly anecdotal, they nevertheless developed an argument — that colonial women often worked outside the home — which has had an enormous and continuing impact upon interpretations of female lives in early America. The first works by trained scholars were two revised doctoral dissertations published in the 1930s: Mary Sumner Benson, *Women in Eighteenth-Century America: A Study of Opinion and Social Usage* (New York, 1935; reprint, Port Washington, N.Y., 1966); and Julia Cherry Spruill, *Women's Life and Work in the Southern Colonies* (Chapel Hill, N.C., 1938; reprint, New York, 1973). These two pioneering efforts still stand almost alone as serious, book-length discussions of colonial women.

The revival of interest in women's history during the past decade has stimulated a number of scholars to enter the field, which had remained largely fallow except for Janet Wilson James's unpublished doctoral dissertation, "Changing Ideas about Women in the United States, 1776-1825" (Radcliffe College, 1954). Recent years have witnessed the publication of such important articles as Nancy F. Cott, "Divorce and the Changing Status of Women in Eighteenth-Century Massachusetts," *WMQ* 3rd ser., XXXIII (1976), 586-614; Mary Beth Norton, "Eighteenth-Century American Women in Peace and War: The Case of the Loyalists," *ibid.*, 386-409; Alexander Keyssar, "Widowhood in Eighteenth-Century Massachusetts: A Problem in the History of the Family," *Perspectives in American History*, VIII (1974), 83-119; Linda K. Kerber, "Daughters of Columbia: Educating Women for the Republic 1787-1805," in Stanley Elkins and Eric McKitrick, eds., *The Hofstadter Aegis* (New York, 1974), 36-59; Kerber, "The Republican Mother: Women and the Enlightenment — An American Perspective," *American Quarterly*, XXVIII (1976), 187-205; and the first five essays in Carol Berkin and Mary Beth Norton, eds., *Women of America: A History* (Boston, 1979). Although the primary emphasis of Nancy F. Cott's excellent book, *The Bonds of Womanhood: "Woman's Sphere" in New England, 1780-1835* (New Haven, Ct., 1977), lies in the early nineteenth century, it is also useful in illuminating the lives of northern women before 1800.

One might suppose that new scholarship on the colonial family would have added greatly to our knowledge of the female members of early American households. Regrettably, though, most of the works on family history have been heavily male-oriented, partly because of the nature of the available sources, but mainly (it must be said) because scholars in the field have not generally asked sex-differentiated questions. Articles by Daniel Scott Smith and Robert V. Wells constitute an exception to this rule; see, in particular, Wells, "Quaker Marriage Patterns in a Colonial Perspective," *WMQ*, 3rd ser., XXIX (1972), 415-442; and Smith, "Parental Power and Marriage Patterns: An Analysis of Historical Trends in Hingham, Massachusetts," *JMF*, XXXV (1973), 419–428. Works on child rearing, too, tend to concentrate on fathers, although they are less subject to a male bias than are other studies of the family. The essays by Joseph Illick and John Walzer in Lloyd deMause, ed., *The History of Childhood* (New York, 1974); Daniel Blake Smith, "Autonomy and Affection: Parents and Children in Eighteenth-Century Chesapeake Families," *The Psychohistory Review*, VI, nos. 2–3 (fall–winter 1977–1978), 32–51; and especially Philip J. Greven, Jr., *The Protestant Temperament: Patterns of Child-Rearing, Religious Experience, and the Self in Early America* (New York, 1978) should be consulted by serious scholars.

PRINTED PRIMARY SOURCES

The scholar searching for references to published and unpublished primary sources can initially rely upon several helpful bibliographies: Harriette M. Forbes, *New England Diaries 1602–1800* (Topsfield, Mass., 1923); Eugenie Leonard, Sophie Drinker, and Miriam Holden, *The American Woman in Colonial and Revolutionary Times, 1565–1800: A Syllabus with Bibliography* (Philadelphia, 1962); William S. Thomas, "American Revolutionary Diaries," *New-York Historical Society Quarterly Bulletin*, VI (1922–1923), 32–35, 61–71, 101–107, 143–147; VII (1923–1924), 28–35; and two by William Matthews, *American Diaries: An Annotated Bibliography of American Diaries Written Prior to the Year 1861* (Berkeley, Calif., 1945), and *American Diaries in Manuscript 1580–1954: A Descriptive Bibliography* (Athens, Ga., 1974).

When one embarks upon the study of women in the past, it is perhaps tempting — because it is also easiest — to look first at the wives and daughters of "great white men." Indeed, historians have often adopted this approach, writing volumes entitled *Alexander Hamilton's Wife* (Alice Desmond; New York, 1952) or *The Women in Their Lives: The Distaff Side of the Founding Fathers* (Frank Donovan; New York, 1966). Current publication projects facilitate this approach, since modern editors, unlike those of the nineteenth century, do not necessarily deem women's letters to be unimportant. Thus in such collections as Julian Boyd et al., eds., *The Papers of Thomas Jefferson* (Princeton, N.J., 1950–), Leonard W. Labaree et al., eds., *The Papers of Benjamin Franklin* (New Haven, Ct., 1959–), and Don Higginbotham, ed., *The Papers of James Iredell* (2 vols., Raleigh, N.C., 1976), one finds much pertinent material. In addition, a number of special volumes of correspondence are relevant to women, in particular Carl Van Doren, ed., *The Letters of Benjamin Franklin & Jane Mecom* (Princeton, N.J., 1950); William G. Roelker, ed., *Benjamin Franklin and Catharine Ray Greene: Their Correspondence 1755–1790* (Philadelphia, 1949); Frances N. Mason, ed., *My Dearest Polly: Letters of Chief Justice John Marshall to His Wife . . . 1799–1831* (Richmond, Va., 1961); and Edwin M. Betts and James A. Bear, eds., *The Family Letters of Thomas Jefferson* (Columbia, Mo., 1966).

In this context the Adams family stands in a class by itself, because so many of its papers have been published. It is, of course, preferable to turn first to the most recent volumes: Lyman H. Butterfield et al., eds., *Adams Family Correspondence* (4 vols., Cambridge, Mass., 1963, 1973), which ends in 1782, and Butterfield et al., eds., *The Book of Abigail and John* (Cambridge, Mass., 1975), which continues to 1784. But for correspondence after 1784 (if one does not want to turn to the originals, available on microfilm), it is still necessary to rely on the earlier editions prepared by Charles Francis Adams: *Letters of John Adams, Addressed to His Wife* (2 vols., 3rd ed., Boston, 1841), and *Letters of Mrs. Adams, The Wife of John Adams* (2 vols., 3rd ed., Boston, 1841). Also available for the later period is Stewart Mitchell, ed., *New Letters of Abigail Adams 1788-1801* (Boston, 1947), which consists of letters written to Mary Smith Cranch. See, too, *Warren-Adams Letters . . . 1743-1814*, Collections of the Massachusetts Historical Society, LXXII-LXXIII (Boston, 1917, 1925), and [Caroline de Windt, ed.], *Journal and Correspondence of Miss Adams, Daughter of John Adams* (2 vols., New York and London, 1841-1842).

But one does not have to look solely at women connected with eminent men to find printed sources for the revolutionary period. Many diaries dating from the latter half of the eighteenth century have been published and are readily available to researchers. A recent compilation of diaries is Elizabeth Evans, *Weathering the Storm: Women of the American Revolution* (New York, 1975). Although it suffers from inadequate editing — including a poor introduction, a failure to indicate the sources of the diaries it reprints, and silent excisions from the originals — the book nevertheless can serve as an introduction to women's private writings in the revolutionary years. Among the most interesting published diaries for the period 1765-1785 are *Jemima Condict, Her Book. Being a Transcript of the Diary of an Essex County Maid during the Revolutionary War* (Newark, N.J., 1930); Alice M. Earle, ed., *Diary of Anna Green Winslow, A Boston School Girl of 1771* (Boston, 1894); Albert C. Myers, ed., *Sally Wister's Journal* (Philadelphia, 1902); John Jackson, ed., *Margaret Morris: Her Journal with Biographical Sketch and Notes* (Philadelphia, 1949); and Raymond C. Werner, ed., "Diary of Grace Growden Galloway," *PMHB*, LV (1931), 32-94, LVIII (1934), 152-189. [Lydia M. Post], *Personal Recollections of the American Revolution. A Private Journal* (New York, 1859), appears to have been altered by its nineteenth-century editor and so should be used with great care. Henry D. Biddle, who prepared *Extracts from the Journal of Elizabeth Drinker, from 1759 to 1807, A.D.* (Philadelphia, 1889), evidently did not change the entries he selected for publication, but he did omit much material of interest to modern scholars. Consequently, historians should rely on the original of this major source, available on microfilm from the Historical Society of Pennsylvania.

The most important surviving diary for the prewar period is Esther Edwards Burr's extended journal-letter to her friend Sarah Prince, 1754-1757, original in the Yale Library, soon to be published in an edition edited by Laurie Crumpacker and Carol Karlsen (my thanks go to Ms. Crumpacker for allowing me to use her typescript of the Burr journal). For the postwar years there are a number of diaries already in print: Ethel Armes, ed., *Nancy Shippen Her Journal Book* (Philadelphia, 1935); [Lucinda Lee Orr], *Journal of a Young Lady of Virginia 1782*, ed. Emily V. Mason (Baltimore, 1871); Lizzie Mason and James D. Phillips, eds., "The Journal of

Elizabeth Cranch," *EIHC*, LXXX (1944), 1–36; "Diary of Mary Orne Tucker, 1802," *ibid.*, LXXVII (1941), 306–338; Sarah Cadbury, ed., "Extracts from the Diary of Mrs. Ann Warder," *PMHB*, XVII (1893), 444–462, XVIII (1894), 51–63; and William Bottorff and Roy Flannagan, eds., "The Diary of Frances Baylor Hill of 'Hillsborough' King and Queen County Virginia (1797)," *EAL*, II, no. 3 (winter 1967), 4–53.

Collections of letters to and from American women are also of great value to the scholar. For the war itself, two volumes are especially important: Herbert T. Wade and Robert Lively, eds., *This Glorious Cause: The Adventures of Two Company Officers in Washington's Army* (Princeton, N.J., 1958), which contains, pp. 167–245, the letters of Joseph and Sarah Hodgkins of Ipswich, Mass.; and Caroline Gilman, ed., *Letters of Eliza Wilkinson, during the Invasion and Possession of Charlestown, S.C. by the British in the Revolutionary War* (New York, 1839; reprint, New York, 1969). Questions have been raised about the reliability of the latter, since Gilman was a well-known novelist, but recent discoveries in Gilman's papers by Ms. Catherine Clinton indicate that the Wilkinson letters are probably authentic. (But for information on two fake diaries, see Mary Beth Norton, "Letter to the Editor," *WMQ*, 3rd. ser., XXXIII [1976], 715–717).

In addition, there are a number of other published sets of relevant correspondence. For teenaged girls, see Mark Van Doren, ed., *Correspondence of Aaron Burr and His Daughter Theodosia* (New York, 1929); "Kennon Letters," published serially in *VMHB*, starting with XXXI (1923), 185–206, and extending beyond the chronological scope of this book; Helen M. Morgan, ed., *A Season in New York 1801* (Pittsburgh, Pa., 1969); John A. H. Sweeney, ed., "The Norris-Fisher Correspondence: A Circle of Friends, 1779–1782," *Delaware History*, VI (1954–1955), 187–232; and J. Hall Pleasants, ed., "Letters of Molly and Hetty Tilghman," *MHM*, XXI (1926), 20–30, 123–149, 219–241, an especially delightful selection. Elise Pinckney, ed., *The Letterbook of Eliza Lucas Pinckney 1739–1762* (Chapel Hill, N.C., 1972), and Simon P. Gratz, ed., "Some Material for a Biography of Mrs. Elizabeth Fergusson, Née Graeme," *PMHB*, XXXIX (1915), 257–321, 385–409; XLI (1917), 385–398; both begin in their subjects' youth and continue into their maturity. Other collections containing interesting material are Mary V. S. White, ed., *Fifteen Letters of Nathalie Sumter* (Columbia, S.C., 1942); J. Lawrence Boggs, ed., "The Cornelia (Bell) Paterson Letters," *Proceedings of the New Jersey Historical Society*, n.s., XV (1930), 508–517, XVI (1931), 56–67, 187–201; Leo Hershkowitz and Isidore Meyer, eds., *Letters of the Franks Family (1733–1748)* (Waltham, Mass., 1968); and John J. Smith, ed., *Letters of Doctor Richard Hill and his Children* (Philadelphia, 1854).

Eliza Southgate Bowne, *A Girl's Life Eighty Years Ago*, ed. Clarence Cook (London, 1888), prints a large selection from the thoughtful letters of an intelligent young Maine woman, and is perhaps the single most significant volume covering the lives of girls in the 1790s and early 1800s. A comparison of Bowne's few surviving letters — in the Townsend Lawrence Papers, New-York Historical Society, and Bedinger-Dandridge Collection, Duke University — with the published text indicates that the editor was scrupulously accurate in his transcription of the original documents, and thus that the edition is entirely trustworthy.

Memoirs written by women themselves or compiled by their descendants are additional valuable sources. Because of nineteenth-century Americans' interest in the Revolution, more works of this sort were prepared than one might otherwise have anticipated. The most important such book has been cited repeatedly in the preceding pages; it is Frederick Tupper and Helen Tyler Brown, eds., *Grandmother Tyler's Book, The Recollections of Mary Palmer Tyler 1775-1866* (New York, 1925). Of the ones composed by eighteenth-century women, the more significant are *Bessie; or, Reminiscences of a Daughter* . . . (New Haven, Ct., 1861); Anne MacVicar Grant, *Memoirs of an American Lady* (Albany, N.Y., 1876); Hannah Adams, *A Memoir of Miss Hannah Adams, Written by Herself* (Boston, 1832); Elizabeth Johnston, *Recollections of a Georgia Loyalist*, ed. Arthur W. Eaton (New York, 1901); and especially William Maxwell, comp., "My Mother: Memoirs of Mrs. Helen Read," *Lower Norfolk County Virginia Antiquary*, printed serially from I (1895-1896), 60-62, to III (1899-1901), 46-50.

Volumes prepared by relatives or friends, bringing together extracts from the woman's writings, can be of similar value to historians. [Margaretta Faugeres, ed.], *The Posthumous Works of Ann Eliza Bleecker, in Prose and Verse* (New York, 1793), is a daughter's tribute to her mother's literary talents. Samuel Hopkins's *Memoirs of the Life of Mrs. Sarah Osborn* . . . (Worcester, Mass., 1799), celebrates the piety of the woman who had helped Hopkins obtain a coveted pulpit (see chapter 5, above). David Ramsay praised his deceased wife in *Memoirs of the Life of Martha Laurens Ramsay* (3rd ed., Boston, 1812), and Herman Mann publicized the patriotism of Deborah Sampson Gannett in *The Female Review: Memoirs of an American Young Lady* (Dedham, Mass., 1797). Other examples of this same genre are William Patten, *Memoirs of Mrs. Ruth Patten, of Hartford, Conn.* (Hartford, Ct., 1834; see also *Interesting Family Letters of the Late Mrs. Ruth Patten* [n.p., 1845]); *The Power of Faith, Exemplified in the Life and Writings of the Late Mrs. Isabella Graham* (New York, 1843); John Frederick Schroeder, *Memoir of the Life and Character of Mrs. Mary Anna Boardman* (New Haven, Ct., 1849); and, for a particularly interesting but little-known woman, Amelia Elizabeth Dwight, *Memorials of Mary Wilder White*, ed. Mary Wilder Tileston (Boston, 1903).

Finally, mention must be made of the closest thing there is to an oral history of the Revolution: Benson J. Lossing, *Hours with the Living Men and Women of the Revolution. A Pilgrimage* (New York, 1889), which recounts in detail (unfortunately, with nineteenth-century emendations) some of Lossing's interviews with aged survivors of the American war for independence. If only he had had a tape recorder . . . .

MANUSCRIPT SOURCES

The major New England repository for the private papers of late eighteenth-century American families is the Massachusetts Historical Society. Unfortunately, the lack of a chronological index to their collections makes it difficult to locate sources when one does not already know the names of appropriate families. The chief collections cited in this study are the Robert Treat Paine Papers, which include much correspondence with Paine's sisters Eunice Paine and Abigail Paine Greenleaf (and his niece, Abigail Greenleaf, Jr.); Sedgwick Papers II and III, in which may be found the letters of Abigail Dwight and her daughter Pamela Dwight Sedgwick; and James M. Robbins Papers, the first six volumes of which are the correspondence of Robbins's great-greataunt, Elizabeth Murray Smith Inman. Nina M. Tiffany, ed., *Letters of James Murray Loyalist* (Boston, 1901), should be used in conjunction with the latter, since it reprints some letters not found in the manuscript collection. The Henry Knox Papers and Timothy Pickering Papers, both valuable for wartime husband-wife correspondence, have been published in microfilm editions, as have the letterbooks of Mercy Otis Warren.

Also of importance at the MHS are the Cushing-Orne Papers, which contain letters written to the Salem teenager Peggy Orne; Gilman Papers, the correspondence of a family divided between Massachusetts and Ohio; Jacob Norton Papers, which include the original diary of Elizabeth Cranch Norton, daughter of Mary Smith Cranch (partly published in *EIHC*; see above); and Harrison Gray Otis Papers, interesting for the courtship of Otis and Sally Foster.

Although the American Antiquarian Society, Worcester, Massachusetts, is primarily known for its collection of printed works, its manuscript holdings are significant. The letters of Sarah Osborn to Joseph Fish are of special importance for students of American religion, since they describe Mrs. Osborn's revival activities in great detail as well as revealing her pious reflections. The extensive Dwight Foster Papers contain much correspondence with his wife, Rebecca, and his young daughter Pamela in the 1790s, while he was away serving in Congress. The diaries of Patty Rogers (1785), Ruth Henshaw [Bascom] (1789–1814), and Sarah Ripley [Stearns] (1799–1801, 1805–1808) give added insight into the lives of young New England women at the end of the century.

At the Essex Institute, Salem, Massachusetts, may be found more material pertinent to republican girls: the correspondence of Eliza Waite, 1786–1792, and the Cutts Family Papers, which include the letters of Mary Carter (of Newburyport) and Hannah Emery (of Exeter), 1787–1791. The diary of the Haverhill housewife Mary Orne Tucker, 1802, was partly published in the *EIHC* (see above); also valuable are two related collections, the Drury Family and Dr. John Drury Papers.

Important manuscript holdings are also located in Cambridge, Massachusetts. The Arthur and Elizabeth Schlesinger Library of the History of Women, Radcliffe College, is of less use than might be imagined, because its unpublished collections concentrate on the nineteenth and twentieth centuries. But it does own the abridged journal of Sarah Ripley [Stearns] for the years 1801–1805; the Poor Family Papers, which include the letters of Lucy Tappan Pierce and her husband, John; the May-Goddard Papers, with more letters of New England schoolgirls at the end of the century; and the fascinating manuscript "Reminiscences" of Eliza Perkins Cabot (b. 1791) in the Cabot Family Papers. At Houghton Library, Harvard, one finds the laconic but useful diaries of Sarah Snell Bryant (the mother of William Cullen Bryant); the lengthy correspondence of Paine Wingate, a New Hampshire congressman, and William Palfrey, a revolutionary activist, with their respective wives and daughters; and the letterbook of Catherine and Mary Byles, 1793–1835.

Outside of Massachusetts are other New England repositories with significant collections. At the New Hampshire Historical Society, Concord, are the Jeremy Belknap Papers, which include the letters of his wife, and especially the Josiah Bartlett Papers, in which are preserved both sides of the wartime correspondence of that congressman and his wife, Mary. The Connecticut Historical Society, Hartford, possesses the diaries of the teenaged sisters Nabby and Betsy Foote, 1775–1776, and the Rhode Island Historical Society, Providence, owns the travel diary of another young New England woman, Susan Lear, 1788, which is primarily important for its firsthand description of Judith Sargent Murray, then Mrs. Stevens. The John Brown and Enos Hitchcock Papers contain interesting family correspondence; the latter is also valuable for information concerning Hitchcock's child-rearing tract, *Memoirs of the Bloomsgrove Family* (1790). But the major collection at the RIHS is beyond question the John Innes Clark Papers, not only because it includes the useful correspondence of Lydia Bowen Clark with her sisters Frances Bowen Moore and Anna Bowen Mitchell, who migrated to South Carolina, but also because it contains a myriad of letters from the Clarks' schoolgirl daughters, Anne Eliza and Harriet, in the 1790s.

There is also much manuscript material available for the study of women who lived in the middle colonies. In New York City several libraries have collections of interest. The DeLancey Family Papers (Museum of the City of New York) include the important copybook "DeLancey Reminiscences," and in the Columbia University Library are the John Jay Papers, with the correspondence of Sarah Livingston Jay, her mother, sisters, and daughters; and the Moore Family Papers, with the letters of Charity Clarke, the home manufacturing activist of the late 1760s. The Gansevoort-Lansing and Hudson Family Collections at the New York Public Library are also valuable, the latter for insights into the lives of several widowed business-women. Three diaries at the NYPL deserve special mention: that of Mary Cooper, the Long Island evangelical, 1768–1773; that of Elizabeth DeHart Bleecker [McDonald], a young matron, 1799–1806; and that of Henrietta Bevier, a student at Sarah Pierce's academy, Litchfield, Connecticut, summer 1809.

The chief repository of interest in New York City, though, is the New-York Historical Society. Many small collections in its miscellaneous manuscripts category are exceptional; these include the letters of Margaretta Akerly, a student at the Moravian Academy; the John Brown Family Papers, the correspondence of a family divided between New Jersey, the Bahamas, and South Carolina, with much information on blacks; the wartime letters of Mr. and Mrs. James Clinton; and papers of Maria and Cornelia Clinton, daughters of Governor George Clinton. Also at the NYHS are the large Bancker family collection (a prime example of how men's letters can serve as sources for women's experience) and the papers of Joseph Reed, which provide information about his lengthy courtship of Esther DeBerdt and are the best single source for the study of the Philadelphia Ladies Association of 1780, which she headed. The Murray Family Papers are directly related to the J. M. Robbins Papers at the MHS, for they center around Elizabeth Murray Inman's brother John and his children. Finally, the typescript "Narrative of Mrs. Abraham Brasher, 1801," is an excellent private memoir of the prerevolutionary and revolutionary years.

In Philadelphia, aside from some papers of various female members of the Bache family (at the American Philosophical Society Library), the chief manuscript collections of interest are housed in the Historical Society of Pennsylvania. These include three collections actually owned by the Library Company of Philadelphia: the Benjamin Rush Papers, with its volume of material pertinent to Elizabeth Graeme Fergusson (vol. 40); the numerous letters of William Dillwyn and his daughter Susanna, beginning in 1778; and the poems of Hannah Griffitts.

The holdings of the HSP itself are of extraordinary importance, especially for the extensive documentation of the lives of the closely allied Logan, Norris, Fisher, and Dickinson families (see glossary of major families and sources for specific collection names). In addition, the HSP possesses the Thomas McKean and Edward Hand Papers, each containing husband-wife correspondence during the war; the letters and diaries of Rebecca Shoemaker and her daughters, Margaret and Anna Rawle (Clifford), 1780–1786; the sixty-year correspondence of Eleanor Parke Custis Lewis and Elizabeth Bordley Gibson; the Emlen Collection, which includes the many commonplace books of the Quaker Anne Emlen Mifflin; the Powel Collection of material pertinent to Elizabeth Willing Powel; the huge collection of Meredith Papers, with the correspondence of Elizabeth Meredith and her daughter-in-law, the writer Gertrude Ogden Meredith; the Parker-Brinley Papers, comprising the letters of women in England, Canada, and New Jersey; and the Samuel W. Fisher Papers, which contain the fascinating extract books and memorial essays prepared by Fisher's mother-in-law, Sarah Rhoads.

Available at the National Archives, Washington, D.C., are the Papers of the Continental Congress, microfilms M-247 and M-332, which include women's petitions to Congress, depositions about British wartime atrocities, and the lists of slaves who embarked from New York City at the end of the war. Also at the archives are the Revolutionary War Pension Applications, film M-804. Although soldiers' widows did not become eligible for pensions in their own right until the 1830s, the affidavits they submitted then are of great interest, reflecting their memories of the long-past revolutionary years.

The Library of Congress Manuscript Division, while not usually noted for its eighteenth-century holdings, has a number of valuable collections. The letterbooks of Christian Barnes, 1768-1783, and Sarah Hanschurst, 1762, give insight into the lives of Massachusetts and New Jersey women, respectively. Elizabeth Foote Washington's revealing journal is located in the Washington Family Papers, and the Peter Force Collection (compiled by the well-known nineteenth-century antiquarian) contains several interesting sets of papers, especially those of William and Esther Atlee of Pennsylvania, in series 9. The large Shippen Family, Pinckney Family, and Galloway-Maxcy-Markoe collections all include many letters from women, as do the small but exceptionally useful Rhodes Family Papers (correspondence of the poor Boston seamstress Mary Rhodes Bagnall) and Rebecca Stoddert Papers, the latter in the miscellaneous manuscripts collection. The papers of James Kent and those of Joseph Galloway contain much material pertinent to Elizabeth Kent and Grace and Betsy Galloway. Finally, the papers of Abigail Adams's sisters, Mary Smith Cranch (Cranch Family Papers) and Elizabeth Smith Shaw Peabody (Shaw Family Papers) allow one to explore the relationship among those three remarkable women.

In Williamsburg, Virginia, both Colonial Williamsburg, Inc., and the Earl Gregg Swem Library, College of William and Mary, have material of interest. The most important collection at Colonial Williamsburg is that of Elizabeth Ambler Brent Carrington, transcripts of which are located at the Virginia Historical Society, Richmond, and the Alderman Library, University of Virginia, with photostats at the LCMD. The letters range from girlish missives written during the Revolution to a series of reminiscences prepared for her younger sister in 1809–1810, and they add greatly to our understanding of the impact of the Revolution on southern women. At the Swem Library, two major collections relate to the female relatives of the distinguished lawyer St. George Tucker: the Tucker-Coleman Papers (on microfilm), which include the correspondence of his wife, Frances Bland Randolph; and the Brown-Coalter-Tucker Papers, which pertain to his daughter Fanny Tucker, the third wife of John Coalter, and her predecessors, Maria Rind and Margaret Davenport. Two other EGS collections with extensive female representation are the Armistead-Cocke Papers and the Blair-Banister-Braxton-Horner-Whiting Papers.

Holdings at the Virginia Historical Society, Richmond, include the papers of the Byrd and Lee families, and the small but interesting Holladay Family Papers. The Alderman Library, University of Virginia, owns one of the few surviving diaries of eighteenth-century southern women, that of Sarah Nourse, 1781–1783, in the Nourse Family Papers, which also contain the courtship correspondence of her son Joseph and Maria Bull. Another set of papers concerning young people at the ALUV is the John H. Cocke Papers, including the letters of his wife, Ann Barraud, and her parents.

The Duke University Library is another major repository of manuscript material. The letterbooks and daybooks of Robert Carter provide a detailed look into the lives of his slaves; so, too, the correspondence of Battaile Muse, a planters' agent in northern Virginia, allows one to learn a great deal about the experience of blacks on a number of different quarters and plantations. The Samuel Smith Downey Papers contain the letters of the North Carolina belle Sally Pomfret, and the Purviance-Courtenay Papers include the fascinating letters of the Maryland revolutionary Samuel Purviance to his wives and daughters. Four other major collections at the DU are closely related to holdings elsewhere in the South: the Eliza Lucas Pinckney Papers, which appear to be leaves from an early letterbook like that edited by Elise Pinckney; the Jacob Mordecai Papers; the Louis Manigault Papers, with the letters of the mature Margaret Izard Manigault; and the James Iredell Sr. and Jr. Papers.

In Raleigh, the North Carolina Division of Archives and History has only a few holdings of private papers, but the three major collections there relate directly to others in the area. The Pattie Mordecai Collection has more letters of Jacob Mordecai and his daughters Ellen and Rachel; and the Charles Johnson Collection includes many letters of the female members of the Johnston/Iredell/Blair family. Finally, the papers of the congressman John Steele, centering on his parents, should be used in conjunction with the John Steele Papers at the Southern Historical Collections, University of North Carolina, Chapel Hill, which focus more on Steele, his wife, Polly, and their daughter Ann, a student at Bethlehem.

At the SHC/UNC are many other important sets of papers. The Mordecai Family Papers, the "Hayes" Collection (Johnston/Iredell), and the Mrs. Francis B. Stewart Collection (Pinckney/Horry) contain further information about those influential families. In the Edmund Kirby-Smith Papers are the letters of Ephraim and Ruth Kirby of Connecticut; in the William Attmore Papers, the correspondence of the sisters Sarah Sitgreaves Attmore and Amaryllis Sitgreaves Ellis, from the 1790s; in the John and Keating Ball Papers, an excellent slave birth register. The lengthy, detailed letters of the young Georgia cousins Eliza McQueen and Mary Ann and Margaret Cowper comprise a large proportion of the Mackay-Stiles Papers. (Other parts of the same correspondence are in the Mackay-McQueen-Cowper Papers, Georgia Society of Colonial Dames Collection, Georgia Historical Society, Savannah.)

Papers of the Pinckney and Manigault/Izard families are found in various libraries in South Carolina: at the South Carolina Historical Society, Charleston, are the Manigault Papers (the letters of Gabriel and Margaret Izard Manigault in the 1780s and 1790s), the Eliza Lucas Pinckney Letters, and the Pinckney Family (Buist Family) Papers. At the South Caroliniana Library, University of South Carolina, are the Ralph Izard Papers (including correspondence with Izard's wife, Alice) and a further installment of the Manigault Papers.

Other collections of interest at the SCL include the Oliver Hart Papers; the "Album" of William Tennent III, which reprises his courtship correspondence with Susan Vergereau; and the Read Family Papers, containing the letters of Catherine Vanhorne Read and her sister Betsy Ludlow. At the SCHS one can find the letters Edward Rutledge addressed to his daughter Sarah in the 1790s, when she was in school in England; the Gibbes-Gilchrist Papers, with the letters of Sarah Gibbes to her son Robert, a Princeton student in the mid-1780s; the Langdon Cheves Collection, including the fragmentary diary of Ann Kinloch, 1799; and finally, the Bowen-Cooke Papers, with letters of Penuel Bowen, the New England clergyman who moved south and opened a school for young ladies in Savannah. His inaugural lecture, "Upon Virtue in general, and female Education & manners in particular," November 1786, is at the Georgia Historical Society.

NOTES

PREFACE

1. Book-length studies of colonial women, some of them very well researched, have tended to be topically arranged compendia of anecdotes or summaries of prescriptive literature. The best of such works are Julia Cherry Spruill, *Women's Life and Work in the Southern Colonies* (Chapel Hill, N.C., 1938; reprinted, New York, 1972); Mary Sumner Benson, *Women in Eighteenth-Century America: A Study of Opinion and Social Usage* (Port Washington, N.Y., reprint, 1966); and Eugenie Leonard, *The Dear-Bought Heritage* (Philadelphia, 1965).

2. This argument is especially evident in Roger Thompson, *Women in Stuart England and America* (Boston, 1974), but it can be discerned, explicitly or implicitly, in nearly every book on American women's history. The emphasis on work comes from the extraordinary influence of two books by Elisabeth Anthony Dexter: *Colonial Women of Affairs*, rev. ed. (Boston, 1931), and *Career Women of America 1776–1840* (Francestown, N.H., 1950).

3. For clear expositions of the theory of decline, see Mary P. Ryan, *Womanhood in America* (New York, 1975), and Ann D. Gordon and Mari Jo Buhle, "Sex and Class in Colonial and Nineteenth-Century America," in Berenice Carroll, ed., *Liberating Women's History* (Urbana, Ill., 1976), 278–300. The notion of domestic feminism has been developed most fully by Kathryn Kish Sklar, *Catharine Beecher: A Study in American Domesticity* (New Haven, Ct., 1973), Nancy F. Cott, *The Bonds of Womanhood: "Woman's Sphere" in New England, 1780–1835* (New Haven, Ct., 1977), and Daniel Scott Smith, "Family Limitation, Sexual Control, and Domestic Feminism in Victorian America," in Mary Hartman and Lois Banner, eds., *Clio's Consciousness Raised* (New York, 1974), 119–136.

4. See Elizabeth Cometti, "Women in the American Revolution," *New England Quarterly*, XX (1947), 329–346; Linda Grant DePauw, *Founding Mothers: Women of America in the Revolutionary Era* (New York, 1975); and Joan Hoff Wilson, "The Illusion of Change: Women and the American Revolution," in Alfred H. Young, ed., *The American Revolution: Explorations in the History of American Radicalism* (DeKalb, Ill., 1976), 383–445.

5. Anne Firor Scott, *The Southern Lady: From Pedestal to Politics, 1830–1930* (Chicago, 1970); William Chafe, *The American Woman: Her Changing Social, Economic, and Political Roles, 1920–1970* (New York, 1972); Jane Abray, "Feminism in the French Revolution," *American Historical Review*, LXXX (1975), 43–62; Patricia Higgins, "The Reactions of Women, with Special Reference to Women Petitioners," in Brian Manning, ed., *Politics, Religion and the English Civil War* (London, 1973), 177–222; Peggy R. Sanday, "Female Status in the Public Domain," in Michelle Rosaldo and Louise Lamphere, eds., *Woman, Culture, and Society* (Stanford, Calif., 1974), 189–206.

6. Although studies of female literacy disagree on the exact percentage of literate women, their findings indicate that, at maximum, about half the women in colonial America could sign their names. See Kenneth Lockridge, *Literacy in Colonial New England* . . . (New York, 1974), 38, 42; Alan Tully, "Literacy Levels and Educational Development in Rural Pennsylvania, 1729–1775," *Pennsylvania History*, XXXIX (1972), 304–305; and Ross W. Beales, Jr., "Studying Literacy at the Community Level: A Research Note," *JIH*, IX (1978), 93–102.

7. Book-length studies now being prepared by such scholars as Mary Maples Dunn, Lyle Koehler, and Laurel Thatcher Ulrich should soon help to fill this gap. See, too, Lois Green Carr and Lorena Walsh, "The Planter's Wife: The Experience of White Women in Seventeenth-Century Maryland," *WMQ*, 3rd ser., XXXIV (1977), 542–571.

CHAPTER ONE

1. The literature on the colonial family is vast. Useful starting places are David Rothman, "A Note on the Study of the Colonial Family," *WMQ*, 3rd ser., XXIII (1966), 627–634; and Rudy Ray Seward, "The Colonial Family in America: Toward a Socio-Historical Restoration of its Structure," *JMF*, XXXV (1973), 58–70. For an example of "my family," see Franklin B. Dexter, ed., *The Literary Diary of Ezra Stiles, D.D., LL.D.* (New York, 1901), I, 25.

2. Samuel Purviance to Betsy Purviance, [c. 1787], Purviance-Courtenay Papers, DU; Caleb Bingham, *The American Preceptor*, 42nd ed. (Boston, 1811), 104. For "our family," see, e.g., Thomas Eliot Andrews, ed., "The Diary of Elizabeth (Porter) Phelps," *NEHGR*, CXIX (1965), 219.

3. Ann Page to Elizabeth Randolph, Nov. 6, 1801, William B. Randolph Papers, box 1, LCMD; Dexter, ed., *Literary Diary of Ezra Stiles*, I, 577; William G. Roelker,

ed., *Benjamin Franklin and Catharine Ray Greene Their Correspondence 1755–1790* (Philadelphia, 1949), 105; Fanny Coalter to John Coalter, March 9, 1804, Brown-Coalter-Tucker Papers, box 2, EGS.

4. William Livingston, "Our Grand-Mothers," *American Museum*, IX (March 1791), 143–144; also printed in *Massachusetts Magazine*, IV (Jan. 1792), 14–15.

5. James Kent, "Chronological Memoranda," May 1, 1799, James Kent Papers, LCMD. For a typical eulogy, see Roelker, ed., *Franklin-Greene Correspondence*, 138. Lonna Malmsheimer, "Daughters of Zion: New England Roots of American Feminism," *New England Quarterly*, L (1977), 491–492, discusses the widespread use of Proverbs 31 in funeral sermons for women.

6. *A Series of Letters on Courtship and Marriage* . . . (Elizabethtown, N.J., 1796), 54–57, esp. 56. The following three paragraphs summarize the findings reported in Mary Beth Norton, "Eighteenth-Century American Women in Peace and War: The Case of the Loyalists," *WMQ*, 3rd ser., XXXIII (1976), 386–398.

7. John J. Smith, ed., *Letters of Doctor Richard Hill and His Children* (Philadelphia, 1854), 141; Elizabeth Drinker, Diary, Dec. 12, 1795, HSP. See also, e.g., B. Crannell to Catherine Livingston, Sept. 3, 1785, Gilbert Livingston Papers, NYPL.

8. Jane Robbins to Hannah Gilman, Sept. 1799, Gilman Papers, MHS; Margret Smith to Samuel Galloway, Sept. 22, 1762, Galloway-Maxcy-Markoe Papers, V, LCMD; Ann Peyton to [Battaile Muse], March 25, 1783, Battaile Muse Papers, DU; Catherine Livingston to [Smith Thompson], Dec. 25, 1806, Gilbert Livingston Papers.

9. John Adams recorded an incident in which his mother asked for such information, but his father refused to give it (Lyman H. Butterfield et al., eds., *Diary and Autobiography of John Adams* [Cambridge, Mass., 1961], I, 65).

10. Elizabeth Powel to Mrs. Page, [1784], Powel Collection, Miscellany, HSP; Peggy Emlen to Sally Logan, Sept. 3rd day morning, [no yr.], Marjorie P. M. Brown Collection, box 1, HSP, "Animadversions on the Affectation of ill-suited Characters among the Female Sex," *American Magazine and Historical Chronicle*, II (1745), 303; [Samuel Quincy] to [Robert Treat Paine], Feb. 2, 1756, Robert Treat Paine Papers, MHS.

11. For "his" estates, see, e.g., "Letters from Mrs. Ralph Izard to Mrs. William Lee," *VMHB*, VIII (1900), 24; for "her" furnishings, John Jones to Polly Jones, Oct. 3, 1779, Seaborn Jones Sr. Papers, DU, and Norton, "Eighteenth-Century American Women," *WMQ*, 3rd ser., XXXIII (1976), 396–397. One of the few men who regularly discussed ordinary household matters during the Revolution was William Palfrey of Massachusetts; see his letters, *passim*, HL.

12. Household size is discussed in Robert V. Wells, *The Population of the British Colonies in America before 1776: A Survey of Census Data* (Princeton, N.J., 1975), 297–333. Problems caused by household composition are evident in [Sarah Nourse] to [James Nourse], Aug. 17, 1783, Nourse Family Papers (no. 3490a), box 1, ALUV; and Abigail Greenleaf to Robert T. Paine, Dec. 10, 1756, Paine Papers.

13. William Duane, ed., *Extracts from the Diary of Christopher Marshall* . . . *1774–1781* (Albany, N.Y., 1877), 157–158; Frederick Tupper and Helen Tyler

Brown, eds., *Grandmother Tyler's Book, The Recollections of Mary Palmer Tyler 1775–1866* (New York, 1925), 142–143, 140, 296 (hereafter cited as Tyler, *Book*).

14. Sarah Snell Bryant, Diary, 1795, *passim*, HL; Mary Cooper, Diary, Dec. 14, 1769, and *passim*, NYPL. For another discussion of northern women's work patterns, see Nancy F. Cott, *The Bonds of Womanhood: "Woman's Sphere" in New England 1780–1835* (New Haven, Ct., 1977), chapter 1.

15. Cooper diary, November 20, 1768; Feb. 12, 1769; Oct. 23, 1768; Sept. 18, 1773.

16. Cooper diary, Dec. [23?], 1768; May 20, 1769; Dec. 15, 1769; April 22, 1769. For some travelers' comments on dirty rural houses, see Francis Baily, *Journal of a Tour in Unsettled Parts of North America in 1796 & 1797*, ed. Jack D. L. Holmes (Carbondale and Edwardsville, Ill., 1969), 45–46; and Max Farrand, ed., *A Journey to Ohio in 1810 as Recorded in the Journal of Margaret Van Horn Dwight* (New Haven, Ct., 1914), 7–8.

17. See, e.g., Matthew Patten, *The Diary of Matthew Patten of Bedford, N.H.* (Concord, N.H., 1903), *passim*.

18. Baily, *Journal of a Tour*, 44; Elizabeth Fuller, Diary, 1790–1792, printed in Frances E. Blake, *History of the Town of Princeton . . . 1759–1915* (Princeton, Mass., 1915), I, 303–304, 316–318, 321; Nabby and Betsy Foote, Diaries, *passim*, CHS; Ruth Henshaw, Diary, July 14, 1789, AAS.

19. J. P. Brissot de Warville, *New Travels in the United States of America 1788*, ed. Durand Echeverria and trans. Mara Soceanu Vamos and Durand Echeverria (Cambridge, Mass., 1964), 208.

20. Dr. Samuel Adams to Sally Adams, Aug. 5, 1778, Sol Feinstone Collection, microfilm, no. 29, reel 1, LCMD; Patten, *Diary*, 6, 16, 19, 22, and *passim*; Lucy Watson, "Account of New Settlers, 1762–1766" (written 1825), HSP.

21. Richard J. Hooker, ed., *The Carolina Backcountry on the Eve of the Revolution. The Journal and Other Writings of Charles Woodmason, Anglican Itinerant* (Chapel Hill, N.C., 1953), 39 (see also 13, 16–17, 33); Clement L. Martzolff, ed., "Reminiscences of a Pioneer [Thomas Rogers]," *Ohio State Archeological and Historical Publications*, XIX (1910), 209.

22. Cuthbert Harrison to Leven Powell, June 22, 1785, Leven Powell Papers, box 2, EGS; Edward Burd to Joseph Shippen, June 24, 1777, Joseph Shippen Papers, in Peter Force Collection, series 8D, no. 163, LCMD; John Coalter, Autobiography to 1787, Brown-Coalter-Tucker Papers, box 1.

23. Elizabeth House Trist, Journal, spring 1784 (typescript), SHC/UNC; Robert Witherspoon, Family Memoirs, Anderson-Thornwell Papers, SHC/UNC. Annette Kolodny has sensitively analyzed female attitudes toward the American landscape in an essay in the forthcoming volume *Language in Women's Lives*, ed. Ruth Borker, Nelly Furman, and Sally McConnell-Ginet.

24. Mary Spence to Mary Hooper, June 22, 1770, Aug. 20, 1773, and George Hooper to same, April 2, 1772, all in James M. Robbins Papers, III, MHS; Mary Emery to a brother, Jan. 14, 1852 (typescript), and Joseph Gilman to Nicholas Gilman, Feb. 23, 1790, both in Gilman Papers.

25. John Hutchens, Autobiography, 6–7, Breckinridge Family Papers, SHC/UNC.

26. On cloth production in the colonies, see Rolla M. Tryon, *Household Manufactures in the United States 1640–1860* (Chicago, 1917), 17–20, 75–99, 202–213; and Arthur H. Cole, *The American Wool Manufacture* (Cambridge, Mass., 1926), I, 5–29.

27. Susanna Dillwyn to William Dillwyn, Jan. 28, 1790, Dillwyn Papers, box 1, LCP/HSP; Hunter Dickinson Farish, ed., *Journal & Letters of Philip Vickers Fithian 1773–1774: A Plantation Tutor of the Old Dominion* (Williamsburg, Va., 1957), 189; Fuller diary, in Blake, *History of Princeton*, I, 311–315, esp. 313, 315. The estimate of a spinner's output is from Tryon, *Household Manufactures*, 118n; it is borne out by the entries in Bryant diary, Feb.–April, 1797, *passim*.

28. Spinning frolics and quilting bees are mentioned in, e.g., Cooper diary, Feb. 3, March 17, and Nov. 14, 1769; and Henshaw diary, Sept. 15, 1789; Sept. 14, Oct. 27, Nov. 4, 1790.

29. Tyler, *Book*, 141; Henshaw diary, Dec. 21, Dec. 31, 1789. For the Henshaws' relationship with Lydia Hawkins, see *ibid.*, April 2, May 17, Sept. 3, Nov. 12, 1790; April 22, July 19, 22, 1791.

30. Nabby Foote diary, August 1775; Betsy Foote diary, Jan.–May 1775, *passim*. See also Elizabeth Hook, Account Book, EI. Patten, *Diary*, 18, 21, 30, 34, 35, 42 shows purchases from his female neighbors, as does Robert Carter, Daybook XIII, 1775–1776, *passim*, Robert Carter Papers, DU.

31. Livingston, "Our Grand-Mothers," *Amer. Museum*, IX (1791), 143; Carl Van Doren, ed., *The Letters of Benjamin Franklin & Jane Mecom* (Princeton, N.J., 1950), 35.

32. Benjamin Hawkins, *Letters of Benjamin Hawkins 1796–1806*, Collections of the GHS, IX (Savannah, 1916), 478 (also 21–22, 57); Anne Mifflin, Journal of Visit to Senecas, October 1803, 28, Logan-Fisher-Fox Papers, box 2A, HSP.

33. Elizabeth Graeme Fergusson, "The Contemplative (or Sentimental) Spinner," in volume labeled "Selections 1797 1799," Elizabeth Graeme Fergusson Papers, HSP.

34. E. H. Wister to [Betsy] Wister, Aug. 15, 1808, Bache Family Papers, APSL. The "lazy hour" phrase comes from Lucy Knox to Henry Knox, Aug. 23, 1777, Henry Knox Papers, microfilm, reel 4, no. 43, MHS. One of the best sources for urban women's work patterns is Sally Logan Fisher's diary, HSP; her comment on ordinarily rising at five o'clock comes on Aug. 9, 1785. See Abigail Adams's description of her daily routine in Stewart Mitchell, ed., *New Letters of Abigail Adams 1788–1801* (Boston, 1947), 91 (hereafter cited as Adams, *New Letters*).

35. Rebecca Stoddert to Elizabeth Gantt, Sept. 15, 1799, Rebecca Stoddert Papers, Miscellaneous Manuscripts, LCMD. Excellent descriptions of city markets are contained in Kenneth and Anna Roberts, eds. and trans., *Moreau de St. Mery's American Journey 1793–1798* (Garden City, N.Y., 1947), 154–155, 316–317; and Alfred J. Morrison, ed. and trans., *Travels in the Confederation (1783–1784). From the German of Johann David Schoepf* (Philadelphia, 1911), I, 112–113; II, 189–190.

36. Hannah Bringhurst, "A Spiritual Diary from the 25th of 3d Mo. 1781, to the

19th of 9th Mo. inclusive," 38, HSP; Fisher diary, April 18, 1785. For urban women's reactions to dirty farmhouses, see Margaret Dwight's comments (n. 16) and those in Trist journal, Dec. 30, 1783, Jan. 1, 8, 1784.

37. Abigail Adams's complaints about servants are especially detailed; see Adams, *New Letters*, 33, 47–48, 68–69, 76, 91. The career of a long-term white female servant is traced in Lucy Searle, "Memoir of Mrs. Sarah Atkins," *EIHC*, LXXXV (1949), 155.

38. The quotation is from Adrian Bancker to Evert Bancker, June 23, 1774, Bancker Family Papers, NYHS. See the letters of Deborah Logan to Mary Norris, Loudoun Papers, box 42, *passim*, HSP. Elizabeth deHart Bleecker [McDonald], Diary, *passim*, NYPL, also mentions large numbers of youthful servants.

39. Descriptions of the daily routines of urban girls are contained in Ethel Armes, ed., *Nancy Shippen Her Journal Book* (Philadelphia, 1935), 220–221; Susanna Dillwyn to William Dillwyn, March 13–23, 1787, Dillwyn Papers; and Jane Lansing to Maria Van Schaick, Oct. 8, 1804, Lansing Family Papers, I, 69, Gansevoort-Lansing Collection, NYPL.

40. Fisher diary, Dec. 27, 1785; Pamela Sedgwick to Elizabeth Mayhew, Aug. 21, 1789, Sedgwick Papers III, MHS; Betsy DeLancey to Anne DeLancey, [c. 1768], DeLancey "Reminiscences," DeLancey Family Papers, MCNY. See also Alice M. Earle, ed., *Diary of Anna Green Winslow, A Boston School Girl of 1771* (Boston, 1894), *passim*, esp. 40, 47.

41. The saga of the Banckers may be traced in Bancker Papers, 1790–1800, *passim*, esp. letters of Polly or Christopher Bancker to Evert Bancker, Feb. 3, 1791; April 16, July 1, Oct. 17, 1794.

42. Such work groups are described in Armes, ed., *Shippen Journal*, 185, and Susan I. Lesley, *Recollections of My Mother* (Boston, 1886), 40. The quotation comes from Constantia [Judith Sargent Murray], *The Gleaner. A Miscellaneous Production* (Boston, 1798), III, 307.

43. William Maxwell, comp., "My Mother: Memoirs of Mrs. Helen Read," *Lower Norfolk County Virginia Antiquary*, II (1897–1898), 26; Fisher diary, Sept. 27, 1788; Abigail Adams to Elizabeth Peabody, June 6, 1809, Shaw Family Papers, box 1, LCMD; Adams, *New Letters*, 5–6.

44. Cf. Bleecker diary, *passim*, with the farm girls' diaries cited in n. 18 above. A city woman expresses regret for not having taught her granddaughter enough about housewifery in Smith, ed., *Hill Letters*, 445.

45. Elizabeth Smith to James Murray, Feb. 7, 1762, Robbins Papers, I; Anna [Bowen] to Lydia Clark, May 31, 1790, John Innes Clark Papers, RIHS.

46. Thomas Pinckney to Harriott Horry, Feb. 22, 1779, Pinckney Family Papers, ser. 1, box 8, LCMD. For other descriptions of the daily routine of plantation mistresses, see Ann Kinloch, Diary, April 1799, Langdon Cheves Collection, SCHS; and Elise Pinckney, ed., *The Letterbook of Eliza Lucas Pinckney 1739–1762* (Chapel Hill, N.C., 1972), 7, 34–35.

47. An excellent sense of the work patterns of plantation mistresses may be obtained by consulting Sarah Nourse, Diary, 1781–1783, Nourse-Morris Papers (no.

3490b), ALUV; Anna Bowen Mitchell to Eliza [Bowen], April 1, 1793, Clark Papers; and Farish, ed., *Fithian Journal, passim,* esp. 38, 44–45, 63, 75, 79 (for the work of Ann Tasker Carter).

48. John Brown Cutting to Thomas Pinckney, Dec. 19, 1794, Pinckney Family Papers, ser. 3, box 6; Harry Toulmin, *The Western Country in 1793: Reports on Kentucky and Virginia,* ed. Marion Tinling and Godfrey Davies (San Marino, Calif., 1948), 28; Farish, ed., *Fithian Journal,* 194; Lucy Armistead to Maria Armistead, Feb. 16, 1788, Armistead-Cocke Papers, EGS. I have pluralized the last two quotations.

49. Hannah Buchanan to Thomas Buchanan, Aug. 13, Sept. 11, Sept. 12, 1809, Hooker Collection, SLRC.

50. Jonathan Jackson to [Hannah Jackson], Feb. 1785, Lee Family Papers, MHS; Edwin Morris Betts and James Adam Bear, Jr., eds., *The Family Letters of Thomas Jefferson* (Columbia, Mo., 1966), 84; Eleanor Parke Custis to Elizabeth Bordley, March 18, 1797, Lewis-Gibson Letters (typescript), I, 31, HSP. The best source for the work of southern daughters is William Bottorff and Roy Flannagan, eds., "The Diary of Frances Baylor Hill of 'Hillsborough' King and Queen County Virginia (1797)," *EAL,* II, no. 3 (winter, 1967), 4–53.

51. Betts and Bear, eds., *Jefferson Family Letters,* 68; Eliza Lucas Pinckney to Daniel Horry, March 7, 1768, Mrs. Francis B. Stewart Collection, SHC/UNC. Contrast these to complaints about daughters in Jack P. Greene, ed., *The Diary of Colonel Landon Carter of Sabine Hall, 1752–1778* (Charlottesville, Va., 1965), I, 553; II, 809.

52. Elizabeth Foote Washington, Journal, summer 1784, spring 1789, Washington Family Papers, box 2, LCMD.

53. Helen Blair to James Iredell, April 20, 1789, James Iredell Sr. and Jr. Papers, DU.

54. See Wells, *Population of British Colonies,* 310–311, on the concentration of slaves in proportionately few households. The findings reported in Sarah S. Hughes, "Slaves for Hire: The Allocation of Black Labor in Elizabeth City County, Virginia, 1782 to 1810," *WMQ,* 3rd ser., XXXV (1978), 260–286, suggest that the experiences of black women on smaller farms and plantations were probably quite different from those outlined here.

55. Detailed lists of women's occupations are in Thomas Middleton, Goose Creek Plantation Book, Nov. 5, 1784, Middleton Papers, SHC/UNC; and Robert Carter, Deed of Emancipation, Aug. 1, 1791, Carter Papers.

56. Edwin M. Betts, ed., *Thomas Jefferson's Farm Book* (Princeton, N.J., 1953), facsimile, 77, pt. 2, 14; List of Negroes Purchased from Col. Fitzgerald, n.d., Muse Papers.

57. Betts, ed., *Jefferson Farm Book,* facsimile, 46, 58; Plantation Work Journal, Nov. 1786–April 1787, George Washington Papers, box 28, LCMD; Greene, ed., *Carter Diary,* I, 568; II, 1137.

58. Alice Izard to Ralph Izard, Dec. 11, 1794, Ralph Izard Papers, SCL. See also Maxwell, comp., "Read Memoirs," *Lower Norfolk Cnty Va. Antiq.,* I (1895–1896),

97; and Hugh Nelson to Battaile Muse, April 12, 1779, Muse Papers. The Muse Papers contain many inventories showing the work assignments of slaves on small quarters.

59. Betts, ed., *Jefferson Farm Book*, facsimile, *passim*; Charles Cotesworth Pinckney, Jr., Plantation Book, 1812, Pinckney Family Papers, ser. 2, vol. 1; Greene, ed., *Carter Diary*, I, 306. For other comments on slave midwives, see Robert Carter, Letterbooks IV, 117, and VII, 20, Carter Papers.

60. James Mercer to Battaile Muse, April 8, 1779, Muse Papers; Betts, ed., *Jefferson Farm Book*, 16. See Farish, ed., *Fithian Journal*, 96, 140, 203; Anna Mitchell to Lydia Clark, April 13, 1793, Clark Papers; and Greene, ed., *Carter Diary*, I, 484; II, 602, 1095–1096.

61. Robert Carter to Thomas Olive, July 24, 1781, to James Clarke, July 28, 1781, Letterbook IV, 93, 95, Carter Papers.

62. Robert Carter to Clement Brooke, Nov. 11, 1776, Letterbook III, no. 2, 76, 78, Carter Papers; Greene, ed., *Carter Diary*, I, 371–372; James Mercer to Battaile Muse, July 10, Aug. 25, 1777, June 13, 1778, Muse Papers.

63. Thomas Clark to Dolly Forbes, Aug. 10, 1768, Robbins Papers, I; Thomas Cullen to Oliver Pollock, July 2, 29, 1783, Oliver Pollock Papers, in Force Collection, ser. 8D, no. 145, vol. 2, LCMD; Dolly Forbes to Elizabeth Smith, Sept. 8, 1769, Robbins Papers, II. On slave women's reluctance to move even from quarter to quarter, see J. H. Norton to Battaile Muse, April 21, May 11, 1782, Muse Papers.

64. William Scarborough to Eliza Gillett, May 15, 1796, Georgia Society of Colonial Dames Collection, GHS; Elizabeth Smith to Isaac Smith, Jr., Aug. [torn], Shaw Papers, box 1; Ann Page to Elizabeth Adams, [c. 1803], Randolph Papers.

65. Cooper diary, Aug. 21, 1769.

66. Cf. Caroline Hazard, ed., *Nailer Tom's Diary* (Boston, 1930), and Harriett Forbes, ed., *The Diary of Rev. Ebenezer Parkman, of Westborough, Mass.* (Westborough, Mass., 1899), with, e.g., Fisher diary.

67. Pamela Sedgwick to Theodore Sedgwick, Jan. 24, 1791, Sedgwick Papers III, MHS; Christian Barnes to Elizabeth Inman, Dec. 3, 1773, Christian Barnes Letterbook, LCMD; Mary Orne Tucker, Diary, May 4, 1802, EI.

68. Anna Mitchell to Lydia Clark, April 13, 1793, Clark Papers; Armes, ed., *Shippen Journal*, 236 (see also 221).

69. Mary Palmer to Abigail Greenleaf, Oct. 12, 1755, Paine Papers; Pamela Sedgwick to Elizabeth Mayhew, Feb. 6, 1785, Sedgwick Papers III; Fisher diary, Jan. 14, 1793; Mary Jones to Fanny Bland, May 10, 1769, Tucker-Coleman Papers, microfilm, reel 1, EGS; Margaret Lowther Page, "To Miss J—— L——," in her Journal and Letters, EGS. The original reads: "From Books and Poetry must turn."

70. Elizabeth Shaw to [Mary Cranch], April 6, 1781; Abigail Adams to Elizabeth S. Peabody, Feb. 4, 1800, both in Shaw Papers, box 1. A boarder's memoir of Elizabeth Peabody is Samuel Gilman, *Contributions to Literature* (Boston, 1856), 220–230. I owe this reference to Lyman H. Butterfield.

71. Eunice Paine to Thomas Paine, June 30, 1753, Paine Papers; Tucker diary, May 1, 1802; Rebecca Foster to Dwight Foster, June 7, 1791, Dwight Foster Papers,

box 24, AAS. On the universality of this devaluation of women's work, see Margaret Mead, *Male and Female: A Study of Sexes in a Changing World* (New York, 1949), 159–160.

72. Elizabeth DeLancey to Anne DeLancey, Dec. 20, 1760, "DeLancey Reminiscences," DeLancey Papers; Elizabeth Meredith to David Meredith, July 12, 1795, Meredith Papers, box 4, HSP; David Ramsay, *Memoirs of the Life of Martha Laurens Ramsay*, 3rd ed. (Boston, 1812), 44; Christian Barnes to Elizabeth Smith, Nov. 24, 1770, Barnes Letterbook. For a unique — and significantly later — expression of pleasure about domestic duties, see Deborah N. Logan, "Biographical Sketches of Life & Character of Dr. George Logan," 1821, Logan Papers, LXI, 161–162, HSP.

73. C[atherine] R[ead] to Betsy [Ludlow], Sept. 16, [1790?], Read Family Papers, SCL; Simon P. Gratz, "Some Material for a Biography of Mrs. Elizabeth Fergusson, Née Graeme," *PMHB*, XXXIX (1915), 277. For the Burr-Prince discussion, see Esther Edwards Burr, Journal-Letters, Nov. 24, 1754 [Dec. 1, 12], YL.

CHAPTER TWO

1. B. Hubbard to Hannah Smith, [Aug.] 20, 1791, Smith-Robert Papers, box 1, NYHS, Eleanor Parke Custis to Elizabeth Bordley, Nov. 4, 1799 (typescript), Lewis-Gibson Letters, I, 67, HSP; Thomas Gisborne, *An Enquiry Into the Duties of the Female Sex* (London, 1797), 4; A. Coxe to Sarah Burd, [1779], Burd-Shippen-Hubley Papers, HSP. For a man's assertion of the superiority of married women, see Robert Treat Paine to Eunice Paine, Nov. 12, 1749, Robert Treat Paine Papers, MHS.

2. Sarah Hanschurst to Sally Forbes, 1762, Sarah Hanschurst Letterbook, Miscellaneous Manuscripts, LCMD. For similar contemporary statements: Alice Izard to Anne DeLancey, Nov. 29, 1772, DeLancey "Reminiscences," DeLancey Family Papers, MCNY; and Elizabeth Smith to Isaac Smith, June 10, 1768, Shaw Family Papers, box 1, LCMD.

3. Rebecca Dickinson, Diary Extracts, printed in Daniel W. Wells and Reuben F. Wells, *A History of Hatfield Massachusetts 1660–1910* (Springfield, Mass., 1910), 206. The unhappy life of Eunice Paine, a dependent spinster, can be traced in Paine Papers.

4. Pamela Sedgwick to Betsy Mayhew, May 25, 1782, Sedgwick Papers III, MHS; Elizabeth Smith Shaw to Abigail Adams Smith, Nov. 27, 1786, Shaw Papers, box 1. But cf. Eleanor Custis to Elizabeth Bordley, Feb. 3, 1799, Lewis-Gibson Letters, I, 64.

5. Elizabeth Foote [Washington], Journal, Nov. 1779, Washington Family Papers, box 2, LCMD; Anne Emlen [Mifflin], Religious Diary, Oct. 1788, Emlen Collection, HSP; Anna Rawle to Rebecca Shoemaker, July 20, [1783], Shoemaker-Rawle Papers, HSP.

6. "Kennon Letters," *VMHB*, XXXII (1924), 160; Hannah Emery to Mary Carter, Oct. 17, 1791, Cutts Family Papers, EI; John A. H. Sweeney, ed., "The Norris-Fisher Correspondence: A Circle of Friends, 1779–1792," *Delaware History*, VI (1954–1955), 228; Eliza Lucas Pinckney to Fanny ———— , [c. Jan. 1745], Eliza Lucas Pinckney Papers, DU. Lawrence Stone, *The Family, Sex, and Marriage in England 1500–1800* (New York, 1977), 270–324, discusses the rise of romantic love as a factor in matrimony.

7. Philander [Jonathan Jackson] to Philocles [John Lowell], March 11, 1763, Lee Family Papers, MHS; John Hook to Charles Hook, Nov. 1, 1779, John Hook Letterbook, John Hook Papers, DU. See also Robert Treat Paine to G[eorge?] L[eonard?], Aug. 7, 1755, and to same, Jan. 1, 1760, Paine Papers.

8. For a contemporary statement of this same interpretation, see Constantia [Judith Sargent Murray], *The Gleaner. A Miscellaneous Production* (Boston, 1798), II, 48–49. One such woman's description of her plight is Justicia Rudolphus to Mr. Armstrong, Oct. 9, 1780, HCA 32/408/3, 28.

9. Elizabeth Graeme to ———— , Feb. 27, 1770, Miscellaneous Manuscripts, HSP. Herman R. Lantz, *Marital Incompatibility and Social Change in Early America*, Sage Research Papers in the Social Sciences, vol. 4, ser. no. 90-026 (Studies of Marriage and the Family) (London and Beverly Hills, 1976), uses newspaper advertisements for runaway husbands and wives in an attempt to measure discord in colonial marriages. Remarks by women on unhappy marriages may be found in Leo Hershkowitz and Isidore Meyer, eds., *Letters of the Franks Family (1733–1748)* (Waltham, Mass., 1968), 28–29; J. Hall Pleasants, ed., "Letters of Molly and Hetty Tilghman," *MHM*, XXI (1926), 36; and [Elizabeth Parker] to [Janet Brinley], Oct. 4, [1798] (typescript), Parker-Brinley Papers, box 2, HSP.

10. The poems by Grace Growden Galloway, or "Blandina," are cited in the following order: "Upon a Time No Matter Where," "Miss Patty & Pheby which once was so gay," "Dear Polly attend," "How happy is the holy Vestals Cot," and "At home at Night alone My Time I spend." Betsy's comment is on a wrapper accompanying the poems. All are in the Joseph Galloway Papers, LCMD.

11. Mary Cooper, Diary, July 13, 1769, NYPL; Mary Russell to Samuel Curwen, Feb. 1757, Curwen Family Papers, III, EI. The latter reference was supplied by Carol Berkin.

12. This discussion of the legal status of colonial women is based upon Richard B. Morris, *Studies in the History of American Law*, 2nd ed. (Philadelphia, 1959), chapter 3, and Marylynn Salmon, "Equality or Submersion? Feme Covert Status in Early Pennsylvania," in Carol Berkin and Mary Beth Norton, eds., *Women of America: A History* (Boston, 1979), 92–113.

13. Charles Biddle, *Autobiography of Charles Biddle . . . 1745–1821* (Philadelphia, 1883), 2. That routine property transactions could take place without a wife's consent was shown when a female Florida refugee told the loyalist claims commission in 1787 that "she never joined in the Sale, was Applied to for that purpose . . . but refused," and the sale nevertheless was completed (AO 12/3, 235).

14. Cf. Mary R. Beard, *Woman as Force in History* (New York, reprint, 1962), and the essay by Marylynn Salmon, cited n. 12 above.

15. Nancy F. Cott, "Divorce and the Changing Status of Women in Eighteenth-Century Massachusetts," *WMQ*, 3rd ser., XXXIII (1976), 586–614, is the best article on colonial divorce. See also Thomas Meehan, "'Not Made out of Levity': Evolution of Divorce in Early Pennsylvania," *PMHB*, XCII (Oct. 1968), 441–464; and Matteo Spalletta, "Divorce in Colonial New York," *New-York Historical Society Quarterly*, XXXIX (Oct. 1955), 422–440.

16. Rachel Wormley to Robert Treat Paine, March 17, 1764 (see also same to same, July 31, Sept. 19, 1762; Dec. 3, 1763), Paine Papers; Cott, "Divorce and Changing Status of Women," *WMQ*, 3rd ser., XXXIII (1976), 598. For an analysis of newspaper advertisements for runaway wives and husbands, see the study by Herman Lantz, cited n. 9 above.

17. Abigail Gardner Drew, Diary, June 4, [no year], AAS; Mary Ellis to Mr. Wirt, April 9, 1802, Baylor Family Papers (no. 2257), ALUV. See Cott, "Divorce and Changing Status of Women," *WMQ*, 3rd ser., XXXIII (1976), 599, and her "Eighteenth-Century Family and Social Life Revealed in Massachusetts Divorce Records," *Journal of Social History*, X (Fall 1976), 31.

18. Ethel Armes, ed., *Nancy Shippen Her Journal Book* (Philadelphia, 1935), *passim*, esp. 233, 234, 267; [Arthur Lee] to Nancy S. Livingston, March 21, 1789, Shippen Family Papers, microfilm, reel 2, 1615, LCMD. Henry Livingston petitioned for divorce in Litchfield, Connecticut, in August 1791. Although the file in the Connecticut Archives does not reveal the outcome of the case, Nancy's mother-in-law referred to the divorce as a fact in a letter printed in Armes, ed., *Shippen Journal*, 287. My thanks to Sheldon S. Cohen and Eunice G. DiBella for their assistance in locating Livingston's petition.

19. Abigail Bailey, *Memoirs of Mrs. Abigail Bailey* . . . , ed. Ethan Smith (Boston, 1815), *passim*, esp. 43–44, 75, 113–114, 189.

20. Lyman H. Butterfield et al., eds., *Adams Family Correspondence* (Cambridge, Mass., 1963), I, 370 (hereafter cited as *AFC*). Similar sentiments were expressed by Sarah Burr Reeve, the daughter of Esther Edwards Burr, in 1779; see Helen Evertson Smith, *Colonial Days and Ways* (New York, 1900), 303–304.

21. Joseph Lathrop, "Remarks on Female Honour," *American Museum*, VIII (Dec. 1790), 281; "Narrative of Mrs. Abraham Brasher, 1801" (typescript), 3–4, NYHS; Eliza Southgate Bowne, *A Girl's Life Eighty Years Ago*, ed. Clarence Cook (London, 1888), 46–47, 50–53; Catherine Read to Betsy Ludlow, Dec. 18, [1787], Read Family Papers, SCL.

22. William Tennent III (Alexis) to Susan Vergereau (Zephyra), [1761], in "Album," 2, William Tennent III Papers, SCL; Eleanor Custis to Elizabeth Bordley, March 20, 1798, Lewis-Gibson Letters, I, 43; Pleasants, ed., "Tilghman Letters," *MHM*, XXI (1926), 131. See esp. the stilted courtship letters of Elizabeth Shipton and Aquila Giles, Aquila Giles Papers, NYHS, partly printed in Morris Bishop, "Love on Parole, 1778–1780," *New York History*, XX (1939), 43–50.

23. Jabez Upham to John Forbes, Nov. 25, 1789, James M. Robbins Papers, VI, MHS; Don Higginbotham, ed., *The Papers of James Iredell* (Raleigh, N.C., 1976), I, 144; Patty Rogers, Diary, Aug. 4, 1785 (see also entry for Sept. 21), AAS.

24. —— to Sally Pomfret, June 7, 1782, Thomas Grafton to same, March 2, 1784, John Wallace to same, May 28, 1783, all in Samuel Smith Downey Papers, DU; Edward M. Riley, ed., *The Journal of John Harrower, An Indentured Servant in the Colony of Virginia, 1773–1776* (Williamsburg, Va., 1963), 118.

25. Riley, ed., *Harrower Journal*, 149, 106, 129, 136–143 *passim*, 159.

26. Janette Day (Barclay) to Elizabeth Smith, June 16, 1769, Robbins Papers, II; same to same, July 30, 1768, *ibid.*, I. For other accounts of the mental state of unwed mothers, see [Elizabeth Parker] to [Janet Brinley?], March 12, 1801, Parker-Brinley Papers, box 2; and Marquis de Chastellux, *Travels in North America in the Years 1780, 1781 and 1782*, ed. and trans. Howard C. Rice, Jr. (Chapel Hill, N.C., 1963), I, 67, 227–228, 231–232, 254.

27. [Mildred Smith] to [Betsy Ambler], 1782, Betsy Ambler to Mildred [Smith], Jan. 10, 1786, Betsy Ambler to Miss [Caines?], 1786 [1789?], same to same, 1792, Betsy Ambler Carrington to Frances Caines, Nov. 1820, Elizabeth Ambler Papers, CW.

28. Robert Treat Paine, Diary (shorthand), spring 1770, *passim*, esp. Feb. 25, 28, Paine Papers. For the premarital pregnancy debate, see Edward Shorter, "Illegitimacy, Sexual Revolution, and Social Change in Modern Europe," *JIH*, II (1971), 237–272; and Louise Tilly et al., "Women's Work and European Fertility Patterns," *JIH*, VI (1976), 447–476. The most comprehensive survey is Daniel Scott Smith and Michael Hindus, "Premarital Pregnancy in America, 1640–1971: An Overview and Interpretation," *JIH*, V (1975), 537–570.

29. Richard Coleman to Elizabeth Holladay, July 23, 1783, Holladay Family Papers, VHS (see also Robert Coleman to same, Dec. 2, 1782). Betsy and Nabby Foote's older sister, Ellen, bundled with her fiancé in 1775; see Betsy's diary, April 22–23, May 11–12, June 11, 1775, CHS. The apologetic stance of young people who were forced to get married is evident in Jemima Condict, *Jemima Condict, Her Book* (Newark, N.J., 1930), 70–71.

30. Stone, *Family, Sex, and Marriage*, adopts this perspective consistently. For a similar approach to American marital decision making, see Neil L. Shumsky, "Parents, Children, and the Selection of Mates in Colonial Virginia," *Eighteenth-Century Life*, II (1975–1976), 83–88.

31. Condict, *Her Book*, 44–45.

32. *AFC*, IV, 335; Abigail Adams to Elizabeth Shaw, March 4, 1786, Shaw Papers, box 1; Stewart Mitchell, ed., *New Letters of Abigail Adams 1788–1801* (Boston, 1947), 109. The courtship can best be traced in Lyman H. Butterfield et al., eds., *The Book of Abigail and John* (Cambridge, Mass., 1976), 333 ff., and Frederick Tupper and Helen Tyler Brown, eds., *Grandmother Tyler's Book, The Recollections of Mary Palmer Tyler, 1775–1866* (Boston, 1925), 77–81 (hereafter cited as Tyler, *Book*). For the Tennent-Vergereau courtship, see "Album," *passim*, esp. 8–9, 34–35, 39, 42, Tennent Papers.

33. Jane Bruce to [Samuel Jones], Oct. 1, 1786; Naomi Smith to Jane B. Jones, c. 1786, both in Miscellaneous Manuscripts, SCL. See also Bruce-Jones Papers, *passim*, SCL. Another elopement that led to a lengthy estrangement between a girl and her parents is described in Hershkowitz and Meyer, eds., *Franks Family Letters*, 116–119, 125.

34. Matilda Schieffelin to John Lawrence, Dec. 4, 1780, Nichols-Shurtleff Family Papers, folder 134, SLRC. Contrite letters to her mother and sister were composed in 1780 by another girl who eloped, the Virginian Courtney Irwin; they may be found in HCA 32/418/21, 53, 58.

35. Alexander McAllister to a brother, Nov. 29–Dec. 6, 1779, Alexander Mc-Allister Papers, SHC/UNC; Carl Van Doren, ed., *The Letters of Benjamin Franklin & Jane Mecom* (Princeton, N.J., 1950), 60 (see also 103); Leonard W. Labaree et al., eds., *The Papers of Benjamin Franklin* (New Haven, Ct., 1959–), XIV, 220–221; XV, 185–186. See also Mary Eddy to Catherine Wister, June 4, 1793, Catherine Wister Bache Papers, APSL.

36. Hershkowitz and Meyer, eds., *Franks Family Letters*, 110; Mrs. George P. Coleman, comp., "Randolph and Tucker Letters," *VMHB*, XLII (1934), 49–50. Other comments on the age of prospective brides may be found in Mrs. Robert Gibbes to John Gibbes, Jan. 3, 1784, Gibbes-Gilchrist Papers, SCHS; and Penelope Dawson to a cousin, [n.d.], Hayes Collection, no. 492, SHC/UNC.

37. Susan Kittredge to Eliza Waite, March 24, 1792 (also Waite to Kittredge, Dec. 18, 1791), Eliza Waite Papers, EI; "Carroll Papers," *MHM*, XI (1916), 273. For another rejection of a suitor on the same grounds, see Anna Bowen to Lydia Clark, May 31, 1790, John Innes Clark Papers, RIHS.

38. Mary Orne Tucker, Diary, April 17, 1802, EI; Charlotte Barrell to Sarah Chace, Oct. 19, 1800, Cheever Papers, AAS; Mary Stevenson to Sarah Bache, Feb. 24, 1764, Sarah Franklin Bache Papers, APSL.

39. Edwin M. Betts and James A. Bear, Jr., eds., *The Family Letters of Thomas Jefferson* (Columbia, Mo., 1966), 50; Cadwallader Colden to Elizabeth DeLancey, [c. 1739], DeLancey Papers. For Shippen, see Armes, ed., *Shippen Journal*, 120; for Lucas, see Harriott Horry Ravenel, *Eliza Pinckney* (New York, 1896), 100.

40. James Iredell Sr. and Jr. Papers, *passim*, DU; Frances Baylor to John Baylor, Nov. 8, 1802, Baylor Papers. Joseph Hawley occasionally addressed his wife, Mercy, as "dear child" (Joseph Hawley Papers, box 2, *passim*, NYPL); the same was true of Joseph Dwight to Abigail Dwight (Sedgwick Papers II, *passim*), and Benjamin Franklin to Deborah Franklin (Labaree et al., eds., *Franklin Papers*, VI, VII, *passim*). But cf. her addressing him the same way, *ibid.*, XII, *passim*. The assistance of Sally McConnell-Ginet has been invaluable in this linguistic analysis.

41. George Logan to Deborah Logan, [April 3?], 1783, Logan Papers, VII, 6, HSP; George Logan to Albanus Logan, Jan. 9, 1800, Maria Dickinson Logan Papers, box 2, HSP. Examples of men assuming their wives missed them are Aquila Giles to Elizabeth Giles, Aug. 10, 1781, Giles Papers, and Mary T. Evans, ed., "Letters of Dr. John McKinly to his Wife, While a Prisoner of War, 1777-1778," *PMHB*, XXXIV (1910), 10.

42. Washington journal, spring 1789, summer 1784. See also Rogers diary, July 19, 1785.

43. See, e.g., Bailey, *Memoirs*, 31; and Catherine Read to Betsy Ludlow, Dec. 8, [no yr.], Read Papers. But cf., for a dominant wife, Condict, *Her Book*, 46–47.

44. Anna Bowen Mitchell to Lydia Clark, Dec. 5, 1792, to Lydia Bowen, March 24, 1793, both in Clark Papers. See also Tucker diary, May 12, 1802.

45. Ravenel, *Eliza Pinckney*, 100.

46. Deborah Norris Logan, "Biographical Sketches of the Life & Character of Dr. George Logan," 1821, Logan Papers, LXI, 160; Jeremy Belknap to Ruth Belknap, April 30, 1772, Jeremy Belknap Papers, NHHS; Sally Logan Fisher, Diary, 5th day [mid-Oct.] 1777, HSP; Washington journal, spring 1789; Anna Mitchell to Eliza B[owen], April 1, 1793, Clark Papers; Mary Dickinson to [John Dickinson], M. D. Logan Papers, box 1.

47. Tyler, *Book*, 180; Butterfield et al., eds., *Book of Abigail and John*, 354.

48. These censuses, upon which other observations in this section are also based, are reproduced in Edwin M. Betts, ed., *Thomas Jefferson's Farm Book* (Princeton, N.J., 1953), facsimile, 5–9, 15–18, 24, 30, 57, 60, 128–129. "Single" as used in this paragraph means an adult woman listed alone without husband or children. The 1810 census grouped tradesmen together instead of listing them with their wives and children, thus inflating the number of women who seem to be unmarried.

49. Inventory of estate of John Morel, June 27, 1777 (typescript), Morel Papers, SHC/UNC; inventory of slaves of Macartan Campbell, Aug. 23, 1792, Pinckney Family Papers, 3rd ser., box 3, LCMD; list of slaves belonging to Joseph Brevard, May 21, 1798, Brevard-McDowell Family Papers, SHC/UNC. On changes in marriage patterns over the course of the eighteenth century, see Allan Kulikoff, "The Origins of Afro-American Society in Tidewater Maryland and Virginia, 1700 to 1790," *WMQ*, 3rd ser., XXXV (1978), 226–259.

50. Christian Barnes to Elizabeth Smith, Oct. 14, Dec. 23, 1769; Feb. 9, May 22, July 6, Nov. 24, 1770; July 25, 1775; all in Christian Barnes Letterbook, LCMD. For the life story of a southern slave likewise parted from his wife, see John Davis, *Travels of Four Years and a Half in the United States . . .* , ed. A. J. Morrison (New York, 1909), 413–424.

51. Betts, ed., *Jefferson Farm Book*, 26, 21 (also, 14, 20, 24–25); Edwin M. Betts, ed., *Thomas Jefferson's Garden Book 1766–1824* (Philadelphia, 1944), 540.

52. The quotations are from H[enry] B[edinger] to Rachel Bedinger, Nov. 14, 1792, Bedinger-Dandridge Papers, DU; and Elizabeth Campbell to James Murray, Dec. 17, 1759, Robbins Papers, I. For Carter, see, e.g., Robert Carter, Letterbooks III, no. 3, 110; VIII, 61; X, 37, Robert Carter Papers, DU.

53. Battered wives: William Read to Jacob Read, Dec. 16, 1795, Read Papers; Jack P. Greene, ed., *The Diary of Colonel Landon Carter of Sabine Hall, 1752–1778* (Charlottesville, Va., 1965), I, 383. Rape: Robert Carter, Letterbook III, no. 3, 35, 45, 57–58, Carter Papers. A fight over a fourteen-year-old girl: *ibid.*, VII, 307. An account of a woman with both black and white lovers: [Janet Schaw], *Journal of a*

Lady of Quality . . . , ed. Evangeline Andrews and Charles Mclean Andrews (New Haven, Ct., 1922), 201. See Gary D. Mills, "Coincoin: An Eighteenth-Century 'Liberated' Woman," *Journal of Southern History,* XLII (1976), 205–222, for the life of a slave woman freed by the white man who fathered her mulatto children.

54. Betts, ed., *Jefferson Farm Book,* 13.

55. Betts, ed., *Jefferson Garden Book,* 540. See also the kinship ties in the plantation register of Charles C. Pinckney, 1812, Pinckney Family Papers, 2nd ser., vol. 1.

56. Betts, ed., *Jefferson Farm Book,* 19.

CHAPTER THREE

1. Hunter Dickinson Farish, ed., *Journal & Letters of Philip Vickers Fithian 1773–1774: A Plantation Tutor of the Old Dominion* (Williamsburg, Va., 1957), 193.

2. See Daniel Scott Smith, "Population, Family and Society in Hingham, Massachusetts, 1635–1880" (unpub. Ph.D. diss., University of California, Berkeley, 1972), esp. 242, and Robert V. Wells, "Family Size and Fertility Control in Eighteenth-Century America: A Study of Quaker Families," *Population Studies,* XXV (1971), 73–83, esp. 75. Abigail Adams's childbearing experience may be followed in Lyman H. Butterfield et al., eds., *Adams Family Correspondence* (Cambridge, Mass., 1963), I, II, *passim* (hereafter cited as *AFC*). For Sally Logan Fisher, see below, pp. 80–83.

3. See Smith, "Hingham, Massachusetts," 333, for white data. The material in these paragraphs and tables has been calculated from Edwin M. Betts, ed., *Thomas Jefferson's Farm Book* (Princeton, N.J., 1953), facsimile, 5–9, 15–18, 24, 30, 57, 60, 128–129, and John and Keating S. Ball, Slave Lists, 1780, microfilm M-1811, 2 reels, SHC/UNC. Richard S. Dunn, "A Tale of Two Plantations: Slave Life at Mesopotamia in Jamaica and Mount Airy in Virginia, 1799 to 1828," *WMQ,* 3rd ser., XXXIV (1977), 32–65, makes useful fertility comparisons. A further analysis of the Ball data is Cheryll Ann Cody, "A Note on the Changing Patterns of Slave Fertility in the South Carolina Rice District, 1735–1865," *Southern Studies,* XVI (1977), 457–463.

4. Esther Burr, Journal-Letters, Jan. 31 [March 8], 1757, YL. On birth spacing: John Rogers, Jr., to Mrs. John Rogers, Sr., June 19, 1787, Hudson Family Collection, box 3, NYPL. An assumption of regular births is evident in Joseph Manigault to Gabriel Manigault, March 18, 1784, and Aug. 4, 1785, Manigault Papers, SCL.

5. Betts, ed., *Jefferson Farm Book,* 46, 43. Intriguingly, a recent article has suggested that an average age of eighteen at first birth for enslaved women — as was the case on Jefferson's holdings — might well imply successful fertility manipulation by the master. See James Trussell and Richard Steckel, "The Age of Slaves at Menarche and Their First Birth," *JIH,* VIII (1978), 477–505, esp. 504.

6. Allyn B. Forbes, ed., "Abigail Adams, Commentator," *Proceedings of the MHS*, LXVI (1936–1941), 137; Stewart Mitchell, ed., *New Letters of Abigail Adams 1788–1801* (Boston, 1947), 36, 41, 52, 244 (hereafter cited as Adams, *New Letters*).

7. S[arah] Cary to Betsy Whiting, March 30, 1791, Blair-Banister-Braxton-Horner-Whiting Papers, box 1, EGS (hereafter cited as Blair-Banister Papers); J. Hall Pleasants, ed., "Letters of Molly and Hetty Tilghman," *MHM*, XXI (1926), 230; Catherine Read to Betsy Ludlow, Dec. 8 [no year], Nov. 29, [1784?], Read Family Papers, SCL. A rare observation on the benefit of menopause for women may be found in Oliver Hart to Joseph Hart, Sept. 15, 1784, Oliver Hart Papers, SCL.

8. On the life expectancy of northern white women, see Smith, "Hingham, Massachusetts," 219–229, and Robert V. Wells, "Quaker Marriage Patterns in a Colonial Perspective," *WMQ*, 3rd ser., XXIX (1972), 422–423. To date, no one has been able to construct a life table for southern white women.

9. Franklin B. Dexter, ed., *The Literary Diary of Ezra Stiles, D.D., LL.D.* (New York, 1901), III, 204; William Bottorff and Roy Flannagan, eds., "The Diary of Frances Baylor Hill of 'Hillsborough' King and Queen County Virginia (1797)," *EAL*, II, no. 3 (winter, 1967), 42–43; Abigail Paine to Robert Treat Paine, Feb. 8, 1748, Robert Treat Paine Papers, MHS; "Letter from Dr. Ramsay to his father-in-law," Dec. 17, 1784, in *American Museum*, IX (April 1791), 198–199; John Coalter to Fanny Coalter, Feb. 3, 1803, Brown-Coalter-Tucker Papers, box 2, EGS.

10. Sarah Jay to Kitty Livingston, July 16, 1783, John Jay Papers, CU; Joyce Myers to Rebecca Mordecai, June 11, [1801], Jacob Mordecai Papers, DU; Lucy Knox to Henry Knox, April 3, 1777, Henry Knox Papers, microfilm, reel 3, no. 148, MHS; Hannah Drury to John Drury, [n.d.], John Drury Papers, III, 23, EI; Helen Tredwell to Hannah Iredell, May 24, 1790, James Iredell Sr. and Jr. Papers, DU (see also same to same, June 16, 1790, *ibid.*).

11. Elizabeth Foote Washington, Journal, summer 1784, Washington Family Papers, box 2, LCMD; Abigail Greenleaf to Robert T. Paine, July 1, 1755, Paine Papers; Mary Grubb to [Sarah Burd], Aug. 19, 1772, and Sarah Burd to Sally [Ewing], [c. Feb. 1774?], Burd-Shippen-Hubley Papers, HSP.

12. Maria Clinton to [Elizabeth Tallmadge], Jan. 3, 1804, Maria Clinton Letters, Miscellaneous Manuscripts, NYHS; Elizabeth Smith to Dolly Forbes, June 22, 1769, James M. Robbins Papers, II, MHS; Edwin M. Betts and James A. Bear, eds., *The Family Letters of Thomas Jefferson* (Columbia, Mo., 1966), 250; F[anny] C[urrie] A[llison] to Margaret Coalter, July 15, 1797, Brown-Coalter-Tucker Papers, box 2. A month later, Margaret was dead.

13. See, e.g., Sally Pomfret to Ann Pomfret, Sept. 24, 1784, Samuel Smith Downey Papers, DU; and Frederick Tupper and Helen Tyler Brown, eds., *Grandmother Tyler's Book, The Recollections of Mary Palmer Tyler 1775–1866* (New York, 1925), 246. Occasionally, of course, mothers did attend their daughters at childbirth (e.g., Mary Norris to [Mary N. Dickinson], April 23, 1791, Loudoun Papers, box 77, HSP).

14. Robert Carter to Stephen Mason, March 9, 1785, in Robert Carter Letterbook

VI, 106, Robert Carter Papers, DU (see also *ibid.*, 31–32, 118). An account of a pregnant slave's childbirth experience is in [Hugh Nelson] to [Battaile Muse], Nov. 30, 1779, Battaile Muse Papers, DU.

15. Dolly Forbes to Elizabeth Smith, Sept. 8, 1769, Robbins Papers, II; Betts and Bear, eds., *Jefferson Family Letters*, 280; Sarah Jay to Susannah Livingston, Sept. 12, 1783, Jay Papers.

16. Joseph Reed to Charles Pettit, May 21, 1771, July 11, 1772, July 2, 1774, all in Joseph Reed Papers, NYHS; Charles Cushing to William Cushing, Feb. 21, 1774, Paine Papers; Robert T. Paine to Eunice Paine, May 17, 1770, *ibid.*; Elizabeth Kent to James Kent, May 29, 1807, James Kent Papers, LCMD. Cf. Catherine Scholten, "'On the Importance of the Obstetrick Art': Changing Customs of Childbirth in America, 1760–1825," *WMQ*, 3rd ser., XXXIV (1977), 426–445, which argues that childbirth was a wholly female affair prior to the nineteenth century.

17. An especially detailed account of a search for a midwife is in Rebecca Stoddert to Elizabeth Gantt, Dec. 30, 1800, Rebecca Stoddert Papers, Miscellaneous Manuscripts, LCMD. For midwives (black and white) attending slave women, see, e.g., John Martin estate accounts, Feb. 11, 1779, Jan. 1784, Telfair Family Papers, box 25, and accounts of Ann Gibbons, July 24, 1754, Aug. 29, 1756, *ibid.*, box 26, GHS. Sally Paine consulted a doctor during her 1777 pregnancy: Sally Paine to Robert T. Paine, Sept. 28, 30, 1777, Paine Papers.

18. Sally Logan Fisher, Diary, April 20, 1794, HSP. See, on doctors: Mary V. S. White, ed., *Fifteen Letters of Nathalie Sumter* (Columbia, S.C., 1942), 51; and Nathaniel Appleton to Noah Webster, July 11, 1790, Noah Webster Papers, box 2, NYPL. On the presence of doctors at slave women's childbeds: Robert Carter Letterbook V, 74, Carter Papers, and Christian Barnes to Elizabeth Smith, Nov. 24, 1770, Christian Barnes Letterbook, LCMD. Cf. Scholten, "Obstetrick Art," *WMQ*, 3rd ser., XXXIV (1977), 426–445, which assumes that women were excluded from births once doctors replaced midwives.

19. Fisher diary, Oct. 16, Dec. 11, 1776; Jan. 8, Feb. 12, March 18, 25, Sept. 4, Nov. 6, 1777; Oct. 10 23, Nov. 13–15, 19, 1778.

20. *Ibid.*, Dec. 15, 1778; Jan. 18, June 10, 20, 29, July 19, 21, Aug. 4, 24, Sept. 3, 21, 1779.

21. *Ibid.*, Sept. 10, Dec. 31, 1780; Jan. 1, 10, 14, 28, Oct. 1, 1781. Billy's recollections of his mother may be found in Nicholas Wainwright, "Memoir of William Logan Fisher (1781–1862) for his Grandchildren," *PMHB*, XCIX (1975), 92–103, esp. 95.

22. Fisher diary, July 14, 1783; Jan. 27, 1784. Also, Sept. 13, 19, 1783, and detailed comments on a friend's death, May 23, 1782.

23. *Ibid.*, Jan. 30, Feb. 25, 28, March 29, July 29, Aug. 14 (the first quotation), 1785; Feb. 19, March 16, April 16, 25, 1786. Her slow recovery is chronicled in May 21, July 24–30, Sept. 15, 1786.

24. *Ibid.*, Feb. 19, April 18, May 24, June 21, 30, July 24, 30, Aug. 10, 19, 1787. For previous references to making baby clothes, see June 29, Aug. 7, 1781.

25. *Ibid.*, March 16, Sept. 23, 28, Oct. 7, Nov. 3, 1788; March 22, 1789; Susanna Dillwyn to William Dillwyn, May 2–27, 1789, William Dillwyn Papers, box 1, LCP/HSP.

26. Sarah Snell Bryant, Diary, July 12, 13, 22, 1798, HL. See Fisher diary, Oct. 5–20, 1779. Other useful comments on lying in and its duration may be found in Thomas Ringgold to Samuel Galloway, March 24, 1772, Galloway-Maxcy-Markoe Papers, XI, LCMD; Adams, *New Letters*, 57; and Eleanor Lewis to [Mary Pinckney?], Jan. 12, 1800, Mrs. Francis B. Stewart Collection, SHC/UNC. Female slaves were expected to return to work soon after births, but they found ways of malingering; see Jack P. Greene, ed., *The Diary of Colonel Landon Carter of Sabine Hall, 1752–1778* (Charlottesville, Va., 1965), I, 496.

27. Judith Mordecai to Joyce Myers, Feb. 8, 1794, Dec. 5, 1792, Mordecai Family Papers, SHC/UNC.

28. Burr journal-letters, April 9 [15], 1756; "Memoir and Journals of Rev. Paul Coffin, D.D.," *Collections of Maine Historical Society*, ser. 1, IV (1856), 404; Esther Atlee to William Atlee, Oct. 7, 1782, William Atlee Papers, in Peter Force Collection, ser. 9, LCMD.

29. Fisher diary, Oct. 13, 1793; Margaret Izard to a cousin, Feb. 28, 1785, Ralph Izard Papers, SCL; Annis Stockton to Elisha Boudinot, Feb. 27, 1786, Elisha Boudinot Papers, Misc. MSS., NYHS. See also Elizabeth Deas to Katherine Thomson, June 15, 1777, HCA 32/447/10, 78.

30. For some very different attitudes toward children, see Nancy F. Cott, "Eighteenth-Century Family and Social Life Revealed in Massachusetts Divorce Records," *Journal of Social History*, X (Fall 1976), 28–29.

31. "It" usage: Fisher diary, Jan. 20, Aug. 12, 1777; Margaret Cowper to Eliza McQueen, Jan. 3, 1799, Mackay-Stiles Papers, SHC/UNC. "Little stranger": Ephraim Kirby to Ruth Kirby, Feb. 4, 1796, Edmund Kirby-Smith Papers, SHC/UNC; Samuel Purviance to Sukey Purviance, Nov. 4, 1770, Purviance-Courtenay Papers, DU. For a humorous comment on the practice of not calling babies by name, see Catherine Byles to Mather Byles, Oct. 7, 1802, Catherine and Mary Byles, Letterbook, I, HL.

32. John Walzer, "A Period of Ambivalence: Eighteenth-Century American Childhood," in Lloyd deMause, ed., *The History of Childhood* (New York, 1974), 380 n. 100; Smith, "Hingham, Massachusetts," 346; Joseph Shippen to Edward Shippen, May 20, 1773, Joseph Shippen Papers, ser. 8D, no. 163, Force Collection. But cf. Sarah Jay to Susannah Livingston, April 29, 1782, Jay Papers.

33. Daniel Scott Smith, "Child-Naming Patterns and Family Structure Change: Hingham, Massachusetts 1640–1880," The Newberry Papers in Family and Community History, no. 76-5, January 1977, *passim*, esp. 3; Smith, "Hingham, Massachusetts," 254. For illuminating comments on lineal naming, see Samuel Purviance to Sukey Purviance, Nov. 4, 1770, Purviance-Courtenay Papers; and Rebecca Shoemaker to Edward Shoemaker, Oct. 26, 1784, Shoemaker-Rawle Papers, HSP.

34. Compiled from Jefferson's censuses; see n. 3 above. Herbert G. Gutman, *The*

Black Family in Slavery & Freedom, 1750–1925 (New York, 1976), 185–201 and *passim*, gives comparable information for other plantations.

35. Smith, "Child-Naming Patterns," tables 2, 6, shows the proportions of Hingham youngsters named for parents and grandparents. On the Jefferson estates, 51 children were named for parents (N = 22) or grandparents, including great-grandparents (N = 29).

36. Charles Carter to Maria Armistead, March 17, 1788, Armistead-Cocke Papers, EGS; Sophia Brown to Susanna Brown, Aug. 1, 1791, June 21, 1792, April 21, 1796, all in John Brown Family Papers, Misc. MSS., NYHS. Notes of sales by Jefferson are scattered in Betts, ed., *Jefferson Farm Book, passim*.

37. Smith, "Child-Naming Patterns," 7. For remarks on the ministerial admonition to "live loose" to one's children: John J. Smith, ed., *Letters of Doctor Richard Hill and His Children* (Philadelphia, 1854), 345; Fisher diary, Sept. 9, 1778, Aug. 22, 1785, Feb. 7, 1794. Parents' difficulty with this teaching is revealed in, e.g., Elizabeth Bowen [Martin], Journal, 1783, EI, and Joseph Greenleaf to Robert T. Paine, March 27, 1755, Paine Papers.

38. John Blair to Mary Prescott, Jan. 15, 1796, Blair-Banister Papers, box 1; Robert Bagnall to Joseph Rhodes, Oct. 20, 1783, Rhodes Family Papers, LCMD; Joseph Reed to Esther Reed, Sept. 22, 1776, Reed Papers.

39. Eliza Lucas Pinckney to Miss B ——, Dec. 2, 1747, Eliza Lucas Pinckney Papers, DU; Sarah Jay to Susannah Livingston, Aug. 28, 1780, Jay Papers.

40. Timothy Barnard to Ebenezer Barnard, March 11, 1786, Ebenezer Barnard Family Papers, LCMD; Worthington C. Ford, ed., *Correspondence and Journals of Samuel Blachley Webb* (New York, reprint, 1969), II, 400; James Kent, "Chronological Memoranda," May 1, 1799, Kent Papers; William Palfrey to Susannah Palfrey, Sept. 19, 1772, William Palfrey Papers, HL.

41. For the hope that women would "make good nurses," see, e.g., Mary Byles to Rebecca Allmon, Sept. 9, 1796, Byles Letterbook I, and Anne Francis to Sarah Bache, March 11, 1807, Sarah Franklin Bache Papers, APSL. Encouragement to nurse is mentioned in S. Peters to Sarah Bache, April 25, 1778, *ibid*.

42. Eleanor Lewis to Mary Pinckney, April 24, 1800, Pinckney Family Papers, 1st ser., box 2, LCMD; Frances Tucker to Frances Tucker, June 11, 1783, Tucker-Coleman Papers, microfilm, reel 4, EGS; Fisher diary, July 17, 1793; Samuel W. Fisher, Memoir of Elizabeth Rhoads Fisher, Samuel W. Fisher Papers, HSP. In an emergency, female friends would briefly suckle each other's babies; see Fisher diary, Aug. 22, 1778, and Sally Paine to Robert T. Paine, May 12, 1776, Paine Papers.

43. Harriott Horry Ravenel, *Eliza Pinckney* (New York, 1896), 151. On Polly Ringgold, see the letters of Thomas Ringgold, Nancy Galloway, and Polly Ringgold, Feb. 5, 1769, March 28, April 14, May 27, 1772, Feb. 8, March 8, 17, 1774, addressed variously to John and Samuel Galloway, in Galloway-Maxcy-Markoe Papers, IX, XI, XIII. For the others mentioned in the text: David Ramsay, *Memoirs of the Life of Martha Laurens Ramsay*, 3rd ed. (Boston, 1812), 26; Greene, ed., *Carter Diary*, I, 512. But cf. Farish, ed., *Fithian Journal*, 39, on southern wet nursing, and

Catherine Ridley to John Jay, Feb. 7, 1792, Jay Papers, on northern wet nursing. The only alternative to nursing was feeding a child on pap; see John Penn to [Joseph Shippen?], July 1769, Shippen Papers, Force Collection.

44. Examples of normal weaning are: Bryant diary, Sept. 2, 12, 13, 1795, and Betts and Bear, eds., *Jefferson Family Letters*, 94. Comments on unusual circumstances are contained in, e.g., White, ed., *Sumter Letters*, 78; and Lucy Pierce to John Pierce, Sept. 17, 1805, Poor Family Papers, SLRC.

45. On timing, see Smith, ed., *Hill Letters*, 27; Betts and Bear, eds., *Jefferson Family Letters*, 191–192; and Joyce Myers to Rebecca Mordecai, June 23, 1800, Jacob Mordecai Papers.

46. Lucy Everett to Rebecca Huse, April 15, 1789, Hale Family Papers, I, 45, LCMD. Instances of abrupt weaning are noted in, e.g., Mabel Webber, ed., "Extracts from the Journal of Mrs. Ann Manigault 1754–1781," *SCHGM*, XX (1919), 131; and Bottorff and Flannagan, eds., "Hill Diary," *EAL*, II (no. 3), 8–9. Women's problems with breast milk after weaning are detailed in Fisher diary, Oct. 11, 12, 1782, and M[ary] Pinckney to Margaret Manigault, March 30, 1797, Manigault Papers, SCL.

47. Gertrude Meredith to William Meredith, Aug. 30, Sept. 4, 1800, Meredith Papers, box 13, HSP; Lelia Tucker to Fanny Coalter, June 5, 1803, Brown-Coalter-Tucker Papers, box 2. An earlier reference to gradual weaning is in Anne Powell to Elizabeth Inman, Feb. 13, 1785, Robbins Papers, VI. See also Elizabeth Drinker, Diary, July 8, 9, 15, 16, 1794, HSP.

48. Margaret Manigault to Alice Izard, June 18, 1801, Manigault Papers, SCL; Eleanor Custis to Elizabeth Bordley, July 2, 1797, Lewis-Gibson Letters, I, 38–39, HSP; Frances Tucker to St. George Tucker, March 22, July 14, 1781, Tucker-Coleman Papers, reel 3; Polly Coalter to Fanny Coalter, April 26, 1805, Lelia Tucker to same, Jan. 20, 1806, and *passim*, 1807, Brown-Coalter-Tucker Papers, box 2.

49. William Palfrey to Susannah Palfrey, April 4, May 10, 1776, Palfrey Papers; Timothy Pickering to Rebecca Pickering, Aug. 30, Dec. 13, 1777, Sept. 11, Aug. 1, 1778, Timothy Pickering Papers, microfilm, reel 1, 60, 78A, 147, 134, MHS. Evidence of a father's later, but growing, attachment to a child is in Burr journal-letters, Nov. 24, 1755 [Jan. 24, 1756].

50. J. T. Ladson to Gabriel Manigault, Sept. 10, 1783, Manigault Papers, SCL; Frances Tucker to St. George Tucker, Oct. 12, 1781, Tucker-Coleman Papers, reel 3; James Kent to Moses Kent, Oct. 13, 1796, Kent Papers; Frances N. Mason, *My Dearest Polly: Letters of Chief Justice John Marshall to His Wife* . . . (Richmond, Va., 1961), 98. Mothers' references to being "plagued" by children are common. See, e.g., Rebecca Stoddert to Mrs. Lowndes, Dec. 15, 1799, Stoddert Papers; Hannah Buchanan to Thomas Buchanan, June 29, 1809, Hooker Collection, SLRC.

51. Margaret Manigault to Gabriel Manigault, Nov. 20–22, Nov. 27, Nov. 23–25, Nov. 28, 1792, Manigault Papers, SCL. But cf. the comments of Rebecca Stoddert on her "brats," in her letters to Elizabeth Gantt, Feb. 23, May 25, 1800, Stoddert Papers.

52. *AFC*, I, 57; Harriott Horry to Eliza Lucas Pinckney, Dec. 7, 1781, Pinckney Family Papers, ser. 1, box 3. For comments on active youngsters: Debby Logan to Isaac Norris, Aug. 28, 1785, Maria Dickinson Logan Papers, box 2, HSP; Sarah Jay to John Jay, May 5, 1786, Jay Papers; Eleanor Lewis to Mary Pinckney, May 9, 1801, Stewart Collection.

53. Household accidents are described in, e.g., Abigail Greenleaf, Jr., to Robert T. Paine, Sept. 12, 1776, Paine Papers; and Thomas E. Andrews, ed., "The Diary of Elizabeth (Porter) Phelps," *NEHGR*, CXVIII (1964), 26, 28, 30, 113, 125.

54. Among the references to "her" babies are Joseph Reed to Charles Pettit, Feb. 28, 1772, Reed Papers; and Isaac Winslow to Margaret Murray, Aug. 25, 1778, Robbins Papers, V. In some families, babies were so much "hers" that the mother named them: e.g., Rebecca Stoddert to Elizabeth Gantt, Jan. 12, 1800, Stoddert Papers.

55. Abigail Greenleaf to Thomas Paine, Jan. 5, 1756, Paine Papers.

56. Benjamin Hawkins, *Letters of Benjamin Hawkins 1796-1806*, Collections of the GHS, IX (Savannah, 1916), 83-85.

57. "My son": Robert Livingston to Gilbert Livingston, Dec. 19, 1779, Gilbert Livingston Papers, NYPL; "his Boys": Debby Logan to [Mary Norris], May 28, 1794, M. D. Logan Papers, box 2; "my Girl": *AFC*, II, 288; "your children" [all daughters]: [John Steele] to Mary Steele, May 15, 1790, John Steele Papers, SHC/UNC.

58. Useful discussions of child-rearing theory are Daniel Calhoun, *The Intelligence of a People* (Princeton, N.J., 1973), 135-155; Peter Gregg Slater, *Children in the New England Mind. In Life and in Death* (Hamden, Ct., 1977); and Philip J. Greven, *The Protestant Temperament: Patterns of Child-Rearing, Religious Experience, and the Self in Early America* (New York, 1977).

59. William Read to Jacob Read, Dec. 29, 1795, Miscellaneous Manuscripts, SCL; Fisher diary, Aug. 7, 1779; Judith Mordecai to Becky Myers, Dec. 5, 1792, Mordecai Family Papers; Burr journal-letters, April 7 [8], 1755, April 9 [16], 1756, May 24 [Sept. 2], 1757; Farish, ed., *Fithian Journal*, 26. Eighteenth-century Americans frequently recalled their mothers as strict disciplinarians; see, e.g., Lucy Searle, "Memoir of Mrs. Sarah Atkins," *EIHC*, LXXXV (1949), 161; and [Susanna Nelson Page] to Lucy Smith Digges, April 10, 1835, Smith-Digges Papers, CW.

60. Catherine Livingston to John Jay, March 29, 1781, Jay Papers; Albert H. Smyth, ed., *The Writings of Benjamin Franklin* (New York, 1905-1906), V, 282. Alexander Graydon, *Memoirs of his own Time . . .* , ed. John S. Littell (New York, reprint, 1969), 21, comments on his grandmother's strictness.

61. Lydia Clark to Mehetabel Higginson, [Oct. 29, 1794], John Innes Clark Papers, RIHS; Timothy Pickering to Rebecca Pickering, June 14, 1777, June 24, 1792, Pickering Papers, reel 1, 42.

62. Fisher diary, Jan. 8, 1785, March 25, 1790; Sarah Gibbes to John Gibbes, Aug. 11, 1783, Gibbes-Gilchrist Papers, SCHS. See also, e.g., Andrews, ed., "Phelps Diary," *NEHGR*, CXVIII (1964), 125.

63. Sarah Osborn to Joseph Fish, Feb. 14, 1760, Sarah Osborn Papers, AAS; Pamela Foster to Dwight Foster, Dec. 22, 1799, Dwight Foster Papers, box 25, AAS; Ann Jay to Sarah Jay, July 27, 1800, Jay Papers. Children's obligations were symbolized in their signature, "your dutiful daughter (or son)," and in the fact that even adults sent "duty" to the parents who sent "love" to them. See, e.g., John Rogers, Jr., to [John Rogers, Sr.], [c. late 1780s], Hudson Collection, box 3.

64. Joseph Rhodes to William Rhodes, Oct. 14, 1785, Rhodes Papers; John Brown to Sarah Brown, Sept. 30, 1781, John Brown Papers, RIHS. See esp. Carl Van Doren, ed., *Correspondence of Aaron Burr and His Daughter Theodosia* (New York, 1929), *passim*.

65. Moses Kent to James Kent, Feb. 28, 1781, Kent Papers; Alice Shippen to Nancy Shippen, Nov. 8, 1777, Shippen Family Papers, microfilm, reel 3, 2195, LCMD.

66. Don Higginbotham, ed., *The Papers of James Iredell* (Raleigh, N.C., 1976), II, 89; Betts and Bear, eds., *Jefferson Family Letters*, 34, 41, 36–37.

67. John C. Symmes to Mrs. William H. Harrison, March 7, 1808, Short Family Papers, box 17, LCMD; James Kent to Elizabeth Kent, April 13, 1804, Kent Papers; Polly Vanhorne to Anne DeLancey, [n.d.], in "DeLancey Reminiscences," De-Lancey Family Papers, MCNY; Pamela Dwight to Betsy Mayhew, Feb. 3, 1771, Sedgwick Papers III, MHS. The toast is recorded in James R. McGovern, *Yankee Family* (New Orleans, La., 1975), 21.

68. Betts and Bear, eds., *Jefferson Family Letters*, 30, 259 (see also 83–84, 218, and, for evidence of how successful this tactic was with Patsy, 154, 166, 260, 303).

69. John Dickinson to Maria Dickinson, Oct. 11, 1787, M. D. Logan Papers, box 1; Timothy Pickering to Rebecca Pickering, Oct. 1, 1781, Pickering Papers, reel 1, 219A; Edward Rutledge to Sarah Rutledge, Oct. 12, 1794, Edward Rutledge Papers, SCHS.

70. *Warren-Adams Letters* . . . , Collections of the MHS, LXXIII (Boston, 1925), 81; Rebecca Stoddert to Elizabeth Gantt, Sept. 15, 1799, Stoddert Papers. On girls living at home: William G. Roelker, ed., *Benjamin Franklin and Catharine Ray Greene Their Correspondence 1755–1790* (Philadelphia, 1949), 114.

71. Alice Izard to Margaret Manigault, Oct. 1, 1801, Manigault Papers, SCL; Fisher diary, Aug. 15, 1793.

72. Quoted in Ravenel, *Eliza Pinckney*, 117.

73. Abigail Greenleaf to Robert T. Paine, March 18, 1755 (in reply to his long disquisition on child rearing, March 7, 1755), Paine Papers. See also the exchange between Abigail Adams and Mercy Warren, *AFC*, I, 85–87; and Ethel Armes, ed., *Nancy Shippen Her Journal Book* (Philadelphia, 1935), 147–149.

74. [Caroline de Windt, ed.], *Journal and Correspondence of Miss Adams, Daughter of John Adams* (London, 1841–1842), I, 83; Elizabeth Smith to Isaac Smith, Jr., Aug. [no yr.], Shaw Family Papers, box 1, LCMD. On different methods for different children: Judith Mordecai to her parents, Dec. 8, 1793, Mordecai Family Papers.

75. Fisher diary, June 1, 1777, Jan. 1, 1786, and *passim*.

76. For fathers' sole control of sons, see, e.g., Mary Rutledge to Sally Rutledge, July 15, 1795, Pinckney Family Papers, ser. 1, box 2; and Hannah Gilman to Peter Robbins, Oct. 29, 1804, Gilman Papers, MHS.

77. Elizabeth Graeme to Mrs. ———, Feb. 27, 1770, Miscellaneous Manuscripts, HSP. On Elizabeth's relationship with her mother: "An Account of the Life and Character of Mrs. Elizabeth Ferguson [sic]," *The Port Folio*, 3rd ser., I (1809), 521–522. See also Washington journal, summer 1784.

78. *AFC*, II, 282–283; Adams, *New Letters*, 77 (see also 8, 56, 76, 162); Alice Izard to Margaret Manigault, June 24, 1801 (see also same to same, July 27, 1801), Manigault Papers, SCL. Husbands expressed their preference for sons in, e.g., Charles Pettit to Joseph Reed, July 18, 1770, Reed Papers; and John Steele to Mary Steele, Jan. 1, 31, 1793, Steele Papers. A rare father who preferred daughters was James Kent (see his letter to Theodorus Bailey, Dec. 31, 1796, Kent Papers).

79. Jane Gaston to William Gaston, Feb. 3, 1795, William Gaston Papers, SHC/UNC; Fisher diary, July 5, 1790; Mrs. Caroline Gardiner Curtis, ed., *The Cary Letters* (Cambridge, Mass., 1891), 111; Eliza Southgate Bowne, *A Girl's Life Eighty Years Ago*, ed. Clarence Cook (London, 1888), 28.

80. *AFC*, I, 325, II, 129 (see also I, 288–289, 297–298, 312–313); Elizabeth S. Peabody to William Shaw, March 20, 1799 (see also hers to Mary Cranch, Jan. 1, 1799, and to William Shaw, Jan. 10, 1799), Shaw Papers, box 1.

81. Sarah Rhoads, "Some account respecting my dearly beloved Daughter Mary Rhoads," S. W. Fisher Papers; Debby Logan to Mary Norris, Dec. 27, 1795, M. D. Logan Papers, box 2. See also Sarah Rhoads, "Respecting my beloved Daughter Elizabeth Fisher," and Samuel W. Fisher, Memoir of Elizabeth R. Fisher, S. W. Fisher Papers.

82. "DeLancey Reminiscences," a copybook in the DeLancey Papers. I owe this important reference to Wendell Tripp.

83. Elizabeth DeLancey to Anne and Alice DeLancey, [Jan. no yr.], Betsy DeLancey to Anne DeLancey, [c. 1768], Elizabeth DeLancey to Betsy DeLancey, [n.d.], all in "DeLancey Reminiscences," DeLancey Papers.

84. Margaret Manigault to Alice Izard, July 29, July 26, 1801, and Alice Izard to Margaret Manigault, July 11, Aug. 17, Oct. 18, 1801, all in Manigault Papers, SCL. It is my intention to edit selections from this extraordinary correspondence for publication.

85. Burr journal-letters, April 10 [12], 1757.

86. Burr journal-letters, Dec. [10], 1756; Oct. 1 [11], 1754; Feb. 12 [15], 1755.

87. Among the published "diaries" that were actually extended letters to friends are Emily V. Mason, ed., [Lucinda Lee Orr], *Journal of a Young Lady of Virginia 1782* (Baltimore, 1871), and Albert Cook Myers, ed., *Sally Wister's Journal* (Philadelphia, 1902). For extensive sets of unpublished correspondence among female friends, see the letters of Peggy Emlen and Sally Logan, Marjorie P. M. Brown Collection, box 1, HSP; Eliza Waite Collection and Cutts Family Papers, EI; and the letters of Margaret Cowper and Eliza McQueen in both Mackay-Stiles Papers, SHC/UNC, and Mackay-McQueen-Cowper Papers, Georgia Society of Colonial

Dames Collection, GHS. For an excellent discussion of such friendships in the nineteenth century: Carroll Smith-Rosenberg, "The Female World of Love and Ritual," *Signs*, I (1975), 1–30.

88. Sophia Brown to Susannah Brown, Oct. 10, 1790, Brown Papers, Miscellaneous MSS, NYHS; Lewis-Gibson Letters, 1794–1854, *passim*; Fisher diary, Feb. 21, 1792. Other references to long-standing female friendships may be found in Bowen [Martin] journal, April 29, 1787; and Harriott Pinckney to [Miss King?], [c. 1767], Pinckney Family (Buist Family) Papers, SCHS.

89. See, e.g., Fisher diary, April 18, Nov. 2, 1789; March *passim*, Dec. 25, 1790, Feb. 5, 1794; Adams, *New Letters*, 78–79; and Rebecca Pickering to Timothy Pickering, Sept. 23, 1782, Pickering Papers, reel 4, pt. 1, 284.

90. Grace Galloway, "A Letter to Miss Nancy Thompson," Nov. 21, 1747, Joseph Galloway Papers, LCMD; Janette Barclay to Elizabeth Smith, Nov. 19, 1768, Robbins Papers, I; "Julia" [Bathshua Pynchon] to Peggy Orne, Jan. 22–31, 1791, Cushing-Orne Papers, MHS.

91. [Margaret Davenport] to [Fanny Currie], May 25–June 2, 1794; F. H. C[urrie] to Margaret D. Coalter, Feb. 9–15, 1795; John Coalter to Margaret Coalter, March 16, April 5, 1795, all in Brown-Coalter-Tucker Papers, box 2.

92. For a typical directive to women to let their husbands be their only true friends, see "Essay on Friendship. Addressed to the Ladies," *Massachusetts Magazine*, VI (Nov. 1794), 683–687.

CHAPTER FOUR

1. There are no systematic American comments on the female role between the sermons of Cotton Mather and the 1770s. The few extended treatments of woman's sphere published in the colonies during that period originated in England or Europe. (See, e.g., "A Letter to a young Lady on her Marriage," *American Magazine and Historical Chronicle*, III [Sept. 1746], 399–404.)

2. These works are conveniently summarized in Mary Sumner Benson, *Women in Eighteenth-Century America: A Study of Opinion and Social Usage* (Port Washington, N.Y., reprint, 1966).

3. [Caroline de Windt, ed.], *Journal and Correspondence of Miss Adams, Daughter of John Adams* (New York and London, 1841–1842), II, 102. See, e.g., Mary Gould Almy, Journal, in Elizabeth Evans, ed., *Weathering the Storm: Women of the American Revolution* (New York, 1975), 252, 253, 255.

4. Charity Clarke to [Joseph Jekyll], Oct. 28, 1771, Moore Family Papers, CU; Carl Van Doren, ed., *The Letters of Benjamin Franklin & Jane Mecom* (Princeton, N.J., 1950), 302; Lyman H. Butterfield et al., eds., *Adams Family Correspondence* (Cambridge, Mass., 1963), IV, 26 (hereafter cited as *AFC*); "Kennon Letters," *VMHB*, XXXI (1923), 305.

5. Lavater, "General Remarks on Women," *Massachusetts Magazine*, VI (Jan.

1794), 20 (also printed, under a different title, in *New York Magazine*, I [June 1790], 335–338); "Animadversions on the Affectation of ill-suited Characters among the Female Sex," *Amer. Mag. & Hist. Chron.*, II (July 1745), 304; Gregory, reprinted in *The Christian's Scholar's and Farmer's Magazine*, I (Sept. 1789), 318.

6. "On Modesty," *The Gentlemen and Ladies Town and Country Magazine*, I (March 1789), 94; "On Modesty," *Columbian Magazine*, IX (Oct. 1792), 239; Mira, "Reflections on the Fair Sex," *Royal American Magazine*, I (May 1774), 188.

7. "Remarks on Female Delicacy," *American Museum*, V (Jan. 1789), 69; "Philo No. XV," *Mass. Mag.*, II (Dec. 1790), 757; "On Politeness," *Amer. Museum*, IV (Sept. 1788), 222; "On Modesty," *The Lady's Magazine*, I (Dec. 1792), 36.

8. Ethel Armes, ed., *Nancy Shippen Her Journal Book* (Philadelphia, 1935), 155; Sarah Cadbury, ed., "Extracts from the Diary of Mrs. Ann Warder," *PMHB*, XVII (1893), 461; Polly Palmer to [Mary Cranch?], July 24, 1766, Cranch Family Papers, 3, LCMD.

9. Eliza Southgate Bowne, *A Girl's Life Eighty Years Ago*, ed. Clarence Cook (London, 1888), 50; [Elizabeth Shaw] to [Miss Hazen], Feb. 10, 1786 (draft), Shaw Family Papers, box 1, LCMD; Amelia Elizabeth Dwight, *Memorials of Mary Wilder White*, ed. Mary Wilder Tileston (Boston, 1903), 160–161.

10. Peggy Emlen to Sally Logan, Jan. 8, 1768, Marjorie P. M. Brown Collection, box 1, HSP; Don Higginbotham, ed., *The Papers of James Iredell* (Raleigh, N.C., 1976), I, 70; Hunter Dickinson Farish, ed., *Journal & Letters of Philip Vickers Fithian 1773–1774: A Plantation Tutor of the Old Dominion* (Williamsburg, Va., 1957), 128; William Bentley, *The Diary of William Bentley, D.D.* (Salem, Mass., 1905–1914), I, 204; M[ary] Ringgold to John Galloway, June 1783, Galloway-Maxcy-Markoe Papers, XVII, LCMD; *AFC*, I, 184. On ordinary women: Mary Beth Norton, "Eighteenth-Century American Women in Peace and War: The Case of the Loyalists," *WMQ*, 3rd ser., XXXIII (1976), 405.

11. *AFC*, I, 302 (see also I, 182, and II, 392); Anne Stokely Pratt, ed., "Nine Letters to Nathan Hale," *Yale University Library Gazette*, XXVI (July 1951), 18.

12. Rebecca Gilman to ———, Oct. 10, 1772, Gilman Papers, MHS; Carl Bridenbaugh, ed., *Gentleman's Progress: The Itinerarium of Dr. Alexander Hamilton 1744* (Chapel Hill, N.C., 1948), 4. Similar references are, e.g., Susan Livingston to Sarah Jay, Oct. 1, 1781, John Jay Papers, CU; and America Lawson to Susanna Campbell, Nov. 20, 1795, Campbell Papers, folder 11, EGS.

13. Armes, ed., *Shippen Journal*, 214; George Barrell to Charlotte Barrell, Aug. 24, 1799, Cheever Family Papers, AAS; Sarah Jay to John Jay, Dec. 10, 1784, Jay Papers. The brief quotations in the first sentence are from Farish, ed., *Fithian Journal*, 179, and Ezekial Freeman to Nehemiah Freeman, Feb. 17, 1789, Minot Family Papers, MHS. And see Maria Seiglearth to Mr. Redhead, Sept. 15, 1778, HCA 32/304/5, 46.

14. "A Father's Advice to his Daughters," *Chris. Schol. Farmer's Mag.*, II (July 1790), 169; Sylvius, Letter to Editor, *United States Magazine*, I (June 1779), 260; Pamela Sedgwick to Theodore Sedgwick, Jan. 31–Feb. 12, 1789, Sedgwick Papers III, MHS; *Letters Written by the Earl of Chesterfield to His Son* (Philadelphia, 1872),

129, 290; Elise Pinckney, ed., *The Letterbook of Eliza Lucas Pinckney 1739–1762* (Chapel Hill, N.C., 1972), 47.

15. *Warren-Adams Letters* . . . , Collections of the MHS, LXXII–LXXIII (Boston, 1917, 1925), II, 129; "A Letter from an American Lady to her son in Europe, on the celebrated letters of the late Earl of Chesterfield," *Boston Magazine*, I (June 1784), 327; also in *Mass. Mag.*, II (Jan. 1790), 36–38. For Abigail's efforts to publish the letter: *AFC*, IV, 59 (see also I, 3͡͡͡͡, 376, 389).

16. *AFC*, IV, 50; III, 147, 214; IV, 506. Another of Mrs. Warren's rare comments on women is in her *The Motley Assembly, A Farce* (Boston, 1779), 5. I owe this last reference to Mary E. Norton.

17. Julian Boyd et al., eds., *The Papers of Thomas Jefferson* (Princeton, N.J., 1950–), XVI, 197; Sarah Jay to John Jay, Nov. 3, 1790, Jay Papers; Mary Murray to James Murray, Jan. 8, 1775, Murray Family Papers, box 4, NYHS; Elizabeth Cushing to William Cushing, April 4, 1773, Robert Treat Paine Papers, MHS. See also, e.g., Rebecca Pickering to Timothy Pickering, Oct. 22, 1787, Timothy Pickering Papers, microfilm, reel 4, pt. 1, 327, MHS; and Rebecca Stoddert to Elizabeth Gantt, Oct. 21, 1799, Rebecca Stoddert Papers, Miscellaneous Manuscripts, LCMD.

18. Mary Gray to Daniel Sutherland, July 25, 1787, AO 13/118, 488; Jane Gordon to John Wilmot and Daniel P. Coke, Nov. 5, 1782, AO 13/73, 586; Joyce Dawson to Lord Dunmore, July 24, 1781, AO 13/28, 220. A more detailed discussion is in Norton, "Eighteenth-Century American Women," *WMQ*, 3rd ser., XXXIII (1976), 404–406.

19. Simon P. Gratz, "Some Material for a Biography of Mrs. Elizabeth Fergusson, Née Graeme," *PMHB*, XXXIX (1915), 402; Mary Kearsley, Testimony, April 28, 1785, AO 12/38, 282; Boyd et al., eds., *Jefferson Papers*, XII, 534; "Letters from Miss Ann Powell Combined in a Journal during a Tour to Niagara and Detroit, 1789," *EIHC*, LXXVI (1950), 343.

20. Elizabeth Fisher to Samuel Fisher, Sept. 19, 1793, Samuel W. Fisher Papers, HSP; Betsy Champion to Ephraim Kirby, Dec. 10, 1782, Ephraim Kirby Papers, DU; Susanna Dillwyn to William Dillwyn, Feb. 12, 1783, William Dillwyn Papers, box 1, LCP/HSP.

21. Anne Nicholas to Fanny Coalter, June 30, 1802, Brown-Coalter-Tucker Papers, box 2, EGS; Abigail Greenleaf to Robert T. Paine, Oct. 23, 1774, Paine Papers; Anna Mitchell to Lydia Bowen, March 24–30, 1793, John Innes Clark Papers, RIHS; E[lizabeth] P[arker] to [Janet Brinley], April 15, [no yr.] (typescript), Parker-Brinley Papers, box 2, HSP; Esther Edwards Burr, Journal-Letters, Oct. 1 [Nov. 9], 1754, YL.

22. Mary Sayre to Joseph Reed, Nov. 9, 1765, Joseph Reed Papers, NYHS; Paine Wingate to Hannah Wingate, Aug. 30, 1789, Paine Wingate Papers, HL. Examples of women's hesitancy at writing to men may be found in Van Doren, ed., *Franklin-Mecom Letters*, 173, 194; Lydia Thayer to Ruth Belknap, Aug. 24, 1777, Jeremy Belknap Papers, NHHS; Eliza Talbot to Enos Hitchcock, Oct. 18, 1789, Enos Hitchcock Papers, RIHS.

23. Betsy Hopkins to Pamela Dwight, Jan. 15, 1774, and Pamela Sedgwick to

Theodore Sedgwick, Jan. 31, 1789, both in Sedgwick Papers III; Mary Dickinson to Isaac Norris, March 14, 1791, Norris Family of Fairhill Papers, I, 77, HSP; Burr journal-letters, April 7 [8], 1755.

24. Elizabeth Foote Washington, Journal, [July 1792?], Washington Family Papers, box 2, LCMD; Higginbotham, ed., *Iredell Papers*, I, 148, II, 392; Frances Norton Mason, ed., *My Dearest Polly: Letters of Chief Justice John Marshall to his Wife* . . . (Richmond, Va., 1961), 344; Augustine Smith to Alice Page, March 22, [1792], Augustine Smith Papers, EGS.

25. [Benjamin Rush], "An Account of the Life and Character of Mrs. Elizabeth Ferguson," *The Port Folio*, 3rd ser., I (1809), 521; Abigail May, Journal-Letters, Aug. 1800, May-Goddard Papers, SLRC. This theme also appeared in poetry; see, e.g., "The Coquette Contrasted," *Col. Mag.*, III (Jan. 1789), 53.

26. Margaret Coalter to John Coalter, Aug. 3, 1795, Brown-Coalter-Tucker Papers, box 2; Elizabeth Shaw to Nabby Adams, Nov. 19, 1785, Shaw Papers, box 1. The same theme appears repeatedly, as in William [Harris] to Peggy [Orne], April 5–20, [179?], Cushing-Orne Papers, MHS; and Mary Dickinson to [Isaac Norris], March 16, [no yr.], Norris Family Papers, I, 71.

27. *AFC*, II, 391, 393n. That Adams was correct in her assessment of the pejorative implications of the attitude toward Macaulay is demonstrated by the comments in John Cotton Smith to James Kent, Sept. 13, 1784, James Kent Papers, LCMD.

28. *Warren-Adams Letters*, II, 101; I, 37, 42–44. The 1768 essay is reprinted in *Amer. Museum*, IV (Aug. 1788), 119. Mrs. Warren also raised the same issue in letters to Abigail Adams; see *AFC*, I, 185–187.

29. *Warren-Adams Letters*, I, 105–107, 115; II, 177, 180, 188.

30. "Vindication of that Sort of Preference which Women are supposed to show for Men of Inferior Talents," *American Magazine*, I (Feb. 1788), 135. On Mercy Warren's ambiguous situation, see also Lawrence J. Friedman and Arthur H. Shaffer, "Mercy Otis Warren and the Politics of Historical Nationalism," *New England Quarterly*, XLVIII (1975), 206–215.

31. Anna Clifford to Rebecca Shoemaker, Oct. 9–18, 1783, Shoemaker-Rawle Papers, HSP; Susanna Dillwyn to William Dillwyn, May 25–June 1, 1786, Dillwyn Papers, box 1; Mary Orne Tucker, Diary, May 3, 1802, EI; L. H. Butterfield et al., eds., *Diary and Autobiography of John Adams* (Cambridge, Mass., 1961), I, 194–195; *Warren-Adams Letters*, II, 380.

32. Boyd et al., eds., *Jefferson Papers*, XIV, 611.

33. Anne Moore to Anne DeLancey, Nov. 2, [no yr., but early 1760s], in "DeLancey Reminiscences," DeLancey Family Papers, MCNY.

CHAPTER FIVE

1. Lavater, "General Remarks on Women," *Massachusetts Magazine*, VI (Jan. 1794), 21. The most detailed discussion of female piety is James Fordyce, *Sermons*

to Young Women (Philadelphia, 1809), II, *passim*. For comments on religion in women's diaries, see, e.g., Thomas Eliot Andrews, ed., "The Diary of Elizabeth (Porter) Phelps," *NEHGR*, CXVIII (1964), 112, 218–219; CXIX (1965), 209, 297, and *passim*; Jemima Condict, *Jemima Condict, Her Book* . . . (Newark, N.J., 1930), 15, 38, 52–53, 56–57.

2. Anne Emlen [Mifflin], "Some Account of My Religious Progress," Emlen Collection, HSP; Elizabeth Foote Washington, Journal, July 1792 [?], Washington Family Papers, box 2, LCMD; David Ramsay, *Memoirs of the Life of Martha Laurens Ramsay*, 3rd ed. (Boston, 1812), 65–208, *passim*.

3. Elizabeth Colden DeLancey to Anne and Alice DeLancey, Dec. 23, 1759 (the quotation comes from a note added later), in "DeLancey Reminiscences," DeLancey Family Papers, MCNY; [Susanna Nelson Page] to Lucy C. Smith Digges, April 10, 1835, Smith-Digges Papers, CW. See Charles Francis Adams, ed., *Letters of Mrs. Adams, the Wife of John Adams*, 3rd ed. (Boston, 1841), II, 229; Franklin B. Dexter, ed., *The Literary Diary of Ezra Stiles, D.D., LL.D.* (New York, 1901), I, 564–565.

4. Eliza Pinckney to Harriott Horry, June 8, 1778, Eliza Lucas Pinckney Papers, SCHS; Washington journal, winter 1792; Peggy Emlen to Sally Logan, Jan. 8, 1768, Marjorie P. M. Brown Collection, box 1, HSP. Men made similar statements; see, e.g., Adrian Bancker to Evert Bancker, Dec. 11, 1774, Bancker Family Papers, NYHS.

5. Sally Logan Fisher, Diary, Feb. 26, 1792, HSP; Elizabeth Drinker, Diary, Dec. 31, 1794, HSP. See Carl Van Doren, ed., *Letters of Benjamin Franklin & Jane Mecom* (Princeton, N.J., 1950), 83–84, for one of the many expressions of the same philosophy by non-Quakers.

6. Lydia Hill Almy, Journal, Feb. 27, 1798, EI. In her autobiographical *Memoirs of Elizabeth Collins* . . . (Philadelphia, 1859), 25–35, a public Friend movingly described the difficulty of making the decision to become a minister. See, in general, Mary Maples Dunn, "Women of Light," in Carol Berkin and Mary Beth Norton, eds., *Women of America: A History* (Boston, 1979), 112–134.

7. Anne Emlen [Mifflin], "Some Account of My Religious Progress," April 13, [1781?], and undated diary extract from early 1780s, Emlen Collection; Fisher diary, March 23, 1781 (see also Oct. 6, Dec. 8, 1778); Anna Rawle, Diary, Sept. 29, March 1, 1781, Shoemaker-Rawle Papers, HSP.

8. William Lumpkin, "The Role of Women in 18th Century Virginia Baptist Life," *Baptist History and Heritage*, VIII (1973), 160–167; Dexter, ed., *Literary Diary of Ezra Stiles*, I, 146–147. For accounts of black women's involvement in the Baptist Church, see Robert Carter, Daybook XV, 15–19, Robert Carter Papers, DU; Oliver Hart to Joseph Hart, April 18, 1785, Oliver Hart Papers, SCL; and Washington journal, July 1792.

9. Mary Cooper, Diary, Nov. 6, 1768; Feb. 19, 1769; July [22?], 1772; Aug. 8 to Oct. 7, 1773, *passim*, esp. Aug. 15, 28, Sept. 12, 16, 19, Oct. 3, NYPL. Mary Maples Dunn suggested this explanation of the division in the congregation.

10. Samuel Hopkins, *Memoirs of the Life of Mrs. Sarah Osborn* (Worcester, Mass., 1799), 49, 51, 71–73; Sarah Osborn to Joseph Fish, May 10, 1761, Sarah Osborn

Papers, AAS. A more extended treatment of Sarah Osborn is Mary Beth Norton, "'My Resting Reaping Times': Sarah Osborn's Defense of Her 'Unfeminine' Activities, 1767," *Signs*, II (1976), 515–529. Such female prayer groups were common; see, e.g., Joshua Huntington, *Memoirs of the Life of Mrs. Abigail Waters* (Boston, 1817), 45–49, and Mary Orne Tucker, Diary, April–May, 1802, *passim*, AAS.

11. Sarah Osborn to Joseph Fish, April 21, 1765; June 17, 1766; [c. July 1766], all in Osborn Papers. See Hopkins, *Osborn Memoirs*, 76–77, 81–82.

12. Sarah Osborn to Joseph Fish, Aug. 9, 1766; Feb. 28, 1767, Osborn Papers. See also same to same, June 17, 1766; [c. July 1766], *ibid.*, and Hopkins, *Osborn Memoirs*, 77–78.

13. The quotations in the following three paragraphs come from Sarah Osborn to Joseph Fish, Feb. 28–March 7, 1767, Osborn Papers, reprinted in Norton, "Osborn's Defense," *Signs*, II (1976), 522–529.

14. Sarah Osborn to Joseph Fish, [c. July 1766], Osborn Papers.

15. Sarah Osborn to Mary Noice, July 9, 1769, Osborn Papers; Hopkins, *Osborn Memoirs*, 83; Dexter, ed., *Literary Diary of Ezra Stiles*, I, 43–44.

16. On the careers of these more prominent female eighteenth-century religious leaders, see their biographies in Edward W. James et al., eds., *Notable American Women 1607–1950*, 3 vols. (Cambridge, Mass., 1971). Nancy F. Cott, *The Bonds of Womanhood: 'Woman's Sphere' in New England, 1780–1835* (New Haven, Ct., 1977), chapter 4, discusses the beginnings of the nineteenth-century female charitable societies.

17. Recent useful studies of widows are Alexander Keyssar, "Widowhood in 18th Century Massachusetts: A Problem in the History of the Family," *Perspectives in American History*, VIII (1974), 83–119, and Susan Grigg, "Toward a Theory of Remarriage: A Case Study of Newburyport at the Beginning of the Nineteenth Century," *JIH*, VIII (1977), 183–220.

18. Cordelia Giles to Aquila Giles, July 13, 1814, Aquila Giles Papers, NYHS; Lucy Everett to Rebecca Huse, Feb. 21, 1803, Hale Family Papers, I, 29–30, LCMD; Harriott Pinckney to Mrs. Favell, March 1763, Pinckney Family (Buist Family) Papers, SCHS; Elise Pinckney, ed., *The Letterbook of Eliza Lucas Pinckney 1739–1762* (Chapel Hill, N.C., 1972), 135, 178.

19. James W. Deen, Jr., "Patterns of Testation: Four Tidewater Counties in Colonial Virginia," *American Journal of Legal History*, XVI (1972), 174–176, and Lois Green Carr and Lorena Walsh, "The Planter's Wife: The Experience of White Women in Seventeenth-Century Maryland," *WMQ*, 3rd ser., XXXIV (1977), 556–557, examine earlier periods, but there is little reason to believe that eighteenth-century practice differed significantly.

20. Juliana Scott to Aquila Giles, March 21, 1800, Giles Papers; Catherine Ridley to John Jay, May 2, 1790, Feb. 7, 1792, John Jay Papers, CU.

21. Lund Washington, Account Book, 1782–1797, notes by Elizabeth F. Washington, box 2, Washington Family Papers.

22. Elisabeth Freeman to Robert T. Paine, June 12, 1758, Robert Treat Paine Papers, MHS; Juliana Scott to Aquila Giles, March 21, 1800, Sept. 10, 1801, Giles

Papers; Catherine Livingston to [Sarah Thompson], Dec. 26, 1806, and *passim*, Gilbert Livingston Papers, NYPL.

23. See Marylynn Salmon, "Equality or Submersion? Feme Covert Status in Early Pennsylvania," in Berkin and Norton, eds., *Women of America*, 96–99, on marriage settlements. Cf. the antenuptial agreement of Martha Jefferson and Thomas Mann Randolph, arranged by her father, in Edwin M. Betts and James A. Bear, Jr., eds., *The Family Letters of Thomas Jefferson* (Columbia, Mo., 1966), 49–50, with some signed by widows: that of Mary Gwynn and James Hudson, [1780], Hudson Family Collection, box 1, NYPL; Jane Donnom and John Bourquin, Aug. 2, 1780, Miscellaneous Manuscripts, SCL; and Agnes Hope and Josiah Bacon, Nov. 25, 1803, Hooker Collection, SLRC.

24. St. George Tucker to John Coalter, Dec. 4, 1808, Brown-Coalter-Tucker Papers, box 2, EGS; Jack P. Greene, ed., *The Diary of Colonel Landon Carter of Sabine Hall, 1752–1778* (Charlottesville, Va., 1965), II, 966; John J. Smith, ed., *Letters of Doctor Richard Hill and his Children* (Philadelphia, 1854), 116, 136. For a girl's rejection of her brother's advice about the need for a marriage settlement, see Francis Dana to Edmund Dana, Jan. 24, 1796, Dana Papers, MHS.

25. Anna Mitchell to Eliza Bowen, April 1, 1793, John Innes Clark Papers, RIHS; Julian Boyd et al., eds., *The Papers of Thomas Jefferson* (Princeton, N.J., 1950–), XV, 95, XIV, 517. For the exchange between John and Abigail Adams, see chapter 2, n. 20.

26. Keyssar, "Widowhood," *Perspectives in Amer. Hist.*, VIII (1974), 99–116. See also James K. Somerville, "The Salem (Mass.) Woman in the Home, 1660–1770," *Eighteenth-Century Life*, I (1974–1975), 11–14. Widows' comments on and attempts to cope with such difficulties are contained in, e.g., Mary Rogers to [Henry Hudson], Nov. 15, 1799, Hudson Family Collection, box 2, and Elizabeth Van Schaick and Gerrit Van Schaick, Agreement, March 28, 1789, Lansing Family Papers, I, 24, Gansevoort-Lansing Collection, NYPL.

27. See Mary Beth Norton, "Eighteenth-Century American Women in Peace and War: The Case of the Loyalists," *WMQ*, 3rd ser., XXXIII (1976), 393–395; and Katherine Allamong Jacob, "The Woman's Lot in Baltimore Town, 1729–97," *MHM*, LXXI (1976), 290–291. On the social pressures brought to bear on working women: Norton, "Osborn's Defense," *Signs*, II (1976), 527, and Lucy Searle, "Memoir of Mrs. Sarah Atkins," *EIHC*, LXXXV (1949), 163.

28. Norton, "Eighteenth-Century American Women," *WMQ*, 3rd ser., XXXIII (1976), 393. On the prostitutes: Frank W. C. Hersey, "The Misfortunes of Dorcas Griffiths," *Publications of Colonial Society of Massachusetts*, XXXIV (1937–1942), 14–25. For women who took over their husbands' businesses: Searle, "Atkins Memoir," *EIHC*, LXXXV (1949), 165; and the papers of Sarah Zane Sr. and Jr. in Coates-Reynall Collection, HSP (on the Marlboro Iron Works).

29. Suky Jervis to John Drury, April 28, [no year, but 1790s], John Drury Papers, III, 23, EI. See Kenneth and Anna Roberts, eds. and trans., *Moreau de St. Mery's American Journey 1793–1798* (Garden City, N.Y., 1947), 156, 302–303, 311, 313; and John S. Ezell, ed., and Judson P. Wood, trans., *The New Democracy in America:*

Travels of Francisco de Miranda in the United States, 1783-84 (Norman, Okla., 1963), 134-135.

30. On teenagers as nurses: Betsy Foote, Diary, May 7, 1775, CHS; William Cranch to Lucy Cranch, June 23, 1792, Cranch Family Papers, LCMD; "Julia" [Bathshua Pynchon] to Peggy Orne, Sept. 14, 1794, Cushing-Orne Papers, MHS.

31. A[nna] H[udson] to Mrs. John Rogers, June 2, 1786, Hudson Family Collection, box 3. For references to these urban nurses, see Fisher diary, Nov. 27, 1779, Aug. 19, Nov. 22, 1781; Elizabeth deHart Bleecker [McDonald], Diary, Sept. 12, Nov. 24, 1802, March 6, 1803, NYPL; and Margaret Manigault to Gabriel Manigault, Nov. 23-25, 1792, Manigault Papers, SCL.

32. Fisher diary, June 8-29, 1782, and *passim*; Frederick Tupper and Helen Tyler Brown, eds., *Grandmother Tyler's Book, The Recollections of Mary Palmer Tyler 1775-1866* (New York, 1925), 223-224 (hereafter cited as Tyler, *Book*); Abigail Greenleaf to Thomas Paine, Nov. 5, 1754, Paine Papers.

33. Dexter, ed., *Literary Diary of Ezra Stiles*, I, 489 (see also 208); Janet Cumming, Testimony, AO 12/50, 347-348, and AO 12/99, 130; Elizabeth Deas to Katherine Thomson, June 15, 1777, HCA 32/447/10, 79. The diary of a midwife, Martha Moore Ballard, is printed in Charles E. Nash, *The History of Augusta* (Augusta, Me., 1904), 229-464.

34. Sarah Osborn to Joseph Fish, May 3, 1759, [n.d., pre-1767], Osborn Papers. See also Hopkins, *Osborn Memoirs*, 20, 59-60, 64-65. The rationale for opening a school is best expressed in Catherine Byles to [Elizabeth] Hurley, Sept. 20, 1799, Catherine and Mary Byles Letterbook, I, HL.

35. Rebecca Pickering to Timothy Pickering, March 20, 1782, Timothy Pickering Papers, microfilm, reel 4, pt. 1, 269, MHS. On Polly Bancker, see chapter 1, n. 41.

36. Mary Bagnall to [William Rhodes], April 13, 1791, and to Joseph Rhodes, Dec. 2, 1784, Rhodes Family Papers, LCMD. Many references to seamstresses may be found in well-to-do women's diaries, letters, and accounts. See, e.g., Bleecker diary, Jan. 23, Feb. 20, 1799, and *passim*; Lelia Tucker to Fanny Coalter, [Jan. 1806], Brown-Coalter-Tucker Papers, box 2. A seamstress's account book is that of Elizabeth Littlepage, 1767, in Holladay Family Papers, VHS.

37. Lyman H. Butterfield et al., eds., *Adams Family Correspondence* (Cambridge, Mass., 1963), I, 47-48; Rebecca Dickinson, Diary, 1787, in Daniel White Wells and Reuben Field Wells, *A History of Hatfield Massachusetts 1660-1910* (Springfield, Mass., 1910), 206; Nancy Rawson to [Eunice Packard], Feb. 1781, Packard Family Papers, Miscellaneous Manuscripts, NYHS.

38. Edward Bridgen to Elizabeth Smith, Jan. 26, 1770, James M. Robbins Papers, II, MHS; Elizabeth Thompson, Testimony, AO 12/46, 77-80; Margaret Hutchinson, Loss Schedule, AO 13/96, 601-602. For the brief descriptions quoted above, see AO 13/125, 639, and AO 12/99, 56. Cf. the circumstances of Margaret Locke, the seamstress, AO 12/38, 350-353. On mantua makers' charges, see Helen M. Morgan, ed., *A Season in New York 1801* (Pittsburgh, 1969), 99, and Eliza Ward to Sarah Brown, Dec. 15, 1799, John Brown Papers, RIHS.

39. "Narrative of Mrs. Abraham Brasher 1801" (typescript), 2, NYHS; Van

Doren, ed., *Franklin-Mecom Letters*, 94, 97–98, and *passim*; Anna Hunter to John Rogers, April 12, 1785, Oct. 8, [1793], Hudson Collection, box 3. Accounts kept by women storekeepers are preserved in Sanders Family Papers, box 2, NYHS (Elizabeth Schuyler Sanders); Alexander Papers, box 68, NYHS (Mary Provoost Alexander); Salisbury Family Papers, AAS (Martha Salisbury); and Susannah Bolton Moore Papers, GHS.

40. Christian Barnes to Elizabeth Smith, Nov. 24, 1770, Barnes Letterbook, LCMD.

41. Max Farrand, ed., *A Journey to Ohio in 1810 as Recorded in the Journal of Margaret Van Horn Dwight* (New Haven, Ct., 1914), 25, 14–15; Maria Clinton to [Elizabeth Tallmadge], Dec. 5, 1805, Maria Clinton Papers, Miscellaneous MSS., NYHS. The extensive papers of a female Charleston tavernkeeper are in the Paul Cross Papers, SCL. And see accounts in travelers' diaries; for example, Marquis de Chastellux, *Travels in North America in the Years 1780, 1781 and 1782*, ed. and trans. Howard C. Rice, Jr. (Chapel Hill, N.C., 1963), I, 71–72, II, 419–420, 512–513, and *passim*.

42. William Palfrey to Susannah Palfrey, June 15, 1779, William Palfrey Papers, HL; William Sullivan to Hitty Cutler, Nov. 28, 1797, Thomas Amory Family Papers, III, MHS; Tyler, *Book*, 97–98. On the Archbald sisters, see Charles W. Janson, *The Stranger in America 1793–1806*, ed. Carl S. Driver (New York, 1935), 21–25, and Catherine Byles to Mather Byles, Aug. 26, 1801, Oct. 7, 1802, Byles Letterbook, I. A detailed description of such a boardinghouse is in Alexander Graydon, *Memoirs of his own Time . . .* , ed. John S. Littell (New York, reprint, 1969), 43, 62–78.

43. Case of Mary Cloudsdall, AO 12/101, 54. Two other loyalist women boardinghouse keepers from New York City were Mary Smith (papers in AO 12/100, 187; AO 13/65, 547, 572; AO 13/67, 192–203); and Mary Airey, who was said to have a "well furnished" house (AO 12/101, 29; AO 12/24, 78–80; AO 13/113, 2–4, 8–9).

44. Pinckney, *Letterbook*, 144 (see 7, 16, 35, 38, for her earlier experience). On Mary Willing Byrd: Chastellux, *Travels*, II, 430–432, and Thomas Anburey, *Travels through the Interior Parts of America* (Boston, 1923), II, 214. The papers of Maria Armistead and Elizabeth Adams, Virginia widows who managed their plantations, are in Armistead-Cocke Papers, EGS.

45. For widows who chose such options: Ferdinand-Marie Bayard, *Travels of a Frenchman in Maryland and Virginia . . . in 1791 . . .* , ed. and trans. Ben C. McCary (Ann Arbor, Mich., 1950), 45–46; Joseph Clay to Edward Telfair, March 30, 1793, Edward Telfair Papers, DU; Ann Banister to Betsy Whiting, July 1, 1790, S[arah] Cary to same, March 30, 1791, M[ary] Burwell to same, Dec. 14, 1791, all in Blair-Banister-Braxton-Horner-Whiting Papers, box 1, EGS.

46. Martha Washington to Fanny [Washington], Sept. 15, 1794 (photostat), Washington Family Papers, box 2. For the Ringgold dispute, see Galloway-Maxcy-Markoe Papers, XIV, XV, *passim*, LCMD, esp. John Galloway to Samuel Galloway, Jan. 18, 1777, Benjamin Chew and James Tilghman, Legal Opinion, May 1, 1777, in XIV, and Anna Maria Ringgold, Deposition, Jan. 22, 1779, in XV.

47. Maria Armistead to Jane Armistead, April 9, 1789, Armistead-Cocke Papers; Polly Bancker to Evert Bancker, March 8, 1800, Bancker Papers; Anna Hunter to John Rogers, [1793], Hudson Family Collection, box 3.

48. Elizabeth Murray to James Murray, Sept. 27, 1754, Robbins Papers, I. See also same to same, May 27, Dec. 4, 1753, April 2, 1754, *ibid.* Biographical information is drawn from Nina M. Tiffany, ed., *Letters of James Murray Loyalist* (Boston, 1901), 103, 105. A more detailed treatment is Mary Beth Norton, "A Cherished Spirit of Independence: The Life of an Eighteenth-Century Boston Businesswoman," in Berkin and Norton, eds., *Women of America*, 46–65.

49. Antenuptial Agreement, Elizabeth Campbell and James Smith, March 13, 1760, Robbins Papers, I.

50. [Elizabeth Smith] to [Christian Barnes], [c. Nov. 1769], Robbins Papers, II; [Elizabeth Inman] to [John Murray], Oct. 9, 1771, *ibid.*, III.

51. Antenuptial Agreement, Elizabeth Smith and Ralph Inman, Sept. 24, 1771, Robbins Papers, III, printed in Norton, "Cherished Spirit," in Berkin and Norton, eds., *Women of America*, 59–62.

52. [Elizabeth Inman] to [Mary Don?], [c. late 1772] (draft), Robbins Papers, IV.

53. Elizabeth M. Campbell to James Murray, March 20, May 12, 1756, Robbins Papers, I; Elizabeth Smith to Christian Barnes, April 24, 1770, Murray Family Papers, box 4, NYHS; Elizabeth Smith to Mrs. Deblois, April 13, 1770, Robbins Papers, II. On Janette Day's school, chapter 2, n. 26. On the Cuming sisters, chapter 6, n. 2. There is a great deal of information on the Murray-Day millinery shop in Robbins Papers, II–IV, *passim,* and Murray Family Papers, boxes 3–4.

54. Elizabeth Inman to John Murray, Sept. 18, 1783, Robbins Papers, VI.

CHAPTER SIX

1. Betsy Cuming to [Elizabeth Smith], Oct. 26, 1769, James M. Robbins Papers, II, MHS. For accounts of these public events in women's diaries and letters, see, e.g., Thomas Eliot Andrews, ed., "The Diary of Elizabeth (Porter) Phelps," *NEHGR*, CXVIII (1964), 220–224 *passim*; Mary Norris to Charles Norris, Oct. 7, 1765, Loudoun Papers, box 77, HSP; Leonard Labaree et al., eds., *The Papers of Benjamin Franklin* (New Haven, Ct., 1959–), XIII, 199.

2. Betsy Cuming to Elizabeth Smith, Nov. 29, 1769, and Anne Cuming to same, Dec. 27, 1769, both in Robbins Papers, II.

3. For some examples of patriot women's activities: Marvin L. Brown, trans., *Baroness Frederica von Riedesel and the American Revolution: Journal and Correspondence of a Tour of Duty 1776–1783* (Chapel Hill, N.C., 1965), 70; Lyman H. Butterfield et al., eds., *Adams Family Correspondence* (Cambridge, Mass., 1963–), II, 295–296 (hereafter cited as *AFC*); Margaret B. Livingston to Robert R. Livingston, Aug. 15, 1776, Robert R. Livingston Papers, NYHS. The later lives of the Cuming

sisters can be traced through their letters to various members of the Murray family, in Robbins Papers, 1780s, *passim*.

4. Franklin B. Dexter, ed., *The Literary Diary of Ezra Stiles, D.D., LL.D.* (New York, 1901), I, 480. A New Jersey girl's work for militia musters is described in Jemima Condict, *Jemima Condict, Her Book* . . . (Newark, N.J., 1930), 38, 42.

5. *New York Gazette and Weekly Mercury*, Oct. 23, 1769; *Providence Gazette*, Jan. 16, 1768.

6. William Tennent III, "To the Ladies of South Carolina," *South Carolina Gazette*, Aug. 2, 1774, reprinted in James H. Smylie, ed., "Presbyterians and the American Revolution: A Documentary Account," *Journal of Presbyterian History*, LI (1973), 370–372. Tennent recorded a somewhat different version on pp. 44–46 of his "Album," in William Tennent Papers, SCL.

7. *Virginia Gazette* (Purdie and Dixon), Jan. 20, 1774; Hannah Griffitts, "Beware the Ides of March," Feb. 28, 1775, Hannah Griffitts Papers, LCP/HSP; "The female Patriots, Address'd to the Daughters of Liberty in America, 1768," printed in *WMQ*, 3rd ser., XXXIV (1977), 307.

8. *AFC*, I, 129–130; Susan Smith, Memoir of Col. David Mason, 1842, Shaw Family Papers, box 4, LCMD; Abigail Dwight to Pamela Dwight, June 14, 1769, Sedgwick Papers III, MHS. For an account of an exemption, see Kemp P. Battle, ed., *Letters and Documents Relating to the Early History of the Lower Cape Fear*, James Sprunt Historical Monograph No. 4 (Chapel Hill, N.C., 1903), 28. But cf. tales of patriot women who secretly drank tea, in Frederick Tupper and Helen Tyler Brown, eds., *Grandmother Tyler's Book, The Recollections of Mary Palmer Tyler 1775–1866* (New York, 1925), 236–237; and William Maxwell, comp., "My Mother: Memoirs of Mrs. Helen Read," *Lower Norfolk County Virginia Antiquary*, I (1895–1896), 98–99.

9. *Boston Evening Post*, Feb. 12, 1770; Peter Force, comp., *American Archives* (Washington, D.C., 1837), 4th ser., I, 891. See also "Ladies of the Association," *WMQ*, 1st ser., VIII (1899), 36.

10. Don Higginbotham, ed., *The Papers of James Iredell* (Raleigh, N.C., 1976), I, 282–286n. The best discussion of both the "tea party" and the print is Inez Parker Cumming, "The Edenton Ladies' Tea-Party," *Georgia Review*, VIII (1954), 289–294.

11. *AFC*, I, 370, 382. Although John laughed off his wife's comments, they seem to have stimulated him to think about the issue of women's political status in the republic. See Charles Francis Adams, ed., *The Works of John Adams* (Boston, 1856), IX, 375–378.

12. The most complete account of home manufactures in this period is Rolla Tryon, *Household Manufactures in the United States 1640–1860* (Chicago, 1917); see esp. 55–57, 87–88, 99–102. For planter attitudes: Lyman H. Butterfield et al., eds., *The Diary and Autobiography of John Adams* (Cambridge, Mass., 1961), II, 216 (the quotation in the text); and John R. Commons et al., eds., *A Documentary History of American Industrial Society* (Cleveland, Ohio, 1910), II, 321–325.

13. Edward M. Riley, ed., *The Journal of John Harrower, An Indentured Servant in the Colony of Virginia, 1773–1776* (Williamsburg, Va., 1963), 121; Robert Carter to William Taylor, Feb. 21, 1775, Letterbook II, 189, Robert Carter Papers, DU. See also, in the Carter Papers, Letterbook II, 116, 122; and Daybook XIII, 114–115, 117–118, 129–130, 171–172.

14. Robert Carter to William Taylor, Feb. 21, 1775, Letterbook II, 189, Carter Papers. See Letterbook III (book 1), 15–17, (book 2), 27–28, and Letterbook V, 11, all in *ibid.* But Landon Carter's slaves were spinning and weaving as early as 1770; see Jack P. Greene, ed., *The Diary of Colonel Landon Carter of Sabine Hall, 1752–1778* (Charlottesville, Va., 1965), I, 362, 525–526, and *passim.*

15. John Hook to Robert McDonald and Co., July 30, 1778, John Hook Letterbook, DU; Thomas Anburey, *Travels through the Interior Parts of America* (Boston, 1923), II, 246. On the Carolinas and Georgia: *Letters of Joseph Clay Merchant of Savannah 1776–1793*, Collections of GHS, VIII (Savannah, 1913), 25; Caroline Gilman, ed., *Letters of Eliza Wilkinson . . .* (New York, reprint, 1969), 105; and John S. Ezell, ed., and Judson P. Wood, trans., *The New Democracy in America: Travels of Francisco de Miranda in the United States, 1783–1784* (Norman, Okla., 1963), 8.

16. Tryon, *Household Manufactures*, 137 (also, 123–132, *passim*). For examples of planters' continuing commitment to home manufactures, see Edwin M. Betts, ed., *Thomas Jefferson's Garden Book 1766–1824* (Philadelphia, 1944), 479, 505; and Charles C. Pinckney, Plantation Book, notes for 1815, Pinckney Family Papers, ser. 2, vol. 1, LCMD.

17. See Gerald Mullin, *Flight and Rebellion: Slave Resistance in Eighteenth-Century Virginia* (New York, 1972), 34–38. A planter's pride in home manufactures is described in Ferdinand-Marie Bayard, *Travels of a Frenchman in Maryland and Virginia . . . in . . . 1791*, ed. and trans. Ben C. McCary (Ann Arbor, Mich., 1950), 81. For comments on the skills of female spinners, see, e.g., Betts, ed., *Jefferson Garden Book*, 466; and Robert Carter, Daybook XIII, 221, and Letterbook V, 14, Carter Papers.

18. *S. C. Gaz.*, Feb. 15, 19, 1768.

19. *Prov. Gaz.*, Nov. 7, 1767; *Bost. Eve. Post*, May 29, 1769. The discussion of spinning bees is based largely on the research of my student assistants Larry Luxenberg and Marilyn Meder.

20. The quotations are from *Bost. Eve. Post*, Sept. 21, 1769; Alice Morse Earle, *Colonial Dames and Good Wives* (Boston, 1895), 242 (see 241–244 in general); *Bost. Eve. Post*, July 3, 1769. Other stylized accounts are in, e.g., *Bost. Eve. Post*, May 22, 29, 1769; *New York Journal*, May 11, 1769; and *Prov. Gaz.*, Aug. 12, 1769. See Tryon, *Household Manufactures*, 105–107.

21. Dexter, ed., *Literary Diary of Ezra Stiles*, I, 8–9 (also 53, 107, 237, 440); *Bost. Eve. Post*, June 19, 1769. In addition: *ibid.*, May 8, June 12, Oct. 30, Nov. 6, 1769.

22. The exchanges are from the *Boston Gazette* and *Massachusetts Gazette*, reprinted in *Prov. Gaz.*, Jan. 2, 9, 1768.

23. Of the twenty-eight spinning bees reported in the *Bost. Eve. Post* in 1769, only five were designated as meetings of Daughters of Liberty. For a hint of regular meetings: *Bost. Eve. Post*, June 12, 1769. On donations to the clergy: Stiles references in n. 21 above. Accounts of prominent men wearing homespun are in Tryon, *Household Manufactures*, 54–55. The quotations are from *S.C. Gaz.*, Feb. 29, Jan. 5, 1768.

24. Elizabeth Ambler Brent to Nancy Fisher, March 1809, Elizabeth Ambler Papers, CW; Alice Morse Earle, ed., *Diary of Anna Green Winslow, A Boston School Girl of 1771* (Boston, 1894), 34, 32; Betsy DeLancey to Anne DeLancey, [c. 1768], "DeLancey Reminiscences," DeLancey Family Papers, MCNY; Betsy Foote, Diary, Oct. 23, 1775, CHS. See also *AFC*, I, 61–62, 173, 178; II, 166–167, 212.

25. Charity Clarke to [Joseph Jekyll], Nov. 6, 1768, June 16, [1769], Sept. 10, 1774, all in Moore Family Papers, CU. See also her letter of Oct. 28, 1771.

26. Charity Clarke to [Joseph Jekyll], Dec. 3, 1769, *ibid.* (see also May 8, 1772).

27. Esther Edwards Burr, Journal-Letters, Nov. 29 [Dec. 20], 1755, YL; Sally Logan Fisher, Diary, Jan. 14, 1777, HSP; Debby Norris to Sally Wister, April 18, 1778, Wister Family Papers, box 20, HSP; Labaree et al., eds., *Franklin Papers*, XII, 318; Abigail Greenleaf, Jr., to Robert Paine, Oct. 8, 1774, Robert Treat Paine Papers, MHS. For a rare example of a woman discussing politics at mid-century, see Leo Hershkowitz and Isidore Meyer, eds., *Letters of the Franks Family (1733–1748)* . . . (Waltham, Mass., 1968), 24–25, 36–37, 40–41, 45–46, 76.

28. Anne Emlen, "On Politicks," Commonplace Book, Emlen Collection, HSP; Elizabeth Feilde to Maria Armistead, June 3, 1776, Armistead-Cocke Papers, EGS; Anne Hooper to Dolly Forbes, Oct. 7, 1768, Robbins Papers, I; L. H. Butterfield, "Annis and the General: Mrs. Stockton's Poetic Eulogies of George Washington," *Princeton University Library Chronicle*, VII (1945–1946), 25.

29. Samuel Adams to Elizabeth Adams, Feb. 26, Nov. 14, 1776 (box 3), Nov. 11, 1780 (box 5), Feb. 1, 1781 (box 6), all in Samuel Adams Papers, NYPL. See also the sets of wartime correspondence cited in chapter 7.

30. Elizabeth Steele to Ephraim Steele, Oct. 25, 1780, John Steele Papers, NCDAH; Gilman, ed., *Wilkinson Letters*, 17. References to public affairs abound in women's papers of the period. See, e.g., Elizabeth Shaw to [Mary Cranch], April 6, 1781, Shaw Family Papers, box 1, LCMD; Harriott Horry to Eliza Pinckney, Dec. 30, 1778, Pinckney Family (Buist Family) Papers, SCHS; and [Penelope Dawson] to Hannah Iredell, [c. Aug.–Sept. 1781], James Iredell Sr. and Jr. Papers, DU.

31. Earle, ed., *Winslow Diary*, 59; Nelly Blair to ———, June 2, 1775, Iredell Papers; [Elizabeth Ambler Brent] to Nancy [Fisher], 1809, Ambler Papers; Jemima Condict, *Jemima Condict, Her Book*, 37, 51. See references to young women's correspondence in n. 27 above.

32. Mary Salisbury to Susanna Shaw, Aug. 2, 1774, Lemuel Shaw Papers, microfilm, reel 1B, 703, MHS; Brown, trans., *Riedesel Journal*, 79, 68 (also, 70, 75–77). See, too, Margaret W. Willard, ed., *Letters on the American Revolution 1774–1776* (Boston, 1925), 334; *AFC*, II, 374; and Nicholas Cresswell, *The Journal of Nicholas Cresswell* (London, 1925), 102, 173.

33. Christian Barnes to Elizabeth Smith, [c. Nov.–Dec. 1769], July 6, 13–28, 1770, all in Christian Barnes Letterbook, LCMD. On the political commitment and physical abuse of other loyalist women, see, e.g., AO 13/14, 393; AO 13/32, 603; AO 13/91, 403; and AO 13/112, 35. But cf. Mrs. A. Pollock to Joseph Hewes, Dec. 23, 1775, Hayes Collection, microfilm, reel 3, 80A, SHC/UNC.

34. Christian Barnes to Elizabeth Smith, Aug. 7, 1768, July 13–28, 1770, both in Barnes Letterbook; "Narrative of Mrs. Abraham Brasher, 1801," 24, NYHS; Ann Ward to Dolly Forbes, June 14, 1774, and [Elizabeth Inman] to [Lady Don], [late 1772], both in Robbins Papers, IV. See also Maria Nevin to Sarah Langdon, Nov. 5, 1769, Langdon Papers, NHHS.

35. Henry Hugh Fergusson, Testimony, Feb. 3, 1785, AO 12/38, 213 (supported by witnesses, 215–221, *passim*); Elizabeth Fergusson to John Young, [n.d.], AO 13/102, 762; Elizabeth Fergusson, "Il Penseroso: or The Deserted Wife," Benjamin Rush Papers, XL, 146, LCP/HSP. See, in general, Simon P. Gratz, "Some Material for a Biography of Mrs. Elizabeth Fergusson, Née Graeme," *PMHB*, XXXIX (1915), 257–321, 385–409; XLI (1917), 385–389. For examples of other marriages broken by politics: AO 12/49, 56–57, and the papers of the Reverend Harry Munro, MCNY.

36. Sally Smith Booth, *The Women of '76* (New York, 1973) is one of the more recent and most comprehensive compilations of such tales. See also Julia Ward Stickley, "The Records of Deborah Sampson Gannett, Woman Soldier of the Revolution," *Prologue*, IV (1972), 233–241; E. Merton Coulter, "Nancy Hart, Georgia Heroine of the Revolution: The Story of the Growth of a Tradition," *Georgia Historical Quarterly*, XXXIX (1955), 118–151; and Charles Coleman Sellers, *Patience Wright, American Artist and Spy in George III's London* (Middletown, Ct., 1976).

37. Paul Smith, "The American Loyalists: Notes on Their Organization and Numerical Strength," *WMQ*, 3rd ser., XXV (1968), 268; statistics on loyalist women's activism compiled by the author from 468 women's claims in AO 12 and 13.

38. Margaret Hutchinson, Claims Papers, AO 13/96, 601, AO 13/70A, 528, 530; Elizabeth Thompson, Claims Papers, AO 13/134, 5, AO 13/136, 7, AO 12/46, 77–79; Lorenda Holmes, Claims Memorial, AO 13/65, 529–530 (for her aunt, see AO 13/67, 194).

39. Nancy Davis, Deposition, Dec. 4, 1841, Revolutionary War Pension Applications and Bounty Land Warrants, microfilm M-804, reel 1541, 18–19, NA; Amy Babcock, Deposition, Sept. 6, 1837, *ibid.*, reel 100, 696; Anna Lawson, Deposition, Dec. 24, 1838, *ibid.*, reel 1533, 550.

40. "Brasher Narrative," 24.

41. *Pennsylvania Gazette*, June 21, 1780, reports on all three projects. The discussion that follows is based largely on the research of my student assistant Peggy Hayes. The one previous detailed treatment of the Ladies Association of 1780 is L. H. Butterfield, "General Washington's Sewing Circle," *American Heritage*, II (Summer 1951), 7–10, 68.

42. "Vision of the Paradise of Female Patriotism. By Clarissa a Lady of this City,"

United States Magazine, I (March 1779), 122–124. Broadsides written by women during the Revolution can be consulted in the Evans American imprint series, nos. 42545, 42847, 43480, and 44247. The papers of the loyalist Hannah Griffitts contain a number of her unpublished commentaries on wartime events.

43. *The Sentiments of an American Woman* can be most conveniently consulted in *PMHB*, XVIII (1894), 361–363. It is reproduced in facsimile in Linda Grant DePauw and Conover Hunt, *'Remember the Ladies': Women in America 1750–1815* (New York, 1976), 93. The broadside has been tentatively attributed to Reed for years; that she wrote it appears certain because the writer of *Sentiments* describes herself as nursing a baby, and Reed was then breastfeeding her youngest child.

44. "Ideas," appended to "Sentiments," *PMHB*, XVIII (1894), 364–366; "Letter from a Lady at Philadelphia, to her best friend in this place," June 28, in *Maryland Gazette*, July 21, 1780.

45. "Letter from Philadelphia," in *Md. Gaz.*, July 21, 1780 (also printed in *Independent Chronicle* [Boston], July 27, 1780); records of canvass, June 1780, Joseph Reed Papers, NYHS. See also the first report of the canvass, *Pennsylvania Packet*, June 17, 1780, datelined June 16.

46. "Letter from Philadelphia," *Md. Gaz.*, July 21, 1780; Anna Rawle to Rebecca Shoemaker, June 30, 1780, Shoemaker-Rawle Papers, HSP.

47. The complete accounts, listing the names of all contributors, are in Reed Papers. *Pa. Gaz.*, July 12, 1780, printed a letter from Esther Reed giving the final totals by district. Butterfield, cited n. 41 above, makes the conversion to specie.

48. "Letter from Philadelphia," *Md. Gaz.*, July 21, 1780. When American troops regained control of the city, they satirized the female collaborators by dressing a woman variously described as a whore or an "old Negro wench" in elaborate style and parading her through the streets on July 4, 1778. There are many accounts of this significant incident; see, e.g., Josiah Bartlett to Mary Bartlett, Aug. 24, 1778, Josiah Bartlett Papers, NHHS; *AFC*, III, 56; Elizabeth Drinker, Diary, July 4, 1778, HSP.

49. "Letter from Philadelphia," *Md. Gaz.*, July 21, 1780; *Pa. Packet*, June 27, 1780.

50. *Continental Journal*, July 13, 1780, remarks reprinted in *Connecticut Gazette*, July 21, and *New Hampshire Gazette*, July 22. The "Letter from an Officer at Camp" appeared in *Pa. Packet*, July 8; *New Jersey Gazette*, July 12; *Ind. Chron.*, Aug. 3; *N.H. Gaz.*, Aug. 5. The following newspapers reprinted *Sentiments: Independent Ledger* (Boston), July 10; *Prov. Gaz.*, July 15; *Massachusetts Spy*, July 21; *Norwich Packet*, July 27.

51. "Letter II from a Lady at Philadelphia to her Friend in this Place," July 6, in *Md. Gaz.*, July 28, 1780 (reprinted in *Ind. Chron.*, Aug. 10, 1780); note of assignments, [June 1780], Reed Papers; Esther Reed to Madam ———, June 30, 1780, Reed Papers.

52. *N.J. Gaz.*, June 28, July 5, July 12 (contains "Sentiments of a Lady in New Jersey"), 1780; *Pa. Packet*, July 8, 1780; John C. Fitzpatrick, ed., *The Writings of*

George Washington (Washington, D.C., 1931–1944), XIX, 72n. Reports of the New Jersey drive appeared in *Ind. Chron.*, July 13, and *Ind. Ledger*, July 17.

53. *Md. Gaz.*, July 14, 1780; Samuel Purviance to David Plunkett, June 24, 1780, HCA 32/441/12, 64–65; *Pa. Packet*, Nov. 4, 1780.

54. Julian Boyd et al., eds., *The Papers of Thomas Jefferson* (Princeton, N.J., 1950–), III, 533n; Thomas J. Randolph, *Memoir, Correspondence and Miscellanies from the Papers of Thomas Jefferson* (Charlottesville, Va., 1829), I, 459–460. See Martha Jefferson to Madam ———, Aug. 8, 1780, Tucker-Coleman Papers, microfilm, reel 3, EGS, for Frances Tucker's copy.

55. H[annah] Corbin to Alice Shippen, [c. July 1780], Shippen Family Papers, microfilm, reel 3, 2101, LCMD; Catharine Greene to Esther Reed, Nov. 31, 1780, Reed Papers. On the reluctance of Massachusetts women to become involved in the campaign, see Samuel Cooper to La Luzerne, July 13, Aug. [17?], 1780, Samuel Cooper Papers, Huntington Library. My thanks to Charles Akers for this latter reference.

56. Fitzpatrick, ed., *Washington Writings*, XIX, 71 (see also 167). For the decision to turn the funds over to Washington, see "Letter II from Philadelphia," *Md. Gaz.*, July 28, 1780.

57. Esther Reed to [George Washington], [July 31, 1780] (draft), Reed Papers.

58. Esther Reed to Joseph Reed, Aug. 22, [1780], *ibid.*; Fitzpatrick, ed., *Washington Writings*, XIX, 350–351; Joseph Reed to Esther Reed, Aug. 26, 1780, Reed Papers.

59. Marquis de Chastellux, *Travels in North America in the Years 1780, 1781 and 1782*, ed. and trans. Howard C. Rice, Jr. (Chapel Hill, N.C., 1963), I, 135; Fitzpatrick, ed., *Washington Writings*, XXI, 101n (see also *ibid.*, 4, 77, 102; XX, 168). And see a note from the committee to Joseph Reed, Oct. 7, [1780], Reed Papers.

60. Fitzpatrick, ed., *Washington Writings*, XXI, 221.

61. *AFC*, III, 580n, 378; Sarah Jay to John Jay, Sept. 22, 1780, and to Kitty Livingston, Dec. 1, 1780, both in John Jay Papers, CU. Rush is quoted in Butterfield, "Washington's Sewing Circle," n. 41 above.

62. "Letter II from Philadelphia," *Md. Gaz.*, July 28, 1780.

63. Gilman, ed., *Wilkinson Letters*, 61.

64. Margaret Manigault to Gabriel Manigault, Nov. 30–Dec. 2, 1792, Manigault Papers, SCL; Susanna Dillwyn to William Dillwyn, May 2–27, 1789, William Dillwyn Papers, box 1, LCP/HSP; Alice Izard to Ralph Izard, Dec. 4, 1794, Ralph Izard Papers, SCL. Men continued their wartime practice of writing about politics to their wives; see, e.g., Theodore Sedgwick to Pamela Sedgwick, 1790s *passim*, in Sedgwick Papers II and III.

65. Bayard, *Travels*, 45; Hannah Emery to Mary Carter, Feb. 10–17, 1788, Cutts Family Papers, EI; Debby Logan to Mary Norris, Feb. 4, 1799, Loudoun Papers, box 42; Abigail Adams to Elizabeth Peabody, July 19, 1799, Shaw Papers, box 1.

66. [Caroline de Windt, ed.], *Journal and Correspondence of Miss Adams, Daughter of John Adams* (New York, 1841–1842), I, 83, 223; *AFC*, I, 329–330; Abigail Adams

to [Cotton Tufts], Oct. 10, 1786, Miscellaneous Letters, MCNY. See esp. Stewart Mitchell, ed., *New Letters of Abigail Adams 1788-1801* (Boston, 1947), *passim* (hereafter cited as Adams, *New Letters*). A challenger to Mrs. Adams's preeminent position among female political commentators was Mary Stead Pinckney, second wife of Charles Cotesworth Pinckney and cousin of Margaret Izard Manigault. See her letters in Pinckney Family Papers, ser. 4, vol. 14, LCMD, and Manigault Papers.

67. Letitia Cunningham, *The Case of the Whigs Who Loaned their Money on the Public Faith Fairly Stated* (Philadelphia, 1783; Evans #17900); Boyd et al., eds., *Jefferson Papers*, XIII, 151, 393. For Abigail Adams's statement that women's influence should not be exercised in public: Adams, *New Letters*, 96.

68. For a positive comment on women's private influence, see, e.g., "An Essay on the Means of Promoting Federal Sentiments," *New Haven Gazette and Connecticut Magazine*, II (1787), 275. The most detailed discussions of the New Jersey episode are Edward Raymond Turner, "Women's Suffrage in New Jersey," *Smith College Studies in History*, I, no. 4 (Northampton, 1916), 165–187, and Mary Philbrook, "Woman's Suffrage in New Jersey Prior to 1807," *Proceedings of the New Jersey Historical Society*, LVII (1939), 870–898. Also useful is J. R. Pole, "Suffrage in New Jersey, 1790–1807," *ibid.*, LXXI (1953), 39–61. My assistant Peggy Hayes did most of the research upon which the following paragraphs are based.

69. The best discussion of the intentions of the New Jersey constitutional convention is in Turner, "Women's Suffrage," *Smith Col. Studs.*, 166–168, 176–179; he quotes the 1800 legislator on 174. For evidence that some women were voting by 1787, see Henry Shinn, "An Early New Jersey Poll List," *PMHB*, XLIV (1920), 77–81.

70. *Centinel of Freedom* (Newark, N.J.), Oct. 18, 1797, quoted in Philbrook, "Woman's Suffrage," *Procs. NJHS*, LVII (1939), 90–91.

71. William Griffith, *Eumenes, Being a Collection of Papers* . . . (Trenton, N.J., 1799), 33; "Friend to the Ladies," in *True American* (Trenton, N.J.), Oct. 18, 1802, quoted in Philbrook, "Woman's Suffrage," *Procs. NJHS*, LVII (1939), 95–96.

72. The best account of the referendum is in Turner, "Women's Suffrage," *Smith Col. Studs.*, 181–185. Richard P. McCormick, *The History of Voting in New Jersey* (New Brunswick, N.J., 1953), 98–100, unfortunately falls prey to the antifemale suffrage propaganda.

73. Eliza Cabot, "Reminiscences," Cabot Family Papers, SLRC; John Frederick Schroeder, *Memoir of the Life and Character of Mrs. Mary Anna Boardman* . . . (New Haven, Ct., 1849), 279. See also Susan I. Lesley, *Recollections of My Mother* (Boston, 1886), 44.

74. John Steele to Ann Steele, Dec. 27, 1800, and Ann Steele to John Steele, Feb. 11, 1801, John Steele Papers, SHC/UNC (see also Ann Steele to Polly Steele, Feb. 29 [*sic*], 1802).

75. Linda K. Kerber has examined the role of the Revolution in American women's collective political memory in a perceptive paper delivered at the Conference on Women in Wars and Revolutions sponsored by Baruch College, CUNY, in May 1978.

CHAPTER SEVEN

1. Two of the most important recent examinations of the Revolution from this standpoint are John Shy, "The Military Conflict Considered as a Revolutionary War," in his *A People Numerous and Armed* (New York, 1976), 193–224; and Ronald Hoffman, "The 'Disaffected' in the Revolutionary South," in Alfred A. Young, ed., *The American Revolution: Essays in the History of American Radicalism* (DeKalb, Ill., 1975), 273–316.

2. Susan Mason Smith, Memoir of Colonel David Mason, 1842, Shaw Family Papers, box 4, LCMD; *Warren-Adams Letters . . . 1743-1814*, Collections of the MHS, LXXII–LXXIII (Boston, 1917, 1925), II, 409–411, I, 59. See further, "Journal of Sarah Winslow Deming, 1775," *American Monthly Magazine*, IV (1894), 45–49; and W. H. Upham, comp., "Extracts from Letters Written at the Time of the Occupation of Boston by the British, 1775-6," *EIHC*, XIII (1876), 153–276.

3. Lyman H. Butterfield et al., eds., *Adams Family Correspondence* (Cambridge, Mass., 1963–), I, 231, 204 (hereafter cited as *AFC*).

4. Lilla M. Hawes, ed., *The Papers of Lachlan McIntosh, 1774-1779*, Collections of GHS, XII (Savannah, 1975), 57–58; Margaret Wheeler Willard, ed., *Letters on the American Revolution 1774–1776* (Boston, 1925), 280; "Narrative of Mrs. Abraham Brasher, 1801" (typescript), 31, NYHS; Ann Eliza Bleecker, *The Posthumous Works of Ann Eliza Bleecker in Prose and Verse . . .* (New York, 1793), 178, 118; Azubah Norton, Deposition, Jan. 7, 1840, Revolutionary War Pension Applications and Bounty Land Warrants, microfilm M-804, reel 1829, 1219, NA (hereafter cited as RWPA). For an analysis of Bleecker's work, see Wendy Martin, "Women and the American Revolution," *EAL*, XI (1976–1977), 323–326.

5. Lyman H. Butterfield et al., eds., *Diary and Autobiography of John Adams* (Cambridge, Mass., 1961), II, 265; Don Higginbotham, ed., *The Papers of James Iredell* (Raleigh, N.C., 1976), II, 239; Elizabeth Farmar to Mrs. [Holroyd?], Oct. 25, 1783, Elizabeth Farmar Letterbook, HSP.

6. Elizabeth Ambler to [Mildred Smith], 1781, Elizabeth Ambler Papers, CW; Higginbotham, ed., *Iredell Papers*, II, 244, 246.

7. Sally Paine to Robert Treat Paine, May 11, 21, 1775, and Abigail Greenleaf to same, Oct. 17, 1775, all in Robert Treat Paine Papers, MHS.

8. Stephen Salisbury to Samuel Salisbury, May 1776, Salisbury Family Papers, AAS; *AFC*, I, 284 (see 276–296 *passim* on the dysentery epidemic, and I, 379–380, II, 23–24, 37, on smallpox). The impact of disease on the northern army is graphically described in the letters of William Bond, 1776 *passim*, microfilm, William Bond Papers, LCMD.

9. The quotation is from St. George Tucker to Fanny Tucker, July 11, 1781, Tucker-Coleman Papers, microfilm, reel 3, EGS. For another expression of the same opinion: *Warren-Adams Letters*, II, 428. The Adams family's inoculation experiences may be traced in *AFC*, II, 37–117, *passim*. Among the women who had to decide to inoculate their children without being able to consult their husbands were Sally Pinckney (see letters of Sept–Oct. 1780, Pinckney Family Papers, ser. 1, box 4,

LCMD) and Esther Atlee (William Atlee to Esther Atlee, April 18, 1781, William Atlee Papers, Peter Force Collection, ser. 9, LCMD).

10. Sally Logan Fisher, Diary, Jan. 17, 1777, April 12, 14, 1779, HSP; Henry Knox to Lucy Knox, April 26, 1777, Henry Knox Papers, microfilm, reel 3, no. 162, MHS; *AFC*, II, 116–117.

11. Martin and Christiana Gatter, Depositions, July 26, 1779, Papers of the Continental Congress, item 53, 236–238, microfilm M-247, reel 66, NA (hereafter cited as PCC). See, in general, 221–253.

12. Rawdon, quoted in Sally Smith Booth, *The Women of '76* (New York, 1973), 105 (see also 106); Varnum Lansing Collins, ed., *A Brief Narrative of the Ravages of the British and Hessians at Princeton in 1776–1777* (New York, reprint, 1968), 14–15; William S. Stryker, ed., *Documents Relating to the Revolutionary History of the State of New Jersey . . .* , New Jersey Archives, ser. 2, I (Trenton, N.J., 1901), 245–246, 351.

13. Depositions of Elizabeth Cain, Abigail Palmer, Sarah Cain, and Mary Phillips, March 22, 24, 1777, PCC, item 53, 29, 31, 35, 37, M-247, reel 66 (see also 33, 39).

14. Elizabeth Drinker, Diary, Dec. 1777–June 1778, *passim*, esp. Dec. 18, 19, 21, 31, 1777; Jan. 1, 8, 16, 19, Feb. 7, 14, March 20, 1778, HSP.

15. [Lydia Mintern Post], *Personal Recollections of the American Revolution. A Private Journal*, ed. Sidney Barclay (New York, 1859), 75, 34, 76 (also, 103–104). Loyalist women's complaints about having to quarter rebel troops in their homes are contained in AO 13/68, 57, and AO 13/91, 284.

16. Fisher diary, Dec. 21, 1776; March 9, Feb. 24, Sept. 25, Dec. 10, 30, 1777; March 14, June 8, 12, 1778; March 23, 1783.

17. [Robert J. Hunter], *Quebec to Carolina in 1785–1786 . . .* , ed. Louis B. Wright and Marion Tinling (San Marino, Calif., 1943), 125; Elizabeth A. Brent to Nancy Fisher, [c. 1810], Ambler Papers. See also Albert Cook Myers, ed., *Sally Wister's Journal* (Philadelphia, 1902). See chapter 2, n. 27, for the story of Betsy's friend.

18. Elizabeth A. Brent to Nancy Fisher, 1809, Ambler Papers; David Ramsay, *Ramsay's History of South Carolina, from its First Settlement in 1670 to the year 1808* (Newberry, S.C., 1858), I, 266. On the war in the South see the essay by Ronald Hoffman, cited in n. 1 above.

19. *Letters of Joseph Clay Merchant of Savannah 1776–1793*, Collections of GHS, VIII (Savannah, 1913), 147 (also 101, 106, 109); Oliver Hart to Joseph Hart, July 18, 1779, Oliver Hart Papers, SCL; Eliza Pinckney to [Mrs. R.E.], Sept. 25, 1780 (draft), Pinckney Family Papers, ser. 1, box 5. See also Julian Boyd et al., eds., *The Papers of Thomas Jefferson* (Princeton, N.J., 1950–), V, 421, 424–425.

20. Caroline Gilman, ed., *Letters of Eliza Wilkinson . . .* (New York, reprint, 1969), 16, 27, 29, 31, 46. See further, "A Woman's Letters in 1779 and 1782," *SCHGM*, X (1909), 125–126.

21. See, in general, Ira Berlin, *Slaves without Masters: The Free Negro in the Antebellum South* (New York, 1974), 15–50; and Benjamin Quarles, *The Negro in the American Revolution* (Chapel Hill, N.C., 1961), 19–32. Of course, northern slaves

fled as well; for an account of one female Philadelphian who left with the British, see James Coxe to ———, Nov. 18, 1778, HCA 32/445/14, 36.

22. Edwin Morris Betts, ed., *Thomas Jefferson's Farm Book* (Princeton, N.J., 1953), facsimile, 29; John Ball, Account Book 1780–1784, John Ball Papers, DU (relationships identified through analysis of John and Keating S. Ball slave birth register, microfilm, M-1811, 2 reels, SHC/UNC).

23. Quarles, *Negro in Revolution*, 163–172, discusses the evacuations and estimates the numbers of slaves who left with the British.

24. These records are in PCC, item 53, 276–294, M-247, reel 66; and Miscellaneous PCC, microfilm M-332, reel 7. The tabulations were done by my assistant Mark Cunha. Two problems should be noted: first, the records are inconsistent, so that not all are equally clear about family relationships; second, since the data were recorded in 1783, they reflect relationships as they existed *in that year*, not perhaps as they existed at the time the blacks fled into the lines.

25. Misc. PCC, book 1, 13, 38, film M-332, reel 7; PCC, item 53, 277, film M-247, reel 66.

26. See, on disease in the runaway camps, Eliza L. Pinckney to [Mrs. R. E.], Sept. 25, 1780, Pinckney Family Papers, ser. 1, box 5; Boyd et al., eds., *Jefferson Papers*, V, 74; Betts, ed., *Jefferson Farm Book*, 505; Ramsay, *History of S.C.*, I, 178–179, 190.

27. "Minutes of Board of Commissioners for Superintending the British Embarkation," April–August 1783, esp. August 7, 2, July 24, 1783, Force Collection, ser. 8D, no. 15 (see also minutes for May 30, 1783).

28. Eliza Pinckney to Thomas Pinckney, May 17, 1779, and Thomas Pinckney to Eliza Pinckney, May 17, [1779], both in Eliza Lucas Pinckney Papers, SCHS. But cf. Frances Tucker to St. George Tucker, July 14, 1781, Tucker-Coleman Papers, reel 3.

29. See Mary Beth Norton, "The Fate of Some Black Loyalists of the American Revolution," *Journal of Negro History*, LVIII (1973), 402–426; Berlin, cited n. 21 above; and James St. G. Walker, *The Black Loyalists: The Search for a Promised Land in Nova Scotia and Sierra Leone 1783–1870* (New York, 1976).

30. The only book-length treatment of army women is Walter Hart Blumenthal's inadequate *Women Camp Followers of the American Revolution* (Philadelphia, 1952), but references to such women may be found in many officers' orderly books and in diaries of private soldiers. The episode in Wayne's command can be inferred from *Orderly Book of the Northern Army, at Ticonderoga and Mt. Independence, from October 17th, 1776, to January 8th, 1777* (Albany, N.Y., 1859), 116, 128. See the statements of camp followers in PCC, item 41, IV, 252, and item 42, VIII, 81, film M-247, reels 50, 56; RWPA, film M-804, reel 2510, 890; and AO 13/24, 359, 386.

31. Mary Beth Norton, "Eighteenth-Century American Women in Peace and War: The Case of the Loyalists," *WMQ*, 3rd ser., XXXIII (1976), 399–403; Mary Beth Norton, "'What an Alarming Crisis Is This': Southern Women and the American Revolution," in Jeffrey Crow and Larry Tise, eds., *The Southern Experience in the American Revolution* (Chapel Hill, N.C., 1978), 217–218.

32. Margaret Gionvaly, Affidavit, Jan. 14, 1786, AO 13/26, 133; Catharine Reading, Affidavit, March 16, 1786, AO 13/25, 398; Mary Hind, Pension Decision, AO 12/99, 35; Anna Jean Simpson, Claims Memorial, Dec. 9, 1784, AO 13/37, 12.

33. Isabella Logan to Charles Steuart, May 20, 1782, Charles Steuart Papers, 5032, 269A, National Library of Scotland; Elizabeth Miller to ———, Oct. 18, 1785, AO 13/131, 382; Elizabeth Deas to James Deas, Nov. 10, 1787, AO 13/137, 114, and James Deas to claims commissioners, May 15, 1788, AO 13/137, 118. See also Hunter, *Quebec to Carolina*, 63.

34. Women's experiences with wartime employment are chronicled in, e.g., Hannah Adams, *A Memoir of Miss Hannah Adams, Written by Herself* . . . (Boston, 1832), 11; [Ruth Patten], *Interesting Family Letters, of the Late Mrs. Ruth Patten, of Hartford, Conn.* (n.p., 1845), 17; and Nicholas Cresswell, *The Journal of Nicholas Cresswell* (London, 1925), 257.

35. [Matthew Patten], *The Diary of Matthew Patten of Bedford, N.H.* (Concord, N.H., 1903), 364; Elizabeth Warren, Deposition, Dec. 6, 1836, RWPA, film M-804, reel 2510, 617; Mary Way, Deposition, Dec. 24, 1836, *ibid.*, 609; Azubah Norton, Deposition, Jan. 7, 1840, *ibid.*, reel 1829, 1219.

36. Higginbotham, ed., *Iredell Papers*, II, 55; Hannah Cochran, Deposition, Oct. 22, 1845, RWPA, film M-804, reel 590, 5; Boyd et al., eds., *Jefferson Papers*, IV, 675, V, 450, 444, 622. See, in general, *Jefferson Papers*, IV–VI, *passim*.

37. The best collection of the letters of an ordinary soldier is that of the shoemaker Joseph Hodgkins and his wife, Sarah, 1775–1779, printed in Herbert Wade and Robert Lively, eds., *This Glorious Cause: The Adventures of Two Company Officers in Washington's Army* (Princeton, N.J., 1958), 167–245. See editorial comment, 55, on the change in their relationship over time. Scattered letters of American sailors and their wives survive in HCA, along with other ships' papers captured by British naval vessels during the war. See, e.g., the following items in HCA 32: 329/10, 29; 357/3, 20; 425/3, 12; 447/1, 24; and esp. 493/6, 7, which include a number of 1778 letters from Newburyport seamen to their spouses.

38. Edward Hand to Kitty Hand, Sept. 26, Nov. 6, 1776, Edward Hand Papers, HSP; Mary Heriot to Bob Heriot, June 3, 1781, Miscellaneous Manuscripts, SCL; Esther Reed to Joseph Reed, June 21, 1777, Joseph Reed Papers, NYHS.

39. James Clinton to Mary Clinton, May 21, 1779, James Clinton Papers, Miscellaneous Manuscripts, NYHS; Peter Gansevoort to Catherine Gansevoort, Aug. 27, 1780, Gansevoort Family Papers, I, 82, Gansevoort-Lansing Collection, NYPL; William Atlee to Esther Atlee, Oct. 15, 1779, Atlee Papers, Force Collection, ser. 9. See also Thomas Wood to Molly Wood, Sept. 24, 1778, HCA 32/493/6, 797, 799, 800. Indications of women's growing financial expertise and independence may be found in, e.g., Mary Morgan to John Morgan, May 14, 1781, Francis Hopkinson Papers, XIII, no. 38, HSP; Worthington C. Ford, ed., *Correspondence and Journals of Samuel Blachley Webb* (New York, reprint, 1969), I, 212; and Elizabeth Birkbeck to Charles Birkbeck, Oct. 28, 1778, HCA 32/493/5, 298.

40. Nina M. Tiffany, ed., *Letters of James Murray Loyalist* (Boston, 1901), 208,

211, 215–216, 246; Elizabeth Inman, Will, May 14, 1785, Murray Family Papers, box 3, NYHS, printed in Mary Beth Norton, "A Cherished Spirit of Independence: The Life of an Eighteenth-Century Boston Businesswoman," in Carol Berkin and Mary Beth Norton, eds., *Women of America: A History* (Boston, 1979), 63–65.

41. Raymond C. Werner, ed., "Diary of Grace Growden Galloway," *PMHB*, LV (1931), 59–60; LVIII (1934), 177. Betsy Galloway recovered her mother's property in 1799 (Horace Binney, *Reports of Cases Adjudged in the Supreme Court of Pennsylvania* [Philadelphia, 1891], 1–23). My thanks to Marylynn Salmon for this reference.

42. Mary Foster to Isaac Foster, Oct. 17, 1779, Isaac Foster Papers, Miscellaneous MSS, LCMD.

43. Fisher diary, Sept. 17, 21, Oct. 18, 1777, and Sept.–Oct. *passim*.

44. *Ibid.*, Nov. 1, Dec. 6, 1777; Feb. 5, May 29, 1778; Sept. 1, 1779; July 15, 1781. Elizabeth Drinker's husband was also among the Virginia exiles; her diary records the journey she and a number of the other Quaker wives undertook to present George Washington with a petition requesting that their husbands be freed. See Drinker diary, Sept. 1777–April 1778 *passim*.

45. Josiah Bartlett to Mary Bartlett, Oct. 11, 1775, [c. Dec. 1775], Aug. 31, 1778, Mary Bartlett to Josiah Bartlett, July 13, 1776, July 3–4, Aug. 28, 1778, and *passim*, all in Josiah Bartlett Papers, NHHS. The same transition may be seen in *AFC*, I, 205, 218, 375. Strikingly, in the 1790s the Adamses reversed the terminology: see Charles F. Adams, ed., *Letters of John Adams, Addressed to his Wife*, 3rd ed. (Boston, 1841), II, 150, and Stewart Mitchell, ed., *New Letters of Abigail Adams 1788–1801* (Boston, 1947), 89.

46. William Palfrey to Susannah Palfrey, [c. Oct. 1, 1778], Aug. 17, 1779, and 1778–1779 *passim*, William Palfrey Papers, HL.

47. William Palfrey to Susannah Palfrey, June 19, 1779, Oct. 10, 1780, Susannah Palfrey to William Palfrey, Sept. 1, 1780, *ibid.* See also their letters of Aug. 9, Sept. 23, 1779; Sept. 10, [c. Sept.–Oct.], Nov. 23, 1780.

48. Timothy Pickering to Rebecca White, Nov. 14, 29, 1775; Timothy Pickering to Rebecca Pickering, June 4, 1777, July 5, 1778, all in Timothy Pickering Papers, microfilm, reel 1, 2, 3, 37, 121A, MIIS.

49. Rebecca Pickering to Timothy Pickering, Oct. 23, 1780, Feb. 27, 1782, Nov. 21, 1789, *ibid.*, reel 4, pt. 1, 206, 263, 336; Timothy Pickering to Rebecca Pickering, Aug. 29, 1783, *ibid.*, reel 1, 308.

50. The quotations are from Sally Paine to Robert Treat Paine, May 12, Oct. 23, 1776, Paine Papers (see also same to same, May 1, June 16, Aug. 18, Nov. 3, 1776).

51. Oliver Hart to Anne Hart, June 12, 1781, Anne Hart to Oliver Hart, July 19, 23, 1781, Hart Papers.

52. Henry Knox to Lucy Knox, July 8, 1776; to Billy Knox, July 11, 1776; to Lucy, July 11, 1776; Lucy Knox to Henry Knox, [July 1776]; Henry Knox to Lucy Knox, July 18, 1776, all in Knox Papers, microfilm, reel 2, nos. 146, 150, 152, 147, 165.

53. Henry Knox to Lucy Knox, March 31, 1777; Lucy Knox to Henry Knox,

June 3, Aug. 23, 1777, *ibid.*, reel 3, no. 143; reel 4, nos. 12, 43. Lucy also managed to save the estate of her loyalist exile father from confiscation; see her letter to Henry, April 3, 1777, *ibid.*, reel 3, no. 148.

54. Thomas McKean to Sally McKean, July 12, July 20, July 30, 1779, Thomas McKean Papers, VI, 23, 25, 27, HSP. On their autumn move, see same to same, Oct. 15, 1779, *ibid.*, 28.

55. Eliza Pinckney to Betsy Pinckney, June 18, 1780, Pinckney Family Papers, ser. 1, box 1; Higginbotham, ed., *Iredell Papers*, II, 258; Thomas Cushing to Deborah Cushing, Oct. 4, 1774, Cushing Family Papers, MHS; Theophilus Parsons to Francis Dana, Aug. 3, 1780, Francis Dana Papers, MHS.

56. Elizabeth Brent to Nancy Fisher, [c. 1810], Ambler Papers.

57. Rachel Wells, Memorial, May 18, 1786, PCC, item 42, VIII, 354–355, film M-247, reel 56. A similar argument was advanced by the loyalist Elizabeth Putnam in a letter to Thomas Dundas, May 7, 1789, AO 13/75, 309.

58. Boyd et al., eds., *Jefferson Papers*, V, 703–704. Hannah Corbin made the same point to her brother Richard Henry Lee, although with greater emphasis on her status as a widow holding a life estate; see James C. Ballagh, ed., *The Letters of Richard Henry Lee* (New York, reprint, 1970), I, 392–393; and H[annah] Corbin to Alice Shippen, March 14, 1778, Shippen Family Papers, microfilm, reel 3, 2118, LCMD.

59. *AFC*, I, 370.

60. *Ibid.*, IV, 328.

CHAPTER EIGHT

1. Some historians have attributed the changes in late eighteenth-century America more to the long-term trend called "modernization" than to the effects of the Revolution. Yet many of the developments in the United States, especially those in the realm of women's education, were closely tied to republican ideology and had no counterpart in contemporary Great Britain. It may well be that the Revolution only accelerated or intensified certain trends already in progress, but that the war had a major impact on women's lives in the following decades appears to me undeniable. On modernization, see Richard D. Brown, *Modernization* (New York, 1975), and Robert V. Wells, "Family History and Demographic Transition," *Journal of Social History*, IX (1975), 1–19. On education, see chapter 9, below.

2. Julian Boyd et al., eds., *The Papers of Thomas Jefferson* (Princeton, N.J., 1950–), XVI, 290; Henry Lloyd to James Lloyd, Feb. 19, 1784, Lloyd Papers, HL.

3. John Page to Augustine Smith, Oct. 10, 1792 (see also Smith's letter to Page, [Oct. 8, 1792]), Augustine Smith Papers, EGS; Elizabeth Meredith to David Meredith, Jan. 6, 1796, Nov. 8, 1795, Meredith Papers, boxes 5, 4, HSP. But cf. the letters of John Lloyd and Richard Champion, in Miscellaneous Manuscripts, SCL.

4. A. B., "Has He a Fortune?" *American Museum*, X (Dec. 1791), 284; Constantia [Judith Sargent Murray], *The Gleaner. A Miscellaneous Production* (Boston, 1798), I, 87.

5. Rebecca Shoemaker to Anna Rawle, May 31–June 1, 1783, and Rawle to Shoemaker, June 7, 1783, both in Shoemaker-Rawle Papers, HSP; Sarah Cadbury, ed., "Extracts from the Diary of Mrs. Ann Warder," *PMHB*, XVII (1893), 460, 459; Marquis de Chastellux, *Travels in North America in the Years 1780, 1781 and 1782*, ed. and trans. Howard C. Rice (Chapel Hill, N.C., 1963), I, 136. See Daniel Scott Smith, "Parental Power and Marriage Patterns: An Analysis of Historical Trends in Hingham, Massachusetts," *JMF*, XXI (1973), 419–428, esp. 425–426.

6. John Coalter to Maria Rind, April 15, 1791; Rind to Coalter, May 3, June 7, [c. July], 1791, all in Brown-Coalter-Tucker Papers, box 1, EGS. Another egalitarian courtship is chronicled in the letters of Rachel Bradford and Elisha Boudinot, Elisha Boudinot Papers, Miscellaneous Manuscripts, NYHS.

7. John Coalter to Margaret Coalter, Tues. night [May 1795], and Margaret Coalter to John Coalter, May 10, 1795, Brown-Coalter-Tucker Papers, box 2.

8. The quotation is from Mary Morgan to Kitty Foley, April 17, 1779, HCA 42/156, entry book, item 21. For men's attitudes toward contraception and childbirth and how they differed from women's, see Jack P. Greene, ed., *The Diary of Colonel Landon Carter of Sabine Hall, 1752–1778* (Charlottesville, Va., 1965), I, 511; and "Narrative of Mrs. Abraham Brasher, 1801" (typescript), 36, NYHS. Lawrence Stone discusses the contraceptive effects of nursing in *The Family, Sex and Marriage in England, 1500–1800* (New York, 1977), 64–65. See also Daniel Scott Smith, "Family Limitation, Sexual Control, and Domestic Feminism in Victorian America," in Lois Banner and Mary Hartman, eds., *Clio's Consciousness Raised* (New York, 1974), 119–136. For a letter assuming that nursing would have contraceptive effects, see Honoria Logan to C. Lawford, April 7, 1777, HCA 32/260/14, 123.

9. Esther Atlee to William Atlee, Oct. 7, 1778, William Atlee Papers, in Peter Force Collection, ser. 9, LCMD; Theodore Sedgwick to Pamela Sedgwick, June 24, 1786, Sedgwick Papers II, MHS.

10. Elizabeth Drinker, Diary, Oct. 23, 1799, and 1761–1783 *passim*, HSP; Margaret Manigault to Mrs. Lewis Morris, Jr., Dec. 16, 1809, Louis Manigault Papers, DU.

11. Kenneth and Anna Roberts, eds. and trans., *Moreau de St. Mery's American Journey 1793–1798* (Garden City, N.Y., 1947), 177–178, 324–325; Daniel Scott Smith, "Population, Family and Society in Hingham, Massachusetts, 1635–1880" (unpub. Ph.D. diss., University of California, Berkeley, 1972), 259; Robert V. Wells, "Family Size and Fertility Control in Eighteenth-Century America: A Study of Quaker Families," *Population Studies*, XXV (1971), 77–79 and *passim*. I wish to thank Professor Wells for making available to me additional data analyzing his sample by marriage (rather than birth) cohorts.

12. Nancy Cott, "Divorce and the Changing Status of Women in Eighteenth-Century Massachusetts," *WMQ*, 3rd ser., XXXIII (1976), 592–594, 613–614; Sheldon S. Cohen, "'To Parts of the World Unknown': The Circumstances of Divorce

in Connecticut, 1750–1797," unpub. paper delivered at Columbia University Seminar on Early American History and Culture, May 1978. Also, Henry Cohn, "Connecticut's Divorce Mechanism 1636–1969," *American Journal of Legal History*, XIV (1970), 35–54.

13. Murray, *Gleaner*, I, 133; "On Connubial Happiness," *Gentleman and Lady's Town and Country Magazine*, I (July 1784), 103. See also, e.g., "On Matrimonial Felicity," *ibid.*, I (Sept. 1784), 193–194; and "Panegyric on the Marriage State," *Columbian Magazine*, I (Oct. 1786), 71–74.

14. "Sermon," *Col. Mag.*, I (Feb. 1787), 272; "Character of a Good Husband," *Massachusetts Magazine*, I (March 1789), 177; "The Philanthropist. No. XIX. Conjugal and Domestick Happiness," *ibid.*, II (July 1790), 393. See also *ibid.*, II (Nov. 1790), 664–666, and *American Magazine*, I (March 1788), 245.

15. E.g., *Amer. Museum*, VI (Oct. 1789), 315; *Lady's Magazine*, I (Dec. 1792), 33–36; *Mass. Mag.*, VI (June 1794), 343–349; and *Col. Mag.*, I (June 1787), 473–475 and IV (Jan. 1790), 24.

16. "On Matrimonial Obedience," *Lady's Mag.*, I (July 1792), 64–67. For similar private comments on marital obedience: "Kennon Letters," *VMHB*, XXXII (1924), 171–172; Ethel Armes, ed., *Nancy Shippen Her Journal Book* (Philadelphia, 1935), 144–145.

17. Paine Wingate to Mary Wiggin, June 9, 1788, and same to Sally Wingate, May 21, 1788, Paine Wingate Papers, HL. Examples of child-rearing advice suggesting that parents be "friends" to their children are *Amer. Museum*, XI (Jan. 1792), 18–20; and *Ladies Monitor*, I (Dec. 5, 1801), 124.

18. William Palfrey to Susannah Palfrey, Sept. 15, 1777, William Palfrey Papers, HL; Mary Cranch to Billy Cranch, April 28, 1783, Cranch Family Papers, 31, LCMD; "Essay on the Proper Management of Children," *Amer. Museum*, X (Aug. 1791), 105–106; Sarah Coombe Shields to ———, [n.d.], Thomas Coombe Papers, HSP.

19. Augustine Smith to Graham Frank, Aug. 17, 1791, Smith-Digges Papers, CW; Sally Logan Fisher, Diary, Sept. 22, 1790, HSP (see also entries for Aug. 28, 1785, and Feb. 4, 1787); Pamela Foster to Dwight Foster, March 17, 1802, Dwight Foster Papers, box 25, AAS. Teaching children by example is advocated in, e.g., Tristam Gilman, *The Right Education of Children Recommended . . .* (Boston, 1789), 10–16; and Nathan Fiske, *The Moral Monitor* (Worcester, Mass., 1801), II, 148.

20. A convenient source of biographical information on Murray is Edward James et al., eds., *Notable American Women* (Cambridge, Mass., 1971), II, 603–605.

21. Debby Norris to Sally Wister, April 18, 1778, Wister Family Papers, box 20, HSP; Constantia, "The Repository. No. XXV," *Mass. Mag.*, VI (Oct. 1794), 595. For a similar attribution of fickleness to men, see Anne Powell to [Betsy Murray Robbins], Aug. 1, 1787, James M. Robbins Papers, VI, MHS.

22. Maria Bronson to Nancy Hopkins, July 6, [1808], Murray Family Papers, box 3, NYHS; Amelia, Letter to Editor, *United States Magazine*, I (June 1779), 264. For charges that the ultimate responsibility for feminine vanity lay with men, see *Amer.*

Mag., I (March 1788), 240; and *Col. Mag.*, III (Feb. 1789), 96–100, and IX (July 1792), 28–30.

23. Daphne, "Sentiments on Libertinism," *Boston Magazine*, I (Aug. 1784), 419–420. Also, *Mass. Mag.*, I (May 1789), 304; *Gentlemen and Ladies Town and Country Magazine*, I (July 1789), 311–312; *Ladies Monitor*, I (Sept. 5, 1801), 39; and Mary Orne Tucker, Diary, May 7, 1802, EI.

24. ——— to Cynthia Winslow, Feb. 5, 1802, Northey Family Papers, box 4, EI; John A. H. Sweeney, ed., "The Norris-Fisher Correspondence: A Circle of Friends, 1779–1782," *Delaware History*, VI (1954–1955), 203; Anne Emlen [Mifflin], "Some Account of My Religious Progress," Emlen Collection, HSP; Nancy Rawson to Eunice Packard, Sept. 30, 1793, Packard Family Papers, Miscellaneous Manuscripts, NYHS. The trend was also apparent in published works; see esp. the same essay, under different titles, in *Mass. Mag.*, III (Feb. 1791), 96–97, and *Lady's Mag.*, II (Jan. 1793), 77–78.

25. Mary V. S. White, ed., *Fifteen Letters of Nathalie Sumter* (Columbia, S.C., 1942), 63, 54–55. On the sex ratio: U.S. Bureau of the Census, *A Century of Population Growth . . . 1790–1900* (Washington, D.C., 1909), 93. New Englanders' complaints about the lack of eligible bachelors may be found in, e.g., Susan Kittredge to Eliza Waite, March 24, 1792, Eliza Waite Papers, EI; and Polly Fales to Hannah Drury, March 24, 1789, Drury Family Papers, EI.

26. Betsy Mayhew to Pamela Sedgwick, June 25, 1782, and Sedgwick to Mayhew, Aug. 10, 1788, both in Sedgwick Papers III; Gertrude Meredith to [Gertrude Parker?], 1806, Elizabeth Skinner to Gertrude Parker, July 9, 1803, and E[lizabeth] P[arker] to Susan [Parker?], Dec. 14, [n.d.], all in Parker-Brinley Papers, box 2, HSP. See also [Bathshua Pynchon] to Peggy Orne, Sept. 30, 1795, Cushing-Orne Papers, MHS. For more on Betsy Mayhew: Frederick Tupper and Helen Tyler Brown, eds., *Grandmother Tyler's Book, The Recollections of Mary Palmer Tyler 1775–1866* (New York, 1925), 66.

27. Robert V. Wells, "Quaker Marriage Patterns in a Colonial Perspective," *WMQ*, 3rd ser., XXIX (1972), 426–427, 433–434; Wells, "Family History," *J. Soc. Hist.*, IX (1975), 11–12; Smith, "Parental Power," *JMF*, XXXV (1973), 425; Eliza Southgate Bowne, *A Girl's Life Eighty Years Ago*, ed. Clarence Cook (London, 1888), 38, 41.

28. "Lines, Written by a Lady, who was questioned respecting her inclination to marry," *Mass. Mag.*, VI (Sept. 1794), 566. A similar poem is "By a Young Lady, on Being Persuaded to Marry for Interest," *Ladies Monitor*, I (Aug. 15, 1801), 16.

29. "Excerpts from the Papers of Dr. Benjamin Rush," *PMHB*, XXIX (1905), 21; "The Competitor, XII," *Bost. Mag.*, III (Nov. 1785), 428 (see *ibid.*, Sept. 1785, 347, for the Harvard identification); David Ramsay, "Address to Citizens of the United States," *Col. Mag.*, VII (Dec. 1791), 376. Michael C. Schaffer discusses the relationship between public and private virtue in his "The Good Citizen of the American Republic, 1789–1800" (unpub. Ph.D. diss., Yale University, 1973), 4–5, 8–10.

30. The best summary of the traditional literature is Mary Sumner Benson, *Women in Eighteenth-Century America: A Study of Opinion and Social Usage* (Port Washington, N.Y., reprint, 1966). See Schaffer, "Good Citizen," 75–77, on women.

31. W. J., "On the Virtues of Women," *Gentleman and Lady's Town and Country Magazine*, I (Dec. 1784), 337; Alphonzo, "An Address to the Ladies," *Amer. Mag.*, I (March 1788), 246. "Happy Influence" appeared in both *Amer. Museum*, I (Jan. 1787), 61–64, and *Mass. Mag.*, VII (July 1795), 220–223; "Advantages to be Derived" was published in *Bost. Mag.*, II (Aug. 1785), 297–298. Two private comments along the same lines are John Coalter to Margaret Coalter, April 29, 1795, box 2, Brown-Coalter-Tucker Papers; and Noah Webster to James Greenleaf, Sept. 20, 1789, Noah Webster Papers, box 1, NYPL.

32. Cf. older pieces reprinted in the 1780s and 1790s, like *Amer. Museum*, V (Jan. 1789), 67–68, or XI (March 1792), 93–94, with comments composed after the war, such as that by George Washington quoted in L. H. Butterfield, "Annis and the General: Mrs. Stockton's Poetic Eulogies of George Washington," *Princeton University Library Chronicle*, VII (1945–1946), 33.

33. See, e.g., Elizabeth Huske to Nelly Blair, Jan. 30, 1786, James Iredell Sr. and Jr. Papers, DU; Hannah Emery to Mary Carter, July 2, 1789, Cutts Family Papers, EI.

34. "Letter from a Chinese Lady, to Mrs. ***** of Philadelphia," printed in both *Col. Mag.*, IV (June 1790), 351, and *Mass. Mag.*, IV (March 1792), 169–170; "Remarks on the Manners, Government, Laws and Domestic Debt of America," *Amer. Museum*, V (March 1789), 269–270. Of many other essays along the same lines, the most important is William Livingston's "Homespun," *ibid.*, X (July 1791), 17–18.

35. "Patriotic and Economical Association of the Ladies of Hartford, in Connecticut," *Amer. Museum*, II (Aug. 1787), 165. See also the following private comments: Mary Norris to Hannah Thomson, Feb. 25, 1787, Logan Papers, LXXIV, 13, HSP; and Susanna Dillwyn to William Dillwyn, Nov. 27, 1788, June 2, 1790, William Dillwyn Papers, box 1, LCP/HSP.

36. James Tilton, "A Oration . . . ," *Col. Mag.*, V (Dec. 1790), 372. Also, *United States Magazine*, I (June 1794), 153–157. For an excellent analysis of the maternal ideal: Linda K. Kerber, "The Republican Mother: Women and the Enlightenment — An American Perspective," *American Quarterly*, XXVIII (Summer 1976), 187–205. See also Ruth Bloch, "American Feminine Ideals in Transition: The Rise of the Moral Mother, 1785–1815," *Feminist Studies*, IV, no. 2 (June 1978), 100–126.

37. "Introduction," *Christian's, Scholar's, and Farmer's Magazine*, I (April–May, 1789), 52; Editors' Preface, *Lady and Gentleman's Pocket Magazine of Literature and Polite Amusement*, I (1796), iii–iv. See also *Lady's Mag.*, I (June 1792), i–v; *Ladies Monitor*, I (Oct. 10, 1801), 73, and I (Nov. 21, 1801), 110.

38. Notes to correspondents, in *Bost. Mag.*, I (Dec. 1783), 42; *Mass. Mag.*, IV (Nov. 1792), 650; and *Lady's Mag.*, I (Dec. 1792), iv. The Ramsay excerpt appeared in *Col. Mag.*, IV (March 1790), 139, and *Mass. Mag.*, III (Dec. 1791), 743. Gannett's story is in *Amer. Museum*, XI (March 1792), 110. For just a few examples of published

accounts of female courage and genius, see, e.g., *Mass. Mag.*, III (March 1791), 165–166; V (March, June, Dec., 1793), 132–133, 136, 329–330, 727, 736–738; and *Col. Mag.*, V (Sept. 1790), 156–157; IX (Nov. 1792), 300–302.

39. Murray, *Gleaner*, I, 30, 308.

40. Sidney, "Maxims for Republics," *U.S. Mag.*, I (Jan. 1779), 19, and *Amer. Museum*, II (July 1787), 80–82; [Caroline de Windt, ed.], *Journal and Correspondence of Miss Adams, Daughter of John Adams* (New York, 1841–1842), II, 147. "The Good Mother" appeared in *Mass. Mag.*, III (April 1791), 233–234; and "Stanzas" in both *ibid.*, V (Nov. 1793), 692–693, and *Amer. Museum*, VIII (1790), Appendix I, 34–35. Wilson's comments on women in his "Introduction" may be consulted conveniently in Robert McCloskey, ed., *The Works of James Wilson* (Cambridge, Mass., 1967), I, 85–89. The passage was also printed in several contemporary magazines.

41. Emily Noyes Vanderpoel, comp., *Chronicles of a Pioneer School from 1792 to 1833 . . .* , ed. Elizabeth C. Barney Buel (Cambridge, Mass., 1903), 214; Bowne, *Girl's Life*, 110. See also Fisher diary, June 1, 1785; and Elizabeth Peabody to Sarah Johnson, April 1811, Shaw Family Papers, box 1, LCMD.

42. Deborah Logan to Albanus Logan, Feb. 3, 1803, Maria Dickinson Logan Papers, box 2, HSP; Sarah Gibbes to John Gibbes, Aug. 11, 1783, Gibbes-Gilchrist Papers, SCHS. See also Abigail Adams's letters to her son John Quincy, in Lyman H. Butterfield et al., eds., *Adams Family Correspondence* (Cambridge, Mass., 1963), III, *passim*, esp. 37, 269.

43. Elizabeth Powel to Enos Hitchcock, May 20, 1790, Enos Hitchcock Papers, RIHS. For other contemporary comments on *Bloomsgrove Family*, see *Papers of Jeremy Belknap*, II, Collections of MHS, XLIII (Boston, 1877), 228, 232; and a review of the book, in *Col. Mag.*, V (July 1790), 47.

44. "On the Supposed Superiority of the Masculine Understanding, by a Lady," *Col. Mag.*, VII (July 1791), 9–11. See also "Reflections on What is Called Amiable Weakness in Woman," *Lady and Gentleman's Pocket Mag.*, I (Oct. 1796), 174–175; and "On Woman," *Mass. Mag.*, VIII (July 1796), 394–396.

45. Abigail Adams to Elizabeth Peabody, July 19, 1799, Shaw Papers, box 1; Amelia Dwight, *Memorials of Mary Wilder White*, ed. Mary W. Tileston (Boston, 1903), 110, 178.

46. Bowne, *Girl's Life*, 60. And see "Letter from Aspasia," *Amer. Museum*, VI (Aug. 1789), 148–149.

47. Bowne, *Girl's Life*, 62; Alice Izard to Margaret Manigault, May 29, 1801 (see also the reply, June 16, 1801), Manigault Papers, SCL. Benson, *Women in Eighteenth-Century America*, 85–92, discusses the response to Wollstonecraft and summarizes her arguments. For a somewhat different treatment of this general topic, see Patricia J. McAlexander, "The Creation of the American Eve: The Cultural Dialogue on the Nature of the Role of Women in Late Eighteenth-Century America," *EAL*, IX (1975), 152–166.

48. Alice Izard to Margaret Manigault, May 29, 1801, Manigault Papers; Bowne, *Girl's Life*, 61–62; Drinker diary, April 22, 1796.

49. The quotations are from Charles Francis Adams, ed., *Letters of John Adams*,

Addressed to His Wife, 3rd ed. (Boston, 1841), II, 139; and Tucker diary, May 10, 1802. Fergusson used Wollstonecraft as an authority for a comment on Mrs. Hester Chapone in her notebook labeled "E. Graeme," Elizabeth Graeme Fergusson Papers, HSP. Powel purchased Wollstonecraft's works in 1799; see her Diary/Almanac, Aug. 2, 1799, Powel Collection, HSP.

50. Dwight, ed., *White Memorials*, 111, 123.

51. Constantia, "On the Equality of the Sexes," *Mass. Mag.*, II (March 1790), 132–135; (April 1790), 223–226. In her introduction Murray explained she had written the essay in 1779.

52. Constantia, "Desultory Thoughts upon the Utility of Encouraging a Degree of Self-Complacency, Especially in Female Bosoms," *Gentleman and Lady's Town and Country Magazine*, I (Oct. 1784), 251–253. For similar viewpoints, see "Second Vindication of the Rights of Women," *Ladies Monitor*, I (Sept. 5, 1801), 35; and "Reflections on What is Called Amiable Weakness in Woman," *Lady and Gentleman's Pocket Mag.*, I (Oct. 1796), 175.

53. Murray, *Gleaner*, I, 167–168; III, 219–220. Murray was more systematic on this subject than was Wollstonecraft, *A Vindication of the Rights of Woman* (New York, 1967), chapter 9, or Charles Brockden Brown, *Alcuin: A Dialogue* (New York, 1971), 16, 40.

54. Wollstonecraft, *Vindication*, 32, for the quotation. "The Influence of the Female Sex on the Enjoyments of Social Life," printed in both *Christian's, Scholar's and Farmer's Mag.*, I (Nov. 1789), 496–497, and *Col. Mag.*, IV (March 1790), 153–154; and Benjamin Rush, "Thoughts upon Female Education," in Frederick Rudolph, ed., *Essays on Education in the Early Republic* (Cambridge, Mass., 1965), 27–28, present the more conservative view. For Murray on the training of wives and mothers, see *Gleaner*, I, 68–69; II, 5–7.

CHAPTER NINE

1. See, in general, Thomas Woody, *A History of Women's Education in the United States* (New York, 1929), I, esp. 106, 138–147, 177–217, 268–273. Kenneth Lockridge, in *Literacy in Colonial New England . . .* (New York, 1974), 52, 57–58, has concluded that women's exclusion from formal schooling was the chief cause of their relative lack of writing skills.

2. Eleanor Lewis to Elizabeth Bordley, March 23, 1806 (typescript), Lewis-Gibson Letters, I, 82, HSP. Mothers often talked about teaching their children to read. See, e.g., Rebecca Pickering to Timothy Pickering, Sept. 8, 1781, Feb. 2, 1782, Timothy Pickering Papers, microfilm, reel 4, pt. 1, 251, 262, MHS; Ann Kinloch, Diary, April 4–10, 1799, *passim*, Langdon Cheves Collection, SCHS; and C[atherine] Read to Betsy Ludlow, Jan. 13, 1805, Read Family Papers, SCL.

3. Frederick Tupper and Helen Tyler Brown, eds., *Grandmother Tyler's Book, The Recollections of Mary Palmer Tyler, 1775–1866* (Boston, 1925), 51, 57, 144, 157 (the

quotation) (hereafter cited as Tyler, *Book*). On teaching by older siblings, see also, e.g., Eunice Paine to Abigail Greenleaf, March 5, 1757, Robert Treat Paine Papers, MHS; and John C. Symmes to John and Charles Short, July 20, 1803, Short Family Papers, box 25, LCMD. Hannah Johnston Iredell taught her niece Nelly Blair to write; see Blair to Iredell, Feb. 22, 1790, James Iredell Sr. and Jr. Papers, DU.

4. Eliza Pinckney to Mary Lucas, [c. Dec. 1746], Eliza Lucas Pinckney Papers, DU; Sarah Snell Bryant, Diary, Feb. 3, March 20, 28, April 12, 1796, Jan. 13, March 31, 1797, HL; Elizabeth L. Johnston, *Recollections of a Georgia Loyalist*, ed. Arthur W. Eaton (New York, 1901), 218; William Gilmore Simms, "Memoir of the Pinckney Family of South Carolina," Pinckney Family Papers, ser. 2, vol. 2, 5, LCMD.

5. Hunter Dickinson Farish, ed., *Journal & Letters of Philip Vickers Fithian 1773–1774: A Plantation Tutor of the Old Dominion* (Williamsburg, Va., 1957), 20; Robert Carter, Daybook XV, 100 (Oct. 16, 1778), Robert Carter Papers, DU. Other references to delayed writing instruction may be found in Catherine Livingston to John Jay, Dec. 30, 1783, John Jay Papers, CU; and Susanna Dillwyn to William Dillwyn, Feb. 14, 1792, William Dillwyn Papers, box 1, LCP/HSP.

6. Edgar W. Knight, ed., *A Documentary History of Education in the South before 1860* (Chapel Hill, N.C., 1949), I, 143–176, *passim*, esp. 170, 176, describes the efforts of Dr. Bray's Associates. On Pinckney, see Elise Pinckney, ed., *The Letterbook of Eliza Lucas Pinckney 1739–1762* (Chapel Hill, N.C., 1972), 12; on Washington, her Journal, spring 1789, Washington Family Papers, box 2, LCMD. One of Hannah Hubbard's letters is printed in Edwin M. Betts, ed., *Thomas Jefferson's Farm Book* (Princeton, N.J., 1953), 41–42.

7. Janet Brinley to Francis Brinley, [c. 1801?], Parker-Brinley Papers, box 1, HSP; Tyler, *Book*, 65; William Maxwell, comp., "My Mother: Memoirs of Mrs. Helen Read," *Lower Norfolk County Virginia Antiquary*, II (1897–1899), 24–25.

8. *Papers of Jeremy Belknap*, III, Collections of the MHS, LIV (Boston, 1891), 233. Woody, *History of Women's Education*, I, 149–153, 213–230, 281–300 discusses adventure schools.

9. On Benezet's school: Woody, *History of Women's Education*, I, 235. Elizabeth Drinker's references to Benezet may be found in her diary, Jan. 31, 1785, Nov. 20, 1793, and Nov. 11, 1798, HSP. The Sally Powel accounts are in Deborah Morris, Account Book, 1759–1786, HSP.

10. Alice M. Earle, ed., *Diary of Anna Green Winslow, A Boston School Girl of 1771* (Boston, 1894), 12, 22, 35; Elizabeth M. Campbell to James Murray, Dec. 3, 1756, James M. Robbins Papers, I, MHS. On the similar education of Hannah Fisher, see Sally Logan Fisher, Diary, May 1, Nov. 13, 1786; Feb. 8, 1788; April 10, 1790; Aug. 3, 1792; Dec. 31, 1793, HSP.

11. Farish, ed., *Fithian Journal*, 21–25, 26, 36, 48–49, 64, 88, 134, 142, 157.

12. Simms, "Memoir of Pinckney Family," Pinckney Family Papers, ser. 2, vol. 2, 2; Eliza Lucas to George Lucas, May 2, [1744], Eliza Lucas Pinckney Papers; Tyler, *Book*, 9, 13, 14, 15–17.

13. Leonard W. Labaree et al., eds., *The Papers of Benjamin Franklin* (New

Haven, Ct., 1959–), VII, 276n; Ann Eliza Bleecker, *The Posthumous Works of Ann Eliza Bleecker* . . . (New York, 1793), i; [Benjamin Rush], "An Account of the Life and Character of Mrs. Elizabeth Ferguson [*sic*]," *The Port Folio*, 3rd ser., I (1809), 521; Pinckney, *Letterbook*, 142. Also, on Harriott, see Harriott Pinckney to Mrs. Favell, March 1763, Pinckney Family (Buist Family) Papers, SCHS, and Thomas Pinckney to Harriott Horry, July 30, Sept. 22, 1776; May 13, June 6, 20, Oct. 10, 1777, all in Pinckney Family Papers, ser. 1, box 6.

14. Eliza Pinckney to Daniel Horry, July 3, [no yr.], Pinckney Family (Buist Family) Papers; Carl Van Doren, ed., *The Letters of Benjamin Franklin & Jane Mecom* (Princeton, N.J., 1950), 45 (also 88, 269); Rachel Sayre to Joseph Reed, May 11, 1764, Joseph Reed Papers, NYHS; Deborah Cushing to Thomas Cushing, Sept. 14, 1774, [c. Aug.–Sept. 1774], Cushing Family Papers, MHS.

15. Mary Meriwether to Lewis Holladay, April 11, 1801, Holladay Family Papers, VHS; Joyce Myers to Rebecca Mordecai, June 23, 1800, Jacob Mordecai Papers, DU; Grace Galloway to Betsy Galloway, April 5, 1780, Joseph Galloway Papers, LCMD; Charles Francis Adams, ed., *Letters of Mrs. Adams, The Wife of John Adams*, 3rd ed. (Boston, 1841), II, 79.

16. Lyman H. Butterfield et al., eds., *Adams Family Correspondence* (Cambridge, Mass., 1963), III, 52; II, 94, 391 (hereafter cited as *AFC*). John's letters eliciting her comments are in *AFC*, II, 76, and III, 17.

17. See a rare exchange in the pages of the *Royal American Magazine*, I (1774), 9–10, 131–132, 178–179.

18. James Fordyce, *Sermons to Young Women*, 3rd Amer. ed. (Philadelphia, 1809), I, 137, 143; John Bennet, "Letters to a Young Lady," *American Museum*, X (Aug. 1791), 74–75.

19. Bennet, "Letters to a Young Lady," *Amer. Museum*, X (Aug. 1791), 75; Alphonzo, "An Address to the Ladies," *American Magazine*, I (March 1788), 244–245; "To a Lady, who expressed a desire of seeing an university established for women," *Amer. Museum*, XI, appendix I (1792), 3. On learned ladies, see Fordyce, *Sermons*, I, 102–103, 151–152.

20. Eliza Southgate Bowne, *A Girl's Life Eighty Years Ago*, ed. Clarence Cook (London, 1888), 104; Adams, ed., *Letters of Mrs. Adams*, II, 278–279.

21. Noah Webster, "On the Education of Youth in America," *Amer. Museum*, XII (Nov. 1792), 282–283; "An Extract," *Lady's Magazine*, I (May 1793), 292; Lavinia, "Dialogue between Mrs. Careless and Mrs. Friendly, upon Female Education," in Caleb Bingham, *The American Preceptor*, 42nd ed. (Boston, 1811), 92.

22. [Penuel Bowen], "Upon Virtue in general, and female Education & manners in particular, Being An Inaugural Disartation . . . ," Nov. 26, 1786, *passim*, esp. 2, 27, 28–29, GHS. The GHS has catalogued this as "anonymous," but the manuscript is in Bowen's handwriting, and he also mentions the school in letters to William Gibbons, Nov. 26, 1786, and to his wife Susannah, Jan. 4, 1787, both in Bowen-Cooke Papers, SCHS.

23. Benjamin Rush, "Thoughts upon Female Education," in Frederick Rudolph, ed., *Essays on Education in the Early Republic* (Cambridge, Mass., 1963), *passim*, esp.

27–30. The most complete discussion of female education in the early republic is Linda K. Kerber, "Daughters of Columbia: Educating Women for the Republic, 1787–1805," in Stanley Elkins and Eric McKittrick, eds., *The Hofstadter Aegis* (New York, 1974), 36–59. See also Ann D. Gordon, "The Philadelphia Young Ladies Academy," in Carol Berkin and Mary Beth Norton, eds., *Women of America: A History* (Boston, 1979), 68–89.

24. Samuel Magaw, "An Address Delivered in the Young Ladies' Academy, at Philadelphia, on February 8th, 1787, at the Close of a Public Examination," *Amer. Museum*, III (Jan. 1788), 25–28, *passim*; Samuel Magaw, "An Address Delivered at the University of Pennsylvania . . . on the 5th of June, 1782," *ibid.*, IV (Aug. 1788), 163–166, *passim*.

25. "Reflections on What is Called Amiable Weakness in Woman," *Lady and Gentleman's Pocket Magazine of Literature and Polite Amusement*, I (Oct. 1796), 75, 77; "A Second Vindication of the Rights of Women," *Ladies Monitor*, I, no. 2 (Aug. 15, 1801), 11–13 (quotation slightly altered for grammatical reasons). Bertha M. Stearns has tentatively attributed "Reflections on Amiable Weakness" to Charles Brockden Brown; see her "A Speculation Concerning Charles Brockden Brown," *PMHB*, LIX (1935), 99–105.

26. *New York Magazine*, IV (Sept. 1794), 569–570; "The Speculator. No. II," *Massachusetts Magazine*, I (Oct. 1789), 619; "The Dreamer. No. VI," *ibid.*, I (June 1789), 370–373. See, too, "On Female Universities and Academies," *Lady and Gentleman's Pocket Mag.*, I (Sept. 15, 1796), 116–118, also attributed to Brown by Stearns (n. 25 above).

27. Anaximander, "The Competitor, No. III," *Boston Magazine*, III (June 1785), 213 (see chapter 8, n. 29, for the attribution to Harvard students); Emily Noyes Vanderpoel, comp., *Chronicles of a Pioneer School . . .*, ed. Elizabeth C. Barney Buel (Cambridge, Mass., 1903), 177–178.

28. Constantia [Judith Sargent Murray], *The Gleaner. A Miscellaneous Production* (Boston, 1798), III, 115, 191.

29. Erasmus Darwin, *A Plan for the Conduct of Female Education . . .* (Philadelphia, 1798), 10–11 (see 13–96 *passim* for the recommended curriculum). See also Thomas Gisborne, *An Enquiry into the Duties of the Female Sex* (London, 1797), 37–92 *passim*; and Hannah More, *Strictures on the Modern System of Female Education* (New York, 1813), 45–50, 71–80. Studies of female education in England concur in the opinion that the late eighteenth century was not notable as a time of reform. See, e.g., Dorothy Gardiner, *English Girlhood at School* (London, 1929), 333–476; and Mary Cathcart Borer, *Willingly to School: A History of Women's Education* (Guilford and London, 1975), 150–227. There was also a lack of reform movements on the continent: see Phyllis H. Stock, "The Theory and Practice of Women's Education in Eighteenth-Century France," *Eighteenth-Century Life*, II (1975–1976), 79–82; and Peter Petschauer, "Improving Educational Opportunities for Girls in Eighteenth-Century Germany," *ibid.*, III (1976–1977), 56–62.

30. Woody, *History of Women's Education*, I, does not ask these questions. Other scholars have incorrectly assumed that because the educators' goals were limited, the

students' education was similarly restrictive (and restricting). See esp. Keith Melder, "Mask of Oppression: The Female Seminary Movement in the United States," *New York History*, LV (1974), 260–279.

31. Franklin B. Dexter, ed., *The Literary Diary of Ezra Stiles, D.D., LL.D.* (New York, 1901), III, 247. Woody, *History of Women's Education*, I, 154–155, 339–349, discusses these first academies. Woodbridge made his claim in his article "Female Education in the Last Century," *American Annals of Education*, 3rd ser., I (1831), 525, published under the pseudonym "Senex." On Dwight's academy, see Charles E. Cunningham, *Timothy Dwight 1752–1817* (New York, 1942), 154–163; on Isabella Graham's, see *The Power of Faith, Exemplified in the Life and Writings of the Late Mrs. Isabella Graham* (New York, 1843), esp. 82.

32. Vanderpoel, *Chronicles*, 395–397, for the 1802 list, and 19–20, for accounts of Litchfield residents' contributions to the academy. A list of pupils from Greenfield Academy, 1804, shows students from various towns in Massachusetts but no other states or foreign countries (see Sarah Ripley's "Abridged Journal," late summer, 1804, SLRC). One of the schools that continues to this day is the Moravian Academy, now College, Bethlehem, Pa.

33. Judith Randolph to Martha Jefferson, Feb. 12, 1785, Nicholas Trist Papers, SHC/UNC, and Vanderpoel, *Chronicles*, 388, contain the quotations. For examples of southerners going north to school, see W. Few to Edward Telfair, July 12, 30, 1801, Edward Telfair Papers, DU; and Eleanor Lewis to Elizabeth Bordley, Aug. 25, 1811, Jan. 3, 1815, Lewis-Gibson Letters, I, 87, 91.

34. Caleb Cotton to his parents, Aug. 6, 1799, Caleb Cotton Papers, SCHS; Penuel Bowen to Henry Hill, Oct. 18, 1786, Bowen-Cooke Papers; Douglas S. Robertson, ed., *An Englishman in America 1785, Being the Diary of Joseph Hadfield* (Toronto, 1933), 6; Kenneth and Anna Roberts, eds. and trans., *Moreau de St. Mery's American Journey 1793–1798* (Garden City, N.Y., 1947), 47; *Letters of Joseph Clay Merchant of Savannah 1776–1793*, Collections of GHS, VIII (Savannah, 1913), 230. The initial advertisement for the Mordecai Academy is reprinted in Knight, *Doc. History*, V, 387.

35. David Ramsay, *Ramsay's History of South Carolina, from its First Settlement in 1670 to the year 1808* (Newberry, S.C., 1854), II, 247; Francis duBose Richardson, "Memoirs of Our Family," 21, SHC/UNC; Clay, *Letters*, 194–195. This point is developed more fully in Mary Beth Norton, "'What an Alarming Crisis Is This': Southern Women and the American Revolution," in Jeffrey Crow and Larry Tise, eds., *The Southern Experience in the American Revolution* (Chapel Hill, N.C., 1978), 222–225.

36. Elizabeth Kent to James Kent, June 7, 1807, James Kent Papers, LCMD. The students at Sarah Pierce's school commented on their homesickness in their diaries; see Vanderpoel, *Chronicles*, 66, 154.

37. [Frances Silvester] to Catherine Van Schaack, [1806], Catherine Van Schaack Papers, Miscellaneous Manuscripts, NYHS; Bowne, *Girl's Life*, 4.

38. [Sarah Brown] to Sally Brown, April 16, 1786, and John Brown to same, March 11, 1786, John Brown Papers, RIHS; Ann Barraud to Nancy Barraud, July

[1801], John H. Cocke Papers, box 1, ALUV (no. 640); Abraham Lansing to Jane Lansing, July 25, 1794, Lansing Family Papers, I, 39, Gansevoort-Lansing Collection, NYPL; Sarah Jay to Maria Jay, Dec. 16, 1794, Jay Papers.

39. Elizabeth Peabody to William Shaw, March 20, Nov. 20, 1799, and to Mary Cranch, March 2, 1803, Feb. 25, 1804, all in Shaw Family Papers, box 1, LCMD; Maxwell, comp., "My Mother," *Lower Norfolk Cty Va. Antiq.*, I (1895–1896), 25, III (1899–1901), 48; John Frederick Schroeder, *Memoir of the Life and Character of Mrs. Mary Anna Boardman* . . . (New Haven, Ct., 1849), 183, 182 (see 79–98 for Mrs. Boardman's schooling).

40. Eleanor Lewis to Elizabeth Bordley, Jan. 3, 1815, Lewis-Gibson Letters, I, 91; Isabella Graham to James Duane, Jan. 22, 1795, March 6, 1796, James Duane Papers, NYHS; Bowne, *Girl's Life*, 8, 11. Stephen Decatur, Jr., *Private Affairs of George Washington* . . . (Boston, 1933), 85, details Nelly's attendance at Mrs. Graham's school.

41. Pelatiah Hitchcock to Enos Hitchcock, Nov. 18, 1788, Enos Hitchcock Papers, RIHS; Elizabeth [Tappan] to John Pierce, [Jan. 30, 1808], Poor Family Papers, SLRC; Anne Iredell to James Iredell, Jr., Dec. 14, 1805, Aug. 27, 1806, Charles Johnson Collection, NCDAH; Susan I. Lesley, *Recollections of My Mother* (Boston, 1886), 33, 50.

42. [Woodbridge], "Female Education," *Amer. Annals of Ed.*, I (1831), 526; Charlotte Barrell to Sally Chace, Oct. 19, 1800, Cheever Family Papers, AAS; Mary Pinckney to Margaret Manigault, March 30, July 13–15, 1797, Margaret Manigault to Alice Izard, June 16, 1801, all in Manigault Papers, SCL; Gertrude Meredith to William Meredith, May 3, 1804, Meredith Papers, HSP.

43. On Elizabeth Murray's education of her nieces, see chapter 5, n. 53, and Mary Beth Norton, "A Cherished Spirit of Independence: The Life of an Eighteenth-Century Boston Businesswoman," in Berkin and Norton, eds., *Women of America*, 51–55.

44. Harriet Clark to Lydia Clark, March 31, 1791, Anne Usher to Harriet Clark, [June 1789], same to Lydia Clark, June 25, 1789, Anne Eliza Clark to John and Lydia Clark, Nov. 16, 1789, all in John Innes Clark Papers, RIHS. On Mrs. Clark's illness, see her letter to Mehetabel Higginson, [Oct. 29, 1791] (draft), *ibid.*

45. Anne Eliza Clark to Harriet Clark, Jan. 7, 1791 [i.e., 1792], Sept. 11, 1791, to Lydia Clark, Sept. 11, 1791, and her letters 1791–1792 *passim, ibid.* For Penuel Bowen's daughter, see Frances Bowen to Susannah Bowen, [c. 1791], Bowen-Cooke Papers. For information on other students at the school that same year: Caroline Gardiner Curtis, ed., *The Cary Letters* (Cambridge, Mass., 1891), 90–91.

46. Anne Eliza Clark to Lydia Clark, Nov. 30, 18, 1794, and 1794–1795 *passim*, Clark Papers. For Harriet Clark's experience at Mrs. Higginson's, see her letter to her parents, Aug. 31, 179–, *ibid.*

47. John Innes Clark to Lydia Clark, Dec. 30, 1792, Eliza Clark to same, Sept. 26, 1791, and the correspondence with Elizabeth Chester, cited n. 51 below, all in Clark Papers.

48. Mabel Haller, *Early Moravian Education in Pennsylvania*, Transactions of the

Moravian Historical Society, XV (Nazareth, Pa., 1953), 22, 13–21 *passim*. For favorable wartime comments on the school, see William Atlee to Esther Atlee, May 15, 1779, William Atlee Papers, Peter Force Collection, ser. 9, LCMD; and William Palfrey to Susannah Palfrey, [Oct.] 23, [1777], William Palfrey Papers, HL. A negative comment is in *AFC*, II, 155.

49. John Steele to Ann Steele, July 22, 1799, John Steele Papers, SHC/UNC; Ephraim Kirby to Jacob Van Vleck, Jan. 25, 1797, Edmund Kirby-Smith Papers, SHC/UNC. A list of the students at the academy is appended to William C. Reichel, *A History of the Rise, Progress, and Present Condition of the Moravian Seminary for Young Ladies at Bethlehem, Pa.* (Philadelphia, 1874).

50. Sarah Jay to John Jay, Oct. 11, 25, 1794; Sarah Jay to Catherine Livingston Ridley, Nov. 25, 1794, all in Jay Papers. Sarah Jay to Maria Jay, April 23, 1791, notes her attendance at Mrs. Graham's school, and same, April 1, 1795, comments on the disapproval of her friends' mothers.

51. Elizabeth Chester to Lydia Clark, Jan. 15, 1791, and [Lydia Clark] to Elizabeth Chester, [Dec. 3, 1790] (draft), Clark Papers. The information on the Chester girls as students is in Reichel, *History*, 329, 336. See also "Description of a Journey to Bethlehem, Pennsylvania," *N.Y. Mag.*, I (Aug. 1790), 458–464.

52. "Letter from a Young Lady at the Moravian Academy," *Amer. Mag.*, I (July 1788), 569–570; "Address of a Young Lady of Fifteen, on her Leaving the Academy at Bethlehem," *Amer. Museum*, VIII (Sept. 1790), 118–119. The place of residence and age of the author of these pieces coincides with the information about Amelia Blakely on the pupil list in Reichel, *History*, 327.

53. Schroeder, *Boardman Memoir*, 307; Ephraim Kirby to Ruth Kirby, July 16, 1797, Kirby-Smith Papers; Maria Jay to Sarah Jay, Nov. 9, 1794, March 29, 1795, Jay Papers. On Ann Steele's leaving school, see John Steele to Ann Steele, Oct. 28, 1799, Steele Papers.

54. Margaretta Akerly to [Catherine Cox], March 23, 1796, Margaretta Akerly Papers, Miscellaneous MSS, NYHS. Haller, *Early Moravian Education*, 240, reconstructs a typical day. See *ibid.*, 233–275, for a detailed account of the curriculum.

55. Reichel, *History*, 109–111, quotes the school journal on the 1791 examinations.

56. Jane Nylander, "Evidence of Accomplishment: New England Schoolgirl Art in the Early Nineteenth Century," unpub. paper delivered at Old Sturbridge Village, March, 1976. Linda Grant DePauw and Conover Hunt, *'Remember the Ladies': Women in America 1750–1815* (New York, 1976), 102–109, reproduces drawings and needlework from the academies. Ruth Henshaw Bascom, whose naive paintings are now well known, attended Leicester Academy. Her diary is at AAS.

57. My thanks to Mary E. Norton for helping me compile these data from the biographies in Edward W. James et al., eds., *Notable American Women*, 3 vols. (Cambridge, Mass., 1971).

58. See their biographies in *ibid.*, *passim*.

59. *Boston Evening Post*, Feb. 2, 1782; *Massachusetts Centinel*, Feb. 19, 26, 1785. (See also *Centinel*, March 2, 5, 9, 12, 30, April 6, 1785, for a continuation of the discussion.) See further Woody, *History of Women's Education*, I, 146, and esp.

Kathryn Kish Sklar, "Public Expenditures for Schooling Girls in Massachusetts Towns, 1750–1800," unpub. paper delivered to the History of Education Society, Boston, Oct. 1976.

60. Woody, *History of Women's Education*, I, 202–206; Carl Kaestle, *The Evolution of an Urban School System: New York City, 1750–1850* (Cambridge, Mass., 1973), chapter 1. Isabella Graham and her daughter Joanna Bethune were active in the charity school movement; see *Power of Faith, passim,* esp. 228–229.

61. Nathan Fiske, *The Moral Monitor* (Worcester, Mass., 1801), II, 231–232. On the same point: Murray, *Gleaner,* II, 7–13. See Maris A. Vinovskis and Richard A. Bernard, "Women in Education in Ante-Bellum America," Working Paper 73-7, Center for Demography and Ecology, University of Wisconsin-Madison.

62. Tyler, *Book,* 193; Ruth Henshaw, Diary, May–June, 1791, June–Aug., 1792, April–Nov. 1796, *passim,* AAS; Elizabeth Bancroft, Diary, Oct. 12, 1793, Sept. 24, 1795, Sept. 6, 8, 1794, AAS.

63. Anne Emlen [Mifflin], "Some Account of my Religious Progress," Emlen Collection, HSP.

64. *Bessie; or, Reminiscences of a Daughter* . . . (New Haven, Ct., 1861), 185; [Woodbridge], "Female Education," *Amer. Annals of Ed.,* I (1831), 525; Tyler, *Book,* 219.

65. Lydia Parker to Cynthia Winslow, Aug. 1807, Northey Family Papers, box 4, EI; Polly Smith to Elizabeth Smith, 1787, and same to —————, 1789 (typescripts), Helen Evertson Smith Papers, box 2, NYIIS. See also William J. Allinson, comp., *Memorials of Rebecca Jones* (Philadelphia, 1849), 187–188.

66. Samuel Mordecai to Rachel Mordecai, May 4, 1809, Mordecai Family Papers, SHC/UNC; Rachel Mordecai to Samuel Mordecai, Feb. 12, 1809, Pattie Mordecai Papers, NCDAH; Ellen Mordecai to Samuel Mordecai, Sept. 12, 1808, Mordecai Family Papers. Jacob's letters to his daughters during their Richmond schooling, 1796–1798, are in both Jacob Mordecai Papers, DU, and Mordecai Family Papers (in latter see esp. his letter of July 3, 1798).

67. Rachel Mordecai to Samuel Mordecai, Jan. 6, July 3, 1811, Mordecai Family Papers.

68. Mary Norris to Hannah Thomson, June 29, 1786, Logan Papers, LXXIV, 8, HSP. On the early women teachers, see Jill Ker Conway, "Perspectives on the History of Women's Education in the United States," *History of Education Quarterly,* XIV (1974), 5; Glenda Gates Riley, "Origins of the Argument for Improved Female Education," *ibid.,* IX (1969), 455–470; and esp. Kathryn Kish Sklar, *Catharine Beecher: A Study in American Domesticity* (New Haven, Ct., 1973).

CONCLUSION

1. Constantia [Judith Sargent Murray], *The Gleaner. A Miscellaneous Production* (Boston, 1798), III, 189; II, 280, 47. Similar optimism was expressed in "An Oration upon Female Education," in Caleb Bingham, *The American Preceptor*, 42nd ed. (Boston, 1811), 47–51.

2. "A Second Vindication of the Rights of Women," *The Ladies Monitor*, I, no. 2 (Aug. 15, 1801), 13.

3. Ann D. Gordon, "The Philadelphia Young Ladies Academy," in Carol Berkin and Mary Beth Norton, eds., *Women of America: A History* (Boston, 1979), 83, 90.

4. Eliza Southgate Bowne, *A Girl's Life Eighty Years Ago*, ed. Clarence Cook (London, 1888), 102.

5. *Letters of Joseph Clay Merchant of Savannah 1776–1793*, Collections of GHS, VIII (Savannah, 1913), 178; Grace Galloway to Betsy Galloway, May 15, 1779, Joseph Galloway Papers, LCMD; Lyman H. Butterfield et al., eds., *Adams Family Correspondence* (Cambridge, Mass., 1963), II, 4, 390.

INDEX

Bethune, Joanna, 273
Bingham, Anne Willing, 190–191
Bingham, Caleb, 4, 266, 273
birth intervals, 72–74
Blair, Helen (Nelly), 77, 98, 172
Blair, Jean, 199, 200
Blakeley, Amelia, 285
Bleecker, Ann Eliza, 199, 262
boardinghouse keeping: as women's occupation, 144–145
Boardman, Cornelia, 278
Boardman, Mary Anna, 193, 278, 285
Boston, Mass.: and Revolution, 156–157, 197, 200–201
Boudinot, Elisha, 84
Bowen, Anna. See Mitchell, Anna Bowen
Bowen, Rev. Penuel, 266–267, 274
boys: and courtship, 51–52, 56; and marriage, 60; education of, at home, 257–258. See also sons
Brackenridge, Hugh Henry, 246
Brasher, Helena Kortwright, 142–143, 283; as teenager, 51; and politics, 173, 176–177; and war, 199
Brattleboro, Vt., 10
Brent, Betsy Ambler. See Ambler, Betsy
Brissot de Warville, Jacques Pierre, 13
Brown, John, 87
Bruce, Jane, 58
Bryant, Austin, 258
Bryant, Cullen, 258
Bryant, Sarah Snell, 83, 258; domestic work of, 10–12
Buchanan, Hannah, 27
bundling, 56
Burr, Aaron, Jr., 73, 83
Burr, Esther Edwards, 73, 119, 170; and Sarah Prince, 39, 106, 108; and child rearing, 83, 96
Byrd, Mary Willing, 145, 226

Cabot, Eliza Perkins, 193
Cain, Elisabeth, 203
Cain, Sarah, 203
Campbell, Thomas, 147, 150
camp followers, 174, 212–213
Carey, Matthew, 246
Carter, Ann Tasker, 96
Carter, Landon, 30–32, 136
Carter, Lucy, 136
Carter, Robert: and slaves, 32, 68; and cloth manufactory, 164; and children's education, 258, 261
Carter, Mrs. Robert Wormeley, 91
Cary (slave), 70
Case of the Whigs Who Loaned their Money on the Public Faith Fairly Stated, The (Cunningham), 190
Chapone, Hester, 282

Charlotte (slaves), 33, 209
Chastellux, Marquis François Jean de, 186, 230
Chester, Elizabeth, 284
Chesterfield, Lord (Philip Dormer Stanhope), 115–116
childbirth, 66–67, 139; deaths in, 75–78, 81, 83. See also pregnancy
child naming, 85–87
child rearing, 93–94; in wealthy and poor households, compared, 84; paternal role in, 94–95, 97–100; maternal role in, 95–96, 99, 100–102; republican, 235–236, 238, 247–249. See also parents
child-rearing literature, 95, 100, 247, 249
children: black, 30, 86–87, 210–211, 258–259; parents on, 85, 92–94; named for relatives, 85–87; deaths of, parents on, 88–90, 103–104; nursed by mothers, 90, 232–233; duty of, to parents, 96–97; parental sex preference for, 102–103. See also daughters; sons
Chloe (slave), 30
cities: white women's domestic work in, 20–26; female wage earners in, 24, 137, 139–145, 147, 149–151, 157; adventure schools in, 259–260
Clark, Anne. See Hooper, Anne Clark
Clark, Anne Eliza, 281–283
Clark, Harriet, 281–283
Clark, John, 281–283
Clark, Lydia Bowen, 281–283, 284
Clarke, Charity, 169–170
Cleaveland, Rev. John, 167
Clifford, John, 43, 230
Cloudsdall, Mary, 145
Coalter, Fanny Tucker, 4, 77, 92, 93
Coalter, John, 4, 77, 135; and wife Margaret, 109, 231–232; courts Maria Rind, 231
Coalter, Margaret Davenport, 77, 120; and childbirth, 78; and female friend, 109; and husband, John, 231–232
Coalter, Maria Rind, 77, 231
Colchester, Conn., 12
Colden, Cadwallader, 61
common law: women's status in, 45–46, 137. See also legal status
Condict, Jemima, 57, 172
Condict, John, 192
Congregational church: women in, 128–132
Connecticut: British raids in, 202; divorce in, 234
contraception, 232–234
Cooper, Mary: and domestic work, 11–12, 34; on unhappy marriage, 45; and New Light church, 129
Corbin, Hannah Lee, 184, 360n.58
courtship, 51–60, 229–231
Cranch, Mary Smith, 36, 57, 236, 276
Creek Indians, 18, 94–95